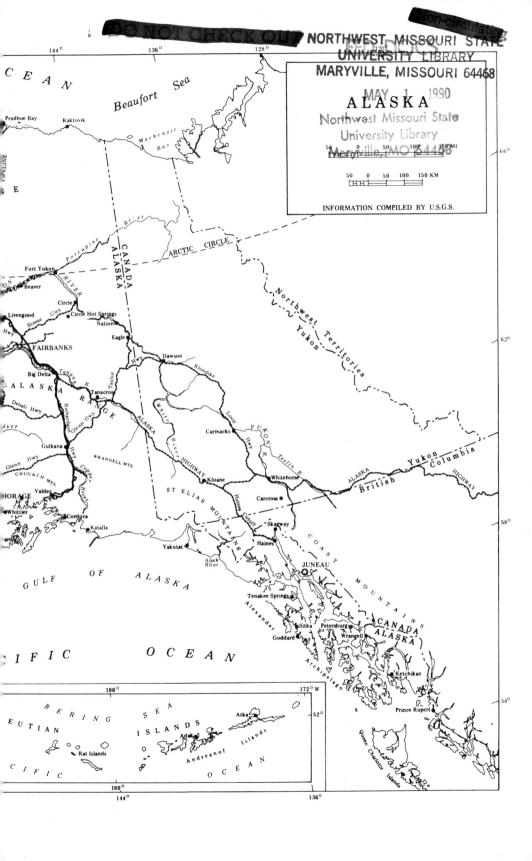

ALASKA

INFORMATION COMPILED BY U.S.G.S.

ALASKA
STATE GOVERNMENT
AND POLITICS

Marble columns mark the entrance to Alaska's state capitol in Juneau.
(Fairbanks Daily News-Miner.)

ALASKA
STATE GOVERNMENT AND POLITICS

Gerald A. McBeath
Thomas A. Morehouse
Editors

University of Alaska Press
Fairbanks

© 1987 by the University of Alaska Press
All rights reserved. First printing.
International Standard Book Number: Cloth 0-912006-20-X
Paper 0-912006-21-8
Library of Congress Card Number: 86-051368
Alaska Historical Commission Studies in History Number 208
Printed in the United States of America

Research and preparation supported by a grant from the
Alaska Historical Commission.

Publication coordination, design and production by Deborah Van Stone
with assistance from K. Fiedler Morack

Cover design by Wanda Seamster

Contents

v

PART THREE: State Government Institutions

Preface

Alaska state government and politics include much that is fascinating: a volatile legislature, dramatic statewide elections, large numbers of independent voters, strong interest groups, and much more. During the first 25 years of statehood, Alaska saw wide swings in state revenues and fiscal policies, shifts in the balance of power between the governor and the legislature, development of an administrative bureaucracy, emergence of a court system recognized as one of the most progressive in the nation, and changing orientations of Alaskans toward their political system.

Unfortunately, no comprehensive treatment of Alaska state government has previously been available. In 1984, the twelve authors of this book—eleven political scientists and one historian—began to discuss and plan a book on government and politics in Alaska. We conducted research and collaborated on this study because of our consuming interest in Alaska's political development. We learned a great deal and believe we acquired a better understanding of the dynamics of state politics.

With this book we present the product of our efforts and hope that it will give others a better understanding of public affairs in Alaska and lead them to share our fascination with Alaska state politics and government.

Each of the authors bears responsibility for his or her own chapter, and each chapter bears its author's particular stamp. Thus, the chapters of this book represent a range of perspectives and vantage points on Alaska state government rather than a single, unified point of view. Our intent is to enrich understanding, not to convert or persuade. The authors are:

Claus-M. Naske, professor of history at the University of Alaska, Fairbanks, is a specialist in regional history and an expert on Alaska history. His numerous published works on Alaska history include *A History of Alaska Statehood*, *E.L. Bartlett of Alaska: A Life in Politics*, *Alaska: A History of the 49th State* (with Herman Slotnick), *Paving Alaska's Trails: The Work of the Alaska Road Commission*, and a forthcoming biography of Ernest Gruening.

Victor Fischer was a delegate to the Alaska Constitutional Convention of 1955-56 and a territorial legislator. He taught at the University of Alaska in Fairbanks and Anchorage in the 1960s and 1970s, and from 1966 to 1976 directed the university's Institute of Social and Economic Research. During this period he published the study, *Alaska's Constitutional Convention*. Since 1980 he has been a member of the Alaska State Senate from Anchorage.

Gerald McBeath, professor of political science at the University of Alaska, Fairbanks, has published several studies on Alaska government and politics, including *Dynamics of Alaska Native Self-Government* (with Thomas Morehouse), *Alaska's Rural Development* (co-editor, with Peter Cornwall), and *Alaska's Urban and Rural Governments* (with Thomas Morehouse and Linda Leask).

David Maas teaches politics and government at Anchorage Community College. He has done extensive research on Alaska Native politics, including research for the Alaska Federation of Natives. His doctoral dissertation concerned the Alaska Native Claims Settlement Act and state politics in Alaska, and he has written articles on those subjects for various publications.

Thomas Morehouse, professor of political science at the University of Alaska, Anchorage, is senior member of the university's Institute of Social and Economic Research. His writings on Alaska government and politics include *Issues in Alaska Development* (with David Kresge and George Rogers), *Alaska Resources Development* (editor and co-author), and *Alaska's Urban and Rural Governments* (with Gerald McBeath and Linda Leask).

Carl Shepro is on the faculty of political science at the University of Alaska, Fairbanks. His research and teaching interests are in the fields of state, local, and urban politics and intergovernmental relations; he has written several articles on these subjects. His doctoral dissertation on political organizations and citizen participation is now being prepared for publication.

Clive Thomas is associate professor of political science at the University of Alaska, Juneau. His major fields of research are interest groups and other political organizations, political development, and state and local politics. Among his publications is *Interest Group Politics in the Western States* (co-editor, with Ronald Hrebenar).

Richard Ender, professor of public policy and administration, is on the faculty of the School of Business and Public Affairs at the University of Alaska, Anchorage. He formerly headed the university's Anchorage Urban Observatory and developed its opinion research program. He recently edited a symposium on energy policies for the Policy Studies Organization and has written extensively on disaster mitigation and public responses to oil and gas development.

Richard Fineberg taught political science on the Fairbanks and Juneau campuses of the University of Alaska and was a free-lance reporter in Alaska for more than a decade. His many articles have appeared in various state and national publications. He is the author of *Chaos in the Capital*, an analysis of state spending patterns in the petroleum era. Since 1983 he has been a budget and policy analyst in the governor's Office of Management and Budget in Juneau.

Stephen Johnson chaired the Department of Political Science at the University of Alaska, Anchorage, from 1984 to 1986. His research and teaching focus on American politics and the legislative process, and he has written extensively on legislatures in the western states.

Gordon Harrison was an associate professor of political science at the University of Alaska, Fairbanks. He taught courses and conducted research for the university's Institute of Social and Economic Research. He has also worked as a consultant to government and industry. His published writings include *Alaska Public Policy* (editor and co-author) and *A Citizen's Guide to the Constitution of Alaska*. Harrison is currently associate director of the governor's Office of Management and Budget.

Andrea Helms, professor of political science at the University of Alaska, Fairbanks, is a specialist in comparative politics and public law. She has written articles on community bases of justice and intergovernmental issues, and is now doing research for a book on domestic violence.

Acknowledgements

We relied on a number of persons and organizations for help in preparing this book. Linda Leask, editor and research associate at the Institute of Social and Economic Research, University of Alaska, Anchorage, reviewed and copyedited every chapter of this book. Since the dozen authors represent a wide range of sensibilities, quirks, and writing styles, her editorial contribution was large. She also helped with logistics and production in ways too numerous to mention. Also critical to production of this book was Sheri Layral, administrative assistant with the Political Science and History Departments of the University of Alaska, Fairbanks. She typed and revised several versions of each chapter with great skill, speed, and patience. Carla Helfferich and Debbie Van Stone of the University of Alaska Press helped in many ways to move the book from manuscript to published form. Wanda Seamster of the University of Alaska's Arctic Environmental Information and Data Center designed the cover.

People engaged in Alaska politics and serving in Alaska government, as well as some no longer actively involved, provided essential assistance. We interviewed many persons, and several Alaskans, including prominent members of the Alaska press, criticized earlier drafts of chapters in this book. The *Fairbanks Daily News-Miner* also generously loaned us a number of photographs used in this book.

Four experts on American state government provided valuable advice and suggestions for improvement of the manuscript: L. Harmon Zeigler, professor and chair, Political Science Department, University of Puget Sound; Victor Jones, professor emeritus (Political Science), University of California, Berkeley; Louis Wechsler, professor of Public Affairs, Arizona State University; and Harold Seidman, professor emeritus, University of Connecticut.

Alaska reviewers included students in the Political Science 210 course at the University of Alaska, Fairbanks campus, during spring semester 1985. They also included the following teachers and school administrators who critically reviewed first drafts of the text as part of their study of Alaska government and politics during the Taft Seminar for Teachers, conducted at the University of Alaska, Fairbanks campus, in summer 1985: Jerry Arthur, Palmer; Glenda Anderson, Lathrop High School, Fairbanks; Michael Blewett, Fairbanks; Mary Bristol, Romig Jr. High School, Anchorage; Judy Carpenter, Valdez High School; Charles Chaffee, North Pole High School; Robert

Chambers, Nenana School; Darrell Coe, Salcha Elementary; Rebecca Gatterdam, Fairbanks; Gerald Gates, Mountain Village School; Don Gray, Lathrop High School, Fairbanks; Mary Hallman, Tri-Valley School, Healy; Glenda Helms, Fairbanks; James Holcomb, Homer High School; Judy Jasperson, Lathrop High School, Fairbanks; Aldean Kilbourn, West Valley High School, Fairbanks; Charles Kingsland, Lower Yukon School District; Jordan Lanz, Stebbins School; Stan Lujan, Aurora School; John Lyle, Kaltag Schools; Sam McCormick, Eielson High School; Robert Mulluk, Kotzebue; John Nagy, Fairbanks; Patrick O'Connell, Soldotna High School; Joyce Ower, East High School, Anchorage; Dorothy Whitaker, Badger Elementary, North Pole; David W. Watkins, Point Hope Schools; Constance Watson, Pennell Elementary, Eielson Air Force Base; and Carl White, Stony River School. We are grateful to them for their time, their cooperation, and their ideas.

Linda Ilgenfritz, personal secretary for the Political Science Department of the University of Alaska at Fairbanks, helped with production of the book. Several department student assistants gathered information for authors, checked facts, and played other research roles: Beverly and Joe St. Sauver, Tom VanFlein, John Brainerd, Mike Balas, and Katharina Tumpek. Christine Gilbert compiled the index.

Others also played an important part in the publication of this book. A grant from the Alaska State Legislature materially assisted the preparation of studies on Alaska government and politics. Special thanks are due Representative Niilo Koponen for his assistance in obtaining this support. The Alaska Historical Commission, directed by William Hanable and Jo Antonson, funded many of the research costs, secretarial expenses, and communication expenses among authors, including two statewide meetings. A second grant from the historical commission helped pay for publication expenses. For the assignment of special assistance, we gratefully thank Lee Gorsuch, Director of the Institute of Social and Economic Research.

An effort of this sort requires many kinds of support, and we were fortunate to have received help from so many sources. Of course, editors and authors cannot be entirely saved from their own errors and omissions, and we acknowledge our individual responsibilities for any that remain.

Introduction

A newspaper publisher asked us how anyone could write a book on Alaska's government and politics when it would be "out-of-date before the ink dried." Seeming to support this view of the volatility of Alaska politics were these disparate events of the 1980s:

- A grand jury investigating alleged improprieties and illegalities in the state's lease of a Fairbanks office building recommended the impeachment of the governor, and the legislature called itself into special session to consider charges of bidrigging and perjury against the chief executive.

- Showing its extreme dependence on a single source of revenue, the state budget dramatically ballooned and shrank when oil prices rose and fell globally.

- A conflict over state spending levels and priorities led to the overthrow of the Democratic leadership in the state house by a coalition of Republicans and Democrats near the end of an especially rancorous legislative session.

- Following a state court decision that overturned the state's fishing and hunting regulations, which gave preference to rural subsistence users, the state Boards of Fisheries and Game opened subsistence fishing and hunting to all residents, urban and rural.

- State troopers rounded up and escorted state legislators back into a legislative session which they were avoiding in order to block a quorum and gain bargaining power in their budgetary struggles with the governor.

The events of Alaska government and politics may seem exceptional, and increasingly they have drawn national attention. Yet they also at times reflect experiences similar to those of the other states. This book looks at state government during the first 25 years of Alaska statehood. It is intended to reveal what is uniquely Alaskan in the state's government and politics, while also showing what Alaska's state government has in common with other state governments.

The setting of Alaska government is distinctive not only in its vast geography, regional variations, and extremes of climate, but also in its social and political dimensions. The four chapters in Part One describe the aspects of the environment most directly relevant to the operation of institutions and processes of government in Alaska—history, constitution, political culture, and state-federal relations.

Chapter 1, by Claus-M. Naske, discusses the history of Alaska from the first contacts between Western explorers and Alaska Natives to statehood. Most attention is devoted to the state's history as first a possession and then an organized territory of the United States. The chapter looks particularly at how Alaskans' experiences under territorial government influenced the state government they established when Alaska entered the union.

Chapter 2, by Victor Fischer, describes the setting of the Alaska constitutional convention, and the proceedings that led to the drafting of the state's constitution in 1955-1956. The chapter also examines key provisions of the constitution and identifies its distinctive features in comparison with the constitutions of the other states.

Chapter 3, by Gerald McBeath, examines the culture of politics in Alaska. It describes unique aspects of Alaskans politically, and it summarizes results of recent survey research, particularly political attitudes of those residing in rural villages. The chapter emphasizes the significant differences between culture and approaches to politics of Natives and of whites and urban Alaskans generally.

Chapter 4, by David Maas, discusses the American federal system generally and its operation in Alaska particularly. The Alaska Native component of the federal relationship complicates the pattern of federalism in Alaska, and the chapter looks especially at the unresolved issues of federal-state-Native government power in the state.

Part Two of the book examines the process of Alaska politics, including political events, opinions and attitudes, interest groups, and organizations that shape government policy.

Chapter 5, by Thomas Morehouse, analyzes Alaska's behavior in state elections since statehood. It shows the decline of party fortunes and the continuing importance of regional factors in electoral contests. It demonstrates the increasing fluidity of politics in Alaska, as parties—weakened as institutions and without coherent bases of support—cannot effectively provide consistent choices among policies and programs.

Chapter 6, by Carl Shepro, investigates party organizations and politics in Alaska. It describes the district roots of parties and discusses the factors—especially the development of the open primary system—that have weakened party influence over time. The chapter also considers the ambivalent attitudes Alaskans have about political parties.

Chapter 7, by Clive Thomas, describes the interest groups that exercise influence on state government, particularly on the legislative branch. It comprehensively covers the different types of interest groups in Alaska—including professional associations, business organizations, labor unions, and civic associations. The chapter examines in detail their lobbying activities in recent years, including legislators' views of who are the most effective. The chapter makes the case that the pressure group system in Alaska is among the strongest in the nation.

Chapter 8, by Richard Ender, examines public attitudes and opinions, and their linkages with public policy in Alaska. It surveys and explains the orientations citizens have toward contemporary political issues, giving special attention to issues of economic development versus conservation.

Chapter 9, by Richard Fineberg, presents a perspective on Alaska's media over the course of statehood. It discusses the organization and functioning of both print and electronic media in the state and includes vignettes of the state's largest and most influential newspapers. The chapter evaluates the independence, accuracy, and fairness of press coverage of Alaska public affairs and the effects of that coverage on political decisionmaking.

Part Three of the text introduces state government institutions. It presents information on the legislature, governor, administrative bureaucracy, and state courts.

Chapter 10, by Stephen Johnson, focuses on the state legislature. It explains the constitutional provisions under which the legislature operates, legislative structure and functions, and political factors that shape the legislative process. The chapter also describes the recruitment of legislators, types of legislators, and their behavior. It looks particularly at the effects of large petroleum revenues on the legislative budgeting process in the early 1980s.

Chapter 11, by Gerald McBeath, discusses the state's chief executive. The chapter considers the history of the governorship through gubernatorial elections, showing the recent impacts of candidate organizations and issues. Focusing on the constitutional provisions for a strong executive, the chapter examines the governor's appointment powers, role as opinion leader and policymaker, and budgetary authority. Brief comments are presented on different styles of past executive leadership.

Chapter 12, by Gordon Harrison, presents a comprehensive survey of the state's administrative system. This chapter treats the origin of the state's executive departments, their executive and legislative linkages, the role of boards and commissions, the process of bureaucratic politics and policymaking, and the accountability and efficiency of the state's large bureaucracy.

Chapter 13, by Andrea Helms, describes Alaska's court system. It discusses the system used to select judges and retention elections for judges. The chapter also discusses court history, structure and operations, and administrative organization and relationships.

The authors present their subjects in their own terms, but some common questions guide the presentations. The most significant question addressed by each author is: What is the difference between the Alaska practice and what one observes in the other American states—and why? This suggests one of the main reasons why we study Alaska—because it has characteristics not found in the other states. Especially is this so of the state's physical geography and pattern of settlements, which have an important influence on the character of the political system.

Alaska's geography and historical settlement patterns are clearly different from those of the other American states. It is partially in response to unique geographic factors that the state's separate political development has proceeded.

Some 375 million acres of land make Alaska America's largest state. Indeed, the land mass is roughly 20 percent of the total size of the continental United States. From Barrow, the nation's northernmost city, to Ketchikan in the southeast, is a distance of over 1,000 miles, and from Eagle on the Canadian border to Attu at the end of the Aleutian Islands is nearly 1,500 miles.

These distances seem greater than they are because there are few means of direct transportation. The land forms of Alaska produce a variegated, rough terrain in a pattern discouraging transportation and human habitation. North America's highest mountain, Mount McKinley, is located in interior Alaska, across which cuts the Alaska Range, the northwestern spur of the Rocky Mountains. The Brooks Range divides the Arctic Slope from the interior. The Kuskokwim Mountains separate western Alaska from the rest of the state, and the Saint Elias and Wrangell Mountains divide southeast Alaska from the great Alaska land mass. North America's mightiest river, the Yukon, flows through Alaska, joining with the Kuskokwim and Tanana to form a vast riverine navigation system that also disrupts land transportation. There are other unusual features of the Alaska terrain. Glaciers cover 3 percent—about 11 million acres—of the land surface, and there are northern deserts and rain forests.

The important political characteristic of Alaska's physical geography is the extent to which areas are isolated from one another. At least 100 of the villages and towns of the state are accessible by only one means of transportation—usually small planes—for much of the year. The great majority of the state's population lives on the road system, but this system does not connect any part of the state directly to the contiguous-48 states. Instead, one must drive hundreds of miles through Canada to reach the Pacific Northwest or upper Midwest.

Extremes of temperature and climate reinforce the effects of physical geography. The Arctic Slope of Alaska has a winter lasting nearly eight months. During four winter months the sun is little more than a blip on the horizon, and during summer months the sun does not set. The long winter cold of the Arctic north has produced permanently frozen ground, called permafrost, which presents difficulties for builders. Midnight sun extends into interior Alaska, the region of the state with the widest swings of temperature (from 60 degrees below zero in deep winter to 90 degrees above in summer). Coastal areas of southeast Alaska experience moderating air currents from the ocean, but there is also much precipitation, gale force winds, and little sun. For most of the state's population, extremes of temperature—and particularly the severity of winter—reinforce the sense of isolation from the contiguous-48 states; they produce the feeling of frontier living, notwithstanding the amenities of urban Alaska life.

Alaska was settled in two quite distinct waves of immigration. Traveling to Alaska across the Bering Land Bridge over a period of thousands of years were the ancestors of today's Eskimos, Indians, and Aleuts (collectively referred to as Alaska Natives). The origin of Alaska Natives was Asia, but their exact points and dates of departure for Alaska are unknown. The physical geography of Alaska insured that they would be dispersed throughout the territory, and that the aboriginal cultures growing in the new land would be separated from one another.

The second wave of settlement occurred at the end of the age of exploration that populated much of the New World with white colonizers. Vitus Bering claims title as first Western explorer to reach Alaska, under the Russian flag, in 1741. This wave of settlement, unlike that of the Native population, was not propelled to Alaska in pursuit of game and fish for subsistence. Instead, white explorers, adventurers, and pioneers arrived mainly in response to global resource demands. Russian traders sailed to Alaska to capture fur seals and other fur-bearing mammals, and the Russian interest in Alaska declined with the decline of the fur market. When whalebone and other whale products attained high market value, northern Europeans and Americans interested themselves in the whales that migrated to Alaska waters. Communities in Alaska became populated during the gold rush at the turn of the nineteenth century. Nome became Alaska's largest city, with nearly 10,000 settlers in 1898-99. Juneau and Fairbanks received their first spurts of growth as mining towns at about the same time. Alaska's marine resources attracted attention from fish canners, and these interests, although not physically resident in Alaska, exercised control over territorial policy. The same was true of companies exploiting wood products in the territory. Logging and fishing were also responsible for the growth of communities of white settlers in southeast Alaska.

Political events and military necessities interrupted this resource-dependent pattern of white settlement. The need for staging areas in the western United States in World War II led to the growth of large military installations in the Anchorage and Fairbanks areas. The Cold War, beginning in the late 1940s, accelerated this development. The growth of military installations not only brought new population to the territory; it also provided a continuing source of income and employment in Alaska communities.

The most recent global economic cycle to affect human settlement in Alaska has been oil. Declining oil and gas reserves in the 1960s, and the increased importation of oil into the United States, made oil exploration in Alaska profitable. The 1968 Prudhoe Bay discovery was an instant bonanza for the new state, and further exploration, development, and construction activities (for example, the trans-Alaska pipeline) brought thousands of new residents to the state. Oil and gas royalties and severance taxes paid for a massive increase in social and economic development, which was a further stimulus to migration from the other states.

Thus, the Alaska Native population settled Alaska and developed independent, subsistence lifestyles, while the majority, white population arrived in Alaska in response to global economic and political cycles. The combination of the white population's resource dependence, and the factors of physical geography and climatic extremes mentioned previously, created a unique path of sociopolitical development from Alaska's purchase in 1867 to statehood in 1959. Moreover, for nearly 100 years, Alaska was more dependent on the federal government than previous territories had been, but its distance and isolation made it the most neglected American territory. During this period, there grew in the territory a powerful drive by white settlers to make Alaska an integrated part of the United States. This drive flowered in the Alaska statehood movement of the 1950s. But as the "last colony" of the United States, in a dependent relationship for nearly a century, Alaska had to build a government system nearly from scratch.

This theme of dependence and reactions to it are explored in several chapters of this book. The chapters also dwell on some larger, universal issues of politics in the American states—regional conflicts and tensions, centralization versus decentralization, development versus preservation, and processes of political development.

Interregional tensions figure prominently in the history of Alaska politics. Strong rivalries, jealousies, and conflicts separate the different regions of the state—southeast, southcentral, interior, western, and the sparsely populated areas of northwest Alaska. The different regions of the state have been in competition for state dollars and programs, a conflict most visible in the battles over the location of the state capital and access to limited fish and game resources, as well as in legislative bargaining over the state's capital construction budget.

Cutting across this regional conflict is a very strong rural-urban tension, perhaps the single most important division in the state over the period of statehood. This tension reflects the different interests and needs of Native, primarily rural, Alaskans as opposed to non-Native, primarily white, urban Alaskans. The values of these communities are dissimilar, as are their resources and power, and competition between them—as well as cooperative relationships—are reflected in the state's political process.

As the state approaches the 1990 census—at which time it is likely that the unified Municipality of Anchorage and its immediate environs will hold a clear majority of the state's population—a third aspect of regional tension will become more important: the division between Anchorage and the rest of the state. Following a strict democratic majoritarian rule, by right the state's largest city should control outcomes, assuming its elected representatives could overcome their own partisan, ideological, and social divisions. Other values and rules, however, call for respect for regions, historical forces, and minority ethnic communities. These tensions and conflicts pervade Alaska politics.

The issue of centralization versus decentralization concerns the locus of power and control. Originally, this issue involved the relationship between Alaska and the federal government. After statehood, the issue shifted to the question of the proper amount of power at the state level—how centralized should state government be? This question figured in several plans for decentralization of state services, as the new state agencies decided how to establish offices and deliver services over the far-flung regions of the state. The topic also figured in discussions about the role of local governments, which under the Alaska constitution are given significant powers and the authority to use them liberally. There was little state-local conflict in the early 1980s, but declining state revenues will likely increase tension in the late 1980s and 1990s.

A related question concerns the maximum extent of self-government available to Alaskans. Several interrelated issues emerge and are addressed in different chapters of this book—opportunities for citizen involvement and participation in public affairs, democratization of policies and programs, and the extent to which popular and organized group demands have a deciding impact on public policies.

The issue of development versus preservation is endemic to and often synonymous with Alaska politics. An argument for statehood was that it would increase opportunity to develop Alaska economically, and this became a key point in subsequent state elections and government policymaking. Few have opposed economic development, and it is almost a consensus issue in the state. Instead, conflict has developed over the rates of economic and population growth, and, more important, over the extent to which the resources of the state should be conserved for use by future generations.

The issue of political development concerns the state polity as a whole. Over the period of statehood, the capability of government and its ability to respond to popular demands and needs have changed. Much of this change is attributable to greater state wealth, particularly in the late 1970s and early 1980s. A large and specialized state government workforce has developed, and it is equipped to handle a broad range of problems. More significant to the process of "institutionalization"—the ability of government to respond to changes in the environment—is the state's having confronted certain crises: first, the adjustment to a situation of independent authority with statehood, and, second, the adaptation to conditions of super-wealth and all this entailed. This series of tests has perhaps occurred earlier in Alaska's history than in those of other states, and the opportunities for crisis testing and hardening of the state's political system continue as the state faces a sharp revenue downturn in the years ahead. In various ways the following chapters explore the question of political development, examining the performance and capabilities of state government as an instrument by which the people of Alaska shape their futures.

ALASKA
STATE GOVERNMENT
AND POLITICS

1
Toward Statehood

Claus-M. Naske

Alaska became the 49th state on January 3, 1959. It had served a long apprenticeship before joining the union. In many ways the federal government had treated Alaska as it had no other territory, establishing government institutions slowly and withholding from it many of the authorities given other territories. When Alaskans had the chance to design their own state government, they intended to create a strong government with independent and vigorous executive, legislative, and judicial branches.

This chapter discusses the history of Alaska from the time of Russian rule up to statehood. It briefly outlines the various phases of Russia's occupation of northern North America. It deals with the American decision to purchase Russian America in 1867, and discusses the difficulties Congress and the executive departments encountered in attempting to devise workable governmental institutions for the nation's only noncontiguous, subarctic, subcontinental possession.

At first, the Army was assigned the job of governing this sprawling landmass, followed for a short time by the collector of customs, and then by the U.S. Navy. In 1884 Congress made Alaska a judicial district with passage of the First Organic Act. It provided the district with an appointed federal judge and various court officials as well as a territorial governor and other functionaries. In 1906 federal legislation granted Alaskans a delegate to Congress, and the passage of the Second Organic Act in 1912 officially made Alaska a territory and gave it a legislature with limited powers. With a large influx of population after World War II came increasing demands for statehood. More than 90 years after the U.S. purchased Alaska from Russia, Congress passed the Alaska Statehood Act, which admitted Alaska to the union and brought with it the promise of a new form of government.

RUSSIAN RULE

Between 1790 and 1840, Russia effectively rivaled Great Britain, Spain, and the United States for control of the resources of the northwest coast of

North America. Russian occupancy of Alaska from the late eighteenth century was the latest and farthest phase of a protracted and extensive eastward expansion the Russians had launched in the mid-sixteenth century. Their advance across northern Asia was speeded by the taiga's abundance of furs, Europe's ready markets, and a lack of foreign competition. Weak Native resistance also helped the Russians in their march of conquest. In 1639, sixty years after they crossed the Ural Mountains, Russian Cossacks and promyshlenniks, or fur hunters, reached the Pacific.

The first Russian approach to Alaska came in 1725, after Czar Peter the Great appointed Vitus Bering (a Dane holding the rank of captain in the Russian Navy) to lead the First Kamchatka Expedition. That expedition was to determine whether Asia and America were connected by land. Peter the Great died on January 28, 1725, but a part of Bering's expedition had already departed, led by Lieutenant Aleksei Chirikov. Bering followed in February.

After many hardships, Bering and his men reached Kamchatka village on the Kamchatka Peninsula in Siberia, thousands of miles east of St. Petersburg, and there built the ship *Gabriel*. He sailed through the strait which later was to bear his name and named Diomede Island. By 1730 he was back in St. Petersburg to report on the results of his voyage. Scholars, however, were disappointed with his findings, because he could not conclusively prove that the two continents were separated. Within a short time, therefore, Bering proposed a second voyage to clear up the matter. The Great Northern Expedition was to be vast in scope. Bering proposed to explore and chart the western coast of America and establish commercial relations with that country, visit Japan and the Amur, and chart the Arctic coast of Siberia. By 1733, detachments of the expedition left St. Petersburg. Bering had the ships *St. Peter* and *St. Paul* built. Bering founded the settlement of Petropavlovsk on the Kamchatka Peninsula, wintered there, and departed from there in May 1741. Bering and Chirikov, his second-in-command, became separated almost immediately, and the latter returned to Kamchatka that same year. Bering's boat shipwrecked on Bering Island, where he died. The survivors returned to Petropavlovsk and brought news of a great landmass across the eastern Pacific Ocean, and numerous samples of sea otter pelts, which were to prove more valuable and marketable than the sable skins which had been the mainstay of the Russian fur trade.[1]

This discovery prompted a fur rush across the Bering Sea via the convenient Aleutian Island chain, giving the Russians a substantial head start on foreign competition. In fact, other nations did not learn of the Russian presence in Alaska until the results of British Captain James Cook's third voyage (1776-1779) were published.

From about 1745, Russian fur hunters harvested off the Aleutians and gradually moved east toward Kodiak Island and southeast Alaska. Russian America had many weaknesses, including labor shortage, natural climatic severity, inadequate transportation, and most critically, insufficient food supply. Also, fur bearers were becoming depleted, there was fierce competition between Russian fur traders, and British and American entrepreneurs were beginning to offer strong competition. Despite all these problems, the Russians established the first permanent settlement in 1784 on the southwestern coast of Kodiak Island at Three Saints Harbor.

Three Saints Harbor remained the company's chief settlement until 1791, when Alexander Baranov, the manager for the largest Russian fur trader, established St. Paul's Harbor at the present site of Kodiak City. It soon became one of the largest settlements in Russian America. Other settlements followed, but the Russian population remained small and scattered; in 1788 the Spanish Captains Esteban Jose Martinez and Gonzalo Lopez de Haro had visited Unalaska and learned that there were approximately 500 Russian promyshlenniks (fur hunters) with twenty ships at seven settlements in Alaska. Czar Paul I organized the harvesting of American fur resources in 1799, when he ended the competition among the various small companies and granted a monopoly to a group of merchants who combined to form the Russian-American Company. The formation of the Russian-American Company halved the population, dropping it to no more than 225 Russians, including fewer than 200 promyshlenniks. The decrease occurred because many small entrepreneurs left Alaska after the monopoly was granted.

Alexander Baranov was chosen to manage the new Russian-American Company, and he dominated the period from 1799 to 1818, which roughly coincided with the first charter of the Russian-American Company. This period was characterized by expansion to California and Hawaii, despite stronger Native opposition and keen foreign competition. When Baranov retired in 1818, the Russian Navy took over control of the colony. The period from 1819 to 1840 was characterized by corporate reorganization, a reorientation of settlement northward and inland, and regulation of foreign competition. Naval officers conducted a conservative administration. Profits from the colony also declined during that period.

By 1833, the Russian-American Company had five administrative units known as counters and two districts with a population of 627 Russians, 991 Creoles (or individuals of mixed Native-Russian blood), and 9,120 Natives. New Archangel (Sitka), Kodiak, Unalaska, and Atka in Alaska, and Ross in California, comprised the five counters. The two districts were the Northern, including Stuart Island and the settlements on the adjacent mainland of Norton Sound in western Alaska, and Kurile, which was centered on Urup (Alexander) Island in the Kuriles. New Archangel Counter predominated, because it was the seat of the governor and the commercial center of the colonies, conducting fishing, manufacturing, lumbering, and sawmilling.[2]

Eventually, Russia was no longer able to compete with the British and American traders because it offered inferior and costlier goods. After it lost the Crimean War to Great Britain and France in 1856, revolutionary changes took place in the country. The Russian government eventually decided to sell Russian America to the United States since the colony by then had become a financial burden.

Rivalry between American whalers and fur traders and their Russian counterparts first drew official attention of the United States to northern North America. Russia's policy of excluding foreign vessels from Russian American waters had displeased Secretary of State John Quincy Adams and led to negotiations that resulted in the Conventions of 1824 and 1825, which admitted American and British vessels to Russian coasts in the north Pacific. By the 1850s expansionists in the United States had renewed their interest in the region and its resources. In 1852 Senators William H. Seward and William M. Gwin sponsored legislation to explore and map the area to facilitate American commerce there. By the middle of that decade, Russian America's potential as a strategic link to Asia had whetted the appetite of many Americans who believed in the manifest destiny of the United States—namely, to occupy the whole hemisphere.

ALASKA BECOMES A U.S. POSSESSION

In 1867, William H. Seward, who by then had become Secretary of State, negotiated the purchase of Alaska from Russia. The reasons for the purchase were complex, but included Seward's belief in the manifest destiny of the United States; the hope that it would give the United States an entry in the Northwest for trade with the Pacific and Asia; the expectation that the deal would sandwich British Columbia between American territory and make inevitable its annexation; the belief that Alaska's resources would more than pay for the $7.2 million price tag; and, last but not least, American friendship for Russia. The new possession was the nation's first noncontiguous territory. Preoccupied with attempts to impeach President Andrew Johnson, as well as with the complex problems of Reconstruction after the Civil War, Congress waited fifteen months to appropriate the $7.2 million purchase money.

THE ARMY TAKES OVER

Seward arranged for the War Department to occupy Alaska until Congress provided a civil government. In the meantime, Alaska was designated a district and not a territory. The difference between the two was that a territory had a representative assembly whereas a district did not. The constitution gave Congress plenary power over Alaska, as it did over all other United States territories. The pertinent constitutional language stated that "Congress shall have power to dispose of and make all needful rules and regulations respecting the territory or other property belonging to the United States." Therefore, on July 27, 1868 Congress extended the customs, commerce, and navigation laws of the United States to Alaska, and designated it as a customs collection district. Much later it was held that by this act and by the "rights, advantages and immunities" clause of the Treaty of Cession, Congress had "incorporated" Alaska, which was an important designation, because it meant Alaska was eligible for statehood at some future time.

The terms "incorporated" and "unincorporated" were devised by the U.S. Supreme Court in a series of decisions in the early twentieth century known as the "Insular Cases." These decisions stemmed from the Spanish-American War of 1898, which had brought the United States possession of numerous noncontiguous territories with large, non-white populations. Congress, reflecting American attitudes of the time, was unwilling to consider these new possessions as potentially entitled to statehood. The Supreme Court, therefore, declared that in some territories, namely Alaska and Hawaii, the U.S. constitution applied fully. That meant Alaska and Hawaii were "incorporated" and thereby entitled to future statehood. Others, like Puerto Rico, were "unincorporated" because the U.S. constitution did not apply fully to them, and they were therefore disqualified from future statehood. Secretary of War Elihu Root reportedly said of this rather nebulous distinction established by the court, "...as near as I can make out the constitution follows the flag—but doesn't quite catch up with it."[3]

The U.S. Army arrived in Alaska in October 1867. After the transfer ceremonies had taken place in Sitka on October 18 of that year, the Army constructed six posts, completed in 1869. One year later it had abandoned all but the one at Sitka because no need existed for the others. From that post, successive Army officers enforced what little law existed, maintained order, aided the short-lived city government of Sitka, and fed the destitute when necessary. In the absence of civil government, the Army officers, in effect, became Alaska's governors. Army officials also concerned themselves with

Indian affairs, maintaining peace with the Natives of southeastern Alaska. Congress had designated the district "Indian Country," a designation that allowed the Army to keep the Natives from consuming alcohol. Enforcing the liquor prohibition therefore constituted the primary administrative problem for Alaska's military commanders. They generally failed. They were marooned on their island posts, and even the occasional help of a Revenue Marine Service vessel could not stem liquor smuggling. Worse yet, the Natives had learned to distill hoochinoo, a vile but potent liquor. No districtwide administration enforced the law, and no one was certain what laws applied in Alaska and precisely which Pacific Coast courts had jurisdiction over what.[4]

CONGRESSIONAL NEGLECT

In fact, Congress had not yet provided Alaskans with any legal means of acquiring title to land, staking mining claims, enforcing contracts, arranging matrimony, bequeathing property, or penalizing any misconduct not defined by the Customs Act of 1868. William H. Seward visited Sitka in 1869 and commiserated with its citizens about their situation. In addressing the town's residents, the former Secretary of State expressed the conviction that Congress would surely provide Alaskans with a civil government during the coming winter, because "our political system rejects alike anarchy and executive absolutism." He also was confident that "the political society to be constituted here, first as a Territory, and ultimately as a State or many States, will prove a worthy constituency of the Republic."[5]

Seward's prophecy and the expectations of Sitka's inhabitants went unrealized. Congress did pass legislation to protect the fur seals in 1870, but did not concern itself with the north in a major fashion until 1884.

In the meantime, Army troops left Alaska in 1877 after experts at congressional budget hearings testified that the soldiers were of no use in Alaska and merely represented an unnecessary expense. Furthermore, the troops were needed to aid in suppressing the uprising of Chief Joseph and his Nez Perce Indian tribe in the Pacific Northwest. The collector of customs and his deputies now were the sole federal representatives in Alaska, but these representatives of the Treasury Department lacked the necessary force to maintain order even in the southeast region. Historian Jeannette P. Nichols reported that the customs collector was "supported by a small armament and two cases of rifles and two cases of ammunition..." to be used to enforce the laws. Soon reports of strife became common and many anticipated bloodshed. In early 1879, after the murder of a white man and alleged threats of violence by Indians, Sitka's residents appealed for British protection. With United States sanction, a British man-of-war steamed to Sitka to protect the settlement. The rumors of an uprising proved to be unfounded, but soon the U.S. Navy assumed administrative responsibilities for the district.

A succession of able Naval commanders ruled southeastern Alaska. The Naval governors controlled the coastal tribes through an Indian police force and an occasional show of force, resorting to punitive action only once. The Navy interfered little with civilian affairs, and intervened only to prevent disorder and violence and to arrest criminals. Since it had mobility, the Navy more effectively administered Alaska affairs than its Army and Treasury Department predecessors had, but it also lacked legal authority. Naval rule ended in 1884, after Congress passed the First Organic Act for Alaska.[6]

THE FIRST ORGANIC ACT

Congress governed Alaska for seventeen years through the administrative expedients of putting first the Army, then the Treasury Department, and finally the Navy in charge. Congress was under growing pressure to provide more government when Presbyterian missionary Sheldon Jackson mounted a petition campaign and when prospectors swarmed into the Juneau area in 1880 after the discovery of gold and organized a mining district. Congress finally passed Alaska's First Organic Act on May 17, 1884. (An organic act provides fundamental authorities for institutions.) A compromise bill, it designated Alaska a civil and judicial district, an unprecedented event, and authorized the president to appoint a governor with few specific powers. It designated Sitka as the capital and prohibited the importation, sale, and manufacture of liquor, "except for medicinal, mechanical, and scientific purposes," and charged the president with making provisions for enforcing the prohibition. There was to be be no county organization, no delegate to Congress, no territorial legislature, no regular system of taxation. The act did not extend the U.S. constitution and laws of the United States to Alaska, as was customary in territorial acts. Instead, "only those laws not locally inapplicable or inconsistent with the provisions of this Act" were to apply to Alaska. Since the constitution did not fully extend to Alaska, federal officials there could not be required to swear that they would support the constitution and laws of the United States. The act provided that they swear "the oaths required by law."[7]

The act provided for one federal territorial district court judge, a marshal and four deputy marshals, a district attorney, a clerk, and four commissioners. The clerk, in addition to his judicial duties, was to record deeds, mortgages, and certificates of mining claims and other real estate contracts as well as registering wills. The marshal, in addition to his traditional responsibilities, also functioned as surveyor-general, while the four commissioners exercised the powers and duties of justices of the peace under the laws of Oregon. During the debate on the Alaska measure, Senator James B. Beck of Kentucky asked Senator Benjamin Harrison of Indiana, the sponsor of the bill, why the laws of Oregon were to apply to Alaska. Beck pointed out that Washington Territory's less complicated statutes would be more suitable for primitive Alaska. Harrison replied that his committee had not studied the Oregon nor Washington laws very carefully. His committee had felt, however, that it was preferable to apply to any territory a code of laws adopted by a mature legislature of a state rather than a code of laws adopted by the immature and imperfect legislature of an adjacent territory. Also, Alaska already had been attached to Oregon for some judicial purposes. Harrison also speculated that the adoption of the Oregon code "was in the mind of the person who framed the original bill, and in...remodeling it, as I presented it to the Senate this session, I took it just as I found it in that respect."[8]

The laws of the United States were to be enforced in Alaska, and wherever applicable, the general laws of the state of Oregon as they existed at the time. Appeals from decisions of the district court of Alaska were to go to the United States circuit court of the district of Oregon. Congress also designated Alaska a land district in which United States mining laws were to apply. Congress decided not to extend the general land laws to Alaska until they had been rewritten; at the time the laws were receiving much public scrutiny due to abuses and land scandals that had occurred in the contiguous states and territories. There seemed to be considerable public sentiment for keeping the remaining U.S. public lands for bona fide settlers. The organic act also declared that "the Indians or other persons in said district shall not be disturbed in the possession of any lands actually in their use or occupation or now claimed by them, but the terms under which such persons may acquire title to such lands is reserved for future legislation by Congress."[9] This provision was to prove very important in the later Alaska Native land claims movement.

Senator Harrison, chairman of the Senate Committee on Territories in 1884, apologized for the severe shortcomings of the legislation. He conceded that "all of the provisions of the bill are inadequate. It is a mere shift; it is a mere expedient; it is a mere beginning in what we believe to be the right direction toward giving a civil government and education to Alaska. I hope more will follow, but the committee in this matter adjudged what they believed to be the probable limit of the generosity of the Senate."[10]

Earl S. Pomeroy, a historian of territorial government, observed that Alaska "stood in an outer political anteroom without the most rudimentary territorial status, governed (when governed at all) more like the Newfoundland fisheries of the seventeenth-century British empire than like a territory.'' Jack E. Eblen, another scholar of territorial government, concluded that the organic act "provided a cruelly modified first-stage government and made no provision for eventual representative government."[11]

Historian Nichols observed that Alaska's Organic Act of 1884 "evolved from a composite of honest intentions, ignorance, stupidity, indifference, and quasi-expediency." In his 1887-1888 annual report to the Congress, the Secretary of the Interior described civil relations in Alaska as "anomalous and exceptional." He referred to the organic act as an "imperfect and crude piece of legislation," because it provided only "the shadow of civil government, without the right to legislate or raise revenue." It had not extended the general land laws to Alaska, but declared the mining laws to be fully operational. It had created a single tribunal "with many of the powers of a Federal or State court, having more extensive territorial jurisdiction than any similar court in the United States, but without providing the means of serving its process or enforcing its decrees." Overall, the organic act has been described as a "legislative fungus, without precedent or parallel in the history of American legislation."[12] But despite all the criticism and the act's inadequacies, it was important because it established the foundation upon which Alaska's governmental structure could later be elaborated, refined, and expanded.

There were some immediate problems, however, because Alaska's residents in 1884 had no means of establishing towns or counties, and no taxes were levied on the inhabitants. As a consequence, no school districts could be created, because the Oregon code allowed only county superintendents to set up such districts. Furthermore, Oregon charged county officials with marriage registration and the execution of probate rights. Such activities could not lawfully be conducted in Alaska since it had no counties. The Oregon code also required that jurors be selected from among taxpayers. Alaska had no taxpayers, and jury trials were therefore unauthorized.[13]

Demands for additional legislation soon arose, but Congress could not be roused until another gold discovery convulsed the district. In 1896, George Carmack and two Indian companions discovered gold near the Klondike, a Canadian tributary of the Yukon River. Not long thereafter, prospectors made additional discoveries in Alaska, near the present site of Nome in 1898 and on the beaches of Nome soon thereafter. In 1902 Felix Pedro discovered gold in the Tanana Valley, which led to the founding of the town of Fairbanks. As a result, the population of the district increased from 33,052, of whom 6,698 were non-Native, in 1890, to 63,592, of whom 34,056 were non-Native, in 1900. This resource wealth and sudden population influx finally persuaded Congress to pay attention to Alaska once again.[14]

MORE GOVERNMENT FOR ALASKA

In 1897, President William McKinley, taking notice of the gold rush, said in his first annual message to Congress that "the conditions now existing demand material changes in the laws relating to the Territory." In 1899, the president again voiced his concern for Alaska problems when he asserted that "a necessity for immediate legislative relief exists in the Territory of Alaska." McKinley asked for a system of local government and at least two federal judges. "I see no reason why a more complete form of territorial organization should not be provided," he added.[15]

Under the McKinley administration the Fifty-fifth Congress (1897-99) passed two major pieces of legislation pertaining to the northern territory. One, enacted before the end of 1898, made various provisions for the construction of railroads and extended the homestead laws to Alaska. The size of the homestead plots, however, was arbitrarily restricted to 80 acres in contrast to the 160 acres allowed in the contiguous states, and the burden of the survey had to be borne by the applicant. The act also provided that Canadian citizens were to be accorded the same mining rights as American citizens were granted in Canada, and goods could be transported duty-free between Alaska and Canadian ports if the Canadians granted reciprocal privileges.[16]

The other major piece of legislation provided for the punishment of crime in Alaska and gave the territory a code of criminal procedure. This act was very complex. It codified the laws of Oregon and modified them for Alaska. Included was a tax system, the first one for the district, which included license fees for occupations and taxes on industry. Funds derived from these taxes were to pay for the government of Alaska, and the surplus was to go into the United States Treasury.[17] This system of taxation, with only minor modifications, persisted for over fifty years.

Congress passed many Alaska bills between 1899 and 1901, including measures pertaining to Native welfare, education, and the fisheries. The act of June 6, 1900 called for moving the capital from Sitka to Juneau (because of the influx of miners to Juneau), although the physical relocation was not accomplished for several years.

Congress also complemented the Penal Code of 1899 with a civil code and code of civil procedure. With this piece of legislation, Congress began to deal directly with the problem of providing a general governmental system for Alaska. It divided the immense judicial district into three parts, and established district courts at Sitka, Nome, and Eagle City on the Yukon, with authority to convene elsewhere when necessary. Within the framework of the Organic Act of 1884, which had established Alaska as a civil and judicial district of the United States, the 1900 act provided for the presidential appointment of three district court judges, who in turn were to appoint commissioners, a function previously exercised by the chief executive. The 1900 act also made possible the incorporation of municipalities for the first time. Communities with 300 or more permanent inhabitants were allowed to organize local governments. It also provided for the establishment of municipal and district schools, and reduced some of the license fees imposed by the Penal Code of 1899. Half the revenues collected from the businesses within incorporated towns were to be returned to the municipalities for educational purposes. The following year Congress authorized the use of such funds in excess of school needs to be spent on other municipal projects. This spate of legislation in the early 1900s was the beginning of statutory local self-government in Alaska.[18]

Congress had relied heavily on the Oregon and California statutes in drafting and enacting the civil and criminal codes. Alaskans at last had been provided with criminal and civil laws and means for their enforcement, local self-government, and a tax system. Still, northern citizens were dissatisfied. Increasingly, they demanded a delegate to Congress, and less frequently, a territorial legislature.[19]

Precedents existed for giving Alaska a non-voting delegate to Congress. The Northwest Ordinance of 1787 had empowered the legislature of the territory northwest of the Ohio River to elect a delegate to Congress. The delegateship first became popularly elective in 1808 in Mississippi territory. A member of the House of Representatives, the delegate was authorized to introduce bills and participate in debate. He received the same pay and enjoyed all the privileges of the other representatives, but he could not vote. The delegate also represented the territory before the executive branch of the federal government. The effectiveness of this voteless delegate obviously depended on his persuasive qualities. Dealing largely with territorial issues, the delegate did not have to take stands on controversial national issues. He thereby avoided the ire some of his colleagues incurred from constituents.[20]

Bills to provide Alaska with a delegate to Congress were repeatedly introduced between 1897 and 1903. These measures made some progress, but not enough for enactment. Ordinarily, Congress authorized the establishment of a territorial legislature before providing for the election of a delegate. In 1903, however, President Theodore Roosevelt pledged his aid in securing a delegateship in a speech he made to Alaskans in Seattle's Grand Opera House. Roosevelt said that those men of his age in the audience, ''will not be old men before they see one of the greatest and most populous states of the entire Union in Alaska.'' This was Roosevelt exaggeration, but taking his cue from the president, Senator Albert Beveridge of Indiana arranged for the Committee on Territories to tour Alaska during the summer of that year. After returning home, the committee reported that Alaska residents felt their social, industrial, and political conditions were little understood in the nation's capital. They requested that Alaska be represented by someone who understood and could authoritatively speak ''concerning their interests.'' Alaskans universally desired delegate representation and only disagreed on the method of selection. Most preferred election, but others argued that the president should appoint the delegate with the consent of the Senate. These individuals were apprehensive about the costs and problems of conducting elections in a huge area with a widely dispersed and unstable population.[21]

The House eventually passed a delegate bill, but when the measure reached the Senate, Orville Platt of Connecticut opposed it. He urged Congress to formulate special policies for governing noncontiguous territories. Platt proposed ''that nothing in this act shall in any way be taken or construed to imply or indicate that the territory embraced in the district of Alaska, or any portion thereof, shall at any time hereafter be admitted as a State.'' James Wickersham, a federal territorial district court judge in interior Alaska, had testified before the Beveridge committee in 1903 in favor of a delegate bill. On hearing of Platt's remark, the judge declared in a speech in Fairbanks that Alaska residents might have to form an independent country in the face of congressional inaction. A Republic of Alaska could adopt a constitution modeled on the federal document, Wickersham said, and could be divided into four states.[22]

During the summer of 1904, the *Valdez News* and the *Skagway Daily Alaskan* suggested that Alaskans establish their own legislature, elect a delegate, and send him to Congress even without the authorization of that body. If their delegate were rejected, northerners should ''go it alone and govern Alaska.'' At a public meeting in Valdez, citizens sent President Roosevelt a telegram on March 4, 1905, his inauguration day: ''On behalf of 60,000 American citizens in Alaska who are denied the right of representation in any form, we demand, in mass meeting assembled, that Alaska be annexed to Canada''—a message that might not impress a U.S. president. As early as 1898, the Dominion government had granted an appointive legislative council to the Yukon Territory. By early 1905, half the council members were elective and Yukon residents had elected a member to Parliament in Ottawa. Newspapers in the United States and Canada commented on the Yukon-Alaska contrast, and the telegram to the president undoubtedly was designed to prod Congress into action.[23]

Congress finally responded, in part because so many individuals claimed to speak for the territory. These included interested west coast Congressmen, the appointive governor, civil and military officials of the federal government employed in the north, the lobbyists for the mining and canned-salmon industries, representatives of steamship and mercantile interests, and Seattle and San Francisco merchants and members of chambers of commerce. Often their voices were contradictory, and it was difficult for Congress and the president to sort out what to believe. In his 1905 State of the Union address, Roosevelt asked Congress to "give Alaska some person whose business it shall be to speak with authority on her behalf to the Congress." In the spring of 1906, Congress passed legislation authorizing Alaskans to elect a delegate.[24]

Some Alaskans were only partially pacified by the delegate bill because they still lacked a legislature. Many others, however, argued that until the territory's population increased and its economy developed further, a legislature would be premature. Territorial Governor John Brady, appointed by President William McKinley and reappointed by President Theodore Roosevelt, became the spokesman for the latter group. He argued that Alaska lacked the necessary population and taxable wealth to support a system of counties and townships. Instead of agitating for home rule, he urged his fellow citizens to lobby Congress and the executive departments to modify the homestead law and support improvements in transportation, communications, agriculture, and education in the territory. Once Alaska possessed an adequate infrastructure and had become home to a large and stable population, the governor said, Congress should skip the territorial government stage entirely and simply admit Alaska into the union as a state.

Assuming that newspaper coverage reflected popular thinking, the majority of Alaskans shared Brady's views in the early part of the new century. Residents of southeast Alaska, however, wanted a legislature for their section alone, maintaining that it would be too expensive and too difficult for a legislature to function over the whole district. Interior residents expressed little interest in a territorial government, and at Valdez and Nome opinions were about evenly divided between those who favored territorial organization and those who opposed it. Among the latter were most businessmen, who feared the enormous costs involved and suspected that they would have to bear the lion's share of the necessary taxes.[25]

President Roosevelt appointed Wilford Hoggatt to the Alaska governorship in 1906. The new chief executive shared Brady's viewpoint, which put him in opposition to Frank Waskey and Thomas Cale, Alaska's first and second delegates to Congress. In the meantime, the president had conferred with

Delegate Cale, and then recommended to Congress that it provide some form of local self-government, "as simple and inexpensive as possible," because that body did not have the time to deal with the details of legislation required for the north. Delegate Cale thereupon introduced two measures to achieve the objective. James Wickersham had drafted one of the bills. Wickersham had come to Alaska in 1900, when President McKinley appointed him to a federal district court judgeship. He had gained a reputation for efficiency, fairness, and courage on the benches at Nome, Eagle, and Fairbanks. Unsuccessful litigants, however, disliked him, and some of those individuals were politically influential, preventing his Senate confirmation as a judge. President Roosevelt, however, liked him and kept him in office through five recess appointments. The judge eventually tired of that game and resigned in 1907. Shortly thereafter, in 1908, he successfully ran for the delegateship and subsequently dominated Alaska politics for a couple of decades.[26]

At first, Wickersham had opposed territorial government, and had written to Governor Hoggatt, criticizing Delegates Waskey and Cale for advocating territorial organization. Alaska was too poor, and its population too sparse and unstable, to sustain organized government. In fact, in his judgment most Alaskans actually opposed territorial organization, although it was always easy to draft Fourth of July resolutions favoring it. But Wickersham changed his mind, and became the champion of the movement for territorial government. The territorial legislature that Wickersham had in mind, however, was a very restrictive one.

In any event, the bill went no further than Senate committee investigation, because its members feared that territorial organization would seemingly promise statehood to a noncontiguous territory, while the House committee thought it would require excessive taxes.[27]

When Cale decided not to run again, Wickersham sought the delegateship and won the 1908 election. He arrived in Washington early in 1909 and wasted no time introducing a bill for territorial government. It was unclear how the new president, William Taft, would regard the measure. His views on the matter were unclear until the end of September, when he addressed a large crowd at the Alaska-Yukon-Pacific Exposition in Seattle. Alaska was too sparsely settled and too sectional to be given a legislature. The president said that federal concern for the district should be centralized in a single department of the government for the time being, presumably the Bureau of Insular Affairs in the War Department. A commission of five or more members, appointed by the president, would exercise local legislative power. Taft said this was practically the same government Congress had given to the Philippine Islands, although the commission there had more legislative authority than he considered necessary for its Alaskan counterpart.[28]

As governor general of the Philippines under President Roosevelt, Taft had implemented the commission form of government. He had gained a reputation as an exceptionally able administrator, and he considered his proposal for Alaska efficient and adequate for the district's needs. In part because of the Philippine analogy, public reaction in Alaska was generally unfavorable and sometimes bitter. For example, an editorial in the *Fairbanks Times* said that President Taft's Philippine experience had been with people who were not born to self-government: "Withhold self-government from a Malay, and he will not know the difference. Deprive an Anglo-Saxon of the same thing, and he feels enslaved." Wickersham remarked that Taft was surprised at the Alaskan reaction. If the president anticipated trouble from the north over his proposal, the delegate concluded, it was likely to occur, for "I intend to make some myself."[29]

If anything, the president's plan for a commission form of government had a unifying effect in Alaska, where many changed from mere interest in a local legislature to active advocacy. This became evident when Wickersham asked his constituents to strengthen his position in Washington by holding mass meetings on October 18, 1909—the anniversary of Alaska Cession Day—and by passing resolutions in favor of home rule. Many citizens complied with his request, and the delegate returned to Washington fortified with these favorable expressions. Others, however, still opposed a legislature and pointed out that it would mean higher taxes.[30] In any event, Congress never enacted President Taft's government plan for Alaska because it was so contrary to all previous American territorial experience, and also because a majority of northern residents opposed it. In addition, Taft had problems with Republican progressives in the Senate and insurgents in the House who regarded him as a conservative in a time of dynamic reform. The 1910 elections brought more progressives and insurgents to Congress, and the Democrats gained control of the House of Representatives. Members of Congress continued to raise questions about Alaska's size, racial heterogeneity, the instability of its population, the level of taxation required for territorial organization, the influence big business would exercise, and the degree of popular support for territorial organization. The doubts, however, did not prevail against the now widely-shared feeling that Alaska should receive a better governmental structure.[31]

ESTABLISHING TERRITORIAL GOVERNMENT

Both houses of Congress finally passed a modified version of the Wickersham bill, and President Taft signed the measure into law on August 24, 1912.

This Second Organic Act defined the structure and powers of Alaska's legislature for the next forty-six years. It authorized a biennial legislature, consisting of a senate of eight members serving four-year terms, and a house of sixteen members serving two-year terms. The existing judicial divisions were made electoral districts as well. Each district received equal representation in the house and senate. Congress earlier had expanded the number of judicial divisions from three to four: the first division was headquartered at Juneau, the second at Nome, the third at Valdez and later Anchorage, and the fourth at Fairbanks. The Senate Committee on Territories had proposed that Alaska should have a unicameral legislature, since senators and representatives represent identical constituencies. Wickersham, however, feared that unicameralism would imperil the measure, and the House did not concur with the Senate. The United States Treasury, as it had with previous territorial governments, was to pay legislative expenses. The appointive governor possessed the item veto for appropriation acts, but had to veto all other measures as a whole. The legislature could override vetoes by a two-thirds vote of each house. Congress retained the authority, never exercised, to disallow any territorial legislation.[32]

The Second Organic Act quickly became famous for the many restrictions it imposed on the legislature, some customary and not objectionable, others serious ones reflecting Wickersham's experiences as attorney, judge, legislator, and property owner. He was afraid, for example, that the legislature might plunge the territory into debt. He thought county government would be too expensive. Other restrictions reflected Congressional attitudes and the objections of miners and businessmen to unlimited legislative power to borrow and spend. Historian Nichols concluded that for the benefit of the "lobbies of the fish conservationists and the big New York game hunters," Congress assigned the regulation of Alaska's fish, game, and fur resources to the federal government. No other organized territory had ever been denied this function.[33]

The legislature was not to alter license taxes imposed by the Penal Code of 1899 and the Civil Code of 1900, nor could the legislature or any municipality assume bonded indebtedness without Congressional consent. No debts were to be incurred except in anticipation of the tax receipts of any one year. Municipal property taxes were limited to two percent of "actual" rather than "assessed" value. Congress also excluded a wide range of local or special laws as specified in the Territories Act of 1886 from the jurisdiction of the legislature. No act organizing county government for Alaska could become effective without Congressional approval. These and other restrictions soon led to agitation for increased powers.

The Second Organic Act specifically incorporated Alaska, although the Supreme Court had already ruled that it had been incorporated since 1868. As mentioned earlier in the chapter, the court had made a distinction between "incorporated" and "unincorporated" territories, holding in essence that "incorporated" territories were destined for statehood, while "unincorporated" territories were forever excluded from that status. The Second Organic Act also gave Alaska a substantially increased, although limited, form of self-government. It was to be another forty-seven years before the territory joined the union.

The territorial legislature was to convene "at the capitol at the city of Juneau, Alaska, on the first Monday in March in the year nineteen hundred thirteen, and on the first Monday in March every two years thereafter." Sessions were restricted to sixty days, but the governor had the authority to call fifteen-day extraordinary sessions.[34]

The first act of the territorial legislature extended the franchise to women, while the second designated legal holidays, including Alaska Day on October 18 of each year. Other legislation established the Alaska Pioneers' Home, created the office of territorial treasurer, regulated the practice of medicine and dentistry, established a modest tax system including a poll tax, made education compulsory, created juvenile courts, and established a system for registering vital statistics. Lawmakers also passed much labor legislation, including a workmen's compensation law. The first ecology measure prohibited the discharge of sawdust and other lumber waste into territorial waters. The legislature also appropriated the magnificent sum of $75, 143.75 for the biennium. Of that amount, at least $11,000 was not expended.[35]

Meeting for the second biennial legislature, lawmakers in 1915 created the offices of attorney general and territorial mine inspector. The next year, Alaskans voted to ban the sale of alcohol. Congress quickly responded to territorial wishes in February 1917 when it passed the so-called "Alaska Bone Dry Law" which became effective on January 1, 1918, more than a year before prohibition became effective nationwide.[36] It soon became evident that Alaskans had acted rashly, because demand for alcohol continued unabated and made enforcement of prohibition almost impossible.

In 1916, Delegate James Wickersham introduced the first Alaska statehood bill on March 30, the forty-ninth anniversary of the signing of the Treaty of Cession. Referred to committee, it was not dealt with.[37]

By an act of March 3, 1917 Congress authorized the Alaska Legislature "to establish and maintain schools for white and colored children and children of mixed blood who lead a civilized life," and to appropriate funds for such purposes. In response, territorial lawmakers created a board of education. In that same session, the lawmakers also established the Alaska Agricultural College and School of Mines at Fairbanks. In 1935, the legislature responded to the request of the alumni and administration of the institution and changed the name to University of Alaska.[38]

In other early actions, the 1917 legislature created a bureau of publicity to promote tourism and economic development, and created Alaska's first primary election, to be held on the last Tuesday in April 1918, and every two years thereafter.[39] In 1919, the legislature established the office of labor commissioner and provided that the territorial mine inspector fill the position ex-officio; it also created the office of commissioner of health, a part-time position with a number of assistant commissioners serving in various parts of the territory.

Subsequent legislatures continued to respond to territorial needs and constituent demands. In 1921, for example, lawmakers put into place a system of business license taxes. The 1920s saw the subsidization of certain air routes, authorization for the Alaska Road Commission, a federal agency, to construct airplane landing fields, and creation of a teachers' pension board and fund.[40]

Over the years, many lawmakers clashed with the federally-appointed governor and wished to emasculate that office. They resented the governor because he represented federal authority in the territory, and many lawmakers alternately complained of federal oppression or neglect. The governor was a symbol of federal power and reminded them of their impotence. In 1923, territorial senator Frank A.T. Aldrich introduced the first of a series of measures that were designed to sharply restrict the chief executive's powers. Others followed in the 1920s. Finally, on January 29, 1957, just before Alaska became a state, the Territorial Affairs Committee introduced the last of these bills, entitled "An Act to reorganize the Territorial Government; creating the office of Administrative Governor, and defining his powers and duties and repealing conflicting laws to the extent of the conflict...."

In essence, these so-called "administrative governor" bills provided for a new office in territorial government. The titles of these measures varied, including "administrative governor," "governor general," "controller," and "controller general." The purpose of these measures, however, was always identical: in each instance the legislature first proposed to appoint the new officer, but then to make the office elective at the first general election following enactment of the measure. The administrative governor was to take over all the duties and functions granted to the federally-appointed governor of Alaska by territorial law. These included power to appoint the commissioners of lands and agriculture, the tax commissioner, the directors of finance and civil defense, and the members of territorial boards and commissions, such as the banking board. The new official also was to administer a number of territorial programs, including rescue and relief of lost persons and emergency relief. None of the measures ever passed both houses of the territorial legislature.[41]

While the legislators and the governor feuded from time to time, the Great Depression began in the contiguous states. It finally affected Alaska in the 1930s. It brought unemployment, and eventually Alaska participated in a modest fashion in some of the many New Deal economic recovery programs. To help ameliorate economic hardships, territorial lawmakers also appropriated funds for direct relief for the needy, and for job-generating programs such as clearing salmon streams, stocking lakes and streams with game fish, and maintaining roads and trails. Revenues continued to shrink as the Depression worsened, and the 1933 legislature created a board of administration and authorized it to "freeze" appropriations in whole or in part when funds for them had not become available. In addition, lawmakers regularly memorialized Congress, asking for more federal public works funds. In 1937, Governor John W. Troy called Alaska's first extraordinary session of the legislature, immediately following the regular session, to enact the territory's unemployment compensation law. Lawmakers also created a department of welfare during that special session.[42]

Of major importance to Alaska's future was the appointment of Ernest Gruening to Alaska's governorship in 1939. He had graduated from Harvard University in 1912 with a medical degree, but never practiced medicine and instead became a journalist and expert on Latin American affairs. That expertise brought him to the attention of President Franklin Roosevelt, and he was appointed advisor to the United States delegation to the Seventh Inter-American Conference held at Montevideo, Uruguay in 1933. The next year the president appointed Gruening director of the newly-created Division of Territories and Island Possessions within the Department of the Interior. After much conflict between Gruening and his boss, Secretary of the Interior Harold L. Ickes, the president decided to kick Gruening upstairs by making him governor of Alaska. The new governor, an intelligent and energetic man, was determined to prove his mettle to the president and to bring backward Alaska into the American political and economic mainstream.[43]

In the process, Gruening clashed with the territorial legislature. Over the years that body created many boards and commissions designed to curtail the governor's authority. The new governor's agenda was an ambitious one: to goad the lawmakers into adopting a modern tax system. He also thought that Alaska should demand statehood.

Alaska's voters declared themselves for statehood in the October 1946 general election, by a vote of 9,630 to 6,822. They also approved a blanket primary by a vote of 12,305 to 3,328. Implemented by the 1947 legislature, this measure eliminated the party primary in which the candidates of the two political parties appeared on separate ballots and voters had to declare party membership in order to vote. Now all candidates would appear on one ballot and no party declaration would be necessary.[44]

The 1949 territorial legislature adopted a modern tax system. Gruening savored the realization of the goal he had set himself in 1939. He generally was happy with the 1949 session because lawmakers also passed other measures he had long sought, such as a public employees retirement fund. It also created the Alaska Statehood Committee, an eleven-member nonpartisan group nominated by the chief executive and approved by the legislature in joint session. The committee was to aid in Alaska's struggle for statehood.[45] When Gruening left the governorship in 1953, after the election of Republican Dwight D. Eisenhower to the presidency, significant strides in the statehood battle had been made, but success seemed to lie in the far future.

Impatient with the lack of progress on the statehood issue in Congress, the 1955 territorial legislature made provisions for holding a constitutional convention. (See discussion of that convention in the chapter on Alaska's constitution.) With renewed vigor, territorial residents pushed for statehood. In Congress, Alaska's delegate, E.L. "Bob" Bartlett, the son of pioneer Alaskans, skillfully managed the statehood campaign. Elected to the delegateship in 1944, Bartlett played a major role in Alaska's battle for statehood.[46]

On May 28, 1958 the House of Representatives passed the Alaska statehood bill by a vote of 208 to 166. The Senate followed suit on June 30 with a vote of 64 to 20, and President Dwight D. Eisenhower signed the measure into law on July 7 of that year. Alaskans went to the polls on August 26 and voted 40,452 to 8,010 for the immediate admission of Alaska. In the November general election voters chose the first officials of the State of Alaska. On January 3, 1959 President Eisenhower signed the proclamation officially admitting Alaska into the union as the 49th state.

CONCLUSION

Alaska had experienced a unique period of Army, Treasury Department, and Navy rule from 1867 until Congress made it a judicial district in 1884. All other territories had been authorized to create their own judicial systems. That was not the case in Alaska, where a federal system had jurisdiction over both territorial and federal matters. All other territories had managed their own fish, fur, and game resources. The federal government performed that function in Alaska until 1960, despite the fact that the territorial legislature had petitioned Congress for decades to relinquish those responsibilities. Territorial municipalities were not allowed to incur bonded indebtedness without Congressional approval. There are many other examples that illustrate how Congress and federal agencies treated Alaska unlike any territory had been treated before.

Alaskans complained long and loudly about this treatment. Congress and the federal government responded favorably to northern needs from time to time, but without relinquishing tight colonial controls. World War II set forces in motion that were to change the north forever. The Japanese occupation of Kiska and Attu in the Aleutian Islands in 1942 resulted in a major American effort to retake the islands. That effort succeeded in 1943. In the meantime, the Army had connected Alaska by land to the contiguous states by building the Alaska Highway in slightly more than nine months in 1942. And although military activities declined sharply after 1943, the subsequent Cold War resulted in the remilitarization of the north. By that time, Alaska's strategic military position at the top of the world had also been recognized.

The postwar military construction boom resulted in a population influx to Alaska. These newcomers, accustomed to participating politically in their home states, were unwilling to endure territorial restrictions. Many actively participated in the statehood drive.

The members of the constitutional convention who met on the campus of the University of Alaska in Fairbanks in the fall of 1955 were acutely aware of territorial shortcomings. They had a good knowledge of the limited functions the territorial legislature and the chief executive exercised. They changed the territorial system by creating a powerful governor and an independent legislature for the new state. They kept the constitution short and entrusted the legislature and governor with implementing it. They also realized, however, that many territorial institutions which had grown and matured from 1912 onward would, with minor changes, serve the future state well. In retrospect, the drafters of the constitution did well in remembering the territorial lessons and incorporating them in the future state's basic document.

ENDNOTES

[1]Peter Lauridsen, _Vitus Bering: The Discoverer of Bering Strait_ (Chicago, IL: S.C. Griggs & Company, 1889), pp. 6-7, 10-11, 32-33, 61-62, 77, 128-129.

[2]The discussion of the Russian background is based on James R. Gibson, _Imperial Russia in Frontier America: The Changing Geography of Supply of Russian America, 1784-1867_ (New York: Oxford University Press, 1976), pp. VII-VII, 3-20.

[3]Claus-M. Naske, _An Interpretative History of Alaskan Statehood_ (Anchorage, AK: Alaska Northwest Publishing Company, 1973), p. 8.

[4]Based on Ted C. Hinckley, *The Americanization of Alaska, 1867-1897* (Palo Alto, CA: Pacific Book Publishers, 1972), pp. 29-131; 15 Stat. 240-242.

[5]William H. Seward, *Speech of William H. Seward at Sitka, August 12, 1869* (Washington, D.C.: Philip & Solomons, 1869), pp. 15-16.

[6]Jeannette Paddock Nichols, *Alaska: A History of Its Administration, Exploitation, and Industrial Development during its first Half Century under the Rule of the United States* (New York: Russell & Russell, Inc., 1963), pp. 59-82. Based on Bobby Dave Lain, *North of Fifty-Three: Army, Treasury Department, and Navy Administration of Alaska, 1867-1884*, unpublished Ph.D. dissertation, University of Texas at Austin, 1974.

[7]23 Stat. L. 24.

[8]Claus-M. Naske, Technical Research Report to the Alaska Court System, *A History of the Alaska Federal District Court System, 1884-1959, and the Creation of the State Court System*, July 1, 1985.

[9]U.S., Congress, House, Committee on the Territories, *Civil Government for Alaska*, Report to Accompany S. 153, 48 Cong., 1 Sess., House Rept. No. 476 (Washington, D.C.: Government Printing Office, 1884), p. 2.

[10]Ernest Gruening, *The State of Alaska* (New York: Random House, 1954), p. 52.

[11]Earl S. Pomeroy, *The Territories and the United States, 1861-1890: Studies in Colonial Administration* (Seattle, WA: University of Washington Press, 1969), p. 2; Jack Eric Eblen, *The First and Second United States Empires* (Pittsburgh, PA: University of Pittsburgh Press, 1968), p. 151.

[12]Claus-M. Naske, *Alaska Federal District Court System*.

[13]Gruening, *State of Alaska*, pp. 58-59; Nichols, *Alaska*, p. 123.

[14]C.L. Andrews, *The Story of Alaska* (Calwell, ID: Caxton Printers, 1938), pp. 181-207.

[15]James D. Richardson, ed., *A Compilation of the Messages and Papers of the Presidents* (New York: Bureau of National Literature, 1912), vol. 8, p. 6269; Ibid., vol. 9, p. 6400-6401.

[16]Gruening, *State of Alaska*, p. 105.

[17]Ibid., pp. 107-113.

[18]Nichols, *Alaska*, pp. 180-183; Thomas A. Morehouse and Victor Fischer, *The State and the Local Governmental System* (Fairbanks, AK: University of Alaska, Institute of Social, Economic, and Government Research, March 1970), p. III-8; 31 Stat. 321-552, 1438; Robert N. DeArmond to Claus-M. Naske, October 6, 1985, personal communication, in author's file.

[19]U.S., Congress, Senate, Committee on Territories, *Conditions in Alaska*, Report to Accompany S. Res. 16, 58 Cong., 2 Sess. (Washington, D.C.: Government Printing Office, 1904), S. Rept. No. 282, p. 29.

[20]Max Farrand, _The Legislation of Congress for the Government of the Organized Territories of the United States, 1789-1895_ (Newark, NJ: William A. Baker, 1896), p. 18.

[21]Gruening, _State of Alaska_, pp. 138-139; _Daily Alaska Dispatch_, May 26, 27, 1903; Clarence L. Andrews, "Alaska and Its Resources," _Alaska-Yukon Magazine_ 8 (1909), p. 263; U.S., Congress, Senate, Committee on Territories, _Conditions in Alaska_, Report to Accompany S. Res. 16, 58 Cong., 2 Sess., S. Rept. No 282 (Washington, D.C.: Government Printing Office, 1904), p. 32.

[22]_Cong. Record_, 58 Cong., 2 Sess., p. 3092; Nichols, _Alaska_, p. 228; _Annual Report of the Governor of Alaska_, 1904, p. 7.

[23]Nichols, _Alaska_, pp. 246-247, 190, 327.

[24]34 Stat. 169-175.

[25]_Annual Report of the Governor of Alaska_, 1902, pp. 14-15, 1905, p. 8; _Conditions in Alaska_, pp. 30-32.

[26]Nichols, _Alaska_, pp. 276-300; Richardson, _A Compilation of the Messages and Papers of the Presidents_, vol. 16, p. 7103; 60 Cong., 1 Sess., H.R. 4820, December 5, 1907, H.R. 17649, February 20, 1908.

[27]Nichols, _Alaska_, pp. 295-303.

[28]61 Cong., 1 Sess., H.R. 10418, June 7, 1909; _Seattle Post-Intelligencer_, October 1, 1909.

[29]Atherton Brownell, "Wanted: A Government for Alaska," _Outlook_, February 26, 1910, pp. 431-434; _Fairbanks Times_, October 3, 1909.

[30]Wickersham Diary, October 13, 18, 1909, University of Alaska Archives, Fairbanks, Alaska; _Annual Report of the Governor of Alaska_, 1911, pp. 31-32.

[31]Nichols, _Alaska_, pp. 304-404.

[32]35 Stat. 839-842; Nichols, _Alaska_, p. 403; U.S., Department of the Interior, _Fact Sheet: Alaska_ (Washington, D.C.: Government Printing Office, 1949), p. 4.

[33]Nichols, _Alaska_, pp. 401-402; Richard A. Cooley, _Politics and Conservation: The Decline of the Alaska Salmon_ (New York: Harper and Row, 1963), p. xvii.

[34]37 Stat. L., 512.

[35]Robert DeArmond, "Alaska: 1867-1959," in _Alaska Blue Book 1973_, ed. Elaine Mitchell (Juneau, AK: Alaska State Department of Education, Division of State Libraries, 1973), p. 144.

[36]Ibid. For a full discussion of prohibition, see Becky Smith, "Prohibition in Alaska," _The Alaska Journal_, Vol. 3, No. 3, Summer 1973, pp. 170-179.

[37]For the details on Alaska's long struggle for statehood, see Claus-M. Naske, _A History of Alaska Statehood_ (Lanham, MD: University Press of America, Inc., 1985).

[38]For details on the history of the University of Alaska, see William R. Cashen, *Farthest North College President: Charles E. Bunnell and the Early History of the University of Alaska* (Fairbanks, AK: University of Alaska Press, 1972).

[39]Robert DeArmond, ''Alaska: 1867-1959,'' p. 145.

[40]Ibid.

[41]Robert DeArmond, ''History of 'Administrative Governor' bills in the Alaska Legislature,'' mimeo. memo to the governor dated February 3, 1957, copy in author's files.

[42]Robert DeArmond, ''Alaska: 1867-1959,'' pp. 145-146.

[43]Based on the author's manuscript and entitled *Ernest Gruening: Alaska's Territorial Governor, 1939 to 1953*.

[44]Robert DeArmond, ''Alaska: 1867-1959,'' p. 147. When Alaska became a state, the primary was once again closed, but was opened again by law in 1967.

[45]Ibid., p. 148.

[46]Ibid. For the details of Alaskan politics in the 1950s, see Claus-M. Naske, *Edward Lewis Bob Bartlett of Alaska...A Life in Politics* (Fairbanks, AK: University of Alaska Press, 1970), pp. 142-174. For an account of the constitutional convention, see Victor Fischer, *Alaska's Constitutional Convention* (Fairbanks, AK: University of Alaska Press, 1975).

2
Alaska's Constitution

Victor Fischer

Alaska's state constitution was written before the territory became a state. In fact, it was created as part of the battle for statehood—a circumstance that greatly influenced its content and character.

One of the chief arguments for statehood was that as a territory Alaska lacked self-determination. Alaska residents had only such rights and privileges as were granted all citizens under the U.S. constitution or were specifically authorized by Congress. A state constitution would define the specific rights and powers of Alaskans as residents of a state and set limits on the powers of state and local governments. Many Alaskans who favored statehood also saw creation of a constitution as a signal to the U.S. Congress that Alaska was ready to join the union.

This chapter presents the context and reviews the content of Alaska's constitution. It looks at the role of state constitutions in general and examines the historical setting in which Alaska's was written. The chapter also surveys the document's principal provisions and their rationales, the changes that have been proposed and enacted, and major issues that remain outstanding.

CONSTITUTIONS IN THE UNITED STATES

The constitution is the basic law of the land under the American system of government. It sets out the structure of government, provides for the performance of government functions, establishes limits on the powers of government, and delineates the rights of the people.

Constitutions create the foundation for state governments. Commonly they establish three branches of government—legislative, executive, and judicial— and spell out the organization and allocation of powers among the branches. While constitutions provide for the exercise of powers by states, they also set limits on their powers and activities. Generally constitutions include a system of checks and balances to keep the respective branches from usurping power or overstepping their appropriate bounds. For example, a governor can veto acts of the legislature; the legislature can reject a governor's executive branch appointees; and the courts may, in the exercise of judicial review, declare acts of the governor or the legislature to be unconstitutional.

Written constitutions in the United States evolved from the British history of constitutionalism and from the British tradition of granting charters to its colonies. At the time of the American Revolution, the colonies drew up their own constitutions. The federal constitution was written in 1787. All 50 states have constitutions; many have dropped their early constitutions and adopted new ones. Some states have had as many as ten constitutions. Alaska and a few other states are operating under their original constitutions.

Past and present state constitutions reflect different periods in American history.[1] The earliest state constitutions, written immediately after the United States won its independence from Britain, gave very strong powers to state legislatures and sharply restricted powers of state governors. These restrictions on executive powers were largely the result of the unpopularity of colonial governors—appointed by the British—who had carried out British orders in the colonies in the days before independence.

By the nineteenth century, states began to see that legislatures could not efficiently carry out administrative functions and could abuse their broad powers. New and revised state constitutions began to limit legislative powers and strengthen executive powers somewhat. In many cases, however, powers that were taken away from the legislatures were not given to the governors but to a wide range of executive officials and commissions that were elected independently. The administrative reform movement of the early 1900s was somewhat successful in halting constitutional changes that diffused executive authority among a wide range of officials, but in general, state governors continued to share power with many others in the executive branch.

The revised state constitutions that restricted legislative power and increased executive authority were much longer and more detailed than the earlier constitutions. The first constitutions had generally contained fewer than 10,000 words; some constitutions adopted in the last half of the 1800s were ten times that long.

By about 1950, a new constitutional reform movement began in the United States. Leaders of the push for changes in state constitutions said that on the whole they were too long; that they included details that belonged in laws rather than in the basic document of government; that they reduced the efficiency of the executive branch by failing to concentrate power with the governor; and that they placed so many restrictions on the powers of state and local government officials that they made effective government hard to achieve.

It was at this point in constitutional history that Alaska's constitution was written. As we will discuss more later, Alaska's constitution incorporated many of the proposed constitutional reforms, including brevity, concentration of executive power with the governor, and a grant of broad home-rule powers to local governments. Over the past 25 years, many states have revised their constitutions—and in some cases adopted new ones—to also include those kinds of changes.

Before turning to a description of Alaska's specific constitutional provisions, we look at the forces that led up to the 1955 constitutional convention and at how the authors of the constitution deliberated over this critical document.

PREPARING FOR THE CONVENTION

Holding an Alaska constitutional convention was first proposed in 1953, but the idea was overwhelmingly rejected by statehood proponents, who believed a convention would delay statehood. By late 1954, however, opinion had turned in favor of a convention. The main reason was that Congress had failed to act on Alaska statehood that year, and it had become clear that several more years might elapse before Congress did act.

So statehood advocates decided to move toward a constitutional convention. Hawaii, which was also being considered for statehood, had held a constitutional convention in 1950. Because the issues of Alaska and Hawaii statehood were intertwined in Congress, it seemed logical for Alaska to also write a constitution and be on par with Hawaii. Also, proponents of Alaska statehood hoped the existence of a constitution for the proposed state would show Congress that Alaska was in fact ready to become a state.

In the 1954 general election in Alaska, a rejuvenated Democratic party took control of both the territorial house and senate and decided that its legislative program would include a call for a constitutional convention.

The Constitutional Convention Act of 1955 called for a convention with an unrestricted legislative mandate "to take all measures necessary or proper in preparation for the admission of Alaska as a State of the Union."[2] The legislature also enacted a districting scheme for delegate elections, selected the University of Alaska campus near Fairbanks as the convention site, and provided for a 75-day session and a 15-day recess for hearings.

DELEGATE ELECTIONS

The legislature fixed the number of convention delegates at 55—the same number as had drafted the U.S. constitution. Seven delegates were to be elected at-large from the whole territory. This measure was intended to counteract the sectionalism among regions of Alaska and to encourage prominent people to run.

Apportionment of the other 48 seats presented a major problem. Previous territorial elections had been held at-large in Alaska's four judicial divisions—which had led to over-representation of the urban centers of Anchorage, Fairbanks, Juneau, and Nome. (For example, in 1955, all ten house members representing the Third Judicial Division were from Anchorage, even though half the votes in the division came from smaller communities.)

Pressure for a different set of districts for the delegate election came from Alaskans who believed in redistricting as a matter of equity and from those who favored it to promote acceptance of the convention and to boost the statehood cause. Opposition to redistricting came from those who did not want a political shift away from urban areas and who—correctly as it turned out—believed that the scheme for electing delegates would be the basis for districting and apportionment under the constitution.

The legislature compromised by providing for election of 15 delegates from newly delineated single-member districts (which had no significant relation to population) and for election of the remaining 33 delegates from the four judicial divisions. The total number of delegates from each division was kept in proportion to the 1950 census reapportionment. Even though limited, this apportionment produced a legislative body that was the most representative group of elected officials in Alaska up to that time.

Delegates were elected on nonpartisan ballots. In modern times, most states have elected constitutional convention delegates on nonpartisan ballots. In Alaska, this approach helped insulate the convention from partisan politics. Democrats, who were in a strong majority in the territorial legislature, also wanted to assure that Republicans were adequately represented in key convention posts—and to thereby avoid giving the convention and the constitution a partisan label.

The delegates elected were a disparate group. As a result of the new districting and nonpartisan election, 24 delegates came from 19 communities throughout Alaska, ranging from Kotzebue and Unalakleet in the west to Klawock and Ketchikan in the southeast. The other 31 delegates came from Alaska's three major cities—Anchorage, Fairbanks, and Juneau.

Matching the geographical distribution of delegates was the variety of their occupations—they included lawyers, businessmen, commercial fishermen, engineers, miners, housewives, ministers, homesteaders, and more. Six were women. Ages of delegates ranged from 29 to 82. Eight had been born in Alaska, although only one was an Alaska Native.

Many delegates had records of public service. They included current or former legislators, mayors, and city council members. Thirty had held or were holding elective office, and fourteen had held or were holding appointive positions at the territorial or local level.

Forty-seven delegates favored statehood at the earliest time. One opposed it outright. The other seven held positions in-between but supported Alaska's becoming a state at some future time.

William A. Egan, a territorial senator who later became Alaska's first state governor, was elected convention president. After the convention, delegates gave Egan much of the credit for its success. They cited his political wisdom, persuasiveness, and ability to bring people together as important factors during the drafting of Alaska's constitution.

DRAFTING THE CONSTITUTION

PREPARATORY WORK

The Alaska Statehood Committee, which had been established by the territorial legislature to promote the statehood cause, contracted with the Public Administration Service (PAS) of Chicago for a series of reports for convention delegates and the public. These included papers on all elements of modern constitutions and the process of drafting constitutions. The statehood committee also hired Thomas Stewart, a former attorney general and territorial legislator, who later became a state superior court judge, to oversee PAS work and to make necessary arrangements for the convention.

CONVENTION TIMING AND SITE

When the delegates set to work on the constitution in November 1955, the fact that Alaska was not yet a state was beneficial. The drafting of the constitution was able to proceed outside the realm of the usual political pressures. The convention had little to do with current affairs; it didn't affect jobs, business, or any present allocation of power. With few exceptions, the pressures from lobbyists and special interest groups that accompany legislative sessions were absent at the convention. The environment of the University of Alaska campus near Fairbanks was also conducive to unity and dedication of purpose among the delegates; there were few distractions.

CREATING THE CONSTITUTION

The delegates found constitution drafting to be a challenging and often arduous task. By the fiftieth day, the convention was meeting in general session from nine in the morning until ten or eleven at night, six days a week. Shortly thereafter, sessions were held on Sundays as well. Toward the end of the convention, delegates often stayed in session until after midnight.

Committees were established to cover all major parts of the constitution. Each committee began its work by studying the Public Administration Service preparatory materials, the National Municipal League's "Model State Constitution," and the Hawaii Constitutional Convention Manual, which summarized the provisions of other state constitutions. Committees could also draw on national experts, who were available as consultants to the convention.

Substantive responsibilities differed widely among committees. In some cases, the basic structure of an article was clear to the committee, and members focused on specific provisions. This was particularly true for the articles on the executive, legislative, and judicial branches.

In other instances, committees had to work from scratch. Often they had little more than examples from other states of what not to do in Alaska, or they had to work with no precedents at all. The committees responsible for drafting the natural resources and local government articles had to innovate more than any of the others.

Committees had to determine what was appropriate constitutional matter and what was legislative in nature and that therefore should not be part of the fundamental document. Faced with examples from many states that had written minutia and special privileges into their constitutions, delegates wanted to keep Alaska's constitution as basic as possible. They believed that in this way the constitution would survive as time went on, and not need revision every time conditions changed.

Once committees had an initial draft of an article, they conducted hearings to obtain the views of other delegates and invited witnesses and the public. The convention recessed for fifteen days on December 20 for a holiday break and to sound out opinion at home. Despite heavy snow storms in some areas, some twenty hearings were held around the territory.

When a committee had completed the article within its jurisdiction, the article was presented on the floor. Every section of every article was thoroughly examined. Frequently, extensive discussions ensued and many amendments were considered before an article was approved in second reading. After all articles had been subjected to and adopted in third reading on the floor, the style and drafting committee assembled the entire constitution.

The formal signing of the constitution by 54 of the 55 delegates[3] on February 6, 1956, was part of the emotional closing ceremonies that attracted attention throughout Alaska.

RATIFICATION AND STATEHOOD

Ratification of the constitution by Alaska voters was closely linked with statehood. As part of the ratification campaign, the convention sponsored printing and distribution of 15,000 copies of the proposed constitution and 100,000 copies of "A Report to the People of Alaska from the Alaska Constitutional Convention."

On the same ballot with the ordinance approving the constitution were the issues of abolishing fish traps[4] and sending two "senators" and a "representative" to Washington under the Alaska-Tennessee Plan to officially lobby for statehood.[5] While the latter proposal was somewhat controversial, prohibition of fish traps was a longstanding battle cry of Alaskans and was included on the ballot to help assure good voter turnout.

Voters ratified the constitution by more than two to one on April 24, 1956. In southcentral and northwest Alaska, the vote was nearly 80 percent in favor. The Alaska-Tennessee Plan passed by 61 percent, while the fish trap ordinance won approval by more than five to one.

Statehood proponents viewed these results as a great victory. Alaska had a constitution for whenever statehood came. In the meantime, the statehood cause had one more solid argument in its favor, and three full-time advocates would represent the statehood effort in Washington. There was yet another positive effect. The writing and ratification of the constitution attracted national attention to the statehood cause. Political scientists, constitutional experts, and public figures all over the country praised the constitution. The convention had been widely covered by the national press, and both the closing of the convention and ratification of the document gave rise to editorials by the *New York Times* and other major papers and magazines across the United States. All of them tied this coverage to strong endorsements of Alaska statehood. Moreover, these statements and editorials were reported on the floor of Congress and printed in the Congressional Record.[6]

Congressional action on statehood came in 1958. The U.S. House of Representatives approved the statehood bill on May 28 and the Senate on June 30. The act of admission specified that Alaska's constitution "is hereby found to be republican in form and in conformity with the Constitution of the United States and the principles of the Declaration of Independence, and is hereby accepted, ratified, and confirmed."[7]

CONSTITUTIONAL PROVISIONS:
POPULAR RIGHTS AND CONTROLS

Alaska's constitution went into effect January 3, 1959, the day Alaska became a state. It contains some significant original provisions as well as a number that are more conventional, patterned on those of the U.S. constitution and other federal and state documents. Basic provisions of Alaska's constitution deal with the people's fundamental rights and controls, including suffrage, direct legislation, and constitutional revision.

DECLARATION OF RIGHTS

Article I of the constitution, the Declaration of Rights, includes the standard protections of personal rights contained in the Bill of Rights of the U.S. constitution and in other state constitutions.

Basic provisions include guarantees of free speech, religion, petition and assembly, due process, and the right to bear arms. Protections are written in against violation of civil rights, double jeopardy and self-incrimination, excessive punishment, unreasonable searches and seizures, and imprisonment for debt. The article covers trial by jury, rights of accused, treason, habeas corpus, eminent domain, and even the traditional proviso on quartering soldiers.

An interesting reflection of the time when the constitution was written is found in Section 7, dealing with due process. A new right was established: the right to fair and just treatment in the course of legislative and executive investigations. This provision was a direct response to the abuses by U.S. Senator Joseph McCarthy, who in the 1950s conducted widely publicized investigations of communism in the United States, often making damaging but unsupported charges against those he questioned. It was copied in a subsequent redraft of the Michigan constitution.

Two amendments to Article I were adopted in 1972. The first banned discrimination on the basis of sex.[8] A new protection against government interference—the right of privacy—was created by the second amendment. Section 22 stipulates that: "The right of the people to privacy is recognized and shall not be infringed." This protection of privacy is not spelled out in the federal constitution, although it is implied in other kinds of guaranteed rights.[9] The provision has influenced legislative and executive policies and actions and was the basis for a 1975 state supreme court decision allowing possession of marijuana for personal use.

SUFFRAGE AND ELECTIONS

Alaskans' right to vote is guaranteed by Article V, which also delineates voter qualifications. Beyond that, the article leaves it to the legislature to provide for elections, voter registration, and limited additional voting qualifications.

Four liberalizing amendments have been made to Section 1 of this article, which establishes voter qualifications. These amendments gave the legislature the authority to modify residency requirements for voting in presidential elections, reduced the legal voting age from 19 to 18, eliminated the requirement that voters had to read or write English, and reduced from one year to 30 days the time individuals had to live in Alaska before being eligible to vote. These changes were in accordance with federal court decisions and federal laws that in recent decades have reduced restrictions on voting.

INITIATIVE, REFERENDUM, AND RECALL

"Direct legislation" provisions allow the people to:

- enact laws through the initiative process
- veto, by referendum, laws passed by the legislature
- remove elected officials through the recall process.

Procedures for using the initiative and referendum are specified in Article XI. Neither initiative nor referendum may be applied to dedication of revenues, appropriation of funds, or to local and special legislation. In addition, initiatives may not create courts, define judicial jurisdiction, or prescribe court rules. The referendum may not be applied to laws necessary for the immediate preservation of the public peace, health, and safety. These kinds of procedures that allow citizens to have a direct say in legislation and in the recall of elected officials have been included in most other state constitutions, particularly in western states.

By 1985, 12 initiatives had gone before Alaska voters, of which five were adopted. Four of the initiatives pertained to moving the state capital, as did two of the five advisory referenda put on the ballot by law rather than by petition. Constitutional referenda have succeeded in both attempts to repeal legislative enactments, one for voter registration and the other increasing legislative salaries.

In the case of recall, the constitution simply provides that all elected officials, not including judges, are subject to recall by voters. Procedures and grounds for recall are left entirely to the legislature.

AMENDMENT AND REVISION

Three methods for changing the state constitution are provided by Article XIII. First, amendments can be initiated by a two-thirds vote of each house of the legislature. Second, the legislature may call a constitutional convention. Third, the state's voters are given the opportunity once every ten years to call a constitutional convention. In each case, changes go into effect only if approved by the voters.

Virtually all state constitutions provide for amendment through constitutional convention or legislative initiative, but the ease or difficulty of implementing those procedures varies among states. All states except one require voter approval of constitutional amendments. The provision that automatically gives Alaska voters a chance to call a constitutional convention every ten years is unusual among state constitutions, although a handful of others also require periodic votes on the question of calling constitutional conventions.[10]

In establishing the procedures for Alaska, the constitutional convention sought to make the amendment process difficult enough to prevent hasty, destructive, or cluttering changes, but easy enough to accommodate the legitimate needs of a changing society.

In all cases, changes are to be initiated by a deliberative body—the legislature or a convention—that can give proposals full consideration. The constitution may not be amended by the initiative process because that would bypass the review and deliberation considered crucial by framers of the constitution.[11]

Twice since statehood, voters have declined to call constitutional conventions. The legislature has never exercised its prerogative to issue a convention call. The people have likewise never used another potential means of effecting constitutional change: using the initiative process to call a convention.

In the first 25 years of statehood, 19 of 26 amendments proposed by the legislature have been ratified by voters; these amendments are reviewed in the individual discussions of articles. Many of the legislature-initiated amendments since 1956 lack the brevity and clarity of original provisions of the constitution. A prime example is the spending limit amendment (Article IX, Section 16) that was hurriedly drafted during a brief special session in 1981.

STRUCTURE OF GOVERNMENT

Each state constitution lays out the basic structure of government and delineates authorities of the various branches and levels of government. The approach, however, varies from state to state.

Alaska's constitution outlines only the general framework of government, providing broad grants of power to each branch and level and leaving enough flexibility to allow for necessary changes.

The writers of Alaska's constitution intended to make each branch of government effective and strong in its own right. Similarly, they saw no conflict in authorizing a major state role in local government and granting maximum self-government at the local level.

LEGISLATIVE BRANCH

Legislative reform was a primary objective of the statehood movement, largely in response to the weaknesses and inadequacies of the territorial legislature. Those shortcomings had been caused by constraints imposed by the U.S. Congress. As a result, the constitutional convention accepted most of the provisions designed to create a strong state legislature.

Article II delineates the basic structure, composition, and procedures of the legislature, and specifies the main legislative power that may be exercised by the governor—the veto.

Legislative Structure. The Alaska Legislature is bicameral and its membership relatively small: twenty senators serving four-year terms and forty representatives serving two-year terms. Proposals for a unicameral legislature were hotly debated during the constitutional convention, but received little support. Vestiges of the unicameral scheme are, however, incorporated in the constitution in the provisions for joint sessions of the legislature to act on vetoes, executive appointments, executive reorganization orders, and martial law.

As discussed more below, the constitution originally called for senators to be elected by geographic area (regardless of the size of area population) and for representatives to be elected on the basis of population. But in 1962 the U.S. Supreme Court ruled that apportionment of state legislatures had to be on the basis of population. As a result of that decision, there was substantial public support in Alaska for creation of a one-house legislature—since in the future senators and representatives would serve essentially the same constituencies. But though an advisory vote showed majority support for this change, the legislature, as might be expected, has refused to propose a constitutional amendment that would establish a one-house legislature.

Legislative Pay. The issue of legislators' pay was a matter of controversy during the constitutional convention, and it continues to be so. While most delegates agreed that the salary should be adequate to attract good legislators, there was also strong sentiment that lawmakers should make a public service contribution. In the end, delegates provided for an annual salary with salary levels to be set by future legislatures.

Lawmakers have found themselves in a quandary about how to provide adequate compensation for legislative service, while not setting salaries that the public considers too high.[12] One way being considered to accomplish this is establishment of an independent salary commission that would set pay without need for legislative action.

Legislative Sessions. The constitution provides for annual legislative sessions. These sessions have traditionally started in January. Although their length was not initially restricted, regular sessions are now limited to 120 days. Delegates to the convention assumed that a long session to organize government might be needed when Alaska became a state, but that thereafter sessions would be relatively brief. With oil development and greatly increased state wealth in the 1970s, a pattern of ever longer sessions developed. The public became critical as sessions beginning in January lasted into late June and July. Legislators themselves saw that lack of a deadline tended to extend sessions. A constitutional amendment establishing a 120-day session limit was overwhelmingly adopted in 1984.

Special sessions may be called by the governor or by vote of two-thirds of the legislature. Because at special sessions called by the governor only bills specified by him can be considered, governors have been able to exert extreme pressure on legislatures to do their bidding at such sessions. The only session convened by the legislature to date was in 1985, when the senate considered impeaching the governor.

A 1976 amendment allows special sessions to consider bills vetoed by the governor after adjournment of the last general session. Its main purpose was to expand legislative opportunities to override vetoes and, secondarily, to discourage the governor from calling special sessions. In fact, legislators have not addressed vetoes in special sessions held since the change became effective. Neither house of the Alaska Legislature may adjourn or recess for longer than three days unless the other concurs.

Interim Committees. The Legislative Council is the committee that conducts the legislature's business between sessions. Other permanent committees that can function during the interim are the Legislative Budget and Audit Committee and the Regulations Review Committee. Standing committees may conduct research, hold hearings, and carry on other business between sessions, but they cannot take final action on bills or other legislative matters.

Vetoes. Once a measure has been approved by the legislature, the governor may exercise a major power he holds under the system of checks and balances—the veto. If he vetoes a non-appropriation bill, the legislature may override his action by two-thirds vote of all members of both houses, in which case the bill becomes law despite the veto. The governor may also strike and reduce items in appropriation bills; these vetoes require a three-fourths vote of the legislature to override.

Alaska's veto override provisions are unusual in that they require the legislature to meet in joint session and to obtain an extraordinary majority of all members—that is, the senators and representatives considered as one body—to override vetoes. This unicameral feature prevents a minority of one chamber (for example, seven senators) from stopping an override. The proportion of legislative votes needed to override governors' vetoes in other states varies, but in most, members of the two houses vote separately rather than as one body.[13]

Alaska's constitution does not permit the "pocket veto," under which a governor can kill a bill by not signing it within a specified period. A bill becomes law if the governor does not sign it within fifteen days while the legislature is in session, and within twenty if it's not.

Impeachment. All officers of the state are subject to impeachment by the legislature. (Recall that impeachment means only to formally charge a public official with malfeasance in office. If an official is impeached, it does not mean that he is removed from office but rather that he is then tried and found guilty or not guilty of the impeachment charges.)

Grounds for impeachment are not spelled out in the constitution, but a motion for impeachment must list the basis for the proceeding. Impeachment originates in the senate by a two-thirds vote of its members. Actual trial on impeachment is conducted by the house, with a supreme court justice presiding, and judgment also requires a two-thirds vote. This assignment of roles reverses the traditional procedure in Congress and most other states, where the house originates impeachment proceedings and the senate holds the trial. In Alaska, action is initiated by the senate because it is considered the more senior body, with greater continuity of membership. Final action is by the house, all of whose members will have been most recently elected, thus better reflecting current popular opinion.

In 1985, Alaska became the first state in more than fifty years to initiate impeachment proceedings against a governor. This action resulted from a grand jury report alleging that Governor Bill Sheffield had lied in statements to the jury concerning a state office building lease and calling on the state senate to consider impeachment for perjury. After two weeks of hearings and deliberations, the senate found there was not sufficient evidence to impeach the governor.

Legislative Apportionment. Apportioning the future state for electing its legislators was probably the most difficult and controversial task of the constitutional convention. The dilemma facing delegates in 1955-56—years before the U.S. Supreme Court's 1962 "one-man, one-vote" decision—was how to allow all Alaskans the fullest measure of representation. They also wanted to make sure that residents of sparsely settled rural areas would be represented in the legislature, which would be dominated by urban areas if population were the only apportionment criterion. Article VI dealt with the problem by allocating house seats chiefly on the basis of population and senate seats mainly on geographic area.

Alaska's legislative apportionment and districting scheme was effectively nullified as a result of the U.S. Supreme Court's 1962 *Baker v. Carr* decision, which said all apportionment would be according to population. Constitutional provisions applicable to the senate became illegal, and even the guidelines for apportioning house seats according to population could not meet the federal court's strict limits on deviation from equal populations. Alaska's practice was modified to conform to the federal decision. Since Article VI is no longer valid, an amendment has been proposed to conform the constitution to actual current practice and to standards applicable under the U.S. constitution. At the same time, Article XIV—Apportionment Schedule—is to be repealed. That article established the district boundaries to be used in the first election after statehood and was designed to be temporary.

The governor and a reapportionment board advisory to him draw up redistricting plans after each 10-year census, to reflect new population patterns. When petitioned by a voter, the superior court may compel the governor to perform reapportionment duties and to correct reapportionment and redistricting errors. The superior and supreme courts have, in fact, been involved in every reapportionment since 1962. While sustaining the governor's reapportionment role, the courts have thoroughly scrutinized challenged schemes, often mandating changes in the governor's reapportionment and redistricting of the legislature.

EXECUTIVE BRANCH

Article III of Alaska's constitution gives very strong power to the state governor. Alaska was among the first states to concentrate executive power with the governor, but many other states have done the same in recent years. This broad grant of power to Alaska's governor was one of the provisions favored by national constitutional experts, but it was also partly a reaction to Alaska's experience with territorial governors, whose effectiveness was hampered by limited authority. Federally appointed territorial governors shared executive power with federal bureaucracies, with boards and commissions created by the territorial legislature to undercut federal authority, and with elected department heads who exercised independent jurisdiction.

Executive Authority. The constitution unequivocally vests all executive power in the governor. A broad grant of authority is given the governor to enforce compliance with constitutional and statutory mandates by any officer of the state and its political subdivisions.

The executive branch is structured to give the governor total control and responsibility. There are no separately elected executive officials. So as to keep the executive branch manageable, there may not be more than twenty principal state departments. All departments are under the governor's supervision, and each department head serves at his pleasure. Where a board or commission is in charge of a department, the executive officer is subject to gubernatorial approval. Reorganization of the executive branch may be made by executive order, subject only to legislative disapproval.

Authority to call the legislature into special session further strengthens the governor's hand. Veto provisions and the executive budget, both discussed elsewhere, are additional elements of executive power.

Regulatory Authority. One constitutional provision pertaining to executive power has created serious conflicts with the legislature: "The governor shall be responsible for the faithful execution of the laws" (Article III, Section 16). At issue has been whether the legislature has the authority to nullify regulations adopted by the executive branch. Legislators have argued that regulations are an extension of the lawmaking power and thus should be subject to legislative veto by resolution. The executive branch has maintained that regulations are a means of executing the laws and thus not subject to legislative veto. The courts have sustained the executive position, as have the voters in turning down several proposed constitutional amendments that would have redressed this balance of power in the legislature's favor.

The question of legislative versus executive authority in drawing up regulations has also come up in other states. In 1985, the Advisory Commission on Intergovernmental Relations reported that 38 state legislatures had established procedures for reviewing proposed regulations.

Term and Tenure. A governor is limited to serving two consecutive four-year terms, but may be elected again after he has spent one term out of office. A governor's term begins on the first Monday in December, making Alaska one of the few states where a governor takes office before January. This provision allows the newly elected governor to have some say on the state budget before the legislature convenes the following month.

Lieutenant Governor. To concentrate executive power, the convention delegates considered simply not creating the position of lieutenant governor. However, there was strong belief that the successor to the governor should be a popularly elected official, so the office of lieutenant governor was established. Candidates for lieutenant governor stand independently in the primary election. The winner in each party is then paired with the party's gubernatorial nominee in the general election. As a result, the governor and lieutenant governor are elected as a team, in contrast to the practice in most other states. Where the two are elected separately, the possibility of partisan strife is created.

Delegates to the constitutional convention knew that lieutenant governors generally perform few useful functions. They wanted Alaska's lieutenant governor to have duties; the constitution therefore gives the lieutenant governor responsibilities for overseeing elections and specifies that additional duties may be prescribed by law or delegated by the governor.[14] These provisions do not change the fact that the duties of the office depend on what the governor wants them to be—and to date these have been very few.

A lieutenant governor has succeeded to the office of governor once in Alaska's brief state history, when Keith Miller became governor in mid-term after Walter Hickel's 1969 confirmation as U.S. Secretary of the Interior. Hugh Wade became acting governor for several months when Governor William Egan became critically ill soon after he took office in 1959.

The constitution leaves further succession to be determined by the legislature. Under existing law, the governor appoints, subject to legislative confirmation, a cabinet member to succeed to the office of the governor and to be acting governor in the absence of the lieutenant governor.

Attorney General. There was considerable debate during the constitutional convention as to whether there should be an elected or appointed attorney general. In the end, the delegates decided that the attorney general would be appointed. The principal consideration for the majority of delegates was maintaining the integrity of the strong chief executive concept, and avoiding dissension at the top levels of the executive branch. Others had argued that election to office would make the state's top legal officer strongly independent of those, including the governor, who administer the laws.

Debate on this point has continued over the years, and constitutional amendments calling for an elected attorney general have been proposed in almost every legislature since statehood. Although commanding much popular support, these proposals have never received the necessary two-thirds vote in each house to be placed before the voters for ratification. Attorneys general are elected rather than appointed in 43 other states.

JUDICIAL BRANCH

Alaska's courts were under the federal court system prior to statehood, so the convention delegates started with a clean slate in creating a strong and effective judicial branch of government. In contrast to the situation in many older states, where state courts can be complex and have separate jurisdictions, Alaska's judicial system is unified: the entire court system is under the rulemaking authority of the supreme court, and the chief justice of that court is the administrative head of all state courts.

Alaska's judicial system, as established by the constitution, consists of a supreme court, a superior court, and other courts to be created by the legislature. The legislature has established an appellate court and district courts.

A key element in assuring judicial independence is the "merit plan" method of selecting and retaining judges embodied in Article IV. Judges are appointed by the governor from nominees presented to him by the judicial council, composed of three lay members appointed by the governor (with consent of the legislature), three attorneys selected by the state bar, and the chief justice, who chairs the council. This scheme makes it likely that only qualified candidates will be selected for judgeships. The alternative of electing judges was overwhelmingly rejected by the constitutional convention as being unlikely to produce a quality judiciary.

Public accountability of appointed judges is also a crucial part of Alaska's judicial system and is achieved through periodic votes of confidence. In retention elections held three years after initial appointment and at six- or ten-year intervals thereafter, judges run on their records and are subject to approval or rejection on a nonpartisan ballot. A judge can also be impeached by the legislature or removed from the bench if incapacitated.

Twenty-one states still elect judges in the 1980s, but in recent times there has been a trend toward appointing judges but keeping public accountability by requiring periodic retention votes.[15] (See the chapter devoted to Alaska's court system for a more detailed description of Alaska's judicial system.)

LOCAL GOVERNMENT

Article X reflects significant constitutional innovation. At the time of the constitutional convention, local government institutions were quite undeveloped in Alaska. There were some city governments, and a few special districts had been established around the major cities. Creation of counties in the territory of Alaska had been prohibited by Congress, so most of Alaska had no local government whatsoever.

While there was clear need for a system of local government, particularly for a regional unit between cities and the state government, delegates concluded that local government systems in other states provided lessons on what to avoid, but offered little guidance on what Alaskans should do. Delegates did not want to simply adopt county governments in Alaska. Counties were thought of as too rigid to meet the wide-ranging conditions in different areas of Alaska. Also, delegates believed that the powers of counties were not broad enough—and that the limits on county powers in other states had contributed to creation of many kinds of local government units and a proliferation of taxing authorities.

The local government article adopted by the convention states that its basic purpose is "to provide for maximum local self-government with a minimum of local government units, and to prevent duplication of tax levying jurisdictions." The local government system that the delegates settled on to achieve those goals recognizes only cities and boroughs as local government units with authority to levy taxes.

The boroughs established by the constitution are regional governments somewhat similar to counties but with potentially broader powers and more adaptability. Boroughs can provide anything from a minimum of services to a whole range of local government services, depending on the choices of local residents and on tax bases in various areas. Likewise, cities can exercise few or many local government powers. The constitution makes a liberal grant of home-rule powers to cities and boroughs.

The constitutional convention saw a state role as critical in making the local government system work. Among the factors arguing for a continuing state responsibility were lack of general government beyond cities, traditional territorial government provision of services outside incorporated areas, and the varying levels of service requirements and local government capability throughout Alaska. Delegates also recognized that further study and planning would be necessary to establish the new governmental system. Finally, there appeared to be a need for statewide overview to assure that matters having effects beyond a particular local area were not determined on a strictly parochial basis. Article X includes a series of provisions fixing the state role in local affairs: a local government boundary commission, a state-level local affairs agency, and legislative responsibility for standards and methods for creating, classifying, and changing boroughs.

Despite the constitutional convention's emphasis on state leadership in establishing the borough system, governors and legislatures have been reluctant to create boroughs, largely because of frequent local opposition to establishment of another level of government. In 1985, there were eleven organized boroughs covering about one-third of Alaska. The rest of the state still has no regional governments; this vast area is known as the unorganized borough.

STATE FUNCTIONS AND RESPONSIBILITIES

Legislative, executive, and judicial powers are broadly delegated by the constitution to the three branches of state government. In contrast to provisions in many other state constitutions, specific functional responsibilities are spelled out in only a few areas: natural resources, public health, education, and public welfare. In addition, the document sets out ground rules for state and local finance and taxation.

NATURAL RESOURCES

Alaska's territorial delegate to Congress, E.L. "Bob" Bartlett, emphasized the need for the constitutional convention to concentrate on lands and resources. Delivering the keynote address at the opening session of the convention on November 8, 1955, he observed:

> ...fifty years from now, the people of Alaska may very well judge the product of this Convention not by the decisions taken upon issues like local government, apportionment, and the structure and powers of the three branches of government, but rather by the decisions taken upon the vital issue of resources policy.

Convention delegates took Bartlett's advice to heart and fashioned the first article in any state constitution that is devoted exclusively to natural resources. With statehood, Alaska stood to receive a federal land grant of more than one hundred million acres and obtain jurisdiction over fish, wildlife, and extensive mineral and timber resources. It was widely recognized that the state's future economic well-being would depend on the effective management of the state's patrimony.

Article VIII establishes a series of principles that reflect the values of the times and a vision of Alaska's future. Section 1 of the article establishes a broad policy to encourage the settlement of state land and development of its resources for maximum use. This presumption in favor of resource development is modified by the statement that such use must be "consistent with the public interest." While this modifier was originally designed to avoid undesirable exploitation of state resources, in the context of development-conservation conflicts it can become an argument for moderating development pressures. A similar balance is struck in Section 3: "The legislature shall provide for the utilization, development, and conservation of all natural resources...for the maximum benefit of its people.'' One can use this language to support just about any position.

The next two sections embody statements of principles that are used in political as well as legal arguments to assert rights to fish and game resources. Section 3 reserves to the people—for common use—fish, wildlife, and waters when these occur in their natural state. Section 4 provides for management of renewable resources on a sustained yield basis, ''subject to preferences among beneficial uses.'' The language in these sections of the constitution has been used in recent years by both supporters and opponents of subsistence laws that give preference in allocation of limited fish and game stocks to certain groups of Alaskans.

A somewhat related provision is contained in Section 15, prohibiting creation of an exclusive right or special privilege of fishery. This was an outgrowth of one of the major issues in the statehood fight: federal authorization of fish traps.[16] The section was amended in 1972 to permit the state to establish a program that restricts entry to the state's commercial fisheries. That has been the only change in the resources article.

Section 6 defines and establishes the state public domain, and Sections 8 and 9 provide for lease, sale, and other disposal of public lands. Together with the land settlement policy stated in the first section, these provisions reflect a general direction of making state lands available for acquisition and development. The state currently has several land disposal programs; there has been much controversy in recent years over whether the state has released too much or not enough land for private ownership. Sections 11 and 12 outline how rights to minerals and coal can be obtained.

Article VIII also includes policies that provide for acquisition of water rights through actual use, public access to navigable waters, reservation of land for public purposes, and others pertaining to resource management and protection of individual rights.

HEALTH, EDUCATION, AND WELFARE

Article VII is the briefest in the constitution. One section covers public education, two sections establish the University of Alaska as a single, unified system of higher education for the state, and two one-sentence sections require that the legislature provide for public health and public welfare. Public money cannot be used for direct benefit of religious or other private schools; that was the only provision of this article that was controversial during the constitutional convention. The functions covered were already being carried out by the territorial government.

Sections 2 and 3 establish the University of Alaska and provide for its management. Lack of a clear definition of the university's relationship to the rest of the state government have, however, led to some bitter disagreements with the governor and legislature about the degree of its autonomy, resulting in several court cases. The main conflicts have been over fiscal and administrative controls and procedures. The governor and legislature have considered the university akin to other state agencies, while the university's Board of Regents has argued for maximum independence.

After court and other battles, the legislature and executive have agreed that the university is different, that it is not a state agency, and that the Board of Regents has greater fiduciary responsibility than executive departments have. In line with this understanding, the university has separate accounting and payroll systems, its own insurance program, and is allowed to invest its funds and retain the earnings.

On the other hand, the university falls within the executive budget act, comes under the legislature's budgeting authority and appropriations, and is subject to the governor's veto power. Since the state's budgetary jurisdiction is clear and the power of the purse provides the ultimate measure of power, it is evident that university autonomy could be severely curtailed, regardless of constitutional provisions, if the governor and legislature chose to do so.

FINANCE AND TAXATION

In Article IX, the constitutional convention provided the legislature with broad discretion to tax and to spend money. Debt ceilings, curbs on rates and types of taxation, and similar restrictions that appear in many older state constitutions were carefully avoided. The principal curbs written into the constitution prohibit the earmarking of funds for special purposes and require voter approval prior to incurring any state or local debt for capital improvements.

Section 7's innovative restriction against dedicating state revenues for specific future purposes was designed to protect the state's freedom and flexibility in financial affairs. Earmarking specific revenues for limited purposes is a long-standing practice in many states, with the result that some legislatures have less than half of the state's income actually available for appropriation. The section was amended in 1976 to allow establishment of the Alaska Permanent Fund; this was in anticipation of oil revenues that would accrue to the state when North Slope oil production began in 1977. (The fund itself is created in Section 15.) Its purpose is to automatically set aside part of the state's oil revenues and to have earnings of the fund available when needed as oil revenues decline.

A limit on state spending was added to Article IX in 1982. This limit was intended to hold down the large increases in state spending that occurred when petroleum income was at its peak. However, the effect of the amendment has been nil to date because state revenues after 1982 were far below the allowable ceiling as a result of declining oil prices.

CONCLUSIONS

Little has happened since the constitution went into effect in 1959 to revise the initial judgment that it provided a solid foundation for the state of Alaska. A conference meeting in Fairbanks in 1976 to review the effectiveness of the constitution found that most problems being encountered under the constitution were matters of legislative and executive implementation and not shortcomings in the document. The conference found that the basic framework established by the constitution was general and flexible enough to allow for adaptation to changing conditions and for resolution of conflicts. Problems that could not be solved under the existing constitution could be dealt with by amendment. Alaskans apparently still agreed with these conclusions in the 1980s: in 1982, they voted against a call for a constitutional convention to review and revise the original constitution.

The local government article provides an example of the flexibility of the constitution. The 1976 conference identified two principal problems with provisions of that article: that the borough concept has not been put into effect in large areas of rural Alaska, and that numerous city-borough conflicts have resulted from their sometimes overlapping authorities.

The first problem resulted from the legislature's creating just one unorganized borough in the vast reaches of Alaska not included in incorporated boroughs. Lack of individual unorganized boroughs in the disparate regions of the state has hindered rural Alaskans from participating in planning and services for their areas, while also making it more difficult to move toward some form of regional self-governance. Several accommodations have occurred. The state has established regional educational and coastal management planning areas within the unorganized borough. The North Slope Borough, covering the huge area north of the Brooks Range, was created under local initiative in 1972. Groups in other rural regions have looked into organizing their own boroughs. The legislature and the state Department of Community and Regional Affairs have also studied the unorganized borough situation, though no action has so far resulted.

City-borough conflicts have been attacked by local action and by constitutional amendment. Constitutional convention delegates had toyed with the idea of abolishing cities and establishing areawide boroughs as the only units of local government. Such a drastic step did not appear to be politically acceptable at the time. However, strife between the two kinds of local governments serving the same urban areas became unacceptable to citizens in several communities in the 1970s, leading to city and borough unification into single home-rule municipalities in Anchorage, Juneau, and Sitka. Other areas have made attempts to consolidate city and borough governments but have not been successful so far.

One constitutional attempt to promote coordination between cities and boroughs was a requirement that city areas were to be represented on borough assemblies by members of city councils; areas outside cities were to be represented by directly elected borough assembly members. It turned out that this structure caused constant friction between the two blocks representing city and non-city parts of most boroughs. A 1972 constitutional amendment eliminating the city representation requirement has reduced dissension on borough assemblies and permitted them to deal more peacefully with areawide matters.

Aside from these problems with the local government article, other kinds of controversies have also brought scrutiny of constitutional provisions. Legislative-executive conflicts at the state level have proved difficult to resolve. Convention delegates had generally assumed that a common purpose would unite these two branches of government and believed that making each strong and independent would make both most effective. Delegates did not anticipate the extent of tensions that have arisen, though it is not likely that the constitution would have been written differently if they had. Problems have been due not to the fundamental law but to struggles for power and ascendancy, together with partisan and personality factors.

There have been numerous lawsuits over the issue of legislative versus executive authority. They have involved executive appointments, administrative regulations, veto power, convening the legislature in joint session, and others. The Alaska Supreme Court has generally ruled on the side of the executive branch, although it did uphold the legislature's argument that while the governor could exercise an item veto over the budget, he could not delete legislative intent.

In a number of instances, the legislature has sought constitutional amendments. It has sought voter approval of authority to veto administrative regulations by legislative resolution; such resolutions do not require the governor's concurrence to go into effect. The voters rejected these proposals in several referenda, as they also did an attempt to require legislative confirmation of executive appointments below the cabinet level. Thus, the strong executive concept written into the constitution has been maintained.

Meanwhile, legislative suspicion and dislike of centralized executive power have spawned another series of proposed constitutional changes—changes that would require election of certain public officials who are now appointed. Since 1961, amendments to elect, rather than appoint, the state attorney general have been introduced in every legislature. There have also been numerous proposals for electing district attorneys. Amendments have been introduced to elect a controller general, an auditor, a treasurer, or a similar official. There was a proposal to elect the Commissioner of Education. None of these amendments were approved by the legislature.

The proposals for electing state officials have been motivated in part by the goal of increasing popular control of government. Other unsuccessful attempts toward this end have called for amendment of the constitution by the initiative process, rather than by legislative action as specified in the constitution.

Proposed constitutional revisions of the legislative branch have involved successful efforts to limit the length of sessions and unsuccessful efforts to change from a bicameral to a unicameral system.

Judicial article changes, actual and proposed, have been minor and procedural in nature. The exception was a proposal to elect supreme and superior court judges; this proposal was not seriously considered. The court system has expanded and changed over time as its caseload has grown tremendously and become more complex. New courts have been created and additional judges appointed, as authorized by the constitution.

A major series of proposed constitutional changes has been directed toward saving revenues from nonrenewable resources—particularly petroleum—for future benefits. The state's Permanent Fund, where a portion of oil revenues are deposited, was created by constitutional amendment in 1976. Governor Sheffield has supported setting aside more oil revenues in a major projects fund. This proposal has not found legislative favor, because it would decrease the amount of money legislators have to spend, because of skepticism and uncertainty about the projects that might be funded in the future, and because of doubts about the value of any such major projects as compared with current service and capital needs.

During the 1970s, several proposals were made to introduce an environmental emphasis into the constitution. No such changes were made then, and no attempts have been made since. Perhaps environmentalists and others recognize that existing provisions of the constitution do not in fact mandate development, but rather allow whatever balance between development and conservation the governor, the legislature, and the people wish there to be.

That flexibility to adapt to changing values and conditions is what the framers of the constitution tried to achieve. It is, of course, too early to make definitive judgments. But it does appear from Alaska's brief history as a state that the constitution can adequately serve the state in the future.

ENDNOTES

[1] The following brief description of state constitutional history is based on a detailed discussion in *The Question of State Government Capability*, a report by the Advisory Commission on Intergovernmental Relations, Washington, D.C., January 1985.

[2] Territory of Alaska, *Session Laws of Alaska*, 1955, Chapter 46.

[3] R.E. Robertson of Juneau refused to sign then but did subscribe to the constitution several years later.

[4] Fish traps in Alaska waters caught huge numbers of salmon and required little labor. They were generally controlled by fishery interests from outside Alaska. Many supporters of statehood saw these fish traps as representing the absentee control of Alaska that existed in the absence of statehood.

[5] In 1796, as part of its battle for statehood, Tennessee elected mock senators and sent them to Congress to lobby for statehood. These lobbyists reportedly were so effective that Tennessee was admitted to the union 65 days later. Proponents of Alaska statehood hoped mock representatives of Alaska could be equally effective.

[6] *New York Times* editorial of April 30, 1956, pp. 182-183.

[7] Alaska Statehood Act, Sec. 1, 72 stat. 339 (1958).

[8] Interestingly, a proposal to include ''sex'' among the Section 3 civil rights protections was defeated by delegates in 1956, when a woman delegate argued that women's rights had been and would continue to be protected by Alaska's legislature.

[9] See Gordon S. Harrison, *A Citizen's Guide to the Constitution of the State of Alaska*, Institute of Social and Economic Research, University of Alaska, 1982, p. 18.

[10] *Book of the States, 1984-1985*, Chapter 3, ''Constitutions.'' Also, Joseph F. Zimmerman, *State and Local Government*, Barnes and Noble Outline Series, Harper & Row Publishers, New York, revised 1976, p. 45.

[11] An initiative was, however, used to put an advisory proposition on the ballot to indicate whether voters wanted the legislature to amend the constitution to establish a unicameral legislature; though this measure carried substantially, the legislature refused to initiate the change. Subsequently, the legislature itself placed a ballot proposition before the voters, seeking guidance on the constitutional question of limiting the length of legislative sessions. Neither proposition was an initiative or referendum as provided for in Article XI.

[12] The public has reacted negatively to high legislative compensation, once rolling it back through a referendum and more recently mounting an initiative to repeal a pay raise.

[13] Harrison, *A Citizen's Guide to the Constitution*, pp. 31-32.

[14]In a symbolic attempt to give purpose to the office, the official was initially designated "secretary of state." However, it was found that incumbents carried on few executive duties and that the name lacked prestige, so a 1970 constitutional amendment changed the name to "lieutenant governor," the term used in other states for the successor to the governor.

[15]*The Question of State Government Capability*, p. 189.

[16]See note 4. Fish traps were abolished with ratification of Alaska's constitution.

3
Alaska's Political Culture

Gerald A. McBeath

Alaska's geographic vastness, cold climate, and resource wealth are unique among the American states. The largest state in land area, Alaska covers one-fifth as much territory as the continental United States. Only Hawaii is as isolated and remote, but Alaska is off the world's sea lanes. No other state has so difficult a climate with such extremes in temperature as does Alaska. This remote northern space contains rich natural resources. Prudhoe Bay is a super-giant oil field, and it is only one part of Alaska's mineral bounty, which includes huge coal reserves, gold, and other scarce minerals. Abundant forests and rich fisheries add to the natural resource base that has made the state's per capita income the highest in the nation.

Are Alaska's politics as unique as her environment? One would expect the environment to strongly influence the context and operation of power in the state. Yet it is people who are in charge of government and politics, and what they think and feel stands between the unique environment of Alaska and the state's political outcomes. This intermediate factor has a special name in the study of politics—political culture—and the objective of this chapter is to describe and analyze what political culture is in Alaska.

"Political culture" has several definitions, both simple and complex. Gayle Patrick is a political scientist who has attempted to produce order from the confusion of various meanings. She points out that the different meanings associated with the concept can be reduced to this definition:

> (T)he set of fundamental beliefs, values and attitudes that characterize
> the nature of the political system and regulate the political interactions
> among its members. At the core of these fundamental beliefs, values,
> and attitudes are those associated with:
> cognition/knowledge-conception of the nature of reality;
> conceptions of the ends/purposes of government;
> conceptions of the nature and scope of power and authority.[1]

To simplify this definition, one can say that political culture refers to the core beliefs, values, and attitudes people have about *why* the state does what

53

it does—its goals and objectives. Political culture also sets out rules and routines for the operation of government, and it describes relationships of individuals and political institutions. For instance, it says whether people should actively participate in politics or sit out the political game.

THREE APPROACHES TO THE CULTURE OF POLITICS IN ALASKA

Several avenues lead to an understanding of Alaska's political culture. The first and most often used is descriptive. What this means is that *images* are created to express how Alaskans behave. A second, less often used method goes a step beyond description, and examines different *patterns* of culture. A leading scholar of American politics, Daniel Elazar, argues that political life has developed in geographic regions and then migrated across space and time.[2] This movement has produced three different patterns of political culture. The third approach is *analytical*. It "measures" political culture by treating samples of the attitudes and beliefs people have toward government and politics.

The best way to understand how people think about politics is to use all three of these approaches. After reviewing each approach to the culture of politics in Alaska, we turn to analysis of the structure of political cultures, recent empirical studies of Alaska political culture (focusing on rural Alaska), and evaluations of stability and change in political cultures.

IMAGES OF ALASKA POLITICAL CULTURE

The way most Alaskans identify themselves—and are identified by others—is through traits and labels that form a word picture of *Alaskan*. How that profile is described varies from author to author, but we tend to see some uniformity of labels in an overview of several works. Describing the state's political culture in 1971, political scientists Thomas Morehouse and Gordon Harrison found Alaskans to be self-reliant, ethnocentric individualists:

> Popular references to the other states—such as the "lower 48," the "smaller states," or simply the "outside"—have a thinly veiled ethnocentric and patronizing tone. Self-imagery of rugged individualism is widespread. Strains of popular thought celebrating rural virtues are associated with a sense of innocence vis-a-vis the rest of the nation. In addition to early American pioneer and Calvinist elements, the political culture of Alaska includes traces of turn-of-the-century populism....[3]

This sense of loyalty to the state, and belief in the superiority of an Alaska lifestyle, seem to be common to newcomers to the state as well as to oldtimers.

People identify strongly with Alaska because it is physically and socially isolated from the other states. Identifying with Alaska means that its goals for development become personal objectives, and its social and political affairs are of high interest—more important even than those of the federal government.[4]

Several popular accounts of Alaska written in the 1970s and 1980s add to these ideas. They use colorful language and picturesque descriptions, as in John Hanrahan and Peter Gruenstein's 1977 book about Alaska:

> An Alaskan is someone who wants to be able to "urinate off his front porch and yell for an hour without anyone answering." ...Call it the spirit of the pioneer, romance, rugged individualism, or the desire to find a little "elbow room," the fact is that Alaska has exerted a powerful pull on the imagination of the adventurous for decades.[5]

Similar images are seen in other non-fiction accounts of the Alaska mystique. Perhaps the most popular (except among many Alaskans, who resent the critical observations and negative connotations of the work) is Joe McGinniss' 1980 bestseller *Going to Extremes*. Discussing the preoccupation many Alaskans have with the state, McGinniss writes:

> One thing I noticed quickly was that Alaska was almost an obsession to many of the people living there. It was not simply a place in which they happened to reside: it was a loved one, a family member, by which their emotions were monopolized; about which they fretted and dreamed.
>
> Alaskans thought about Alaska, and talked about it, all the time. The world beyond its borders was called Outside—spelled, even in the newspapers, with a capital O. It was a world which Alaskan residents had willingly left behind, and what happened there now did not concern them, except insofar as a given event might somehow have an effect upon Alaska.[6]

Associated with this preoccupation is a sense of danger and excitement, which one does not find in any other American state (or in many foreign countries, for that matter). McGinniss nicely expresses the essence of the difference between Alaskans and other Americans by saying: "It was as if the boundaries within which the normal range of human activity occurred had been, in Alaska, not just extended, but removed."[7]

Those writing on Alaska do not always agree about what makes the state and its residents unique. There is a tendency, however, for them to select traits Alaskans *learn* by living in this unique environment—particularly influential are the extreme climate, physical isolation, sparsity of population, and varied physical geography. Of course, some observers find Alaskans to be unique because of what they are, not what they do. Clearly, Alaska Natives have distinctive political lifestyles based on their socio-cultural dissimilarity from whites, whether newcomers or long-term residents. Also, a few writers have speculated that Alaska attracts individuals who are different psychologically—in the sense that they are less or more stable emotionally than "normal" Americans. This theory has not been tested empirically.

A recent academic paper by sociologist Lee Cuba attempts to organize the various observations of Alaska behavioral traits.[8] The author describes the study as an examination of "residential identification in Anchorage, Alaska," and the terms of research apply mostly to southcentral Alaska (which has about half the population of the state). Inferences can be drawn for other regions of Alaska, though.

The first of three distinctive aspects of Alaska life is language. Cuba believes there is a special "frontier vocabulary" of the state that is different in three areas from words used in other states. Alaskans distinguish themselves from those living "Outside," and, as mentioned before, they use (sometimes admittedly) derogatory expressions about the rest of the nation such as the "lower-48" (a term which, however, has a clear geographical origin). Alaskans are likely to draw distinctions among residents based on years of residence in the state, and this distinction is still used by politicians in campaigns. (However, it has less effect than it did formerly, because of the high mobility of the state's population in recent years.) A common distinction Alaskans made in earlier times, before construction of the oil pipeline in the mid-1970s brought so many new people to the state, was between old-timers—the real Alaskans known as "sourdoughs"—and newcomers, referred to as "cheechakos." Although Alaskans identity with the state as a whole, they also have strong city or regional identifications, such as with Anchorage or southeast, which make them appear parochial and provincial to newcomers to the state. Too, several words and phrases related to climate figure prominently in the Alaska vocabulary—such as "freeze up," "break up," "termination dust," "ice fog"—words that (for perhaps obvious reasons) are heard rarely if at all outside Alaska. Rural areas use other expressions based on different socio-economic factors and on racial lines.

A second distinctive aspect of Alaska life Cuba finds is physical and psychological isolation, making it necessary for newcomers to "reorient" themselves to the state.[9] One manifestation is greater self-reliance than one might see in other communities, where families are close by and roots deep. A related but contradictory trait is the general friendliness of Alaskans, their willingness to be open and accepting of strangers, and eagerness to help others when in need. (The contrast Cuba makes here is with attitudes in large cities such as Los Angeles, New York, and Chicago, and not with those in rural mountain states such as Idaho, Montana, and Wyoming.) Mutual aid is institutionalized in the volunteer fire associations of Alaska towns and cities. The *ambivalence* that these contradictory dispositions reflect is different from attitudes seen in other states.

A third aspect of Alaska life Cuba describes is a sense of dislocation in time, felt strongly by newcomers to the state, but persisting and possibly increasing somewhat until one has been in the state many years.[10] The overall severity of winter in Alaska induces this feeling, but it is the length of winter and limited daylight that are most responsible. Cabin fever affects those spending much time indoors; it implies deep claustrophobia, because it is not possible to go outdoors often during inclement winter weather, and because nights appear to last forever. Less well known, because its effects are largely benign, is "sun fever," the exhilaration and energy associated with the long daylight hours of late spring and summer.

Cuba found no significant differences in group characteristics (such as sex, age, and ethnicity) between those who identified themselves as Alaskans (and mentioned some of the defining characteristics of Alaskans) and those who did not. The single most important difference was length of residence, suggesting again that Alaska political culture is *acquired* upon exposure to the Alaska environment. This finding is at variance with the other two ways of understanding Alaska political culture.

PATTERNS OF CULTURE

Describing images of Alaska political culture is easy, and there is an intuitive sense of accuracy about it. Relying on such descriptions, however, fails to predict public policy preferences and outcomes other than obvious ones such as stance on development. One cannot say whether Alaskans, because of traits of openness and friendliness, will be more inclined to support social welfare policies than are Vermonters, for example. Another method of determining the political culture of an area is more directly linked to public policy formation. This method was developed by Daniel Elazar, a political scientist at Temple University, who has specialized in studies of comparative state government. He suggests that American political culture is a compound of three political subcultures that he calls moralistic, individualistic, and traditionalistic.[11] These subcultures are the result of interplays among nationalities and religious groups that settled the United States and the diverse continental environments they encountered over time. As state and local governments were formed by different groups throughout the United States, distinct political subcultures grew and expanded.

The moralistic culture began in New England. There, Puritans and other religious groups founded "communities of saints" to save a degenerate world. They viewed politics as a search for the good society and the perfect commonwealth. Government was a positive instrument for promoting the public's social and economic welfare, and governmental intervention in social and economic affairs was always justified. In moralistic cultures, individual participation in politics was encouraged: it was a civic duty, a responsibility to be conducted honestly and selflessly. Group participation (such as through political parties), on the other hand, was suspect. The moralistic culture was ambivalent about changes in the status quo and about bureaucratic as opposed to communal means of achieving goals.[12]

The individualistic political culture originated in the middle Atlantic states; it is the most "privatistic" of the American political subcultures. The political arena is a marketplace, in which private interests compete for utilitarian ends. Government ensures that the marketplace remains open and works; government intervenes in social and economic affairs infrequently and does so in support of private interests. Even politics is sometimes viewed as a form of business: political parties are like business corporations, and are the subject of loyalty. Participation in politics is not encouraged, and citizens view political activity as a job for professionals, an activity that is inherently "dirty" (because compromises are made and less than the whole truth is learned). Because of the personalistic nature of the individualist political culture, attitudes toward formal organizations, such as bureaucracies, are also ambivalent.[13]

The final, traditionalistic subculture arose in the American South; it is elitist with a paternalistic view of the political system as a "commonwealth." It is based on pre-industrial values stressing an ordered hierarchy of social dominance in which interpersonal and family socio-political ties are most important. The traditional culture confers power only on small, closed circles of established elites. Popular participation is discouraged in this culture, and the government is expected to play a role in maintaining traditional patterns of life. Political parties and other organized groups or institutions, including bureaucracies, are relatively unimportant because of their potential competition with the elite-ordered political world.

The political culture of white residents of Alaska corresponds best with the "individualist" culture.[14] The kind of individualism found in Alaska is not the same as that of the middle Atlantic states, but it more clearly resembles that type than it does either of the other types. But it is not in accord with images of Native culture and society in Alaska.

Political culture labels, however, should do more than sort states into categories. There is a relationship between types of political culture and public policy choices.[15] In Alaska, the strong popular support for the state's Permanent Fund dividend program (which makes direct cash payments to Alaskans) can be explained in part by the individualist culture of the state, which incorporates a large measure of greed. Even more to the point, the state in the mid-1980s boasted the nation's largest Libertarian party and the largest percentage of independent voters. A 1984 study on public participation bears out the relationship between Alaskans' political independence and support for the dividend program. Three-fourths of the respondents agreed with the statement "the dividend program keeps politicians from getting into the Permanent Fund Savings because they would have to fight it out with the Alaska public first." And 59 percent affirmed the statement "giving money directly to Alaska residents is better than letting the legislature decide how to spend it."[16]

One difficulty in political culture studies is that there are no pure culture types. State and national political cultures are mixed, and it is difficult (and less than precise scientifically) to identify the leading aspect or main bias of a type. A second difficulty in the use of patterns is that they lack empirical support. One cannot easily say if the geographic area that has been called traditional, for example, holds individuals whose behavior conforms to the requirements of the type. For these among other reasons, patterns tend to be employed most effectively in descriptive studies of American state politics.

ANALYTICAL TYPES

A third method of understanding political culture in regional settings is roughly analytical. This approach is based on studies of national character of the 1930s and 1940s. Social scientists puzzled over the survival of British and American democracies through the traumas of the Depression—when the German and Italian systems failed and fascism developed. The early, war-time studies were primarily anthropological and tried to explain the quite different kinds of governmental systems by different child-rearing practices. Post-war studies, particularly *The Authoritarian Personality*, a study of fascism by T.W. Adorno and others, used systematic techniques based on new developments in political sociology and social psychology (such as the sample survey) but did so with only one population.[17] These different explorations came together in *The Civic Culture* study of 1963. It framed behavioral hypotheses and theories and tested them on probability samples in five different societies—the U.S.,

Great Britain, West Germany, Italy, and Mexico. Authors Gabriel Almond and Sidney Verba focused on the orientation of citizens toward the political system and on the individual as a political actor. They found that political cultures varied across countries, and they expressed this variation with the terms participant, subject, and parochial.[18]

Almond and Verba pointed out two characteristics of the American civic culture: it was both an allegiant and a participatory political culture. Compared with citizens of the other four cultures, Americans had highly favorable opinions about their form of government; 85 percent spontaneously mentioned governmental and political institutions as among the things of which they were most proud.[19] Compared with respondents of the other four countries, Americans also had a strongly activist orientation toward government and politics. Fifty-one percent—compared to 39 percent of British respondents and smaller percentages in the other countries—felt that the good citizen was one who participated actively in community affairs.[20] Moreover, Americans were very confident of their ability to influence the conduct of government by their actions—over three-fourths of the American respondents felt that way compared with much smaller proportions among British and other respondents. Thus the political culture of the United States, according to Almond and Verba, was distinguished by a high degree of support for political institutions and an activist view of the individual in relation to the governing process. But the study also found that Americans were inclined to be critical of how well government provided services.

The civic culture study was both praised and damned by professionals. It was a large step forward in the comparative evaluation of societies and in cross-national research generally. However, the relatively small size of the probability sample in each country—1,000 respondents—made it difficult to conduct any sub-group comparisons. In the U.S., this meant that the political culture of America's black minority could not be treated separately. Later studies pointed out substantial differences between black and white Americans in socio-economic status, democratic characteristics, and most important, in attitudes toward authority.[21]

A more substantial criticism of the civic culture model concerned how it explained political orientations. The focus of the approach was on childhood socialization experiences, which fostered both self-expression and interpersonal trust. That approach de-emphasized political influences and this made the study irrelevant in periods of crisis or change. Changes in political events and issues in the period since the study was completed, especially responses to revelations about government actions during the Vietnam War and the

Watergate scandal, have produced corresponding changes in American political culture—such as lessened confidence in political institutions.[22]

We have looked at three ways to organize attitudinal and perceptual data about Alaska, and have seen that the way we organize information influences the findings. The descriptive approach encourages us to pay attention to peculiar factors, the oddities of Alaska political life. This approach is corrected by the second method—seeking patterns, based on the responses of individuals to environmental constraints. The approach we use most in the rest of this chapter is that of Almond and Verba in their study *The Civic Culture*. It is explicitly comparative and systematic and relies on empirical studies. That study emphasizes orientations individuals have about others as political beings, and their attitudes toward rules, procedures, and institutions. To collect information in these areas, we developed a survey research questionnaire on political cultural attitudes (including some questions drawn from the 5-nation study) and asked survey questions of a random sample of rural Alaskans, supplemented by a small sample of urban Alaskans. We will turn to our findings after reviewing the way Alaska's political culture is organized.

STRUCTURE OF ALASKA'S POLITICAL CULTURE: CLEAVAGES IN THE STATE POLITY

There are certain common cleavages in the structures of political cultures. First, as political scientist Gaetano Mosca points out in *The Ruling Class*, in all societies there is a basic distinction between the culture of those holding power and the powerless. Second, traditional carriers of the region's or country's culture differ from its new members, who may not have learned the traditional culture (or are settlers carrying different cultural traditions) and who may challenge its force. A third distinction is among the policy preferences and attitudes of different groups of the population. Briefly we will survey these divisions in the Alaska political culture.

In most societies, those who hold power and are responsible for government decisions develop outlooks on politics that are different from those held by persons who are at the margins of political activity. The division is between an "elite" and a "mass" culture, and political systems can be readily classified according to the character of the relationships between the two cultures.[23] Part of the folklore of Alaska politics is the degree of homogeneity between the two, which is attributed to the impacts of the harsh environment and sparse population. Extremes of climate in most regions of the state, and particularly the long winters with limited daylight, are said to inhibit the differences between elites and masses (except to the extent that elites can afford to winter in Hawaii while masses "freeze in the dark!"). The need for companionship is said to break down artificial barriers erected by different political ranks or functions. Also, the need for assistance in difficult environmental conditions is thought to erase rank and prestige concerns and emphasize ability. The sparse population puts natural limits on distinctions between elites and others, for in most of the state's communities, numbers are too few to permit much layering within the political community.

For statewide and big city affairs, however, this is not the case. Most of the state's population lives in urban areas where there are political distinctions between leaders and followers. In Anchorage and Fairbanks, relations between leaders and followers are not greatly different from what they are outside Alaska. The first-name relations and friendships many rural and small town Alaskans have with political leaders are unusual in the increasingly urban American politics and society of the late twentieth century.

The second gap or fracture in Alaska's political culture is between Natives (Eskimos, Indians, or Aleuts) and non-Natives. This division in Alaska, more so than in any of the contiguous-48 states, resembles the distinction between traditional communities and modern, nationalizing elites in developing Third World societies. Alaska Natives are like Third World peoples in that they possess and value their aboriginal cultures. Most have strong feelings about their primordial social and group identities, and loyalty and commitment to traditional ways of life. (However, it should be kept in mind that these differences between Natives and non-Natives in most respects have lessened over time, with the greatest erosion occurring in Alaska cities.)

Before the Alaska Native land claims movement began in the mid-1960s, Alaska Native political cultures were for the most part regional and village in nature, notwithstanding shared symbols and rituals among, for example, the broad groupings of Inupiat and Yupik Eskimos, and Athabascan and Tlingit Indians. With formation of a statewide land claims movement and a federated organization of Alaska Natives, these local and regional cultures took a loose statewide form. An "Alaska Native" viewpoint developed on a range of issues, although Native opinion was divided on some issues. On other issues a cohesive Native viewpoint conflicted with ideas of established (primarily white) state leaders.

Some conflicts between modern Western and traditional Native political cultures in Alaska result from enduring differences of political values. For example, most Native cultures have historically prized communal use of land more highly than do modern Western political cultures. The "ownership" of land has been a less congenial concept to Natives than stewardship over property on behalf of the broad community. But since passage of the 1971 Alaska

Native Claims Settlement Act (ANCSA), which awarded ownership of 44 million acres of land to Alaska Natives, private land ownership has increasingly become the norm. Western cultures tend to value individual ownership and use of land, even when private land uses might be at variance with broader community or public interests.

Concepts of authority to rule also vary between Native and non-Native Alaskans. Most Native authority systems emphasize decisionmaking by consensus. Leadership is somewhat dependent on age and family position, as well as on ability—for example, awarding authority to the most skilled hunter. This authority system is opposed to the more market-oriented concepts used by Westerners, which suggest that leaders ought to be selected on the basis of popular support and expertise. Thomas Berger, who in the mid-1980s conducted a review of ANCSA, has summarized Native cultural distinctiveness this way:

> I have found that the culture of Native people amounts to more than crafts and carvings. Their tradition of decision-making by consensus, their respect for the wisdom of their elders, their concept of the extended family, their belief in a special relationship with the land, their willingness to share—all of these values persist in one form or another within their own culture, even though they have been under unremitting pressure to abandon them.[24]

The cleavage between Natives and non-Natives is the largest division in the Alaska polity, of far greater importance in public policymaking than the gap between elites and others. In general, these are the only two cleavages in Alaska political culture, if by "culture" we mean core beliefs that are shared by members of a society. If we expand the meaning of cultural differences to include those of opinion and attitude, then we would find additional cleavages in the Alaska political system—for instance, the division of public opinion between advocates of rapid resource development and environmental preservation. For definitional clarity, we treat such practical differences as matters of opinion and attitude that may not endure over time. (The public opinion chapter covers these topics at length.) Our discussion canvasses the middle ground between enduring cultural cleavages (e.g., the traditional versus modern dichotomy) and attitudes toward different policies. This middle ground covers the domain of political beliefs about government and political interrelationships. Specific questions we ask include: Do Alaskans have a high or low level of trust in government? Is there consensus in the power and authority system of the state? How much knowledge is there of roles, institutions, and actors? How much support do political leaders and organizations have? Our approach synthesizes the various methods of understanding political culture described earlier. We combine description with analysis of differing conceptions of political order. This approach follows most closely Almond and Verba's insights about the intervening effect of beliefs on attitudes and actions. Looking at political beliefs of Alaskans will tell us whether cultural differences are likely to be translated into consensus or conflict.

EMPIRICAL STUDIES OF ALASKA'S POLITICAL CULTURE

Little empirical research has been done on Alaska's political culture. A data collection enterprise like the 5-nation study discussed earlier is not feasible in Alaska, given the high cost of survey research in remote environments. However, a recent study of citizen participation in rural Alaska institutions, broadened to include several urban sites, provides data with which we can make *inferences* about the political beliefs of Alaskans. Particularly, the study points out areas of consensus or conflict.

Information for the next several sections of the chapter was collected throughout Alaska in 1984. The survey focused on community residents, and interviewers talked with randomly selected respondents in 25 villages, towns, and cities. The relatively small sample size (230 respondents), however, limits the extent to which we can make comparative observations. Because the original sample represented just rural Alaskans (urban areas were added later), Natives and other rural Alaskans are overrepresented in the survey. The survey included questions about public trust and family empathy; the individual's role in Alaska's political processes; knowledge, trust, and level of support for different political institutions and organizations in the political world; and orientations toward democracy.[25] Findings of the survey are presented below in Tables 3.1 through 3.12 and in accompanying text discussions that include information not shown in the tables.

BOUNDARIES OF TRUST

Political trust affects the boundaries of the political system. If Alaskans were suspicious and fearful of others, that would connote the presence of cleavages in the political system that would lead to sharply different interpretations of how government should act. Based on answers of respondents in rural and urban sites, it would seem that the typical Alaskan is not fearful of others.[26] Alaskans are likely to be open and accepting of others, even if they are not kin or friends. Much of the evidence for this impression is indirect and is based on responses to questions about who respondents might turn to for help if they had difficulties with organizations. Table 3.1 shows who the respondents said they would first ask for help if they had difficulty with any of the organizations listed at the left end of the table.

Table 3.1
Who Helps Solve Problems With Organizations

Organization	Family	Friend	Official	Teacher	Other
City council	4.8%	14.3%	38.1%		42.9%
Native village corp.*	17.4	8.7	21.7	—	34.8
Native regional corp.*	5.3	10.5			52.6
Advisory Sch. Bd.*	18.5	3.7	22.2		55.6
District Sch. Bd.	3.3	10.0	16.7	13.3	53.3
			N=221		

*Item asked only of rural residents.

In all cases, a large share of respondents said they would turn first to officials with the organizations or to others outside their circle of family and friends for help. These results are particularly interesting in light of the fact that many rural respondents had relatives working for local government—relatives they could ask to intercede on their behalf. For respondents to indicate that their horizon of trust extends beyond family and friends—and that they would not necessarily turn to family and friends even if they worked for the organization in question—suggests a less parochial world view than impressionistic accounts of Alaska political culture might portray.

This relative openness to others might be due to the attitude that in sparsely populated and physically isolated places, everybody should be considered. A good example of this attitude can be seen during village potlatches, when persons who have been drinking make speeches. Everyone, no matter how inebriated or otherwise distracted, is heard out. Another explanation of openness toward others and acceptance of their advice and intercession is tied to the fractionated pattern of local socio-political power. The idea behind this explanation seems to be that contact with others protects one against local instability or conflict. Table 3.2 presents perceptions of respondents about factionalism in local and regional councils. Only 43 percent of the respondents answered these questions, and knowledge of differences among leaders lessened when we asked about regional organizations. Too, urban residents were much less familiar with the situation of power in local organizations.

Table 3.2
Perceptions of Conflict in Local and Regional Councils

Organization	% Perceiving Conflict in Org.**	% Perceiving Factionalism
City council	51.9%	62.5%
Village corp.*	48.2	36.8
Regional corp.*	27.3	—
Advisory Sch. Bd.*	27.7	50.0
District Sch. Bd.	31.4	40.0
IRA*	37.5	62.5
	N = 105	

*Only rural residents were asked about conflict in these organizations.
**The first question asked "Do people disagree about who should run the organization," and the second asked "Do the same people disagree about who should run it, or are there different people?"

Nonetheless, there was a definite perception of conflict and factionalism, strongest for the most public bodies—city and village councils that by definition have to accommodate all residents. The conflicts respondents described often involved members of the same family taking both sides of an issue or dispute. (Familial power rivalries are quite strong, and conflict among extended family members has great consequence in local politics.) Several respondents cited such family conflicts as a reason to support individuals other than family members for leadership positions.

A final indirect question concerning the boundaries of trust asked respondents why they picked the kinds of leaders they did. This line of questioning sought to establish the degree of democratic orientation among rural and urban Alaskans, but the choices offered respondents, and their reactions, also inform us about their perceptions of trust. Table 3.3 shows reasons respondents cited for choosing leaders.

Urban and rural Alaskans generally gave the same answers to this question, with the single exception that more rural than urban residents thought training by elders was a good reason to make someone a leader. Rational and legalistic criteria were preferred over those of family and friendship. However, we should note that respondents commented on how they would be likely to behave. We have no systematic data on how perceptions of trust steer actual behavior.

Table 3.3
Reasons for Selecting Leaders

Reason	% Calling this a "good" reason	% Calling this the "best" way
Family connections	10.2%	1.0%
Experience	91.5	85.7
Friendship	11.7	1.0
Because elders trained them	45.3	7.4
	N=203	

ALASKANS AS POLITICAL AGENTS: SENSE OF POWER AND PARTICIPATION

Trust usually depends to some degree on a sense of power over one's environment and others, and one's ability to control important outcomes. Given the individualist ethos of Alaskans, we expected to find a high degree of efficacy (the term social scientists use to describe having a sense of power) among respondents. We asked several general and specific questions to determine what level of efficacy Alaskans thought they had. In examining affairs close to home—such as whether residents could get rid of a bad teacher or principal in the local school—we found a high level of efficacy: only 7.4 percent of respondents thought this would be impossible; 23.6 percent thought they could do it with a bit of effort; and 53.4 percent felt it would be an easy task. Rural Alaska residents were significantly more confident of their abilities to fire bad teachers or principals than were urban residents, but a strong majority of the city respondents had confidence in their ability to control outcomes. Questions in two other areas—ability to use land the way residents wanted to and finding help getting jobs—elicited similar responses.

General questions on the availability and use of democratic procedures such as voting inspired responses similar (if not even more positive) to those found elsewhere in the U.S. For example, 93 percent of our respondents said that voting "matters," and 92 percent believed that "voting changes things." There was nearly universal agreement with the statement that residents of Alaska have a "say" in public policy through voting. As is typically the case, however, the actual rate of participation (and thus the opportunity for influence) was much lower. A majority had not voted in the preceding 18 months, although there had been elections for local or regional offices in all communities during that period. Nearly 90 percent of those who had voted had done so most recently in the 1982 state elections. Three-fourths claimed to have voted in all office elections in 1982, and 85 percent to have voted on the two major ballot propositions. Table 3.4 presents information on participation in affairs closer to home—local board and council meetings.

Table 3.4
Participation in Local and Regional Boards and Councils

Organization	% Attending at least one Meeting**	% Talking at/ outside Meeting
City council/assembly*	60.2%	58.2%
Village corporation	49.5	61.4
Regional corporation	38.4	41.0
Adv. School Board	34.4	43.8
District School Board*	30.4	54.8
IRA-Traditional council	45.6	47.4
Regional non-profit corp.	18.5	42.9
	N=197	

*Only questions on city councils and district school boards were asked in urban areas.
**Average attendance is much lower.

Rural and urban residents were quite different in attendance at council meetings. A majority of the small urban sample had never attended a council or assembly meeting, but two-thirds of the sample of rural residents had. As we expected, participation varied between private and public organizations. Obviously, non-Natives were not likely to attend meetings of village and regional ANCSA corporations or Native councils. In large villages, there was a wide array of teams, councils, and committees that made it possible for every adult to be involved in some way. There was also higher participation in local than in regional councils. The greatest number of respondents had attended at least one local council meeting. Measures of frequency, however, showed that few respondents had attended such meetings more than once or twice in the previous year. Less than one-quarter of the respondents attended local or regional council meetings regularly.

Although rural respondents claimed to have attended meetings more often than did urban residents (whose participation was about the same as that of urban residents in the contiguous-48 states),[27] they rarely spoke up at those meetings. The greatest percentage had spoken out at meetings of village ANC-SA corporations and town councils, where the setting was comfortable and there were few formal or other intimidating contacts with outsiders. A large percentage had talked to members of boards or councils before or after meetings. This "participation through discussion with leaders" is probably the easiest (and perhaps the most effective) way for rural Alaskans to make their views known. For rural Natives, who are the vast majority of residents in communities with populations under 1,000, speaking out in public may be embarrassing. Some rural Natives lack fluency in English (most meetings are conducted in English), or they may be uncomfortable before those they do not know well. Talking with leaders is akin to the visiting traditions and practices found in most villages.[28]

It is necessary to distinguish between rural and urban rates of participation, and between local and regional levels of activity in Alaska. But the overall impression we gain from comparative data is that Alaskans have a somewhat greater sense of power over their socio-political lives than other Americans do. They are more likely to participate in local affairs and to value that participation than are other Americans, but the difference is not substantial.[29]

KNOWLEDGE AND SUPPORT OF COMMUNITY ORGANIZATIONS

In the 25 Alaska communities surveyed, we interviewed leaders and officials of all community organizations, and then formed profiles of organizational activities in local contexts. In several places we observed meetings of organizations, screened organizational files, and even learned something of the history of organizations. Because in most cases interviewers had visited the communities two years previously and talked to political notables then, we had a good sense of the change in influence within organizations over time.

Having tested the climate of organizational activity in each community,[30] we asked randomly-selected community respondents their perceptions of groups and organizations. The broad purpose of this questioning was to determine how much residents knew about boards and councils, what attachments (if any) local people had toward these organizations, and whether they thought them effective.

Table 3.5 presents information on the extent to which residents knew about the general purposes and activities of community organizations.

A majority of respondents were familiar with what the city (or village) councils did and for what purposes. Most had a very basic understanding of school boards' functions. However, less than half of the respondents (including both

Table 3.5
Knowledge of What Community Organizations Do

Organization	% Correctly identifying an objective of organization
City council	71%
Village ANCSA corporation*	46
Regional ANCSA corporation*	43
Advisory School Board*	75
District School Board	67
IRA-Traditional council*	43
Regional non-profit corporation*	43
	N=214

*Questions asked only of rural residents.

Natives and non-Natives) understood what Native governments did. This finding does not square well with the so-called ''strong tradition'' of tribal government in rural Alaska. Among rural respondents we also noted a degree of confusion about the functions of village and regional ANCSA corporations, and about the differences between city councils (as chartered entities capable of regulating local behavior and receiving state funds) and IRA/traditional councils.

We expected that there would be greater satisfaction with the activities of local than regional councils, but this was not what we found, as indicated in Table 3.6. The highest proportion of respondents said regional nonprofit corporations were doing a good job.

Overall, respondents tended to favorably evaluate the work of community organizations. Complainers were in the minority. Rural residents were somewhat more positive about community organizations than were respondents from Alaska cities—a finding possibly influenced by disinclinations to give negative responses in Native culture. And, Native governments appeared to be evaluated less positively than were public organizations, but the differences were quite small and not significant statistically. The most popular government bodies were local school boards. Most respondents understood what they do, and clearly valued their work. Schools (and churches) have been in villages for generations. They are established and accepted, in contrast to ANCSA corporations and other organs of self-determination which are relatively new to rural areas.

Table 3.6
Evaluations of Community Organizations

Organization	% Believe org. does "Good Job"	% Find nothing to dislike
City council	78.2%	52.5%
Village corporation*	69.4	63.1
Regional corporation*	73.3	39.1
Advisory School Board*	81.1	71.7
District School Board	85.9	62.1
IRA-Traditional council*	73.2	73.0
Regional non-profit corp.*	92.3	72.7
	N = 208	

*Questions asked of rural residents only.

Rural and urban Alaskans have a basic familiarity with their community organizations, and they tend to trust them. The level of support is higher than one would expect to find in large U.S. cities. This support appears to be a consequence of scale. The finding from the Alaska survey confirms the assessment of a group of political scientists who have studied political participation in seven nations:

> [P]olitical activity—at least that kind of activity that involves dealing with the problems of the local community in cooperation with one's fellow citizens or as an individual in face-to-face contact with a government official—is fostered in small communities and becomes more difficult as the scale of community grows.[31]

KNOWLEDGE AND SUPPORT OF STATE AND FEDERAL GOVERNMENT

Participation and attitude studies in the contiguous-48 states find that citizens are best informed about the federal government. Most know who the president is, and at least half can identify one of their congressmen. Levels of information about state and local assemblies are generally far lower, and few respondents to the typical sample survey can name the councilman or alderman who represents them to city hall. We did not collect information on whether respondents in urban areas knew the names of local officials, and thus lack a comparative base on levels of perception about different governmental bodies. However, we did ask all respondents if they knew who represented them in

Table 3.7
Knowledge and Perception of State and Federal Officials

Level of Government	% Knowing Name	% Saying officials try to meet needs
State legislators	82.1%	81.9%
State governor	72.3	84.3
U.S. representative	61.9 (at least one name)	87.4
U.S. senator	68.3	91.0
	N=213	

Juneau and in Washington, D.C., and we also asked a series of questions about the performance of the state and federal governments. Table 3.7 summarizes what we found.

The significant rural-urban differences in Alaska were not reflected strongly in respondents' attitudes toward government performance. We found only one statistically significant difference in urban and rural Alaskans' knowledge of officeholders and perceptions of effectiveness: rural residents evaluated the governor's performance more favorably than did urban residents.

Interviewers polled residents during the spring of 1984, at a time when legislators were in session but gearing up for the fall election campaign (a campaign in which the governor and one of the state's senators were not running). The name recognition of Alaska's political leaders at the state and federal level seems high when compared to what has been found in surveys outside Alaska. (Recall that 50 percent of Americans polled in recent years did not know the name of their representative in Congress.) Of greater significance is the generally very high degree of satisfaction respondents expressed with both state and federal government performance. Given the bad press the federal government has in Alaska, the finding that nearly 90 percent of respondents were satisfied with work their representatives in Washington have done seems contradictory—until one remembers that a similar pattern has been found in other states. Citizens tend to support their individual congressmen but simultaneously complain about federal government actions.

A final question asked respondents which level of government they thought would be most likely to help them if they had problems—for example, problems with roads in their community. Three-fourths of all respondents (and 95 percent of the small sample of urban residents) thought the federal government would be most helpful, compared with only 22 percent who thought the

Table 3.8
How Should Leaders be Selected?

Method	% Saying "Good"	% Saying "Bad"
Voting	72.2%	14.6%
Having a board/council pick them	41.4	32.3
Having elders/experienced people pick them	44.9	32.7
Having people take turns in the job	28.6	53.5
	N=212	

state government might assist. If we compare respondents' perceptions of the effectiveness of local organizations with that of state and federal bodies (Tables 3.6 and 3.7), we find similar levels of satisfaction. In view of the vast resources expended in Alaska by both federal and state governments, these high levels of support come as no surprise.

DEMOCRATIC ATTITUDES OF RURAL AND URBAN ALASKANS

Perhaps the interesting differences between political attitudes and values of urban and rural Alaskans, and between attitudes of Alaskans and other Americans, do not actually influence how Alaskans construct their political lives. To understand Alaskans' orientation toward rules and procedures our 1984 survey asked: What is the best way to select leaders? Who should have the most say in community affairs? What is the best way to voice your views? Tables 3.8 through 3.12 and text discussions of related points not shown in the tables summarize the findings.

Obviously, voting was the preferred way to select leaders: for nearly two-thirds of all respondents it was the first choice, followed (at 23.9 percent) by "letting the board or council" select leaders. Rural and urban Alaskans were united in their evaluation of voting, but opinions diverged on the other methods cited in Table 3.8. Urban residents disliked the notion of selecting their leaders indirectly. A method one might think would be popular with rural Native respondents, letting the elders make such decisions, was cited as a good method by less than half the respondents (including less than half the Native respondents). Several respondents mentioned that it might be a nice way to select leaders, but that it would be impracticable.

Table 3.9
Who Should have the Most Say in Community Decisions?

Choice	% Saying "Good"	% Saying "Bad"
Elected leaders	55.1%	17.7%
Everyone in community	73.8	10.9
Elders	45.9	20.1
Experts from outside community	14.6	69.8
		N=210

A second question asked who should determine community priorities and actions. The question was intended to measure how much faith individuals had in their elected leaders, and also the extent to which the consensus model was attractive and useful to them. Clearly "everyone" was the leading choice of respondents; 65 percent made that their first choice, followed, at 22.4 percent, by elected leaders. Community residents were less inclined to select elders as decisionmakers for issues of substantial impact. In fact, nearly one-fifth of all respondents (and over three-fifths of urban residents) thought it undesirable to give elders the most influence. "Experts," however, were far and away the least popular decisionmakers, with nearly three-fourths of all respondents (and slightly more urban than rural residents) opposing their influence.

Support for community participation and rule was very strong. Respondents' views on the proper pace of decisionmaking showed the nature of this support.

When asked to choose among the three alternative paces of decisionmaking listed in Table 3.10, the majority of respondents, both urban and rural, opted for a slow decisionmaking pace. The single significant difference between responses of urban and rural residents related to postponing decisionmaking. Twice as many rural residents as city residents thought it was "good" to postpone decisions if necessary.

The respondents also were of the opinion that Alaskans should pay attention to "everyone" while making decisions. Neither urban nor rural respondents said communities should be particularly responsive to special interests, but rural residents did say they would respond to the needs of Native culture. However, when asked what the single most important thing in decisionmaking was, 83 percent of the respondents said the needs of everyone

Table 3.10
Pace of Decisionmaking Activity

Pace	% Saying "Good"	% Saying "Bad"
Talk over the issue quickly, so other things can be done	12.4%	70.6%
Talk over the issue slowly, so views of all are represented	81.4	4.9
Postpone decision as needed	42.8	33.5
	N=218	

Table 3.11
Criteria of Decisionmaking

Criterion	% Saying very important	% Saying not important
Keep what is best for everyone in mind	79.3%	1.0%
Keep needs of those most concerned in mind	48.1	9.8
Keep needs of Native culture in mind	63.8	7.4
	N=223	

should be uppermost—another statement in favor of citizen participation at the local level.

A final set of questions concerned how individuals might express their views and develop influence. Given the sparse population of all Alaska communities except Anchorage, and the "friends and neighbors" values that seem to describe small town and village political encounters, we thought we might find that voting and other routine procedures of American society might be less valued than personal ties. In fact this was not the case, as indicated in Table 3.12.

Most respondents (more than 82 percent) thought voting was a good way to express views, but when asked to compare it to other methods, the largest

Table 3.12
Methods of Voicing Opinion in Alaska

Method	% Saying "Good"	% Saying "Bad"
Voting	82.2%	5.8%
Going to meetings	60.1	16.7
Talking with board members	63.7	10.4
Talking with other people before/after meetings	74.1	10.7
Writing letters to leaders	60.4	15.1
Calling state legislators	38.3	21.9
	N=207	

number of respondents (47.8) preferred "talking to leaders." Overall, voting was a close second (36.8 percent) except among urban residents, who felt it was the best influence strategy. Few respondents rated formal means such as writing or calling political representatives highly.

These survey data are a useful addition to information provided in other approaches taken toward understanding Alaska political culture. First, they suggest that while there are differences between the participation orientations of Alaskans and other Americans, these differences are not substantial. The "civic culture" of the United States extends to the North and is practiced there. Second, there are significant differences between the traditional political cultural characteristics of Native Alaskans (most of whom live in rural areas) and those of non-Natives.

STABILITY AND CHANGE IN ALASKA'S POLITICAL CULTURE

How orientations and values of citizens change over time is perhaps the most interesting question in the study of political culture. How much of the "pioneer" Alaska culture will be left at the end of the twentieth century? Will the state retain its distinctive Native culture? Which parts (if any) of the fragments of individualistic attitudes Alaskans have toward government will survive into the next century?

Regional political cultures in the United States have ecological roots. More so than is the case in most American states, Alaska's political culture is dependent on a geographic location—on the development of human population in a unique environmental setting. That setting is the source of the most distinctive political culture in the state—that of Native Alaskans. For example, the slow, almost glacial, process of discussion involving everyone in the community expresses Native cultural attitudes—so that a decision appears to be made only when it has been fully implemented. Given little change in population dynamics, a continuation of this distinctive set of cultural attitudes would be likely. However, communication technology has changed greatly as the state—including its rural regions—has jumped rapidly into the high-tech future.

Outside the villages of Native Alaska, one sees immigrants from different parts of the contiguous-48 states. Then it is important to examine political demography. With population movement, political culture changes, but it does so in a predictable direction.

Our inability to trace large differences between the civic culture of Alaskans and other Americans is perhaps an indication that Alaska has grown more like the rest of the U.S. (been "nationalized" as it were) over the period of statehood. In 1959 Alaska was a parochial symbol of the last frontier. There was a conception of difference, some mystification, and a series of myths— Native society as pristine, highly traditional, and white pioneers as stalwart, fiercely independent individualists. The nationalization of Alaska's political culture has meant the spread to Alaska of national symbols—as for example the punk rockers in small villages. It also has meant the appropriation for a national audience of peculiar Alaska events—such as construction of the trans-Alaska oil pipeline and Native whaling. Any of the epic events can be manipulated to create an image of Alaska behavior. The flinty-eyed trapper, dog musher, subsistence fisherman—real types in Alaska but limited in numbers—then become symbols outside Alaska. But the change is less from developments within Alaska than from trends in the contiguous 48 states, which have effects on Alaska.

CONCLUSION

Studies of political culture tend to refer to two areas—the political culture of nation states, such as Japanese, Chinese, German, or American cultures; and the political culture of geographic regions within states. A few tentative steps have been taken toward creating a file of materials on American state cultures, as for example in studies by political scientists Elazar and Kincaid.[32] But no systematic work has been done on the differences in political cultures among American states.

Thus, there is little material against which one can compare knowledge of Alaska cultural attitudes. It is difficult to say what is the same, and what is different, about Alaskans' attitudes and orientations toward government and about the role of the individual in the state's political process. We know some of the respects in which Alaska's government is different. Most prominent is the sheer size of public sector activity in Alaska compared to private economic activity, which makes government more significant and dramatically increases its role as employer and its general welfare functions. That high level of government activity is the major reason why the average Alaskan has greater awareness of state government than do residents of other states.

On the basis of what others have said about Alaska's political culture and on our own research, we conclude that the unique environment of Alaska—its mind-stretching vastness, climatic extremes, physical isolation—is the most important determinant of the state's political culture. In response to that environment, there is an Alaska Native culture. In a political sense, this culture emphasizes values in the land (and all the land supports) and in consensus. Survey research documents the obvious in this respect: Native Alaskans prize their communal resources and values and seek their perpetuation. Survey research also documents that in many respects the bearers of Native culture are little different from other Alaskans.

What this chapter indicates that is not so obvious is that urban non-Natives, who make up the large majority of Alaska's population, participate somewhat more in government affairs than do other Americans. There is evidence in Alaska of environmental learning in the social sense: greater reliance on others, openness, a greater sense of power, and participation. Each of these values and beliefs is practiced to a somewhat greater extent in Alaska than in other U.S. political communities. But the overall direction of activity—and rates of participation—are not strongly different from those in the contiguous-48 states.

Alaska political culture is a response of humans to unique environmental events and occurrences. The learning process distinguishes two groups on the basis of time. Alaska Natives have orientations to politics that are considerably different from those of other Americans, but the differences are lessening as Natives have greater contact with non-Natives, particularly in urban locales. Non-Native Alaskans have attributes somewhat different from those of citizens of Seattle, Houston, or New York. In theory (or myth), these differences are large indeed; in practice, beliefs of Alaskans and other Americans as they relate to policy choices do not appear greatly dissimilar.

ENDNOTES

[1]Gayle M. Patrick, "Political Culture," in Giovanni Sartori, ed., *Social Science Concepts* (Beverly Hills, CA: Sage Publications, 1984), pp. 297-98.

[2]Daniel J. Elazar, _American Federalism: A View from the States_ (New York: Thomas Y. Crowell, 1963).

[3]Thomas A. Morehouse and Gordon Scott Harrison, "State Government and Economic Development in Alaska," in Gordon Scott Harrison, ed., _Alaska Public Policy_ (College, AK: Institute of Social, Economic and Government Research, University of Alaska, 1971), pp. 18-19. The authors' comments about Alaskans' ethnocentricity are somewhat controversial. Others point out that "Lower 48" is simply a way of indicating the continental U.S., which is south of Alaska and therefore lower.

[4]Morehouse and Harrison, "State Government and Economic Development in Alaska," p. 20.

[5]John Hanrahan and Peter Gruenstein, _Lost Frontier_ (New York: W.W. Norton & Co., 1977), p. 13.

[6]Joe McGinniss, _Going to Extremes_ (New York: New American Library, 1980), p. 37. Many Alaskans would argue with that assessment by McGinniss: Even after many years in the bush or urban Alaska, they still miss, correspond with, and dream of their former homes. An experienced rural teacher, John Lyle, points out that sometimes Alaskans' preoccupation with their state is a convenient veil behind which to hide from their responsibility as citizens of a larger U.S. and world.

[7]McGinniss, _Going to Extremes_, p. 73.

[8]Lee J. Cuba, "Reorientations of Self: Residential Identification in Anchorage, Alaska," Unpublished paper. 1982.

[9]Ibid., p. 11. There is a trend seen in both the bush and in cities of suspicion and distrust of newcomers and transients, related to increasing rates of rape, suicide, drug and alcohol abuses, domestic violence and other violent crimes. The paradox of violence amid friendliness is more evident in Alaska than in other mountain states experiencing slower rates of change.

[10]Ibid., p. 14. The impact of length of residence on values is noted carefully in a study of the impact of oil development on Fairbanks. The author remarks: "the more recent immigrants...are noticeably more attracted to immediate income gains, a challenging or exciting job, and less attracted to a self-reliant lifestyle." See Jack Kruse, "Urban Impacts of Oil Development—The Fairbanks Experience," _Alaska Review of Social and Economic Conditions_, Vol. 13, No. 3 (December 1976) p. 2. Published by the Institute of Social and Economic Research, University of Alaska.

[11]Elazar, _American Federalism_, p. 13.

[12]Ibid., p. 264. Also, see John Kincaid, ed., _Political Culture, Public Policy and the American States_ (Philadelphia: Institute for the Study of Human Issues, 1982), p. 18.

[13]Kincaid, _Political Culture_, p. 19.

[14]Ibid., p. 20.

[15]See, among others, Ira Sharkansky, "The Utility of Elazar's Political Culture: A Research Note," _Polity_ 2 (Fall 1969), pp. 66-83.

[16]Gunnar Knapp, et al., "The Alaska Permanent Fund Dividend Program: Economic Effects and Public Attitudes," unpublished report (Anchorage: Institute of Social and Economic Research, University of Alaska, 1984).

[17]T. W. Adorno, et. al., *The Authoritarian Personality* (New York: Harper, 1950).

[18]Gabriel Almond and Sidney Verba, *The Civic Culture* (Princeton, NJ: Princeton University Press, 1963). In their conceptualization of civic culture, Almond and Verba blended the Weberian types of authority and the Parsonian pattern variables into three types of political culture: parochial, subject, and participant. Together, these composed the mix that was a "civic culture." The persistence of traditional and parochial attitudes toward authority fused with participant ones. Thus from parochial orientations would come passivity, traditionality, and commitment to a local place. From subject orientations would come involvement, trust, and competence. From participation would come political activity, involvement, and rationality.

[19]Almond and Verba, *The Civic Culture*, p. 231.

[20]Almond and Verba, *The Civic Culture*, p. 275.

[21]For example, Dwaine Marvick, "The Political Socialization of the American Negro," in Edward C. Dreyer and Walter A. Rosenbaum, eds., *Political Opinion and Behavior: Essays and Studies* (Belmont, CA: Wadsworth Publishing Company, 1970), pp. 161-79.

[22]Alan I. Abramowitz, "The United States: Political Culture under Stress," in Gabriel A. Almond and Sidney Verba, eds., *The Civic Culture Revisited* (Boston: Little, Brown, 1980), pp. 188-93.

[23]Lucien Pye and Sidney Verba, *Political Culture and Political Development* (Princeton, NJ: Princeton University Press, 1965), p. 16.

[24]Thomas R. Berger, "Alaska Natives and Aboriginal Peoples around the World," report presented at the Tanana Chiefs Conference, Fairbanks, Alaska, March 13, 1984, p. 10.

[25]The research team collecting data was led by Gerald McBeath, Carl Shepro, and Tony Strong. Research was supported by a grant from the Alaska Council on Science and Technology to the University of Alaska's Department of Political Science at Fairbanks. Assisting in this research were Professor Marc Stier, and the following university students: James Kacur, Beverly St. Sauver, Joseph St. Sauver, Julie Goodrich, Beth Allman, Jerry Domnick, Rose Domnick, and Michael Balas. Two researchers were fluent in Alaska Native languages.

[26]Both Anchorage and Fairbanks were added to the original sample of rural and road system places. The total number of interviews conducted in the state's two largest cities, however, was around 50, comprising just under one-quarter of the sample (in contrast to the 53 percent of the 1980 census population represented by the two cities). For this reason, and for the obvious problems of small sample size, we have couched our observations regarding urban attitudes and values in careful terms.

[27]See particularly Sidney Verba, Norman H. Nie, and Jae-on Kim, *Participation and Political Equality: A Seven-Nation Comparison* (Cambridge: Cambridge University Press, 1978), pp. 270-71.

[28]Eric Madsen, "Decision-Making in a Rural Alaska Community," in Ray Barnhardt, ed., *Cross Cultural Issues in Alaska Education*, vol. II (Fairbanks, AK: University of Alaska, 1982), pp. 106-119.

[29]Verba, Nie, Kim, *Participation and Political Equality*, p. 273.

[30]We checked our list of community organizations with village informants (whom we had interviewed about organizational history), and then asked all respondents a series of questions regarding each organization on the list.

[31]Verba, Nie, Kim, *Participation and Political Equality*, p. 277.

[32]Kincaid, *Political Culture*, p. 178.

4

Federalism In Alaska

David C. Maas

Government power in Alaska and the rest of the nation is divided among federal, state, local, and Native American governments. This chapter describes our federal system of government—how it is structured, how it has changed over time, how decisions are made under this system, and what questions about the division of powers remain unresolved.

We start by discussing federalism in the United States as a whole and then look specifically at how the federal system operates in Alaska. We use a case study of passage of the Alaska Native Claims Settlement Act to illustrate how public decisions are made.

In the United States in general in recent decades, scholars have paid close attention to the changing division of responsibility and power between the federal government and the fifty state governments. We also discuss that shifting federal-state relationship; in Alaska there have been and continue to be disagreements and uncertainties about where lines should be drawn between federal and state authority.

But probably the most complex, unresolved questions about government power in Alaska in the 1980s have to do with potential powers of Native governments, particularly in relation to state authority. How much power Native governments in Alaska will ultimately have will be decided by future court rulings, by Congressional actions, by other federal and state actions, and by decisions and activities of Native groups. Because this process of allocating government power will be played out in Alaska over the coming years, we also examine powers of Native American governments in the U.S. as a whole, comparing those powers with the current and potential status of Native governments in Alaska.

A good example of the kinds of Native government issues that are yet to be resolved is a current lawsuit testing the authority of the Native village of Tyonek. In September 1982, Tyonek sought to evict two non-Native couples from the village. By controlling immigration, village leaders said they hoped to protect their "culture, economy and heritage from exploitation and infringement by outsiders."[1] In response, those being evicted brought a lawsuit, charging that Tyonek's action was racially discriminatory and unconstitutional.

The case has not yet been decided; without arguing the merits of the case on either side, we can point out that it raises an important question: which government should exercise which power? We acknowledge the power of government to set geographic boundaries, but which level of government should have the authority to control immigration into a community? This chapter can not answer that question, but it will provide the necessary background for understanding the issues involved in the division of government powers in the United States in general and Alaska in particular.

TYPES OF GOVERNMENTS

BACKGROUND

In 1781, the original states established the first national government in the United States under the Articles of Confederation. That document created a weak national government with almost no authority over the powerful and essentially independent state governments. The national government could not regulate commerce and could not constrain states to obey national laws. Establishing foreign trade and maintaining domestic order were difficult under those circumstances.

By 1785, a number of states agreed that the Articles of Confederation should be revised and the national government strengthened. The national Congress called for a Constitutional Convention, which was held in Philadelphia in 1787. Out of that convention came the Constitution of the United States. The constitution went into effect in 1789 and remains in effect today, with few amendments.

NATIONAL AND STATE GOVERNMENTS

The new government system established under the U.S. constitution is known as federalism, which can be defined as a "political organization in which the activities of government are divided between regional governments and a central government in such a way that each kind of government has some activities on which it makes final decisions."[2]

Unlike the Articles of Confederation, the new constitution divided sovereignty between the national government and the states. A government with sovereign powers is one that exercises the ultimate authority in some areas, even though another government may have the ultimate say in other areas. Very broadly speaking, the original distinction between national and state powers was that the national government was given the authority to control commerce and foreign affairs while the states were left with wide authority to control their domestic affairs.

LOCAL GOVERNMENTS

The U.S. constitution does not specifically mention local governments. State governments, under terms of their own constitutions, create and control local governments. Although these local governments are not therefore "sovereign," a number of state constitutions—including Alaska's—give local governments the authority to exercise substantial control over their own affairs.

A web of state-local relations has been established over the past 200 years. And although historically there was little contact between the national government and local governments, in recent decades direct federal aid to local governments has also created complex national-local relations.

NATIVE AMERICAN GOVERNMENTS

Another form of government in the United States that is recognized as having some sovereign powers is Native American government—government established by the aboriginal peoples of this country. A variety of court decisions and federal laws and policies over the history of the United States have established that Native American governments have authority over the internal affairs of Indians and other Native Americans, but even today the extent of this authority remains unclear in a number of areas. Because Native American governments are in many respects different from state and local governments, we discuss Native governments in a separate section after looking at the other levels of government.

NATIONAL AND STATE POWER

Under federalism both the national and the state governments hold certain sovereign powers. But there is also a provision in Article VI of the U.S. constitution that says the constitution and the federal laws written in accordance with it are the ultimate laws of the land. This means, for instance, that while the state and national governments can at times both pass laws on the same subject, if provisions of those laws conflict it is the federal law that will prevail.[3]

Apart from this assertion of the broad supremacy of federal law, the U.S. constitution delegates certain specific powers to the federal government and implies others. Article I of the constitution specifically gives the national government authority to levy taxes, control foreign and interstate commerce, issue money, and declare war, among others. Articles II and III enumerate other federal powers.

Article I also includes a provision known as the "elastic clause," which gives the U.S. Congress authority to "make all laws necessary and proper" for carrying out its specified powers and responsibilities. The powers that can be implied from that clause, when coupled with the federal government's authority to control commerce and other specific powers, are very broad.

Powers not specifically assigned to the national government under the constitution were left to the state governments. These so-called "reserved" powers (reserved because they were left to the states after national powers were specified) are substantial. They include power to establish domestic law, provide for public safety, health, education, and other services, and regulate business within their areas of jurisdiction. During much of the history of the United States, state governments held the most political power. States established their own voting requirements and apportioned their legislatures under their own systems.

Throughout the nineteenth century the federal government operated under a fairly narrow interpretation of its powers. Congress confined most of its attention to internal improvements, subsidies, tariffs, currency, and the acquisition and disposal of public lands.[4]

But in the twentieth century, through a more liberal interpretation of its delegated and implied powers—and through its constitutional responsibility for protecting certain basic rights of all U.S. citizens—the federal government expanded its domain.[5] Federal civil rights laws, the U.S. Supreme Court's "one man, one vote" ruling, welfare and other social service programs, and environmental protection standards are just a few examples of the ways in which the federal government increasingly moved into domestic areas.

Despite the loss of some of their powers, state governments today remain integral parts of the American federal system. Many states, as we discuss in other chapters, have improved their judicial, executive, and legislative operations in recent times. The federal government could not carry out its programs without the help and cooperation of state governments; as federal programs have expanded, so has the role of state governments in carrying out those programs. States can and do carry out their own programs and laws in some of the same areas as the federal government, as long as those state measures do not conflict with federal ones.

The Reagan Administration in the 1980s has attempted to shift some public responsibilities back to the states, to reduce federal regulations and spending, and to move cases involving the issues of abortion, prayer in schools, and school busing from the national to the state courts. How successful these attempts to reduce federal and promote state activities will be remains to be seen—but in any event they represent a shift from the federal policy that has prevailed for the past several decades.

FEDERAL POWER IN ALASKA

The actions of the federal government affect all the states in hundreds of ways. But for a number of reasons the federal government has been and remains particularly visible in Alaska.

Since World War II Alaska's strategic location has meant that the U.S. Department of Defense is very active here, although not as active in recent years as was true earlier. Before 1959 there was no state government in Alaska. The federal government owned virtually all the land and managed the resources—often to the dissatisfaction of local residents. Today 60 percent of the land in the state is still federal land; there have been and continue to be bitter conflicts between the state and the federal government over management of those vast lands.[6]

Alaska's large Native population has also increased federal activity in Alaska. The federal government provides medical and other federal services for Native Americans nationwide and in Alaska. Also, the federal government was heavily involved in settling land claims of Alaska's aboriginal peoples. (See later discussion of passage of the claims settlement act.) It will likewise be a key player in determining the powers of Native governments in Alaska.

Aside from these broad areas in which the federal government exercises authority in Alaska, we can also see examples of the influence of specific federal powers. Two of the most important bases of the formal power of the federal government are the commerce clause in Article I of the constitution and the Fourteenth Amendment to the constitution.

The commerce clause gives the federal government the power to ''regulate Commerce with foreign nations, and among the several states, and with the Indian tribes.'' In the nineteenth century the national government used the commerce power mainly to restrain the states in the regulation of trade and business; under the Articles of Confederation the states had established various barriers to trade among the states. But in the twentieth century that power has been more broadly interpreted to mean that Congress has the authority to enact ''all appropriate legislation'' for the ''protection and enhancement'' of commerce.[7] Many federal laws affect Alaska commerce. Examples include the Export Administration Act, which prohibits the export to foreign countries of oil from Alaska's North Slope, and the Jones Act, which requires that all ships carrying goods between domestic ports be built and registered in the United States.

The Fourteenth Amendment to the constitution, enacted soon after the end of the Civil War, entitles all U.S. citizens to rights of life, liberty, property, and due process of law. It was originally intended to protect the rights of former slaves who were now citizens. The U.S. Supreme Court has over the years selectively applied these rights to state residents.

In Alaska, application of this amendment means that each of the state's periodic redistricting plans has to be submitted for approval to the U.S. attorney general or the U.S. District Court for Alaska. The federal Civil Rights Act—which is based on Fourteenth Amendment protections—enables federal examiners to closely watch the process of voter registration and elections in Alaska and other states. In a recent application of the Fourteenth Amendment's equal protection clause, the U.S. Supreme Court overturned the state's original Permanent Fund distribution plan, which would have paid higher dividends to those who had lived in Alaska longer.[8]

We could cite many more examples of the effects of federal action in Alaska; the above brief examples are intended just to show a sampling of national government power in Alaska.

LOCAL GOVERNMENT POWERS

Local governments, while lacking an independent source of power, are key providers of public services across the United States. In most areas of the country local governments directly provide police and fire protection, water and sewer systems, education, parks and other recreation areas, and housing and urban renewal programs. They spend about 20 percent of all government money spent in the United States—although, as we will discuss later, much of the money that local governments spend in the 1980s comes from the state and federal governments.

There are many types of local government units around the country, including municipalities, counties, boroughs, townships, school districts, and various special districts. A given type of unit may provide just one or a whole range of public services.

LOCAL GOVERNMENT IN ALASKA

The state constitution of Alaska gives local governments the potential for substantial power. One recent study of state-local relations found Alaska—along with Texas, Maine, California, Connecticut, and Michigan—at the forefront of constitutional and statutory grants of power to local governments.[9]

Only the Pennsylvania constitution grants as much financial discretion to local communities as does the Alaska constitution.[10] Only in Alaska, Montana, and Pennsylvania are the major powers of government decentralized. And in Alaska, conflicts over the powers and boundaries of local governments are initially settled in the legislature, not in the courts.[11] This system can be an advantage to local governments because the Alaska Municipal League and some individual municipalities strongly represent local government interests during legislative sessions.[12] (Of course, decisions of the legislature about local governments can still be appealed to the courts.)

But like all states, Alaska does set important limits on the potential powers of its local governments. State limits on local authority are discussed in detail in the chapter on Alaska's constitution; here we mention a few of the chief controls. Local governments are subject to state law; for instance, state law limits the amount local governments can collect in property taxes. The state constitution gives the state government the authority to approve creation of new boroughs and changes in boundaries of existing local units—although, as noted above, legislative decisions can be appealed. Also, local governments in Alaska are liable to suit, which often means that the courts become involved in local disputes.

The potential for local power and the reality of local government are very different in urban and rural areas of Alaska. In much of rural Alaska there are no organized city or borough governments—mostly because there are not adequate tax bases to support such government. In many rural areas the state government, and, in some instances, the federal government, directly provide services that local governments would provide elsewhere.

In these rural areas there are a number of local entities that, in the absence of cities and boroughs, perform limited local government functions. These include, for example, Regional Education Attendance Areas (REAAs), which are large, regionally controlled school districts. School boards for these districts are elected locally, and these boards have a substantial say in the operation of schools under their jurisdiction. But REAAs are funded entirely with state money, and the state imposes a number of restrictions on school board powers.[13] Other kinds of organizations that carry out local government functions—with federal and state grants—are the nonprofit Native associations and health corporations formed under the terms of the Alaska Native Claims Settlement Act.[14]

A separate and increasingly important issue in rural Alaska is potential power of Native governments—traditional village councils and councils formed under the terms of the federal Indian Reorganization Act (IRA). Up through the mid-1980s, Native government powers have been restricted by lack of money and by uncertainty about the extent of those powers. The state government recognizes only organized cities and boroughs as local government units. The federal government, while it has historically recognized Native governments, has yet to decide how much power it will accord Native governments in Alaska. We discuss these questions about Native government in detail in a later section of this chapter.

In urban Alaska, by contrast, local governments in many respects operate as local governments elsewhere in the country do. They raise a significant share of their own operating money, but also rely on federal and state monies. Some urban governments provide a whole range of services, while others provide just education and a few other basic services.

The most powerful local governments in Alaska are a handful of unified municipalities and one borough that operate under home-rule charters. Those charters essentially allow them to assume any powers not prohibited them by state law and to broadly control their own affairs—much as state governments are allowed to assume any power not reserved to the federal government or in conflict with federal law.

INTERRELATIONSHIPS AMONG GOVERNMENTS

We've looked broadly at the division of power among national, state, and local governments. However, federalism is not a static system with each government operating independently. It is instead a dynamic process of conflict, bargaining, and compromise among governments. In the U.S. today, the national government needs the state governments to administer its programs, the states need national programs and money, towns and cities rely on state and federal aid, and state and national leaders in turn need the cooperation of local officials. Governments at every level are deeply involved in public affairs, and policy areas in which one government acts alone are the exception.

INTERGOVERNMENTAL REVENUE

More than anything else, increased federal revenues and increased federal aid to state and local governments have changed the relations among various levels of government in this country since the 1930s. In earlier times, the federal government raised less money than state and local governments did, and kept most revenues for its own operations. State and local governments raised most of their own money, although there was some state aid to local governments.

In 1929, federal, state, and local governments in the U.S. took in about $10 billion. Local governments raised and spent about half that public money. By 1983, U.S. governments at all levels took in nearly $1 trillion, with the federal

Table 4.1
General Revenues, All Governments, 1983 (in billion $)

| | From Own Sources | Intergovernmental Aid | | | Total |
		From Federal Govt.	From State Govt.	From Local Govt.	
Federal Revenues	$482/100%	—	—	—	$482/100%
State Revenues	$218/75%	$69*/24%	—	$3/1%	$290/100%
Local Revenues	$179/60%	$21/7%	$98/33%	—	$298/100%
Total General Govt. Revenues	$879				

*State governments pass on an estimated 20 percent of federal aid they receive to local governments—so directly and indirectly (through state governments) federal aid amounted to about 11 percent of local revenues in 1983.

Source: U.S. Department of Commerce, Bureau of the Census, _Statistical Abstract of the United States_, 1986.

government collecting the lion's share. Local governments that year spent only about 20 percent of public money in the U.S.—and 40 percent of local government money came from the federal and state governments.

Table 4.1 shows how much in general revenue governments collected across the country in 1983, and how much of that revenue was passed down from one government to another. Of the roughly $900 billion all governments took in that year, the federal government collected $482 billion and passed on about $90 billion, or 19 percent, to state and local governments. Federal aid that year made up nearly 25 percent of state revenues, and combined federal and state aid made up 40 percent of local revenues.

So it is apparent that the federal government has become the dominant tax collector, and that the state and local governments have come to rely heavily on federal aid. The Reagan Administration in the 1980s has attempted to reduce the federal government's role in collecting and distributing revenue—but the trend of the past 50 years is not readily reversed.

FEDERAL GRANTS

Federal aid to state and local governments is chiefly in the form of grants. Grants are used for a variety of purposes—to funnel money to states and localities, to equalize financial resources among governments, to establish administrative standards, and to further national objectives.[15] (Another significant but smaller source of federal aid is federal loans.)

There are three broad types of grants: categorical grants, block grants, and revenue sharing. Categorical grants are federal monies for specific programs or activities—the interstate highways program, for instance, or the Medicaid or Aid to Families with Dependent Children programs. These programs are administered by state governments and generally paid for in part with state money. Block grants are—as the name implies—blocks of money that can be used at the states' discretion for more general purposes; for example, block grants could be used for community development or improving community health. These grants are more popular with states than are the categorical grants. The last kind of federal grant is general revenue sharing. Shared revenue is money that the federal government passes on relatively free of restrictions; how much revenue a state or community receives depends on population and other factors.

State governments pass on to local governments about 20 percent of the federal monies they receive.[16] There are also dozens of federal grant programs that are administered directly by local governments.

These federal grants to state and local governments totaled less than $2 billion in 1948. By 1983, federal grants totaled $90 billion, and rose to $98 billion in 1984, despite curbs the Reagan Administration imposed on growth in domestic aid.[17]

FEDERAL REGULATION OF STATE AND LOCAL GOVERNMENTS

As the national government expanded its operations dramatically over the past half century, it also greatly increased its regulation of the activities of state and local governments. The growth in federal regulation followed major social and political trends.

One trend that prompted an increase in federal regulations was the growth of the civil rights movement in the 1950s and 1960s. As more and more Americans were drawn into that movement, the federal government became increasingly involved. Federal laws and other actions to protect civil rights meant that the federal government began monitoring state and local elections and other areas that had previously been left largely to the states. Similarly, the environmental protection movement of the 1960s and 1970s led to federal laws for the protection of air, water, and other parts of the environment—and these laws were put into effect with many regulations.

Another factor that led to increased federal regulation was the proliferation of federal grant programs. As the programs multiplied so did the pages of the federal register (where regulations are initially published) and the Code of Federal Regulations. Finally, as the U.S. Congress has become more independent and powerful than it was in earlier times, it has pushed for more control and reform—which has led to yet more federal regulations.[18]

There are four types of intergovernmental regulation: direct orders, crosscutting requirements, crossover sanctions, and partial preemptions.

Direct orders are legal commands from one government to another. These are powerful but seldom used tools. Examples include the federal government's order that state and local governments may not discriminate on the basis of race, color, sex, or national origin. Another instance of a direct order is the U.S. Supreme Court's recent decision that national wage and hour restrictions now apply to all public employees at every level of government service.[19]

Crosscutting requirements are standards that apply to all federal programs. Most common among these are standards for protection of the environment, for hiring of minorities, for freedom of information about most federal operations, and certain administrative and related requirements.

Crossover sanctions force state and local governments to meet the requirements of one federal program in order to keep money for another federal program. For instance, in 1975, the federal government threatened to cut off federal aid for all health services to those states that did not have health planning processes in place.

Partial preemption rests on the supremacy of national law and the delegation of responsibility. In Alaska, for example, Congress has reserved the right to protect subsistence resources of rural Alaskans on federal lands. However, the state was given the authority to manage fish and wildlife on federal lands, as long as it gives subsistence uses priority.

IMPLICATIONS OF CHANGING FEDERAL ROLE

The growth of federal spending and regulation has had a number of consequences. Chief among these are changes in intergovernmental relations, conflicts between the federal and the state governments, and increased interstate and interlocal cooperation.

We have already mentioned the changes in intergovernmental relations in the U.S. in recent decades. States have become the intergovernmental managers of national programs. They often determine who is eligible for federal money, and insure that communities and private citizens comply with federal law. States

Table 4.2

Direct Federal Expenditures and Federal Grants in Alaska (1983) (in millions of dollars)

Budget Classification	Amount
Military Salaries and Wages[1]	$ 474
Direct Payment to Individuals[2]	273
Civilian Salaries and Wages	276
Other Operating Expenses[3]	500
Total Operating Expenses	$1,523
Federal Grants	$ 546
Total Federal Money	$2,069

[1]Includes military retirement.

[2]Examples are Medicare, Social Security, Veterans' compensation, unemployment, civilian retirement, and disability.

[3]Expenses are procurement, construction, and the like.

Source: Table compiled from the U.S. Department of Commerce, Bureau of Census, *Consolidated Federal Funds Report*. (Fiscal Year 1983) Volume II. Subcounty Areas.

pass on a share of federal money they receive to local governments, and have become increasingly important sources of local money in their own right.

National-local relations, which were almost non-existent in the nineteenth century, have also multiplied, with federal aid the linchpin between the federal government and thousands of local governments across the country. Dozens of federal grant programs bypass state governments and go directly to local units. These grants have stimulated the growth of community services and local government employment; in the early 1980s there were more local government employees than combined totals of federal and state employees.

Increased federal aid accompanied by increased federal control has inevitably led to conflicts among levels of government. A study done for the National Governors' Association found that states objected to the lack of coordination among federal programs, the intrusions on state authority, prescriptive federal regulations, excessive paperwork for federal programs, long approval procedures, and inconsistency of federal actions.[20]

Alaskans and other Americans frequently bristle under federal actions and regulations, charging—among other things—that some federal requirements do not apply to local situations and that they create inefficiencies. State and local governments have complained that while national laws are often built on the premise of state and local cooperation, the regulations that accompany the laws often seem to assume that state and local governments will not act fairly or responsibly.[21]

Another consequence of the expansion of federal activity has been increased political activity by and cooperation between state and local governments. Thirty states, including Alaska, and a few large cities maintain liaison offices in Washington, D.C. These offices follow activities of Congress and serve as forums for communication and coordination between private and public interests at the state, local, and federal levels.[22] States and communities also have a number of public interest organizations that lobby Congress, act as clearinghouses for information and sponsor research, and enable state and local governments to act in concert in their dealings with the federal government.

INTERGOVERNMENTAL RELATIONS IN ALASKA

The things we've said about intergovernmental relations nationwide apply generally to Alaska; below we look more specifically at the relations between the various levels of government in Alaska.

FEDERAL MONEY IN ALASKA

Federal money has historically been important to Alaska, although in the early 1980s that importance was overshadowed by very fast growth in the state government's petroleum revenues.

It is not only federal grant money that comes into Alaska; most federal money in the state is for direct federal operations. As we mentioned earlier, the federal government has long played an active role in Alaska. Alaska's strategic location means substantial military spending in Alaska. The federal government also has vast land holdings in Alaska, so federal spending by the Department of the Interior is also significant.

Per capita federal spending in Alaska is among the highest in the nation—which follows, given Alaska's small population and the high level of federal operations here. Table 4.2 shows direct federal spending and federal grants in Alaska in 1983. Of the nearly $2.1 billion total, the federal government itself spent about 75 percent for its own operations and programs. Wages paid to military and civilian employees, and costs of construction and other operations, accounted for most of the spending. Direct federal payments to individuals for Social Security and other programs made up most of the rest.

Federal grants to state and local governments in Alaska totaled $546 million, or about 25 percent of direct and indirect federal spending in the state that year. About half the federal grant money went for education and transportation, and another 20 percent for social and medical assistance programs. The remaining federal grants went for general revenue sharing and a variety of land, water, and wildlife conservation and management programs.

FEDERAL LAND IN ALASKA

Ownership of land in Alaska has historically had and will continue to have important effects on intergovernmental relations. The three major land owners in Alaska are the federal government, which will ultimately own about 60 percent of the land in the state, the state government, which will own 28 percent, and the Native corporations formed under the terms of the claims settlement act, which will own more than 11 percent. (The remaining lands, which are less than one percent of the total, belong mainly to municipalities and private citizens.)

The federal government will play an instrumental role in future use and development of natural resources in Alaska, given its large land holdings. Most federal land in Alaska today falls within the national conservation systems—chiefly parks, wildlife refuges, and forests. Development on national conservation lands is restricted in various ways. Invariably national decisions about use of federal lands in Alaska will affect oil and gas leasing, mining, logging, hunting and fishing, subsistence activities, and recreational pursuits. Those future decisions will reflect national interests as Congress and federal officials see them—and those will not always correspond with the interests of Alaska residents.

State management of its own large land holdings will not always mesh with federal management, given the history of bitter conflicts between the two governments over the best uses of Alaska lands. The other big players in land management decisions will be the Native corporations. Important private interests—including environmental organizations and business groups—that have lobbied government over land issues in the past will continue to do so.

Many groups—Alaskans and other Americans, Native groups, federal, state, and municipal agencies, environmentalists, and business interests—will be battling for control of Alaska lands. There is an opportunity, however remote, for cooperation among the big land owners in the state. The Alaska National Interest Lands Conservation Act (ANILCA) of 1980 established the Alaska Land Use Planning Council. It has members representing state and federal government and the Native corporations. Its budget is small and it is essentially a weak organization with an ambiguous role—but it can at least serve as a forum for discussions among various interests.

STATE-LOCAL RELATIONS IN ALASKA

Although the state constitution gives local governments the potential for a large measure of control over their own affairs, the state government plays a very active role in local affairs in the state. As we noted earlier, the state decides what new local governments will be created and what their boundaries will be. In many areas of rural Alaska there are essentially no local governments, and the state directly provides a number of services to those areas. Since 1978 the state has made land grants to local governments, thus putting land for a variety of public purposes into local hands.

The most important influence of state government on local governments in Alaska in the early 1980s was money: very large state petroleum revenues that the state shared with local governments. Between 1976 and 1982, per capita state operating aid to local governments increased from $51 to $211 and per capita capital grants grew from virtually nothing to more than $700. That state aid allowed local governments to cut taxes at the same time they substantially expanded services. In the early 1980s, the largest municipalities in the state—those with significant tax bases of their own—relied on the state for 40 percent or more of their operating money. Some small, rural municipalities relied almost exclusively on state money.[23]

The state in the past decade has been the major source of money for education, health, social welfare, and transportation programs in Alaska. Holding the purse strings has given the state a substantial say in local affairs—it has at times been auditor, reviewer, inspector, and rulemaker. But in some instances the state has not demanded tight oversight of its money. For example, in the early 1980s, the state legislature made large grants to all the municipalities in the state—based on population—to use largely as they chose. The state also made many large grants for capital projects local governments had requested, without closely questioning the rationale for those projects.

A broad indication of the effects of large petroleum revenues in the early 1980s is that in 1982, state and local governments in Alaska combined spent nearly $8,000 per resident. On the national average, state and local governments combined spent less than $2,000 per resident—or about one-fourth the Alaska total.

By the mid-1980s the state's oil revenues had dropped sharply with the falling price of oil. By the 1990s production from Prudhoe Bay will also be down sharply. Local governments in turn face life with much less state money. Just how declining state revenues will change the state's role in local affairs remain to be seen—but it will undoubtedly be a much smaller role.

TRIBAL GOVERNMENT IN THE AMERICAN SYSTEM

Another form of government in the United States that we have not yet talked about is tribal government—government of the Indian and other aboriginal peoples of the United States. We discuss these Native governments separately, because they are in many respects different from other governments in this country—but they are nevertheless part of the American federal system. In Alaska in the coming years, federal and state officials and Native groups will be determining the extent of power of Alaska Native governments.

Federal law is the supreme law for American Indians as it is for all other Americans. But the federal government has a special relationship with American Natives—a relationship that is sometimes described as a "trust" relationship—under which the federal government has complete control over Native peoples but also provides for their protection and welfare. Examples of federal provision for Native welfare include the education and health programs provided for Native peoples by the federal Bureau of Indian Affairs.

Despite the supremacy of the federal government, it has long been federal policy to accord Native peoples the right to control their own internal affairs—what David Case, an author of a text on American law as applied to Alaska Natives, classifies as internal sovereignty.[24] In an 1831 case, the U.S. Supreme Court held that Indian tribes were "distinct, independent political communities." The court said:

> A weaker power does not surrender its independence—its right to self-government—by associating with a stronger, and taking its protection.[25]

But the extent of that self-government is even today not always clear, because federal policies have not been consistent. As Case notes, "generalizations about the scope or nature of Native sovereignty are somewhat perilous; they must take into account not only detailed statutory schemes but sometimes conflicting congressional policies and inconsistent court decisions."[26]

At various times, Native self-government has been defined as giving Natives the right to determine their own forms of government, manage their internal relations, decide who can belong to their communities, impose taxes, regulate property, and oversee the conduct of their members.

At issue in some instances has been the power of state governments over Native people living in communities with tribal governments. Here again federal decisions have not always been consistent. One federal law gives some states—including Alaska—broad authority to enforce certain civil and criminal laws on reservations and other Indian lands. But that law prohibits states from taxing or otherwise regulating the use of Indian lands held in trust and has been interpreted as leaving "civil regulatory matters, such as taxing and zoning" in the hands of Native governments.[27]

Broadly speaking, federal decisions over the years have tended to authorize greater degrees of self-government for tribes living on reservation land. As we discuss below, the absence of reservations in Alaska—there is only one small reservation in southeast Alaska—has complicated issues of self-government for Alaska Natives.

NATIVE SELF-GOVERNMENT IN ALASKA

The federal government was for a number of years undecided about whether Alaska Natives constituted Indian "tribes" subject to the same general policies as other Native Americans because, among other things, Alaska Natives have always been organized around villages rather than tribal groups, as are most other Native Americans. That indecision was largely resolved in 1936, when Congress passed the Alaska Reorganization Act.

That act extended the 1934 Indian Reorganization Act to "Indians in Alaska not heretofore recognized as band or tribes...."[28] Congress had passed the Indian Reorganization Act (IRA) to strengthen tribal governments in the United States by establishing means for them to adopt federally recognized constitutions and bylaws, to obtain federal charters for Native businesses, to exercise land controls, to get federal loans, and to have legal counsel.

Today issues of Native government in Alaska are complicated by several factors.[29] Not the least of these is the fact that in the United States as a whole, Native government jurisdiction has often (although by no means always) been held to apply mainly on reservation lands; reservation lands are reserved for the use of American Indians, but title to those lands is still held by the federal government. In Alaska there is only one small reservation. All other Native land in Alaska belongs to Alaska Natives outright, under terms of the 1971 Alaska Native Claims Settlement Act (ANCSA). Private Native corporations formed under that act hold and manage the land.

The jurisdiction of Native governments over ANCSA lands has not yet been determined. At least two village corporations formed under ANCSA have dissolved themselves and turned their lands over to local tribal governments—not only to put the lands under tribal jurisdiction but also because under the corporate system there is the potential for the lands to fall into non-Native ownership. Other corporations are considering similar moves as part of a growing Native sovereignty movement in Alaska.

Another complication of Native government in Alaska is that there is no general agreement over which organization should have tribal standing. In the mid-1980s there are two types of Native government organizations in Alaska—traditional councils and councils formed under terms of the Indian Reorganization Act. The traditional councils are, as their name implies, the historical Alaska Native governments, built on local traditions. They are eligible for federal services and can at least theoretically exercise the powers of self-government we have talked about. There were 125 traditional councils in Alaska in 1986.

The IRA councils are generally more formally organized than traditional councils, having federally approved constitutions and bylaws. About 70 IRA councils existed in Alaska in 1986. Historically, traditional councils have focused on internal matters and IRAs have conducted business enterprises. But in many cases actions by either kind of council have been quite limited, due to lack of money and other problems.[30]

In the 1980s some Native councils began to test their powers. Earlier we mentioned the case in Tyonek, where the IRA council expelled two non-Natives from the village in an "attempt to protect its culture, economy, and heritage from exploitation and infringement by outsiders."[31] That action engendered a lawsuit on which there has not yet been a ruling. In 1983 the IRA council of Kotzebue passed a Native Employment Rights Ordinance that requires local employers "to give preference to Natives in hiring, promotion, training, and all other aspects of employment." The legality of that ordinance has not yet been tested, nor have its effects been clear. These IRA council actions and others in the future will help define the limits of Native sovereignty in Alaska.

A final complication of Native self-government in Alaska is that the state government recognizes only cities and boroughs as local governments in Alaska. It has been the past and continuing policy of the state to encourage Native villages to incorporate under state law, and dozens have done so over the years. Native sovereignty groups find these state-chartered governments unsatisfactory as Native governments because they can be controlled by non-Natives.

The State of Alaska in the early 1980s asked the U.S. Department of the Interior not to approve any new IRA constitutions until some of the issues of Native government have been resolved. And, through early 1986, the Interior Department had not in fact approved new IRA constitutions.

Overall then, there are significant unresolved questions about the powers of Native government in Alaska in the 1980s. Ongoing actions of IRA councils, court rulings, Congressional and Interior Department policies, and other factors will all influence Native government powers in Alaska. A critical factor will be the extent to which more lands now owned by private Native corporations are shifted to control of Native governments. If a significant share of the 44 million acres owned by Native corporations were shifted to tribal control, the legal basis for Native government powers on those lands would be strengthened.

CASE STUDY: ALASKA NATIVE CLAIMS SETTLEMENT ACT

So far we've described the elements of the federal system, discussed how powers are divided among governments, and looked at some of the relationships between them. Below we offer an example of federalism in action: the development, passage, and provisions of the 1971 Alaska Native Claims Settlement Act (ANCSA). This act is one of great political and historical significance and it demonstrates the dimensions and complexities of policymaking in a federal system.

HISTORY

By the time of World War II Alaska Natives were in a vulnerable and in many ways tragic situation. Their culture had been challenged by outside forces and many of their traditions lost. Like Indians throughout the United States, Alaska Natives were served by a smorgasbord of federal services and subject to a variety of pressures.

But in some respects Alaska Natives had historically been even more disadvantaged than other Native Americans—because the federal government had been slow to recognize Alaska Native groups as "tribes" entitled to the same benefits and provisions for self-government as other Native Americans.

Alaska Natives were, however, in a better position vis-a-vis the land. Alaska Natives had never signed treaties giving up any rights to land. While by 1940 other Native Americans had long been largely confined to reservations established by the federal government, Alaska Natives still enjoyed almost undisturbed use and occupancy of vast expanses of Alaska lands. Geography and political inattention to Alaska up to that point partly accounted for that land status.

And, Congress had said several times—first in the Alaska Organic Act of 1884—that Alaska Natives were not to be "disturbed in the possession of any lands actually in their use or occupation or now claimed by them...." Exactly what that meant was ambiguous, given the uncertain legal status of Alaska Natives and other factors, but it at least provided some recognition of potential Native land claims and reserved to future Congresses the right to settle such claims.

So at the outset of the war Native rights and interests were weak and ill-defined, the result not only of government hesitation, but also the fact that

Alaska Natives had not yet actively pressed for their rights. After World War II federal officials became more aware of the strategic importance of Alaska. That realization, coupled with the influx of people and money into the territory, made it feasible for Alaska to begin moving toward statehood.

Alaska Natives played an insignificant role in the drive for statehood, but that movement did affect the political development of the Natives—because it exposed them to many public statements about democratic principles like consent of the governed and self-determination and to complaints about economic discrimination and lack of self-government in the territory. (See chapters 1 and 2 for discussions of the statehood movement.) They later applied those same principles to their own land claims movement.

LAND CLAIMS MOVEMENT

Alaska became a state in 1959. The most important effect of statehood on Alaska Natives was that it increased pressure on lands they had historically used. The Alaska Statehood Act gave the new state government rights to select about 104 million acres in Alaska.

Inevitably the state selected land used by Natives. At the same time, in the early 1960s, several proposed federal projects—including a plan by the Atomic Energy Commission to create a deepwater port in northwest Alaska by exploding an atomic device—aroused Native opposition. That opposition eventually led to formation of a number of Native regional organizations to protect aboriginal lands and to encourage unity and resistance.[32]

By the late 1960s the state had selected about 12 million acres and Native organizations had claimed most of the land in the state. The Secretary of the Interior decided to stop all transfers of land to the state government and most other land transactions in the state until Native land claims were settled; that action became known as the "land freeze."

PASSAGE OF THE ACT

In 1966, frustrated by the land freeze, the commissioner of the Bureau of Indian Affairs, an Assistant Secretary of the Interior, and a U.S. senator from Alaska began working on a settlement of Native claims—without Native participation. Native reaction was swift. In late 1966 Native organizations from around the state met and agreed to create the Alaska Federation of Natives, an umbrella group to represent all Alaska Natives in the land claims battle.

The discovery of huge quantities of oil on Alaska's North Slope in 1968 was the catalyst that set in motion the forces that would lead to settlement of Native land claims. Powerful interests wanted that North Slope oil to be developed. Oil companies hoped to build a pipeline to carry that oil south across Alaska—but such a pipeline would cross lands under claim by Native groups. The state government also stood to gain by development of North Slope oil, because it had tentative title to the lands above the Prudhoe Bay field; development of the oil would mean revenues for the state. And President Richard Nixon was committed to the development of American energy sources and the proposed trans-Alaska pipeline was to be an integral part of that effort.

But actual passage of the act was due in large part to the skill and prescience of leaders of the Alaska Federation of Natives. They hired attorneys with national reputations and with access to national circles of decisionmaking.[33] They also gained the support of other, often disparate groups—including the Episcopal and Presbyterian churches, the American Federation of Labor, and the National Association for the Advancement of Colored People (NAACP).

AFN lobbyists applied pressure on Congress. Initially they worked with the Senate and Henry Jackson, chairman of the Senate's Interior and Insular Affairs Committee. Because of their inexperience, Native leaders did not at first understand the traditional role of the House of Representatives in drafting legislation and the institutional jealousy between the two houses of Congress— and the personal differences between Jackson and Wayne Aspinall, chairman of the House's Committee on Interior and Insular Affairs.

But by 1971 it became clear that Aspinall was the key to a Congressional decision on land claims. He eventually supported Native claims because he realized the trans-Alaska pipeline would not be built without a settlement of those claims. But he had to be convinced that Alaska Natives would use their settlement lands and money to become an integrated part of Alaska's economy.

Nor did Native leaders overlook the President in their drive for a claims settlement. Don Wright, president of the AFN, wrote a letter to President Nixon's special counsel, pointing out a recent federal district court ruling affecting necessary federal permits for the proposed oil pipeline.[34] Residents of Stevens Village had brought a suit to halt issuance of pipeline permits because the village claimed lands the pipeline would cross. The court had held that because the lands were under unresolved Native claims, the pipeline permits could not be issued.

And AFN exerted pressure on state officials and representatives of the oil companies. AFN argued that settlement of Native claims would be in the interest of the state government and the oil companies. It would mean the end of the land freeze that had halted state acquisition of land, and it would mean the resolution of serious legal bars to construction of the pipeline. AFN also bargained with conservationists who had belatedly entered the battle and who wanted large areas of Alaska land considered for inclusion in parks and other

national conservation units. (Conservation groups did succeed in having a provision inserted in the final act that called for study of large areas of Alaska
for possible inclusion in national conservation areas. That provision led to bitter
conflict between the state and federal governments and ultimately resulted in
passage of the 1980 Alaska National Interest Lands Conservation Act, which
added about 104 million acres to national conservation units in Alaska.)

Finally all the parties understood that the way to get what they wanted was
to support the settlement of Native land claims. A number of bills with widely
varying land and money settlements were introduced in Congress, but because
of the mounting pressure for approval of the trans-Alaska pipeline, Native
leaders were able to hold out for a generous settlement.

On December 18, 1971, the Alaska Native Claims Settlement Act became
law. In exchange for extinguishment of Alaska Native aboriginal land claims,
Natives received rights to select 44 million acres and nearly $1 billion.

ANCSA AND FEDERAL DECISIONMAKING

Passage of the settlement act satisfied at least some of the demands of all
the interested parties. The claims movement and the terms of the claims settlement act tell us much about federal policymaking.

First, decisions under federalism are not made in a vacuum; they are
influenced by ideas and attitudes that are distinctly American. ANCSA is a
testament to American capitalism and its reliance on private organization and
competition. The act requires that land and money awarded Alaska Natives
be handled by private Native corporations organized under state law. The
regional corporations formed under ANCSA were to be mainly concerned with
profitmaking investments, while village corporations were to guide the development of Native communities.[35]

The American faith in competition and private industry are juxtaposed with
the support of law, particularly constitutional law. One of the strongest elements
of the Natives' claims was the legal principle of aboriginal ownership of land.
Groups with the support of the law are more likely to gain access to decisionmakers in the federal system.

Development and passage of the claims settlement act also demonstrates many
elements of the policymaking process in the United States. Power to accomplish
a goal like passing a major piece of legislation is distributed among a variety
of private and public organizations; it is worth emphasizing that federal policy
is not made just by government entities. Private resolution and initiative are
very influential in decisionmaking processes. Many private groups were involved in pressuring Congress for a settlement and in affecting its terms.

The central actors in the claims settlement process were key congressional committees, the U.S. Department of the Interior, the Nixon Administration, the Alaska Federation of Natives and a number of regional Native leaders, representatives of the oil and other industries, environmental organizations, and state officials.

But it was Congress that ultimately controlled the process. Members of Congress structured hearings on claims legislation and had the final say in the terms and conditions of the settlement. We would expect this to be true in a situation involving Native affairs; Congress has reserved to itself the right to handle Native affairs in this country. In other kinds of legislation—those involving transportation or health, for instance—Congress might defer more to desires of state or local entities.

Despite Congress's dominant authority, all interested parties took part in negotiation, bargaining, and compromise. No one interest was clearly subordinate to the others. For example, in 1969 the State of Alaska held up the negotiations when Governor Keith Miller withdrew a previous state offer to include some future state oil revenues in the cash settlement. In 1970 a new governor and congressional representative from Alaska were elected. They agreed to include a share of state revenues in the settlement—and then negotiations began again in earnest. So in this case, the state had the power to restrain national decisionmaking.

Actions that led to the passage of ANCSA, while involving many interests, were orchestrated by a few AFN officials and Native regional leaders. The leaders learned quickly how to use the American political and legal processes. They were particularly effective in Alaska because of the absence of cohesion in the state legislature, weak political parties, and a political culture that can best be described as individualistic—a culture in which "primary public relationships are products of bargaining among individuals and groups acting out of self-interest."[36]

Native village leaders, in contrast to the regional leaders, played a minor role in the claims settlement process, for a number of reasons. Regional and village ties were tenuous. Communication and transportation were difficult and expensive; television had only recently been introduced and telephones were few. The *Tundra Times*, a Native newspaper, was an important source of information for regional and state representatives, but that information seldom reached the village level. Most village leaders were concerned with internal affairs—as they had traditionally been.

Another important reason that village leaders were little involved was that once the process of negotiation truly began, it was a fast-moving, high stakes game that left no time for bringing villages into the process. The results of this lack of village involvement in the process became evident in the 1980s, when many village leaders spoke out against the ANCSA system for managing Native lands. They believe that the Native corporations established under the act do not provide adequate protection for Native lands, because the corporations can lose those lands in a number of ways.

In summary, looking at development and passage of ANCSA gives us a good idea of the kinds of interests that participate in federal decisionmaking, the effects of circumstances and attitudes, and the restrictions on power of any one entity, whether it be public or private.

CONCLUSIONS

We've seen in general how government power is divided under the American federal system, and what forces affect public policymaking. What we have not discussed to this point are the broad questions that political scientists and others interested in the government system argue: who should govern? At what level is government power best placed in a democracy?

The answers to those questions generally fall between two extremes. At one end are those who believe public decisions should be made in a "...small state in which the people can easily be assembled, and each citizen can—without going to too much trouble—get acquainted with all the others."[37]

At the other end of the spectrum are those who favor "...the strengthening of those elements of the political order which tend toward the creation of a constituency of the entire nation. These include the party system, the presidency, and the national government."[38]

So we have Americans who want power to be devolved to the lowest level possible, and those who want it to become more centralized and in the hands of national institutions.

There are a number of advantages to government at the local level. Local officials can be more responsible and responsive because they better understand local conditions, interests, and needs. Public decisions made locally can therefore be more effective and applicable. And local responsibility can tend to increase local political participation. The citizenry becomes more informed and gains a sense of political equality. Under ideal conditions of local government, a citizen learns that "he has to take into account wider matters than his own immediate private interests if he is to gain cooperation from others and he learns that public and private interests are linked."[39]

However, while strong local decisionmaking may be ideally preferable, in reality it may be hard to achieve. Public policies often affect not just one but many communities and will not be determined in individual communities. For instance, the question of whether the State of Alaska should continue to subsidize rural energy costs will be decided not in Emmonak or Nome but by the Alaska Legislature or the state courts.

Further, in the United States today, all communities are linked by a complex web of economic connections; no community is autonomous. Decisions about use of natural resources, prices of goods, and other elements of the economy will be influenced by national and international markets or the actions of corporate managers. Thus, we can speak of "community" power only in a relative sense.

Another realistic limit on powers of local governments is that in the United States over the past 200 years there has been an ongoing centralization of power. That centralization has occurred because of changes in our national economy and society that were beyond the control of local leaders.[40] Inevitably, much future change will also be beyond the control of local communities.

Thus we face a dilemma. If we argue that local government—which offers the best opportunity for the most citizens to participate—cannot always be effective, is the only alternative the ultimate centralization of all government power?

Federalism may in fact offer a partial solution. Our system of government is, despite its tendency toward centralization, a compromise between the two extremes. Local governments are most perspicacious about local needs, but their strengths are limited by the realities of modern societies. The federal government, while remote from the concerns of local citizens, offers the justice of constitutional law and the defense, commerce, economic, and other capacities of national organization and leadership.

One of the most important aspects of federalism is that divisions of power are not absolute—there is, notwithstanding the ultimate authority of the federal government, room for negotiation and compromise. Powers exercised by any particular level of government can and have changed with changing social and political forces in our country. What is crucial to continuing democracy in the United States is that citizens at the community level participate: that our system of government should draw its power and initiative from our towns, our neighborhoods, and our workplaces.[41]

ENDNOTES

[1]Quoted in *Anchorage Daily News*, October 20, 1983.

[2]William H. Riker, "Federalism" in F.I. Greenstein and Nelson W. Polsby, *Handbook of Political Science. Volume V. Governmental Institutions and Processes.* (Reading, MA: Addison-Wesley Publ. Co., 1975), p. 101.

[3]See Joseph F. Zimmerman, *State and Local Government*, Chapter 2, "National-State Relations" (New York: Barnes and Noble Books, revised 1976) for a more detailed discussion of the division of power between national and state governments.

[4]See Theodore Lowi, *Incomplete Conquest: Governing America*. Second Edition (NY: Holt, Rinehart & Winston, 1981), p. 92.

[5]For an analysis of factors that contributed to the shift of power to the federal government, see the study by the Advisory Commission on Intergovernmental Relations, *The Federal Role in the Federal System: The Dynamics of Growth* (Washington, D.C.: U.S. Government Printing Office, 1977); also see ACIR, *The Question of State Government Capability*, 1985, Chapters 1 and 2.

[6]For a discussion of those federal-state conflicts over land management, see Richard A. Cooley, "Evolution of Alaska Land Policy," in *Alaska Resources Development* (Boulder, CO: Westview Press, 1984).

[7]*National Labor Relations Board v. Jones and Laughlin Steel Corporation*. 301 U.S. 1. 57S. Ct. 615 (1937), 3.

[8]*Ronald M. & Patricia L. Zobel v. Thomas Williams*. 457 U.S. SS.72 Lawyer Edition, 2nd 672. 02S. Ct. 2309. The Permanent Fund is a special state fund where a portion of the state's petroleum revenues are deposited. Since the early 1980s, the state has annually distributed a portion of the Permanent Fund earnings to Alaska residents.

[9]See Joseph Zimmerman, *State-Local Relations* (New York: Praeger, 1983). Only the most powerful local governments in Alaska, the unified municipalities and the home-rule cities and boroughs, actually exercise a substantial measure of their potential power.

[10]See Alaska Constitution, Article IX "Finance and Taxation," Section 9 "Local Debts" and Section 10 "Interim Borrowing."

[11]For example, see Article X of the Alaska Constitution and its provision for a local boundary commission and the right of the legislature to override its decisions.

[12]See Clive Thomas, "Interest Groups in Alaska: An Initial Investigation," paper presented at the Annual Meeting of the Western Political Science Association, Seattle, WA, March 24-26, 1983. The Alaska Municipal League is identified as one of the most influential lobbying groups in Juneau.

[13]See F. Darnell, "Education Among the Native Peoples of Alaska," *Polar Record*, Vol. 19, No. 122, 1979, p. 443.

[14]For further discussion of the kinds of entities that exercise some local government functions in rural Alaska, see Chapter 10, "Forms of Rural Government," in *Alaska's Urban and Rural Governments*, by Thomas A. Morehouse, Gerald A. McBeath, and Linda Leask (Lanham, MD: University Press of America, 1984).

[15]See Michael D. Reagan and John G. Sanzone, *The New Federalism*, Second Edition, (NY: Oxford University Press, 1981).

[16]ACIR, *The Question of State Government Capability*, p. 7. Figures as of the early 1980s.

[17]However, in constant dollars—dollars adjusted for price inflation—there was a decline in aid after 1981. See ACIR, *Significant Features of Fiscal Federalism*, 1982-83 Edition, p. 120.

[18]These reasons for the growth in federal regulations are found in Advisory Commission on Intergovernmental Relations, *Regulatory Federalism: Policy, Process, Impact and Reform* (Washington, D.C.: U.S. Government Printing Office, 1984), pp. 65-70.

[19]*Garcia v. San Antonio Metropolitan Transit Authority, et al.* (February 19, 1985).

[20]Quoted in Parris N. Glendening and M.M. Reeves, *Pragmatic Federalism*, Second Edition, (Pacific Palisades, CA: Palisades Publ., 1984), p. 108.

[21]For an elaboration of this point see G. Kem Lowry, Jr. and Norman H. Okamura, "Institutionalized Evaluation and Intergovernmental Relations: The Case of Coastal Zone Management," *Publius* 13 (Fall 1983): 79-80.

[22]See Glendening and Reeves, *Pragmatic Federalism*, p. 106.

[23]Figures from "Effects of Petroleum Revenues on State Aid to Local Governments in Alaska," by L. Leask, in *Alaska Review of Social and Economic Conditions* (Institute of Social and Economic Research, University of Alaska, September 1983).

[24]For a detailed discussion of the history of federal actions regarding Native government in the United States, see David S. Case, *Alaska Natives and American Laws* (Fairbanks, AK: University of Alaska Press, 1984).

[25]*Worcester v. Georgia*, 31 U.S. (6 Peters) 515, 559-560 (1832).

[26]See Case, *Alaska Natives and American Laws*, p. 440.

[27]Ibid., pp. 451-453.

[28]The Alaska Reorganization Act, P.L. 538, 74th Congress, May 1936.

[29]The following discussion is based in part on analysis in Case's *Alaska Natives and American Laws*.

[30]See also discussion of IRA and traditional councils in Chapter 10, "Forms of Rural Government," in *Alaska's Urban and Rural Governments*.

[31]Quoted in *Anchorage Daily News*, October 20, 1983.

[32]Two national organizations that helped Alaska Natives organize were the Association of American Indian Affairs and the Indian Rights Association. The Association of American Indian Affairs (formerly the American Association of Indian Affairs) was founded in 1923 when officials from the American Indian Defense Association and the National Association on Indian Affairs decided to merge. The AAIA "...provides legal and technical assistance to Indian tribes throughout the United States in health, education, economic development, resource utilization, family defense, housing and the administration of justice." *The Encyclopedia of Associations*, p. 929. The Indian Rights Association was formed in 1882 and is composed of "...individuals interested in (the) protection of the legal and human rights of American Indians and promotion of their spiritual, moral and material welfare." *Encyclopedia of Associations*, p. 722.

[33]AFN was represented by Ramsey Clark, former U.S. Attorney General, and Arthur Goldberg, former U.S. Supreme Court Justice and later U.S. Ambassador to the United Nations.

[34]Letter from Don Wright to Len Garment, December 6, 1970.

[35]See the report accompanying Senate Bill 35, Committee on Interior and Insular Affairs, "ANCSA 1971," *Report Together with Additional and Supplemental Views*, October 21, 1971, pp. 105-106.

[36]Daniel Elazar, *American Federalism: A View From the States* (NY: Thomas Y. Crowell, 1966), p. 79. See also his *Cities of the Prairie: The Metropolitan Frontier and American Politics* (NY: Basic Books, 1970). For a study that looks at the effects of different political cultures on public policy see John Kincaid (ed.), *Political Culture, Public Policy and the American States* (Philadelphia: Institute for the Study of Human Issues, 1982).

[37]Jean Jacques Rousseau, *The Social Contract* (Chicago: Henry Regnery Co., 1954), p. 101.

[38]Grant McConnell, *Private Power and American Democracy* (NY: Vintage Books, 1966), p. 368.

[39]Carole Pateman, *Participation and Democratic Theory* (NY: Cambridge University Press, 1970), p. 23.

[40]See Glendening and Reeves, *Pragmatic Federalism*, p. 333.

[41]For further discussion of that point, see Sheldon Wolin, "Revolutionary Action Today," *Democracy* (Fall 1982).

5

Alaska's Elections

Thomas A. Morehouse

The character and outcomes of Alaska's elections are shaped by the state's changing electoral demography, campaign methods and technology, and state election rules. This chapter shows how Alaska's elections changed in the first 25 years of statehood, and how they compare to elections in the American states generally.

Elections are the means by which citizens take part in choosing the leaders who set official policies for nations, states, and communities. In the American states, elections are the most common way that people participate in government.

Elections would serve these purposes most effectively if large numbers of informed citizens went to the polls to choose between competing candidates offering clear choices for future policy. Ideally, the winning candidates would form a unified governing coalition: officials identified with one of the major political parties would lead both executive and legislative branches of government. In this way, officials could be held accountable in the next election for the record of government as a whole and for their individual performances.[1]

These conditions are rarely if ever fulfilled in American elections (or in elections generally). In most state elections, half or fewer of the eligible voters actually go to the polls on election day. Party competition in state executive or legislative elections is often weak and sometimes absent altogether. Candidates tend to avoid committing themselves to party or other programmatic positions. And the elections increasingly result in state governments being divided along party lines, with one party controlling the governor's office and the other controlling either or both houses of the state legislature.

Below we examine the extent to which these different electoral patterns apply in Alaska. First, we broadly discuss the social and institutional setting of Alaska elections. Then, we examine in detail changing patterns of "turnout"—or public participation—in elections, party competition for office, and party control of state government.

THE SETTING AND CONTEXT OF ALASKA ELECTIONS

ELECTORAL DEMOGRAPHY

By "electoral demography" we mean analysis of the social characteristics of a voting-age population that may shed light on its political orientations and voting patterns. Ultimately, we are interested in knowing such things as how likely people are to turn out to vote, which party people are likely to identify with and support, and what general policy preferences they are likely to have. Without survey data, what can be learned from demographic analysis is limited. Nonetheless, we can trace changes in Alaska's population over time, make comparisons with other states, and show some significant differences among the populations of Alaska's major regions. The resulting demographic profile will provide useful background for subsequent analysis of electoral returns.

Between 1960 and 1980 Alaska's population became more like that of the United States as a whole and even more like that of the mountain states, the region that has historically been most similar to Alaska in population and economy. During the twenty-year period, the ratio of men to women in Alaska evened out somewhat; the age structure of the population became more balanced; and Alaskans proportionately became a less transient, more settled people. Also, like Americans elsewhere, fewer Alaskans were married (or they married at a later age) and more were divorced or separated.

On the other hand, Alaskans in 1980 were still younger, better educated, and more mobile than the populations of other states. Alaska still had proportionately more males than other states had. There was also a significantly higher proportion of Native Americans in Alaska's population. And Alaska's rapid growth rate of the 1960-80 period—among the very highest of the states— even accelerated during the early 1980s as the state spent billions of dollars of petroleum revenues.

In the mid-1980s, as at the beginning of statehood, the "typical" Alaska voter was a relatively young, well-educated person who tended to be on the move in pursuit of economic opportunity in the north. But the 1980s Alaskan was likely to be a few years older, better educated, and wealthier.

These demographic changes were concentrated in Alaska's two major cities—Anchorage, with over 40 percent of the state's population in 1980, and Fairbanks, with about 13 percent. Map 5.1 shows the major regions used in the electoral analysis below. (The regions are aggregations of the state's election districts.) We have split the Anchorage and Fairbanks districts out of the southcentral and central regions to show how much they differ from the rest of the state in both their population and voting patterns. Alaska's younger, more mobile, and better educated voters were concentrated in Anchorage and

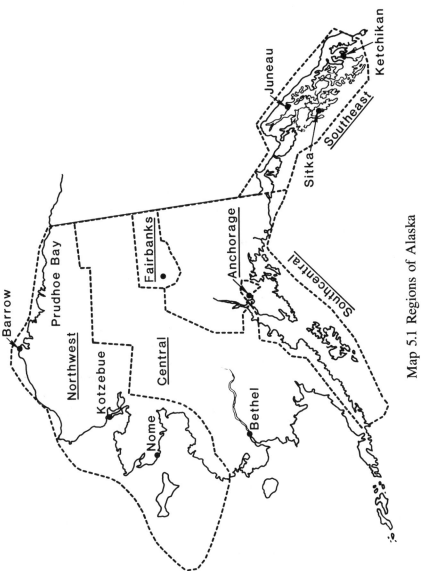

Map 5.1 Regions of Alaska

Fairbanks in 1980. Alaskans in the central and northwest "bush" Native regions, on the other hand, tended to have much less education and to include disproportionately large numbers of unmarried young men. In the predominantly non-Native southeast and southcentral regions, 1980 populations were somewhat older and more settled than those of Anchorage and Fairbanks. In the southeast, there was an unusual concentration of highly educated people in Juneau, the state capital.

These brief regional descriptions indicate that our "typical" Alaska voter in the mid-1980s was most likely to be an Anchorage or Fairbanks resident who was not representative of Alaskans in other parts of the state. In fact, the voters of Alaska's two major urban centers differed from their small town and rural counterparts in several ways that might have been politically significant. In the United States generally, youth, wealth, education, and mobility are associated with political change and a shift toward more conservative political preferences. In Alaska, these distinguishing characteristics of the rapidly growing urban population may have reinforced the state's traditional regional divisions. We might, therefore, expect some substantial regional variations in turnout, party preferences, and voting on statewide candidates and ballot issues in Alaska during the first quarter century of statehood. We might also expect to find growing complexity and perhaps conflict in Alaska's electoral experience.

ELECTION CAMPAIGNS

Growth and change in Alaska's population between 1960 and 1985 were accompanied by changes in the ways candidates attempted to influence and attract voters. Two parallel developments affected campaign methods in Alaska during that period. First was the growth of the population and its continued and increasing concentration in and around Anchorage and Fairbanks. Second was the use of new communications technology and methods, including satellite television, that allowed communication with even the most remote parts of the state.

These changes meant that impersonal, professionally produced television appeals increasingly replaced personal contact by candidates for political office, especially in the larger Anchorage and Fairbanks electoral "markets," and in statewide elections. Just as Alaska's population became more like that of the nation as a whole, so Alaska's election campaigns became more like those of more populous states.

Yet, with only about 500,000 residents in the mid-1980s, Alaska was still small enough so that candidates could personally meet a larger proportion of the electorate than was possible in most other states. This kind of "friends and neighbors" politics, however, which was common throughout the territorial period and in the early years of statehood, was increasingly rare in Anchorage and Fairbanks. Together the two accounted for 60 percent of the state's population in 1985. In rural and small town communities, it was mainly in legislative and municipal elections, as opposed to state elections, where the old-style politics survived.

A further development in Alaska that changed the way candidates communicated with voters during the first 25 years of statehood was the continued erosion of the major political party organizations. (See related discussion in the chapter devoted to Alaska's political parties.) In Alaska, as elsewhere, weak political parties resulted in "party-less" campaigning—elections in which individual candidates formed personal campaign organizations and made individual appeals, often failing to identify themselves with either major party in their campaign advertising. This fading of party organizations and appeals was part of a broader erosion of party loyalty among voters. As we will see below, it was reflected in an increase in ticket-splitting and divided stated government.

Other indicators of change in Alaska elections during this period are the levels and sources of campaign financing. In Anchorage from 1974 to 1984, the average amount spent by primary winners in both primary and general elections for the state house increased (in 1984 dollars) from about $10,000 per candidate to over $46,000. In state senate races, the corresponding increase was from under $22,000 to over $68,000. These are real increases—adjusted to account for inflation—of 367 percent and 216 percent, respectively.

As the costs of campaigns soared, the funding sources on which candidates depended changed radically. Organized contributors and special interests almost totally displaced individual contributors as significant sources of campaign funds. In 1978, contributions of unions, initiative committees, lobbyists, corporations, and other groups accounted for about one-third of all campaign expenditures for state offices. In 1980, they accounted for over half; and in 1982, a big year for statewide initiative campaigns, these special interest contributors covered over 90 percent of all reported campaign costs.[2]

Thus, as candidates increasingly ignored their fading party organizations, they turned to more expensive communications technology and depended on organized, special-interest sources of campaign financing. During this century, these forces transformed relationships between candidates and voters in all states. They caught up with Alaska in recent times, changing the nature of this state's election campaigns in little more than a generation.

ELECTION RULES

A third part of the setting of Alaska's elections is election rules. By rules we mean requirements for legislative districting and apportionment, voter registration, getting on the ballot, and voting in primary and general elections. These rules can have important effects on voter turnout and choice and on who is elected to office.

1. *Legislative districting and apportionment.* Because of uneven, rapid population growth, the Alaska Legislature was reapportioned to revised districts six times during the first twenty-five years of statehood. Under the state constitution, the governor—not the legislature, as is usually the case in other states—has the power to reapportion the legislature, on the advice of a reapportionment board appointed by him.[3] Typically, the governor's reapportionments during this period were followed by partisan political disputes in which the governor was challenged by legislators or party officials.

The perceived stakes in reapportionments are seats in the legislature that might, depending on the reapportionment plan, more likely be captured by one party than by the other. The outcomes could, therefore, affect the balance of competition between the parties and, ultimately, party control of the legislature or the government as a whole. Another political effect of reapportionment often cannot be avoided. This is the change and disruption in precinct and district boundaries, which can undermine voters' familiarity with candidates and officials and increase turnover in office.

2. *Voter registration.* Registering to vote was first required of Alaskans for the 1970 elections. Before then, a person desiring to vote merely had to appear at the polls and sign the voting list. Alaska's registration laws are now like those of most other states. In order to be a registered voter, a person must have lived in the state and the election district for at least 30 days and must register at least 30 days before the election. The most important electoral effect of registration (aside from minimizing fraud, which is the principal justification for the requirement) is reducing voter turnout. This effect can be negligible or significant, depending on how difficult or easy it is for a person to register and on the characteristics of voters. Generally, people with lower levels of education and income are less likely to register.

3. *Getting on the ballot.* Once a person registers and goes to the polls, there is the question of the range of choices he or she will have among party-sponsored and independent candidates. All states have restrictions on whose names can be placed on the ballot, and these restrictions often handicap prospective third-party and independent candidates. Until 1983, Alaska law required that if third-party or independent candidates wished to be on the ballot,

they had to first obtain signatures equal to three percent of the number of voters in the previous general election. Also, to be recognized as a "political party," a third party had to have won at least ten percent of the popular vote in the last gubernatorial election. (The Libertarian Party in Alaska met this requirement in the 1982 gubernatorial election, which will be discussed in detail below.) These were onerous requirements, and they were challenged in the Alaska Supreme Court. In 1983, the court ruled against both requirements, and the legislature moved shortly thereafter to reduce them to more acceptable levels.[4]

4. *Primary and general election requirements.* If a primary election is closed, voters must be registered in a party, and they can choose candidates only in that party's primary. If the primary is open, voters can choose which party primary they wish to vote in without having registered in either party. In the open primaries of some states, voters must publicly choose one party's ballot; in other states, they receive both ballots and, using one and discarding the other, preserve the secrecy of their choice. Alaska (and only one other state, Washington) has the most open form of the open primary, the blanket primary. Here, voters receive ballots including candidates of both parties and can vote for Democratic candidates for some offices and Republicans for others, as they wish. Alaska's blanket primary makes it especially easy for voters belonging to one party to "cross over," voting for candidates of the other party whom they perceive to be weak (and thus easier to beat in the general election), or whom they consider especially attractive.[5]

There is also a minimum legal age for voting in Alaska as in all other states. Under Alaska's constitution, 19-year-olds were originally permitted to vote in state and local elections; in 1970, an amendment lowered the voting age to 18 years. Then in 1971, the U.S. constitution was amended to permit 18-year-olds to vote in all states.

Taken together, these requirements probably have negative effects on voter participation in Alaska elections. Reducing the residency requirement from one year (which it was until 1972) to 30 days made it possible for many more Alaskans to go to the polls. Alaska has an unusually large proportion of recently arrived residents. But the very people who make up the expanded electoral base—new residents, who have been in the state for less than one year—are also less likely than longer-term residents to be familiar with or involved in state and local politics and, therefore, less apt to vote. A similar observation could be made about 18-year-olds. National surveys show that voting turnout generally increases with age (until the mid-60s age group), and that the youngest eligible voters are least likely, of all age groups, to go to the polls and vote.[6]

Thus, the voting population base has expanded, but the newly enfranchised groups are disproportionately likely not to vote.

LEVELS OF PARTICIPATION: TURNOUT

Turnout is usually measured as the percentage of the *voting-age* population that votes in a given election. Another measure of turnout is the percentage of *registered* voters who actually vote. Both measures have their weaknesses. The voting-age criterion may not adequately account for institutionalized people, noncitizens, residency requirements, and other factors that reduce the effective population of eligible voters. And the registered voter criterion depends even more precariously on widely varying registration laws among the states and on voter registration lists that are not consistently kept current and accurate. With these limitations in mind, we will make use of both measures in the examination of turnout in Alaska.

FACTORS AFFECTING TURNOUT

Turnout can rise or fall, depending on voting and election rules, level of party competition, and the characteristics of voters. Registration may be the most substantial deterrent nationwide, causing as much as a 10 percent decline in turnout where registration rules and procedures are most restrictive.[7] Other studies have found that party competition historically has been the chief factor explaining varying levels of turnout. The positive link between competition and turnout has been especially strong "where parties reach out to specific groups, especially those who are otherwise less likely to vote."[8] And still other studies have found that differences in race, age, income, and educational level account for half or more of the variation in the voter turnout rates of the states.[9] There remains a great deal of uncertainty and controversy about what affects turnout. However, even if we accept all of these factors as affecting turnout, they should all tend to increase (or at least not decrease) turnout in Alaska. Alaska's registration requirements are not unusually difficult, competition is relatively intense, and the state's majority urban population ranks well above average on socioeconomic measures.

TURNOUT IN ALASKA

While turnout in presidential elections steadily declined throughout the United States from 1960 through 1976, turnout in Alaska held relatively steady and then turned up significantly in the early 1980s. Table 5.1 shows that even while

Table 5.1
Turnout of Voting-Age Population in Presidential Election Years,
1960-1984, Alaska, Mountain States, and United States

Year	Alaska	Mountain States[1]	United States
1960	53.0%	68.7%	62.8%
1964	51.6	68.5	61.9
1968	55.8	65.5	60.9
1972	52.2	59.2	55.2
1976	50.7	56.8	53.5
1980	59.8	54.1	52.6
1984	60.0	NA	53.0

[1]Mountain states are Idaho, Montana, Wyoming, Utah, Colorado, Arizona, and New Mexico.

Sources: Derived from Alaska Division of Elections, U.S. Bureau of the Census.

turnout of the voting-age population in the United States and the mountain states dropped between 1960 and 1976, Alaska's turnout still lagged by several percentage points. In 1980 and 1984, however, Alaska's turnout was 10 percentage points higher than in 1976, while turnout in the mountain states and the United States as a whole either flattened out or continued to drop closer to the 50 percent level.

The substantial decline from 1968 to 1972 in all three cases may in part be explained by the lowering of the voting age to 18 years and the lack of strong competition (as reflected in pre-election polls) in the 1972 Nixon-McGovern presidential race, as compared to that of the Nixon-Humphrey race four years earlier. Another factor was the much-discussed alienation of the American voter during that period. In Alaska, there was the possible additional effect of the new registration requirements, first imposed two years earlier.

Table 5.2 compares turnout, again of the voting-age population, in presidential and gubernatorial election years in Alaska from 1960 through 1984. Alaskans, like voters elsewhere, voted more in presidential years than in gubernatorial years—until 1982. From 1960 to 1978, gubernatorial election turnout ranged from one to seven percentage points lower than turnout for the previous presidential election. During those years, the average difference was about five percentage points. Then, surpassing even the substantial leap to nearly 60 percent in presidential turnout in 1980, two-thirds of Alaska's voting-age

Table 5.2
Turnout of Voting-Age Population in Presidential and Gubernatorial
Years, 1960-1984, Alaska

Year	Pres. Election	Gov. Election	Percentage Difference
1960	53.0%		
1962		47.3%	−5.7%
1964	51.6		
1966		46.8	−4.8
1968	55.8		
1970		48.6	−7.2
1972	52.2		
1974		47.4	−4.5
1976	50.7		
1978		49.9	−0.8
1980	59.8		
1982		66.5	+6.7
1984	60.0		

Source: Derived from Alaska Division of Elections

population turned out in the 1982 gubernatorial election year, reversing the pattern of over two decades.

The increased turnout in 1980 might be attributed in some part to the stabilizing of Alaska's population growth during the few years after the pipeline was built and before heavy spending by state government again led to high levels of immigration. But even with the population surge of the early 1980s—bringing many newcomers, presumably less likely to vote—the turnout rate soared in the 1982 gubernatorial year and held at the 60 percent level in the 1984 presidential election.

Rates of turnout among *registered* voters in Alaska's regions from 1974 to 1984 are shown in Table 5.3. These rates parallel the corresponding figures for turnout among the *voting age* population presented in the preceding tables.[10] The state's registered voters turned out at increasing rates over that decade, with gains in virtually all regions. Two of the elections during this period, those in 1978 and 1982, were unusual. We have already commented on the surge in turnout in 1982. The 1978 decline in turnout in all regions may be attributed largely to population movements in and out of the state during the pipeline construction years. Many new voters came into the state in the early-to mid-1970s and left when construction ended in 1977. It is likely that many of them remained on voter registration lists for the 1978 elections, which would have artificially depressed the turnout rate.[11] The smallest decrease was in the southeast, historically a high turnout region, where a 1978 ballot initiative placing special financial restrictions on any capital move undoubtedly had special attraction for voters of that region. The southeast, moreover, was the region most remote from and least affected by pipeline construction activity during the previous four years.

The cause of Alaska's high turnout rates in the early 1980s obviously lies in Alaska, rather than in national trends, since presidential election-year turnout in the United States continued at relatively low levels. In Alaska, there were some unusually competitive races for the U.S. Senate, for governor, and for the state legislature. But a more basic explanation may be that increasing numbers of Alaskans perceived greater stakes and benefits in voting. Their state government was now spending billions of dollars in oil revenues, and intense and competitive electoral politics tended to expose and aggravate Alaska's regional divisions. We will explore this proposition further in discussion of "Election Outcomes" below, following discussion of interparty competition.

INTERPARTY COMPETITION

Interparty competition involves the competitive character of electoral contests and the choices of parties and candidates available to a state's voters. There are many ways to define and measure interparty competition in state politics: by voter identification with parties, frequency of both parties fielding candidates, turnover in offices, closeness of elections, and division of control of legislative and governors' offices, among others.[12] Here, we will examine

Table 5.3
Turnout of Registered Voters by Region, 1974-1984

	1974	1976	1978	1980	1982	1984
State	58.2%	61.5%	54.5%	62.7%	74.9%	69.1%
Region						
Southeast	61.2	65.0	62.0	68.0	80.9	67.8
Southcentral	65.3	68.7	61.9	70.8	76.9	70.0
Anchorage	56.7	60.7	51.9	60.6	72.2	69.4
Central	64.0	65.7	57.4	66.6	76.8	71.0
Fairbanks	54.5	57.6	50.2	58.7	72.7	69.7
Northwest	60.0	61.9	56.8	64.2	78.7	62.0

Source: Alaska Division of Elections

some causes and correlates of interparty competition and look at some electoral indicators of interparty competition in Alaska between 1960 and 1985.

PATTERNS IN THE STATES

Generally, the states with the most interparty competition are more urban and industrial, and their populations tend to divide more definitely into separate socioeconomic groups than is the case in the less competitive states. These differences in state socioeconomic characteristics have diminished, however, as population shifted in recent times from the more competitive "Frost Belt" states in the northeastern U.S. to less competitive "Sun Belt" states in the south. Overall, party competition has been increasing in state elections and, on balance, Democratic candidates for state legislatures and governors' offices have been the beneficiaries. This is mainly because older Republican states of the north have become more competitive with the New Deal electoral "realignment" of the 1930s, in which the nation as a whole became more Democratic. The southern Democratic states have been much slower to change. More recently, however, interstate migration and electoral "de-alignment"—the weakening of party loyalties and the crumbling of the old New Deal electoral coalition—have further reinforced competition between the two major parties in virtually all states.[13]

INTERPARTY COMPETITION IN ALASKA

Alaska reflects many of the political and socioeconomic characteristics of the western states, and it can be classified as a competitive two-party state. As we look more closely at Alaska, we will see some important variations within the overall pattern of competition, including increasing differences between urban and rural regions and in levels of competition for statewide and sub-state legislative offices.

In presidential elections from 1960 to 1972, Alaskans divided their votes between candidates for the two major parties much as did voters in the nation as a whole. Table 5.4 shows that during those years, a majority of Alaskans voted for a Democrat only once (Johnson in 1964), although the 1960 Kennedy-Nixon and 1968 Humphrey-Nixon elections were close in Alaska, as they were in the rest of the country. In 1976 and subsequent elections, Alaska became more strongly Republican in its presidential voting than the United States, much like the mountain states region.

Table 5.5 shows the two-party division of the presidential vote by regions within Alaska from 1960 through 1984. As in the state as a whole, there were steep Democratic declines, or Republican gains, in all regions. The

Table 5.4
Percentage Democratic Vote[1] in Presidential Elections: Alaska, Mountain States, and United States, 1960-1984

Year	Alaska	Mountain States	United States
1960	49.1	46.4	50.1
1964	65.9	56.6	61.3
1968	48.8	41.8	49.6
1972	37.3	33.9	38.2
1976	38.1	42.5	51.1
1980	32.7	32.2	44.7
1984	30.7	33.1	41.0

[1]Percentage of total votes for Democratic and Republican candidates; excludes votes for minor-party and independent candidates.

Source: U.S. Bureau of the Census

predominantly Native northwest region (including Nome, Kotzebue, and Barrow), was the only Alaska region to give most of its votes to Democratic presidential candidates in the 1972, 1976, and 1980 elections. The central region, also mostly Native, followed next in Democratic presidential preference. In contrast, urban Alaska, centering on Anchorage and the southcentral region, saw the greatest Republican gains and corresponding Democratic declines during that period.

The pattern of Democratic losses and Republican gains also shows up, although not as dramatically as in presidential elections, in elections to the

Table 5.5
Percentage Democratic Vote[1] in Presidential Elections: State and Regions, 1960-1984

Year	State	Southeast	Southcentral	Anchorage	Central	Fairbanks	Northwest
1960	49.1	49.6	52.2	46.5	49.6	51.2	46.2
1964	65.9	71.1	66.5	59.9	77.8	59.6	80.8
1968	48.8	50.1	47.7	48.5	51.6	44.4	56.4
1972	37.3	41.3	34.4	31.3	43.9	41.2	51.9
1976	38.1	39.3	36.1	35.0	46.1	39.4	55.2
1980	32.7	40.0	25.7	28.1	53.0	31.3	51.4
1984	30.7	39.6	25.0	29.0	38.1	30.2	40.4

[1]Percentage of total vote for Democratic and Republican candidates; excludes votes for minor-party and independent candidates.

Source: Alaska Division of Elections

Table 5.6
Winning Candidates for Statewide Offices in Alaska, 1958-1984

Year	Governor		U.S. Senator		U.S. Representative	
	Name	% of Vote[1]	Name	% of Vote[1]	Name	% of Vote[1]
1958	Egan (D)	60.2	Bartlett (D)	84.9	Rivers (D)	57.5
			Gruening (D)	52.6		
1960			Bartlett (D)	63.4	Rivers (D)	56.7
1962	Egan (D)	52.3	Gruening (D)	58.1	Rivers (D)	54.5
1964					Rivers (D)	51.5
1966	Hickel (R)	50.9	Bartlett (D)	75.5	Pollock (R)	51.7
1968			Gravel (D)	54.7	Pollock (R)	54.2
1970	Egan (D)	53.2	Stevens (R)	59.6	Begich (D)	55.1
1972			Stevens (R)	77.3	Begich (D)	56.2
1974	Hammond (R)	50.1	Gravel (D)	58.3	Young (R)	53.8
1976					Young (R)	71.0
1978	Hammond (R)	65.9[2]	Stevens (R)	75.8	Young (R)	55.5
1980			Murkowski (R)	53.9	Young (R)	74.1
1982	Sheffield (D)	55.4[2]			Young (R)	71.1
1984			Stevens (R)	71.3	Young (R)	56.5

[1]Percentage of total votes for Democratic and Republican candidates; excludes votes for minor-party, independent, and write-in candidates.
[2]These were elections in which substantial portions of the vote went to third party, independent, or write-in candidates. Hammond's plurality in 1978 was 39 percent, and Sheffield's in 1982 was 47 percent.
Source: Alaska Division of Elections

statewide offices of governor, U.S. senator, and U.S. representative (Table 5.6). The most competitive elections from 1958 through 1984 were those for governor. Democrats won four elections and Republicans won three during that period. In five of those elections, the winning majority was 55 percent or less.

In U.S. Senate elections, there was a swing from strong Democratic to strong Republican voting. Both U.S. Senate seats were held by Democrats through the 1960s (until a Republican appointee, Ted Stevens, replaced Democrat Bob Bartlett, who died in office in 1968), and their electoral margins were substantial. In the 1970s, each party held one U.S. Senate seat. After 1980, both were held by Republicans. Since the winning candidate usually won heavy majorities, the balance of electoral strength moved decisively toward the Republicans in these elections.

Elections to Alaska's one seat in the U.S. House of Representatives during this 25-year period went alternately to Democrats and Republicans, paralleling the U.S. Senate elections. First dominated by the Democrat Ralph Rivers, the seat was held next by a Republican and then by a Democrat in the late 1960s and early 1970s. After the death of Democrat Nick Begich in 1972, Republican Don Young carried most of his six elections through 1984 by substantial margins.

Table 5.7

Average Percentage Democratic Vote[1] in State Legislative Elections:
State and Regions, 1960-1984

Years	State	Southeast	Southcentral	Central	Fairbanks	Northwest
1960-66	49.6	57.1	47.8	61.4	51.1	68.3
1968-74	52.0	59.3	51.1	57.6	50.0	83.5
1976-82	50.1	71.0	43.1	50.2	52.7	83.7
1984	44.5	69.3	44.1	56.6	36.3	88.5

[1]Percentage of total vote for Democratic and Republican candidates; excludes votes for minor-party and independent candidates.

Source: Alaska Division of Elections

If strong electoral competition does contribute to higher turnout, that effect was weak or obscured in Alaska's statewide elections through 1984, except for several races for governor. Most of the U.S. Senate and House races reflected weak party or candidate competition. Yet, turnout rates held steady in the 1960s and 1970s and rose significantly in the 1980s. To the extent that competition is a factor in turnout, it may be found in sub-state elections for the legislature, which occur in every election year, as well as in races for governor.

Overall, elections to the state legislature were very competitive throughout the first 25 years of statehood. These results, presented in Table 5.7, show a close partisan division of the vote statewide, but much less competition within individual regions.[14] The Native northwest region was most consistently and strongly Democratic in legislative elections. In two legislative election years, 1974 and 1980, no Republican ran in any state legislative race in the northwest, and, often, specific races there were uncontested by Republicans. This absence of Republican opposition also occurred with some frequency in legislative races in the Democratic southeast in the late 1970s and early 1980s. The most competitive regions were Fairbanks and central. The southcentral region (including Anchorage in this table) was the only region where Republicans gained and held a decisive electoral edge from the mid-1970s through 1984.

The figures in Table 5.7 specifically for the 1984 election (all the others are three-election averages) show the weight of the southcentral/Anchorage and Fairbanks votes in the state totals. They also suggest that, given their concentration in the state's largest urban centers, many Republican votes for legislators may have been "redundant" or "wasted" compared to Democratic votes, which were more evenly spread throughout the state's election districts. Thus, while winning 56 percent of the vote statewide, Republican candidates captured less than half of the total number of available legislative seats in 1984.

Another possibility is that legislative districting by the governor helped create such redundant or wasteful concentrations of voters likely to vote for legislative candidates of the other party. We will take a closer look at this possibility below in discussion of party control of state government.

We can divide the first 25 years of statehood into two major eras of growth and change—the relatively slow-moving period of the 1960s and the continuing boom period of the 1970s and early '80s, after the discovery of Prudhoe Bay, pipeline construction, and billion-dollar state capital budgets. Table 5.8 shows changes in the average Democratic vote for all statewide (governor, U.S. senator, and U.S. representative) and all legislative offices for the 1958-72 and 1974-84 periods, which roughly correspond to the major eras of growth.

Table 5.8
Average Percentage Democratic Vote [1] in Statewide and Legislative Elections: State and Regions, 1958-1972 and 1974-1984

	1958-1972		1974-1984	
	Statewide Elections	Legislative Elections	Statewide Elections	Legislative Elections
State	53.2%	50.1%	38.7%	50.0%
Southeast	58.3	56.7	45.9	70.3
Southcentral				
(incl. Anchorage)	49.0	49.1	35.2	44.1
Central	62.0	59.3	44.5	53.8
Fairbanks	51.5	49.7	38.2	51.3
Northwest	63.9	71.5	50.4	87.7

[1]Percentage of total vote for Democratic and Republican candidates; excludes votes for minor-party and independent candidates.

Source: Alaska Division of Elections

Probably the most significant feature of the table is the divergence in statewide and legislative election patterns from the earlier to the later period. In 1958-72, there was close correspondence in voting for statewide and legislative offices in all regions of the state. In the state as a whole, the parties were very competitive in both kinds of elections, though not, as we have seen, in all individual races for specific offices. In each of the regions, statewide and legislative elections exhibited parallel divisions of party voting. Those parallels sharply diverged in the 1974-84 period. Alaska voters in all regions became much more likely to vote split tickets—to vote in much larger proportions for Republicans for statewide office while continuing to vote for Democrats, by large or competitive margins, for the legislature. Thus, Alaska patterns during that period appear to reflect similar developments in the western states generally.

Table 5.9

Votes in State General Elections by Region, Selected Years 1960-1984

Year	No. of Votes State	Percentage of Votes					
		Southeast	Southcentral	Anchorage	Central	Fairbanks	Northwest
1960	50,343	23.0	16.7	32.1	8.1	14.1	6.1
1968	82,886	19.6	15.1	37.6	6.8	15.2	5.8
1978	129,705	16.5	17.0	41.0	7.7	14.3	3.4
1984	211,009	14.5	19.1	43.1	6.2	13.7	3.5

Source: Alaska Division of Elections

In statewide elections between 1974 and 1984, Democratic voting eroded substantially while Republican voting correspondingly increased in all regions. In legislative elections, Democrats held their own or increased their margins in the southeast, Fairbanks, and the northwest regions while losing ground in the southcentral/Anchorage region and the central region outside Fairbanks.

Anchorage and the southcentral region accounted for almost two-thirds of the total state vote in 1984 (Table 5.9), and population growth in these areas continued to lead the state in the mid-1980s. Republican voting is, therefore, likely to remain strong in statewide elections in future years, and, with legislative reapportionment, more legislative seats may be won by more Republican candidates from the Anchorage region as well.

Republican dominance in presidential and statewide elections in Alaska in the 1970s and 1980s does not represent an electoral monopoly, as the competition in gubernatorial and state legislative elections demonstrates. Even the strong Republican showings in U.S. Senate and House races during that period do not necessarily mean continuing weak competition from Democrats. Republicans gained control of two of those offices only after popular Democratic incumbents died in office. There has been a succession of weak Democratic candidates for the U.S. House and Senate in the 1970s and 1980s, but the Democrats may once again field strong candidates who can appeal to voters whose party loyalties are weak or non-existent.

PARTY IDENTIFICATION AND THIRD-PARTY VOTING

Voter registration by party is another indicator of the level of party competition in the states. Ideally, it would measure the extent to which each of the parties can claim a consistent following of voters. In reality, this is not the case. A growing number of voters have weak or no party identifications— increasingly identifying themselves as independents—and many states do not require registration by party.

Table 5.10
Party Registration, Statewide and Regions, 1974, 1984

| | 1974 Percentages | | | | 1984 Percentages | | | |
	Dem.	Rep.	N-P[1]	Other	Dem.	Rep.	N-P[1]	Other
Statewide	29.0	15.6	53.7	1.7	23.6	20.0	53.2	3.3
Regions								
Southeast	29.6	13.2	56.0	1.2	25.0	14.6	57.6	2.8
Southcentral	30.0	15.5	52.6	1.8	20.9	19.9	55.4	3.8
Anchorage	26.5	17.6	54.2	1.7	22.7	23.4	50.9	3.0
Central	38.4	13.3	46.4	1.9	31.9	12.7	52.5	2.9
Fairbanks	24.4	14.9	58.6	2.1	21.5	19.7	54.6	4.2
Northwest	46.5	13.5	38.7	1.4	37.8	12.3	46.4	3.5

[1]N-P=Nonpartisan

Source: Alaska Division of Elections

Table 5.11
Third-Party and Independent Voting in Alaska Presidential and Gubernatorial Elections

| | Presidential Elections | | | Gubernatorial Elections | |
Year	Candidate/Party[1]	% AK Vote	% U.S. Vote	Candidate/Party[1]	% AK Vote
1968	Wallace (AI)	12.1	13.5		
1970				Anderson (AIP)	1.5
1972	Shmitz (AI)	7.3	1.4		
1974				Vogler (AIP)	5.0
1976	MacBride (L)	5.3	0.0		
1978				Kelly (AKP)	12.3
1980	Clark (L)	11.7	1.2		
	Anderson (IA)				
1982				Vogler (AIP)	1.7
				Randolph (L)	14.9
1984	Bergland (L)	3.1	NA		

[1]AI=American Independent; L=Libertarian; IA=Independents for Anderson; AIP=Alaskan Independence Party; AKP=Alaskans for Kelly and Poland.

Source: Alaska Division of Elections, U.S. Bureau of the Census

A majority of voters statewide, and in every region but one (northwest), registered as "nonpartisans" in both 1974 and 1984. (Table 5.10.) From the 1970s to the 1980s, Democratic registration declined and Republican registration rose, each by about five percentage points. There were especially sharp Democratic declines in the urban southcentral region and the rural or "bush" northwest and central regions. In these bush regions, there were also unusual increases in nonpartisan registration. Anchorage showed a significant gain in Republican registration, while its Democratic and nonpartisan lists showed losses.

About 10,000 Alaskans registered under "third party" labels and a variety of other group and individual designations in 1984. The single largest group of these voters, about three thousand, identified themselves as Libertarians. The Libertarian Party appeal has been strong in Alaska, compared with its appeal in other states.

Alaska voters were attracted to third-party and independent candidates in presidential elections more than were voters in the United States generally from 1968 through 1984. (Table 5.11.) In the 1968 election, George Wallace's 13.5 percent of the national vote signaled his powerful appeal among Americans in general, and he ran nearly as well in Alaska. In the 1970s and 1980s, American Independent and Libertarian candidates, and Independent John Anderson, did better in Alaska than they did nationally. The best Alaska showing by any third-party or independent candidate for governor was Libertarian Dick Randolph's in 1982, when he captured 15 percent of the statewide vote.

In Alaska, as is generally true elsewhere, third-party, independent, and write-in campaigns are improbable ventures, given election laws, realities of campaign financing, and voter habits, among other factors. But such campaigns have not been altogether quixotic in Alaska, given the state's relatively fluid, independent electorate.

ELECTION OUTCOMES

This final part focuses on election outcomes in Alaska during the first 25 years of statehood. We look first at party control of state government, including effects on state legislative elections of "coat-tails," incumbency, and reapportionment. Then, we turn to interactions of parties, candidates, and issues in the case of the 1982 race for governor.

PARTY CONTROL IN THE STATES

Increasingly common in the states in recent years has been the situation in which one of the major parties occupies the governor's office while the other controls one or both houses of the state legislature.[15] Such divided control has, in fact, become the most common pattern in state government.

Ticket-splitting, a key manifestation of party disintegration, may be a major cause of divided party government in the states.[16] Voters do not look for "responsible parties" or "party governments;" they look instead to individual candidates and issues that have themselves become detached from organized party bases.

An important force behind ticket-splitting is the electoral power of incumbency. In all of the states, it has become increasingly difficult to dislodge incumbents from state legislative offices. From the mid-1960s through the early

Table 5.12
Divided Control of Alaska State Government, 1959-1986

	Total Years	Unified	Divided
1959-1968	10	8	2
1969-1980	12	0	12
1981-1986	6	0	6
Total Years	28	8	20
Percentages	100%	29%	71%

1980s about 90 percent of incumbent state legislators seeking re-election were re-elected.[17] Voters have become increasingly inclined to vote for the more familiar candidate, usually the incumbent, regardless of party.[18]

Institutional obstacles, weak parties, independent or nonpartisan voters, power of incumbency, and ticket-splitting have had strong disintegrative effects on electoral politics; they have produced divided governments not only at the state level but at all levels in the American political system.

PARTY CONTROL IN ALASKA

These disintegrative forces emerged in Alaska's electoral politics roughly during the same period they appeared most clearly on the national scene—the late 1960s and the 1970s. In Alaska, their appearance was probably accelerated by the petroleum boom of the 1970s and 1980s, which brought increased growth, diversity, and conflict to Alaska political life.

During the post-World War II period, states outside the south experienced divided party control of the governor's office and the lower house of the legislature about half the time.[19] In Alaska from 1959 through 1986 there was such a division nearly 60 percent of the time. If state senators are included in the calculation, divided party control occurred about 70 percent of the time in both Alaska and the country as a whole in recent decades (Table 5.12).

The most striking thing about Alaska's record of party control is the complete change from the 1950s to the 1970s and 1980s. Alaska's Democratic leaders during the first decade of statehood had been the most prominent leaders of the statehood movement during the 1950s. Democrats controlled the governor's office and both houses of the legislature most of the time in the 1960s. (Except for two U.S. House terms at the end of the 1960s, Democrats controlled Alaska's three seats in the U.S. Congress as well.) Then, from 1969

Table 5.13
Average Net Gains and Losses of Legislative Seats by Winning Party
in Presidential and Gubernatorial Elections, 1960-1984

	Average Net Change in Senate	Average Net Change in House
1960-1984		
Presidential Elections	.7	4.7
Gubernatorial Elections	2.0	2.0
1960-1972		
Presidential Elections	1.3	7.0
Gubernatorial Elections	4.7	8.3
1974-1984		
Presidential Elections	0	1.7
Gubernatorial Elections	-.7	-4.3

through 1986, there were no instances of "unified" party control of state government at all. Governors elected under one party's banner invariably confronted legislative leadership from the other party.

This dramatic reversal in the pattern of control went further than the change from unified to divided *party* control of state government. In the 1980s, the legislative parties were further split into bi-partisan *coalitions*, which were formed in both the house and the senate. These coalitions formed largely as a result of regional and interfactional conflict over the issue of how to divide the petroleum-revenue bonanza.[20] (See further discussion of these coalitions in the chapter on Alaska's legislature.)

Neither presidential nor gubernatorial coat-tails were long enough during that period to produce solid legislative majorities that might have helped organize unified party governments. Table 5.13 shows the average number of state legislative seats picked up by the winning parties in presidential and gubernatorial elections from statehood through 1984. Over the whole period, the winning presidential party averaged less than one additional seat in Alaska's senate (out of an average of twelve up for election) and slightly less than five additional seats (out of forty) in Alaska's house. In the last 10 years of that period, winning presidential parties gained no seats in the state senate and fewer than two seats in the state house. And winning gubernatorial parties actually lost ground in both the senate and the house. National, statewide, and local elections in Alaska—as elsewhere—have become increasingly separate and insulated from one another as voters shed party loyalties and routinely split their tickets.

Incumbency is an additional factor reinforcing split-ticket voting in Alaska as it does elsewhere. Table 5.14 shows the difference in the party turnover of state legislative seats with and without incumbents running for re-election in the 1962 through 1984 elections. When incumbents ran in either house or senate races, they lost their seats to the opposition party candidate only about one-fifth of the time. But when senate and house incumbents did not run, their party's new candidates lost to the opposition party candidates nearly one-third of the time.[21]

Legislative incumbents who are vulnerable tend to be from the largest and fastest growing urban areas, where voters are generally less familiar with public officials. This is clearly the case in Alaska, where incumbent losses in recent times were disproportionately concentrated in Anchorage and Fairbanks. These two cities accounted for about two-thirds of incumbent losses, but only about half of the contested legislative seats, through 1984.

Newcomers have had somewhat more opportunity to be elected to the legislature in Alaska than is the case elsewhere. In the states generally, about one-third of the members of each new legislature in recent decades have been newcomers—just over one-third in state houses, and just under one-third in state senates.[22] In Alaska, as shown in Table 5.15, there has been more turnover in the house—an average of about one-half of each Alaska house between 1962 and 1984 consisted of newcomers—and about the same amount of turnover as nationally in the Alaska senate. The table also shows that turnover rates slowed in the Alaska Legislature from the 1960s to the '70s and '80s.

Reapportionment can be a threat to incumbency rule in Alaska's legislature, especially in the senate. Table 5.15 shows that in Alaska's six reapportioned legislatures through 1984, an average of 38 percent, or eight of the state senators, were newcomers, as opposed to 23 percent, or five, in non-reapportioned legislatures. It does not appear, however, that the reapportionment power of the governor had much positive partisan effect on this pattern. If governors were able to increase the electoral chances of their party's legislative candidates through any form of gerrymandering, the effects do not stand out in the election results. In the five legislatures reapportioned by Democratic governors, there were total net *losses* of eleven Democratic house seats and six Democratic senate seats. In the one legislature reapportioned by a Republican governor, there were only modest Republican gains—five house

Table 5.14
Effects of Incumbency in Alaska State Legislative Elections, Selected
Elections, 1962-1984

	House			Senate		
	Total Seats	Turn-Overs	Percent	Total Seats	Turn-Overs	Percent
Incumbents Running	192	41	21%	50	11	22%
Incumbents Not Running	87	27	31%	22	7	32%

Table 5.15
Newcomers to Alaska State Legislature, 1962-1984

	House	Senate
Total Period	49%	32%
1962-70	52%	36%
1972-84	46%	27%
Reapportioned	51%	38%
Non-Reapportioned	46%	23%

seats and one senate seat. Although it is possible that reapportionment may be an instrument for limiting the losses of legislative seats by the governor's party, it does not appear to be an effective tool of party control in Alaska state government.

The higher turnover in reapportioned legislatures may be attributable simply to the fact that reapportionment creates new districts and constituencies. Thus, incumbent legislators will be more vulnerable to electoral challenges and, as a result, more likely to be defeated or less likely to seek re-election in the first place.

THE 1982 GENERAL ELECTION

Alaska's 1982 election represents an especially valuable opportunity for examining relationships between candidates, issues, and regional voting patterns.

There was a vigorous three-way race for governor. There were also several controversial ballot measures, or "propositions," and some of them were strongly divisive regionally. Further, candidates chose to or were forced to take stands, particularly on these regionally sensitive issues. These conditions make it possible to trace some of the effects of candidate-issue interactions and determine how they help shape electoral outcomes in Alaska's regions.

In the race for governor, Democrat William Sheffield was elected with a 47 percent plurality over Republican Tom Fink (38 percent) and Libertarian Dick Randolph (15 percent). Voters also cast ballots on eight propositions, four of which are of interest here: a constitutional amendment limiting increases in state spending, an initiative claiming state ownership of most federal lands in Alaska ("tundra rebellion"), an initiative abolishing special subsistence hunting and fishing preferences for rural Alaskans, and a measure authorizing the legislature to spend money to move the state capital from Juneau to a new site at Willow, north of Anchorage. The statewide vote on these propositions was as follows:

	For	Against
Spending Limit	61%	39%
Tundra Rebellion	73%	27%
Subsistence Repeal	42%	58%
Capital Move	47%	53%

In the election campaign, the two major party candidates took strong, conflicting positions on two of these propositions. Democrat Sheffield opposed the subsistence preference repeal and the capital move, and Republican Fink favored them. Both of these propositions reinforced another political division in Alaska, that between urban and rural regions, or primarily between Anchorage and the rest of the state. The proposition to repeal the subsistence preference represented a direct threat to the interests of Native Alaskans, who are the majority population in the "bush"—the northwest region and the central region outside Fairbanks. The proposition to move the capital was the current version of a measure that has appeared on the ballot in various forms six times since statehood. In 1982, as in all previous elections in which it has appeared, the capital move proposal reflected economic, political, and social cleavages between the Anchorage area and much of the remainder of Alaska. In part because of these cleavages and the candidates' positions on the issues, Fink was widely perceived as the candidate from Anchorage. Sheffield was widely but perhaps more vaguely perceived as the candidate for Alaska regions outside Anchorage and immediately surrounding areas. (Both Sheffield and Fink are long-time residents of Anchorage.)

The following figures show how voting on the four propositions in the state's 27 election districts related to voting for governor. The districts are identified by region. (In Figures 5.1 through 5.4 the election districts in the northwest and central regions are combined into a single "bush" region.) The figures relate district and regional votes *against* the proposition to district and regional votes *for* Sheffield: Sheffield took positions against the capital move and against repeal of subsistence preference. Negative votes on those two propositions can, with some license, be characterized as more "liberal" and thus closer to Sheffield's perceived orientation than to Fink's "conservative" image. There are very high correlations between the proposition vote and the Sheffield vote.[23]

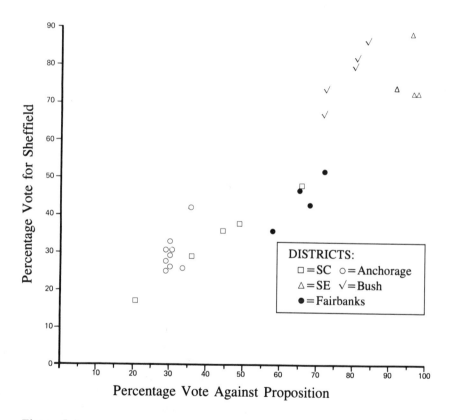

Figure 5.1
Relationship Between Sheffield Vote and Capital Move Vote, 1982 Election

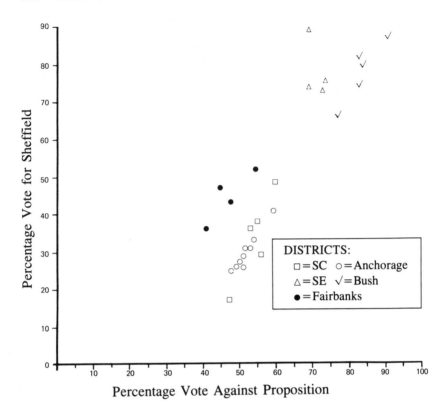

Figure 5.2
Relationship Between Sheffield Vote and Subsistence Preference Repeal
Vote, 1982 Election

In two cases—capital move and subsistence preference—not only is the *statistical relationship* strong between the pro-Sheffield and anti-proposition vote, but the apparent *electoral effect* was also substantial.

Figures 5.1 and 5.2 show that voting against these measures by southeast and ''bush'' voters most clearly differentiated them from voters elsewhere in the state. (Fairbanks voters also voted heavily against the capital move.) These same southeastern and bush districts also gave Sheffield his heaviest majorities. The significance of these issues for voters of these regions, and the stands taken on them by the two candidates, probably were major factors in increasing 1982 registered voter turnout in the southeast and northwest regions by more than 15 percentage points over the average of the previous four elections (see Table 5.3, above).[24]

The strong regional differences on the capital move and subsistence preference issues were to be expected. These issues represented direct threats to southeastern and bush interests, respectively. It may not have been expected, however, that the regional vote on these issues would be so strongly related to the vote for governor, apparently even to the extent of directly reinforcing the vote for Sheffield. Since the two major candidates explicitly differentiated themselves on these issues, it appears that the strong votes against the propositions actually increased Sheffield's expected majorities in the southeast and bush regions.

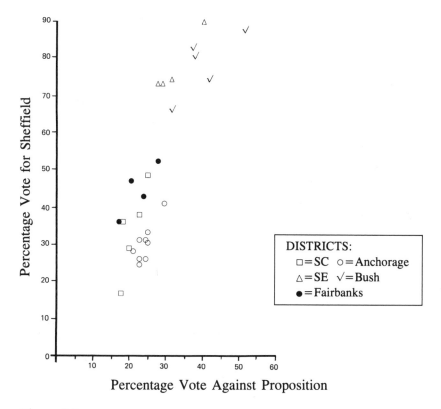

Figure 5.3
Relationship Between Sheffield Vote and Tundra Rebellion Vote, 1982 Election

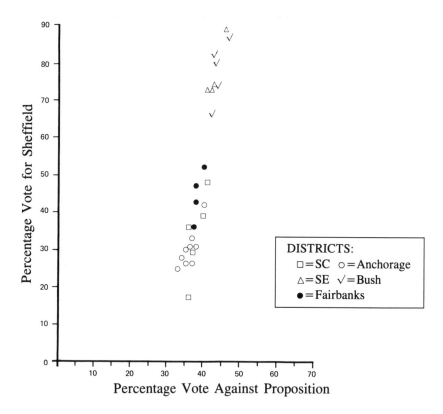

Figure 5.4
Relationship Between Sheffield Vote and Appropriation Limit Vote, 1982 Election

Although smaller in magnitude, there were also "expected" regional differences in voting on the tundra rebellion and appropriation limit propositions (Figures 5.3 and 5.4). The strongholds of the pro-tundra rebellion and pro-spending limit votes were southcentral, Anchorage, and Fairbanks. While the southeast and bush regions also supported the rebellion and the limit, neither were quite as strongly for these propositions as were the other regions. In contrast to the capital move and subsistence preference cases, most voters in all regions voted for the rebellion and the spending limit.

Thus, the ballot issues on which the two major candidates most clearly differentiated themselves—capital move and subsistence—appear to have worked

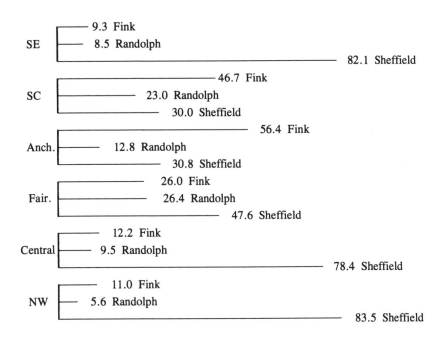

Figure 5.5
Percentage Distributions of Votes for Governor by Region, 1982 Election

more strongly for Sheffield in the threatened southeast and bush regions than they worked against him in the regions that went to Fink (southcentral and Anchorage). Voting on two other propositions (tundra rebellion and spending limit), although highly correlated with the gubernatorial vote and reflecting "expected" regional differences in political or ideological orientations, had little or no apparent electoral effect.

Libertarian candidate Randolph's role in this electoral interplay was effectively that of "spoiler" insofar as Republican Fink's candidacy was concerned. Randolph and Fink tended to appeal to the same side of the political spectrum. Thus, Randolph probably took more votes away from Fink than from Sheffield. If so, Randolph hurt Fink in every region, particularly in southcentral and Anchorage, where Fink would have had to win by huge margins to overcome Sheffield's overwhelming support in southeast and the bush (Figure 5.5).

Randolph also edged Fink in Fairbanks, Randolph's hometown. To win the election, Fink would have needed less than two-thirds of Randolph's 29,000 votes. If Randolph had not run, Fink could have won the votes—particularly in Anchorage, southcentral, and Fairbanks—necessary to edge Sheffield statewide. In any case, the Randolph vote and the regionally divisive capital move and subsistence preference votes appear sufficient to account for Sheffield's victory.

Only once before Sheffield's 1982 victory did a candidate win a statewide election while losing in both the Anchorage and southcentral regions. This happened in 1960, when Democrat Ralph Rivers was re-elected to his second term in the U.S. House over Republican Ron Rettig. After the mid-1960s, it became increasingly difficult for candidates to win statewide if they lost by a significant margin in Anchorage alone. Thus, Sheffield's statewide electoral majority in 1982 was built on a winning regional voting pattern that is unlikely to appear soon again in Alaska's elections.

CONCLUSIONS

Alaska's social and economic growth and diversification during the first 25 years of statehood were reflected in the state's elections. Unified leadership under the Democrats, the statehood party, gave way within a decade to a more fragmented and volatile pattern of control of statewide and legislative offices. The whole electoral pattern became increasingly complex in the 1970s and 1980s. As the state's electoral politics changed, they became more clearly like those of the rest of the states. At the same time, the traditional Alaska phenomena of "small town" and regional politics persisted, though in diminished and modified form. Political parties became increasingly weak organizers of voters, candidates, and election campaigns.

Today voters' party loyalties are slight or non-existent. A majority of Alaska voters in the late 1980s continue to register as independents and nonpartisans. These weak party ties are reflected in a widespread and growing tendency toward split-ticket voting. Reinforcing the split-ticket vote is the power of incumbency. State legislators in particular enjoy lengthening tenure in office, and voters show increasing inclinations to re-elect incumbents regardless of party. The power of incumbency is not yet as strong in Alaska as it is in most other states, but it appears to be growing.

With fading parties and party loyalties, national electoral trends have decreasing influence on state elections, and, similarly, statewide elections have little effect on legislative and other elections within the state. These factors also increase Alaska's electoral similarities to the states generally. Neither a president's nor a governor's coat-tails seem sufficiently long to consistently pull other party candidates into supporting offices. As candidates have become increasingly detached from party organizations and programs, so also have electoral races become more insulated from one another. Voters in Alaska, like those elsewhere, tend to vote for individual candidates, not for parties or party programs.

Thus, strong interparty competition, as measured by relative shares of total votes in any given election or series of elections, does not necessarily refer to vigorous majority-opposition party contention. Increasingly, it means merely that a fluid and shifting electorate has divided its votes over time in ways that maintain the viability of candidates wearing either party's label. Such "competition" also does not necessarily stimulate turnout, as participation rates in national and state elections indicate. It is instead the intensity of individual races, the salience of electorally related issues, and the sense of civic duty that motivate voters to go to the polls, despite the institutional obstacles and other "costs" of voting. Recent high turnout rates in Alaska can, in part, be attributed to increases in perceived stakes in elections that have involved controversial issues, including subsistence preference laws, a proposed capital move, and the spending of billions of dollars in petroleum revenues. These issues have also aggravated Alaska's traditional regional divisions.

One of the most critical outcomes of the electoral dynamics summarized above is the growing incidence of divided party government. As often as not, governors confront legislatures controlled in part or whole by opposition parties or unfriendly coalitions, and policy leadership and direction become obscured in complex legislative and executive gaming, bargaining, and conflict. This situation contrasts sharply with the elusive ideal of unified government, which envisions a governor and legislative leaders from the same party cooperatively developing policies consistent with their party's program and then standing before the electorate to account for their collective decisions. A further departure from the ideal of unified government occurred in Alaska in the early 1980s, when cross-party coalitions formed in both houses of the legislature. This most recent political adaptation occurred largely as a product of interregional and interfactional conflict over the issues of saving, spending, and distributing Alaska's petroleum revenue windfall.

ENDNOTES

[1]The characteristics and especially the limitations of the "party government" model in American politics are discussed fully by Frank J. Sorauf, *Party Politics in America*, Fifth Edition (Boston: Little, Brown and Company, 1984), pp. 388-414.

[2]Alaska Public Offices Commission figures reported in "AkPIRG Legislative Alert," Anchorage, December 14, 1984.

[3]See Gordon S. Harrison, *A Citizen's Guide to the Alaska Constitution* (Anchorage: University of Alaska, Institute of Social and Economic Research, 1982), pp. 57-62.

[4]*Vogler v. Miller* (Alaska, 651 P. 2d 1).

[5]Although little is known about crossovers in primary elections, "it does appear that few voters shift primaries in a deliberate effort to choose the weaker candidate. They are much more likely to shift because they are particularly attracted to a candidate in the other party or because the other party has closer, more interesting primary contests." Malcolm E. Jewell and David M. Olson, *American State Political Parties and Elections* (Homewood, Ill.: The Dorsey Press, 1982), p. 109.

[6]See Jerry Hagstrom, "Baby Boom Generation May Have to Wait a While to Show its Political Clout," *National Journal*, No. 17, Vol. 16 (April 28, 1984), p. 809. In national and state elections from 1932 to 1982, turnout of voters aged 18-29 lagged behind national averages by 11 to 17 percent.

[7]John F. Bibby et al., "Parties in State Politics," in Virginia Gray, Herbert Jacob, Kenneth Vines, *Politics in the American States* (4th ed., Boston: Little, Brown and Co., 1983), p. 64; also Richard G. Niemi and Herbert F. Weisberg, *Controversies in Voting Behavior* (2nd ed., Washington, D.C.: Congressional Quarterly Press, 1984), p. 26.

[8]Niemi and Weisberg, *Controversies in Voting Behavior*, pp. 23-30.

[9]Thomas R. Dye, *Politics in States and Communities* (4th Ed., Englewood Cliffs, N.J.: Prentice-Hall, Inc., 1981), p. 69.

[10]Registered voter turnout rates are consistently higher because they are calculated on a smaller population base than that including all Alaskans over age 18.

[11]Alaska voter registration lists were purged (inactive voters' names were deleted) only every four years until after the 1978 election, when the purge period was shortened to two years.

[12]Jewell and Olson, *American State Political Parties and Elections*, p. 4.

[13]Ibid., p. 44.

[14]We have not analyzed individual races at the election district level. Therefore, these observations about "competition" in legislative elections refer to the aggregate pattern of party voting for both house and senate seats by statewide and regional electorates; they do not refer directly to the level of competition in individual legislative races.

[15]Jewell and Olson, *American State Political Parties and Elections*, p. 232.

[16]Ibid., p. 237.

[17]Bibby, "Parties in State Politics," p. 150-152.

[18]Jewell and Olson, *American State Political Parties and Elections*, p. 214.

[19]Ibid., pp. 232-233.

[20]See Thomas A. Morehouse, ed., *Alaska Resources Development: Issues of the 1980s* (Boulder: Westview Press, 1984), pp. 176ff.

[21]These figures do not include the first two legislative elections, when 'incumbency' was still very fluid, or five elections immediately after redistricting and reapportionments, when incumbents and specific seats were recombined.

[22]Jewell and Olson, *American State Political Parties and Elections*, p. 229; Bibby, "Parties in State Politics," p. 156.

[23]Correlation coefficients, or "r" values, are: capital move, .93; subsistence preference, .88; tundra rebellion, .86; and spending limit, .94.

[24]Table 5.3 shows that registered voter turnout in these two regions settled back to previous levels in the 1984 election. Although turnout increased in all regions in 1982, the extent of the increase in the more transient and growing southcentral, Anchorage, and Fairbanks regions is probably overstated because of unpurged and inflated registration lists for these places in previous years.

6

Alaska's Political Parties

Carl E. Shepro

Alaska political parties face environmental, historical, and cultural circumstances that set them apart from other state, as well as national, parties. The sparse population of Alaska and its concentration in a few urban centers would seem to link people to parties. But the vast size of the state isolates both the statewide and national party representatives from constituents on the local level. Size also contributes to the rivalries between geographical regions, which make concerted action by statewide political party leadership difficult.

Parties in Alaska, like those in most western states, operate within the reform tradition of American politics—a tradition designed to insulate "good government" from the influences of partisan politics.[1] The major political parties in the western states had already been established by the time of the reform period (roughly from the 1890s to the 1920s) and had only to adapt themselves to the reformist mood. However, parties in Alaska organized and carved out a role for themselves after reformist principles had taken root. The new Alaska constitution, a reformist document, made all Alaska political parties compete in an electoral arena that was supportive only of the two major parties and detrimental to challenges by third parties.[2] Also, parties in Alaska had to establish themselves in nonpartisan electoral systems at the local levels and nominate candidates through open primaries rather than by conventions, which would have provided for a measure of party control over this process. They had to face these restrictions while attempting to build party organizations capable of making statewide policy decisions.

Finally, parties in Alaska have had to organize themselves in a population that is culturally and socially diverse. The percentage of Native Americans in the electorate is the highest of any state, and newcomers to the state are proportionately more numerous than elsewhere.

This chapter examines how these factors—ecological, historical, cultural—influence the structure of Alaska political parties and their role in Alaska politics. Too, the chapter looks at how Alaska political parties are different from and similar to those in other states.

Table 6.1
Index of State Laws Regulating Parties (Western States Only)

State	State Comm. Selection[1]	State Comm. Composition[2]	State Comm. Meeting Date[3]	State Comm. Internal Rules[4]	Local Comm. Selection[5]	Local Comm. Composition[6]	Local Comm. Internal Rules or Activities[7]	Cumulative Regulatory Index Score[8]
				Minimum Regulators[9]				
Alaska								0
Hawaii								0
New Mexico							X	1
				Moderate Regulators[9]				
Colorado	X	X	X	X	X	X	X	8
Idaho	X	X			X	X	X	8
Utah	X	X		X	X	X	X	8
Montana	X	X			X	X	X	9
Nevada	X	X		X	X	X	X	9
Washington	X	X			X	X	X	9
				Heavy Regulators[9]				
Oregon	X	X	X	X	X	X	X	10
Arizona	X	X	X	X	X	X	X	11
California	X	X		X	X	X	X	11
Wyoming	X	X	X	X	X	X	X	12

[1]State law regulates the manner of selecting the parties' state central committees.
[2]State law regulates the composition of the parties' state central committees.
[3]State law regulates when the parties' state central committee will meet.
[4]State law regulates internal procedures of the parties' state central committees.
[5]State law regulates the manner of selecting the parties' local organizations.
[6]State law regulates the composition of the parties' local organizations.
[7]State law regulates internal rules or activities of the parties' local organizations.
[8]Scores are determined by state regulatory actions in the seven areas examined. Minimum score is 0; maximum score is 14.
[9]"Minimum" regulators are defined as having an index score of 0-4; "moderate" regulators are those states having index scores of 5-9; and "heavy" regulators are those states having index scores above 10.
Source: *Intergovernmental Perspective*, Fall 1984, Vol. 10, No. 4, p. 12.

PARTY ORGANIZATIONS IN ALASKA POLITICS

State legislatures define what party organization will look like, as well as what functional authority parties will have in each state.[3] In many states, political parties function as organs of the state. Their shapes and duties are determined in the same manner as are those of local governments. In other states, parties are responsible for their own organization. Who determines party organization is thus one measure of the strength of parties within a state.

In Alaska, statutes address the party role in elections and nominations. Statutes also prohibit partisan electoral activity by public school teachers and by members of the state Board of Education. Parties can determine their own structures and areas of operation, instead of having this done by the legislature. This provision gives the appearance of providing for relatively strong party organizations in Alaska.

Table 6.1 compares state laws regulating party rules and structure in the western states. Alaska and Hawaii allow parties the most freedom to set rules

Table 6.2
State Laws Governing Party Roles in Electoral Process (Western States Only)

State	Nominating Convention[1]	Party Endorsement[2]	Closed or Partly Open Primaries[3]	Sore Loser Provision[4]	Straight Party Ballot[5]	Cumulative Party Support Index Score[6]
			Generally Unsupportive			
Alaska						0
Hawaii						0
Montana						0
Idaho				X		2
Nevada			X			2
Washington				X		2
			Moderately Supportive			
Arizona			X	X		4
California			X	X		4
Oregon			X	X		4
Wyoming			X		X	4
			Generally Supportive			
Colorado	X	X	X	X		8
New Mexico		X	X	X	X	8
Utah	X	X		X	X	8

[1] State allows/requires nominating conventions.
[2] State's parties make candidate endorsements before the general election.
[3] State has a closed primary or requires voters to acknowledge a party preference.
[4] State has a "sore loser" provision.
[5] State provides a straight party voting mechanism on its ballot.
[6] Scores are determined by the state's positions on the five issues examined. Minimum score is 0; maximum score is 10.
Source: *Intergovernmental Perspective*, Fall 1984, Vol. 10, No. 4, p. 13.

and structure. Of the contiguous western states, only New Mexico comes close to allowing parties as much freedom to establish their own internal rules and structure as do the two newer states.

Other states impose more regulation on parties; the table divides them into "moderate" and "heavy" regulators. Washington state statutes, for example, establish a party organization system for each major party.[4] Washington statutes establish a convention system paralleling that of party organization, except that conventions are denied the power to nominate when that process is done via primary elections. Washington is classified as a moderate regulator. At the opposite end of the organizational continuum from Alaska are states like California and Wyoming, which regulate most or all major aspects of party organization.

Table 6.2 shows to what extent laws in western states support party roles in the electoral process. Alaska is among the least supportive. As in Hawaii, Montana, Idaho, Nevada, and Washington, parties in Alaska may not endorse candidates prior to the general elections. Primary elections are open. Voters need not state party preference, and there is no provision for voting a straight party ticket on the ballot. By contrast, Colorado, New Mexico, and Utah have laws that are much more supportive of party roles in elections.

Party structure is always influenced to an extent by the organization of elections, as political scientist Frank Sorauf notes:

> The party organizations created by the states have in common one dominant characteristic: They match the voting districts and constituencies of the state. They form great step pyramids as they reflect the myriad, vast numbers of officeholders....[5]

Alaska is no different from other states with respect to this generalization.

Figure 6.1 compares the organization of Alaska political parties with typical party organizations in other states. Alaska political parties resemble those in other states at the lowest levels of organization—the precinct or ward and the legislative district levels. Most states have intricate party structures above the local district or precinct level, which incorporate local party bodies into larger intermediate (or regional) levels, and which reflect the prevailing electoral arrangements. No similar intermediate structure exists in the Alaska parties. The intermediate electoral level in Alaska is the judicial district, but no party structure matches the state's four judicial districts. Instead, the next level on which Alaska parties are organized is the state central committee for each party. These committees are too far removed from the legislative districts and precincts to centralize operations from the local levels. As a result, local organizations vary in effectiveness from district to district.[6]

Republican and Democratic parties in Alaska have similar structures. Both lack administrative and electoral arrangements at the borough level, which would correspond with the county level in other states. This leaves them with few connections between the precinct committeemen on the one hand and the state committees on the other. Contact between the opposite ends of the organizational spectrum is limited—even though precinct committeemen are considered essential to the party organization. Moreover, executive directors of both parties see their organizations as just resuming activity in the mid-1980s after a prolonged period of ineffectiveness and lack of statewide organization.[7]

Other party activists offer different reasons for the lack of integrated party organizations in Alaska. One party leader saw the sparse population of the state, spread over such vast distances, as limiting party communication.[8] Also, in the absence of regional party organizations, parties focus on election districts (each district has approximately 7 thousand to 8 thousand voters). This means there is a very small pool of active partisan identifiers per district, resulting in small and ineffective precinct organizing party support on a local level.

Figure 6.1

Typical Party Organization

State Committee
Congressional District Committees
County Committees
Intermediate Committees (City, Legislative, Judicial)
Ward Committees
Local Party Committeemen (Ward, Precinct)

Source: Frank J. Sorauf, *Party Politics in America*, 1972.

Alaska Republican/Democratic Party Organization

State Central Committee
Legislative District Committees
Precinct Committees
(Party Clubs)

Source: League of Women Voters, 1972.

The lack of regionally based party structures is a product of recent developments in most parts of the state. For example, until redistricting following the 1980 U.S. census, the Fairbanks North Star Borough was represented by a regional legislative district electing three senators and six representatives. Voters cast ballots equal to the number of positions open, and the top vote getters won. In practice, this was a type of proportional representation system. Legislative behavior followed the electoral arrangement: members of the Fairbanks delegation acted as a delegation, instead of as individuals representing single legislative districts. Each party (including the Libertarians) maintained a common office and staff. After reapportionment and the formation of single-member districts in 1981, this system collapsed.

Formal structures established by the parties in Alaska are complemented by informal organizations: Republican women's clubs, youth groups (Young

Democrats and Young Republicans), and Gruening, Bartlett, and Egan Clubs of the Democratic Party. Such groups are seldom fully integrated into the formal structure of the party organizations in most states. They may contribute tendencies toward ideological divisions within parties.[9] However, in Alaska, the Democratic issue clubs serve a quasi-official party role by assisting in policy formulation, and this system partly overcomes the lack of a county-level organization in interior Alaska. Informal organizations exerting similar influences on both Democratic and Republican parties exist in California (where parties are viewed as being relatively weak) and in New Mexico (where parties are viewed as being relatively strong).[10]

In short, Alaska parties are skeletal structures. No statutes require any particular kind of structure or functions, and party organization reflects the state's electoral arrangements. There is a pretense of central direction at the top. Little continuing activity outside the election cycle, and nothing at all resembling a party machine, exists at the bottom. In between top and bottom, at the regional (borough) level, there is no uniform electoral structure throughout the state, and this lack has a decentralizing effect on political parties.

PARTY IN THE ELECTORATE: PARTISAN IDENTIFICATION

Partisan identification refers to how much the voter identifies with a particular political party. Is the voter a registered supporter of a party, or, if not, does he nevertheless lean toward that party—and how strongly? These questions are important for the political stability of a state and for the ability of leaders to encourage citizens to follow the leaders' initiatives.[11] In general, studies of how Americans perceive parties demonstrate that partisan political identification has declined over time. Table 6.3 shows that the percentages of voters who identify themselves as Democrats and Republicans declined between 1960 and 1980, while the proportion who think of themselves as independents rose.

Data presented in the chapter on elections show that partisan identification in Alaska has diverged somewhat from national patterns. Alaska Democrats declined by approximately 5.3 percent from 1970 to 1984, and Alaska Republicans increased .4 percent during the same period. Nonpartisan registration did not change significantly during that period, but minor parties grew by about 2 percent.

Statewide electoral data create the impression that Alaska is a two-party competitive state. Although the majority of the registered voters (53 percent) are nonpartisan, they vote for candidates of one of the two major parties in most elections. However, analysis of regional patterns of voting shows a different picture of partisanship.

Table 6.3
Party Affiliation, 1960-1980

	1960	1964	1968	1972	1976	1980
Democrats	47%	53%	46%	42%	48%	44%
Independents	23	22	27	31	29	30
Republicans	30	25	27	27	23	26

Source: American Institute of Public Opinion (Gallup Poll) cited in Frank J. Sorauf, *Party Politics in America*, 5th Ed. (Boston: Little, Brown & Co.), 1984, p. 140.

Party registration in urbanized, primarily non-Native areas of Alaska has become more balanced over time. All these areas—southeast, southcentral (including Anchorage), and central (including Fairbanks)—lost Democratic registrants proportionally, and gained Republican registrants. Republican gains in Anchorage outpaced those in the rest of the state. Also, urban areas were more likely to show declines in nonpartisan registration, and to show significant increases in third-party registration.

Meanwhile, in rural northwest and central Alaska, the percentages of registered Republicans and Democrats declined and proportions of nonpartisan and third-party members increased.

In short, the changes in registration at the statewide level are the result of important regional changes and shifts. But, our ability to track these changes over the period of statehood is inhibited by two factors. First, the state Division of Elections did not begin periodically purging voter registration lists until 1974, and accuracy of data in the earlier periods is suspect. Second, electoral districts were redrawn in 1974, 1976, and 1982, and these changes have had the effect of making all regions appear more competitive.

The important point about party registration in the state is that Alaskans are not very partisan. There have been regional changes and changes in the two-party balance, but a majority of voters still indicate that they follow no particular party. This situation prompts two questions: why do a majority of Alaskans lack an identification with political parties, and what is the nature of the partisanship of the minority who are comfortable being called Democrats or Republicans?

Broadly, three factors explain lack of partisanship in Alaska: political culture, history, and electoral institutions. The cultural explanation, discussed at length in the chapter on Alaska political culture, points to Alaskans' penchant for identifying themselves as individualists. In the electoral context, they are happiest when identified as independents, free of any organizational influence.

The historical explanation extends the logic of Sorauf's comment: "Party organization must and will reflect the political culture and the socioeconomic conditions of the time. As they change, the parties also change."[12] Individuals acquire a partisan identification as a consequence of their interactions with parents, peers, and parties themselves, within a historical context. The Alaska political community formed in the twentieth century, a period of reformism in American politics that was especially pronounced in the western states. Because they organized late, Alaska parties were less able than those of other western states to socialize voters into a partisan identification.

The most compelling explanation for the high rate of nonpartisanship in Alaska, however, is institutional. It is a commonplace of politics that voters are influenced strongly by the rules and structure of the system. In Alaska, existing rules either discourage party affiliation or fail to reinforce it if already formed. Voters participate in elections where party labels are absent or downplayed. This situation applies even to statewide contests for national office, an aspect of Alaska politics with parallels in other western states.[13] The single most important institutional factor is the state's open (blanket) primary, discussed earlier. In use before statehood and re-adopted in 1967, this method of nominating candidates for public office—from state legislature to U.S. senate—discourages affiliation with political parties. Alaska presents the least supportive milieu for state and local party activities.[14]

Perhaps what requires explanation is not the high percentage of nonpartisanship in Alaska, but the substantial minority of Alaskans who do identify with parties. Three factors seem to explain this party affiliation: cultural politics, demographic change, and campaign behavior.

Until recently, rural areas of Alaska, particularly the central and northwest regions, had a higher than average rate of partisan identification. A close look at precinct-by-precinct data from the 1950s and 1960s shows that several villages were unanimous in their partisanship, and more often than not the identification was Democratic. There are economic reasons for this partisanship. For example, during the 1960s the War on Poverty—the product of a national Democratic administration, implemented through a state Democratic administration—brought visible benefits to rural areas of the state and mobilized Natives in the process. Economic benefits that resulted from the various War on Poverty programs influenced many rural voters to line up behind the Democratic party, much as the New Deal policies of the 1930s brought minorities into the Democratic coalition.

Alaska Native cultural politics likely have an important role in this development of partisanship too. The political party is a western symbol in Native villages, but one which has been appropriated by leaders and made part of community life. The Democratic and Republican labels are not used as statements of coherent ideologies or even programs of economic benefits. Instead, Native leaders link values of the community, such as protection of land and continued ability to use the species found on it, with party symbols.

A second explanation for partisanship is demographic. From 1958 to 1985, the population of Alaska grew rapidly. Between 1970 and 1980, Alaska's population grew 32 percent statewide; most growth was in predominantly non-Native, urbanized areas. Anchorage's population increased by 37 percent, to total 173,992, and the Fairbanks North Star Borough's increased 18 percent, to 54,000. The state population rose very quickly in the 1980s, increasing 30 percent between 1980 and 1984. Again, most of that growth was in urban areas—particularly Anchorage, where population grew 40 percent and reached nearly a quarter of a million.

Growth in population in the 1970s and early 1980s was largely a result of Alaska's oil boom and the many new jobs created. However, migrants attracted by jobs were not a mirror image of the old population of the state. Instead, they brought with them political norms and behaviors from their states of origin. Other states have stronger party systems than Alaska, and the migrants were socialized into parties differently from Alaskans. Electoral statistics demonstrating significant Democratic losses in party registration and increases in the numbers of Republican identifiers in Alaska may reflect the political affiliations of migrants from different states.

A third reason for the continued identification of some Alaskans with political parties has to do with election campaigns: in some campaigns, parties are the most significant force. Customarily, we explain voters' behavior in election campaigns by the combined impacts of personalities (candidates), issues, and organizations. Given the sparse population of Alaska, personalities have often had a strong impact on elections. Issues too are powerful motivators of the vote, as illustrated by the 1982 election. (See discussion of issues in the 1982 campaign in the elections chapter.)

However, in the absence of strong personalities and issues, parties remain as symbols in statewide and federal contests. As the strongest available force in some elections, they may influence voters. Parties attract most support, however, when they are linked with policies and personalities. That link is most readily accomplished through activities of party in government, a consideration to which we now turn.

PARTY IN GOVERNMENT

Alaska's major parties have had no more success as vehicles to achieve responsible party government than have parties in other states. Parties in Alaska have not been a strong mechanism for executive or legislative leadership and direction.

Interparty coalitions have controlled the state legislature at various times since statehood, but coalitions have been especially frequent in the 1980s. The basis of coalition formation has been economic interest, not ideology: who should benefit from state oil revenues that reached billions of dollars in the early 1980s? (See related discussion of coalition formation in the chapter on the Alaska Legislature.)

The lack of ideological motivation for coalition formation sets Alaska apart from interparty coalitions in other western states. For example, an ideological split developed within the Democratic party of Washington state in 1951. A coalition of 8 Democrats and 21 Republicans organized the 46-member senate in opposition to the partisan standards of organization.[15] The California legislature underwent a similar experience in 1980, when Democrat Willie Brown was elected Speaker of the Assembly by a 51-24 vote margin. His majority included 23 Democrats and 28 Republicans.[16]

The major difference between coalition building in Alaska legislative politics, and that in legislatures of some other western states, appears to lie in the ability of the Alaska builders to focus on distribution of economic benefits. Also, Alaska coalitions last longer. In the California and Washington cases, normal partisan lines of legislative organization re-established themselves quickly. In the Alaska case, parties have been unable to consistently organize either house of the legislature.

An additional reason why partisan organization in the Alaska Legislature is difficult is that procedural rather than nominal majorities are required in each house.[17] Neither party has commanded a substantial majority in any recent session of the legislature. While 11 seats in the Alaska State Senate provide a party with a nominal majority, a procedural majority of 14 votes is necessary to take action on bills. Thus, coalitions must be formed, and they remain basically the same over time.

The chapter on elections discusses past problems in executive leadership of the party within the state legislature. The winning gubernatorial candidates over the past 10 years have actually lost seats in both the senate and the house, instead of having any coattail effect on legislative elections. The incumbent in the mid-1980s, Bill Sheffield, has made it clear that he considers his role to be one of unifying the Democratic party. He has actively supported candidates at the statewide and local levels by making public appearances at fundraisers, and he has personally contributed to their campaign chests. These practices have antagonized some Republican activists in the state, while bringing forth praise from their Democratic counterparts.[18] The governor has also used patronage as a means of establishing, or re-establishing, party unity.

Alaska's constitution provides for a unified executive, as described in the chapter on the state constitution. In theory the governor has wide-ranging powers of appointment, and could forge an effective party-oriented administration through skillful use of appointment powers. Over the statehood period, however, gubernatorial use of appointment powers to weld a partisan administration has been mixed. Governor Jay Hammond, a Republican who was himself independent of party forces, followed a bipartisan appointment pattern (thereby earning the enmity of some party activists) to accomplish a legislative program from 1974 through 1982. Democratic Governor Sheffield, who took office in 1982, has opted to use party as an important criterion in filling the some 1,000 posts exempt from the state civil service regulations. The result has been confrontation with the coalitions controlling both houses of the legislature. (The 1984 senate organization was blatantly anti-executive branch; the house's organization was only somewhat less so.) Overall, instead of unifying the Democratic party in state government, these attempts have exacerbated existing divisions between leadership in the legislative and executive branches.

Governor Sheffield's attempts to strengthen the Democratic party go against the national trend, which has been toward weaker political parties with less influence over nomination and election of candidates. However, in Alaska in the past few years, parties have become increasingly important vehicles for funneling campaign contributions to candidates, because they are not subject to the same restrictions as are other campaign contributors. But the most important sources of campaign money in Alaska in recent times have been political action committees, construction-related businesses, oil companies, and labor unions.[19]

In addition to party's role in administrative and legislative organization, party also has some influence over judicial appointments. Sorauf notes that at the appellate level in state courts across the country, party affiliation does have an indirect impact on judicial decisionmaking. Democratic and Republican judges tend to make decisions recognizably supportive of party values.[20] The Alaska governor has some latitude in making judicial appointments, but must choose from lists prepared by the Alaska Judicial Council. (See a detailed discussion of the appointment process in the chapter on Alaska courts.) In most administrations since statehood, the party registration and partisan beliefs of judicial applicants have been important factors in appointment decisions. However, the ensuing judicial behavior may not reflect distinctly Alaskan political culture. Effective use of the nomination power to further partisan ends in the state appears extremely doubtful.

THIRD PARTIES IN ALASKA POLITICS

In many respects, activities of third parties in Alaska resemble those in other western states. The third parties most active in the 1980s appear to be more conservative in their ideological focus and choice of issues than was the case in early periods.[21]

Alaska has been a seat of power for the Libertarian Party of the United States. The first Libertarian to serve in a state legislature was elected in Alaska, and Alaska was a key state in the presidential campaign of Ed Clarke in 1980. In addition, Dick Randolph of Fairbanks captured 15 percent of the statewide vote in the 1982 gubernatorial contest—a significant portion of the vote, given the record campaign expenditures by the two major party candidates. Randolph's was far and away the best showing, based on percentage of the total vote, of any Libertarian candidate in any state.

Given these past successes, and the general perception of party activists that the Alaska Libertarians have been better organized than the Republicans and Democrats, the inability of the party to elect more members at the state level requires explanation. One possible explanation is that the party's strength has been based on the idiosyncratic leadership of its major candidate in the state, Dick Randolph. (In 1986, this statewide Libertarian leader, who entered politics as a Republican, returned to the fold as a Republican candidate for governor; party fortunes dipped as a result.)

Second, the Libertarian Party's organizational strength may be more potential than actual. Libertarian campaigns have been individual efforts on the part of candidates, and not coordinated by any statewide or even local organization. Unlike the National Libertarian Party, which has focused on attempts to organize the party and achieve access to the ballot in several states, the Alaska affiliates have focused on such procedures as the initiative process; such practices have not increased the number of Libertarian partisans.[22] A third explanation for the failure of the Libertarian Party to elect statewide candidates is that Randolph's role in the 1982 campaign might have been a fluke. The lineup of issues and opposition candidates in that gubernatorial race may have given Randolph the leverage he needed to win a significant number of votes; his party label may have been immaterial to the outcome. (Randolph's role in the 1982 election is discussed more in the chapter on elections.)

The other third party in Alaska politics that has gained access to the ballot is the Alaskan Independence Party—led by another Fairbanksan, Joe Vogler.

This party, with its distinctive policy of urging separation of Alaska from the United States, has been a regular feature of Alaska elections since statehood. Like third parties in most states, the AIP receives a minimal share of the total vote, and has not achieved success anything like that of the Libertarians.

Third parties in Alaska are more important than in the other western states, because the Libertarian Party has succeeded in advancing ballot initiatives. The best example of this is the tax repeal initiative of 1979, which spurred legislative repeal of the state income tax.[23] Alaska third parties are distinctive because of the way in which they represent aspects of the Alaska political culture, such as individualism and anti-federalism. (See the chapter devoted to Alaska's political culture.) Finally, third parties have practical electoral effects as spoilers in close electoral races, taking votes away from one or the other of the major party contenders.

SUMMARY AND CONCLUSIONS

By most measures of party strength used in national studies, Alaska's political parties are weak vehicles for electoral competition, for voter identification, and for control and direction of government.

Alaska parties appear to be the most disintegrated of American state party systems. At the local level, they barely exist except at election time. There is a missing link at the regional (borough) level where most state parties have some strength. The top, disclaimers to the contrary notwithstanding, has little influence over the bottom.

The picture of party in the mind of the average Alaska voter is blurred and indistinct. Fifty-three percent lack a stable party identification and are guided in electoral choices by other factors—personality and style of candidates, group and regional interests, and issues. Indeed, Alaska can boast the highest rate of nonpartisanship in the nation, which is attributable to individualism and historical and institutional factors. The open (blanket) primary is the most important factor weakening the parties: voters may select any combination of candidates, without attention to partisanship.

Yet a substantial minority of Alaskans still accept party cues in voting and other political behavior. Why? Some are Natives who acquire party identification through cultural processes. Others are migrants who brought their party affiliations from other states. And even in a fragmented electoral environment such as Alaska's (see the elections chapter) party identification and other factors that were historically important still play a role.

Parties in Alaska do not govern, despite recent serious attempts to do so. Coalitions have dominated the legislature in the 1980s. The state administration, with 1,000 jobs available for patronage, is buffered from party signals by civil service protections. The judiciary too is protected from partisan control, if not from partisan influence.

Yet although they are weak, parties continue to operate in Alaska and to exercise some influence on voters. Some tentative speculations about how they may function in Alaska's political system are:

1) Parties may provide, in the minds of the voters, an indication of candidates' positions on issues. The 1982 gubernatorial election is a case study of how voters make correlations between parties, candidates, and issues.

2) The recent propensity of the legislature to form coalitions, the tendency of some elected officials (for instance, former governor Hammond) to act in bipartisan rather than partisan fashion in making appointments, and the anti-party aspect of elections in Alaska all suggest that factions play an important role in the politics of the state. Alaska politics can be compared to those of one-party or nonpartisan states where factional divisions rather than partisan divisons are found. Parties in Alaska may act more as umbrella organizations that facilitate elections rather than as objects of intellectual or emotional identification.

3) In some regions of the state, particularly rural areas, party labels may have little or no meaning as ideological (or even economic) symbols. Rural voters identify with parties for qualitatively different reasons than do urban voters.

4) Although the foregoing discussion emphasizes the substantial differences between Alaska parties and those of other states, there are also important similarities. California, for example, has weak political parties in terms of organization and voter identification, as do Washington and Oregon. Third parties continue to influence California politics, as they do those of Colorado. Coalitions do appear in the legislatures of other states, although for ideological rather than economic reasons.

Our analysis strongly suggests that Alaska's political parties are the weakest among all the states. This weakness can be attributed to several unique characteristics of the state—its culture, its sparse population spread over a vast terrain, and its rapid growth. But the single most important reason why Alaska parties are weak is that the rules, practices, and institutions of the Progressive Era, are, for historical reasons, more pronounced in Alaska than in the other states.

ENDNOTES

[1]Richard Hofstadter, *The Age of Reform* (New York: Vintage Books, 1955), p. 32.

[2]Frank J. Sorauf, *Party Politics in America*, 5th ed. (Boston: Little, Brown Co., 1984), p. 40.

[3]Ibid., pp. 65-85.

[4]Daniel M. Ogden and Hugh A. Bone, *Washington Politics* (New York: New York University Press, 1960), pp. 25-26.

[5]Frank J. Sorauf, *Party Politics in America*, 2nd ed. (Boston: Little, Brown & Co., 1968, 1972), p. 67.

[6]Interviews with party activists from both Democratic and Republican parties in Fairbanks and Anchorage, May and June, 1985.

[7]Interview with Paul Quesnell, executive director of the Alaska Democratic Party, Anchorage, Alaska, February 13, 1985. Interview with Ken Stout, chairman of the Alaska Republican Party, Anchorage, Alaska, February 12, 1985.

[8]Statement of Glenn Juday, president of the Gruening Democratic Club, Fairbanks, Alaska, June 26, 1985.

[9]Sorauf, *Party Politics in America*, 2nd ed., pp. 82-83.

[10]See Katherine Wallace, *California: People, Politics, and Government* (New York: AMSCO School Publications, Inc., 1980), pp. 141-143; Terry Christensen and Larry N. Gerston, *Politics in the Golden State: The California Connection* (Boston: Little, Brown & Co., 1984), pp. 40-42; and F. Chris Garcia and Paul L. Hain (eds.) *New Mexico Government* (Albuquerque: University of New Mexico Press, 1981), pp. 228-231.

[11]Martin P. Wattenberg, *The Decline of American Political Parties: 1952-1980* (Cambridge, MA: Harvard University Press, 1984), p. 12.

[12]Sorauf, *Party Politics in America*, 2nd ed., p. 83.

[13]The 1984 Democratic primary campaign of Tom Dahl for Alaska's lone congressional seat demonstrates this pattern. Apparently in response to the large number of nonpartisan registrations, Dahl campaigned for the party nomination without identifying himself as a Democrat. Ogden and Bone (see note 4) discuss the phenomena in other western states.

[14]Timothy Conlan, Ann Martino, and Robert Diglar, "State Parties in the 1980s: Adaptation, Resurgence and Continuing Constraints," in *Intergovernmental Perspective* 10 (Fall 1974), 4: 11-13.

[15]Ogden and Bone, *Washington Politics*, p. 18.

[16]Christensen and Gerston, *Politics in the Golden State*, pp. 126-136. (See note 10.)

[17]Thanks are due to Patrick O'Connell, former Republican state representative, for this insight.

[18]Feelings about Governor Sheffield's intervention divided neatly on party lines: Republicans were very much in opposition and Democrats were strongly supportive. Additionally, Republicans used the occasion to indicate they would have welcomed gubernatorial support in the Hammond administration, which was nominally but not actively Republican.

[19]For a detailed look at who pays for political campaigns in Alaska, see Larry Makinson, *Open Secrets: The Price of Politics in Alaska*, 1986. Published with funding from The Project For Investigative Reporting on Money in Politics and other sources.

[20]Sorauf, *Party Politics in America*, 5th ed., p. 383.

[21]Ibid., pp. 48-49.

[22]Interview with Mike Prax, chairman of the Interior/Fairbanks Libertarian Party, Fairbanks, Alaska, October 13, 1985.

[23]Dick Randolph, *Freedom for Alaskans* (Aurora, IL: Caroline House Publishers, Inc., 1982), pp. 70-71.

7

Interest Groups and Lobbying in Alaska

Clive S. Thomas

Pick up any Alaska newspaper, turn on any statewide radio or television news program, and the chances are that there will be at least one story about interest groups trying to get the state government to do something they support. Or, as is often the case, they may be working to get the government to block or repeal some action they oppose. The news story might be about a coalition of development groups supporting the proposed Susitna hydroelectric project and the environmentalists opposing it; or the groups for and against the most recent plan for funding education in the state; or about the opposing forces in the latest round in the battle over the state's subsistence law. The issues and the organizations may change, but the involvement of groups in the policymaking process is constant.

It has long been recognized by politicians and students of politics that interest groups play a very important role in the complex process of making public policies. This role is especially significant in the United States at both the federal and state levels and particularly in Alaska. Several political observers have, in fact, concluded that interest groups in Alaska are among the most powerful in the nation.[1]

Since interest groups exert considerable power in determining what government does or does not do in Alaska, understanding something about these groups will tell us a lot about Alaska politics and how political power is distributed in the state. One of the purposes of this chapter is to discuss what the status of interest groups in the state's political system tells us about the nature of Alaska politics. A second purpose is to place Alaska interest groups in context by comparing their operations with those of interest groups in other states. Essentially we ask the question: How different is activity among Alaska interest groups? The third purpose of this chapter, and the one to which we devote most of our attention, is describing the types of groups that make up the interest group scene in Alaska and explaining the methods they use in attempting to achieve their goals.

First we need to define what we mean by *interest groups* and distinguish between them and *lobbies*. Probably the most generally accepted definition of interest groups is political scientist David B. Truman's. He defines them as "any group that is based on one or more shared attitudes and makes certain claims on other groups or organizations in the society."[2] To put this in more concrete terms, we can also think of interest groups as any association of individuals, whether formally organized or not, that seeks to influence public policy. That definition would include everything from groups like the Alaska Federation of Natives to various sectors of government itself at the federal, state, or local level. One type of organization specifically excluded from the category of interest groups, however, is political parties. The type of activity undertaken by political parties differs from that of interest groups in two fundamental ways. Although interest groups try to influence public policy (and particularly who gets elected to make that policy) they do not seek to directly operate government. In contrast, political parties actively seek to win elections so they can directly control and operate government. Political parties also usually have broader support and wider policy goals.

A lobby is similar to but not the same as an interest group. Lobby is a collective term for one or more groups concerned with promoting the same general area of public policy, though these groups may or may not be in agreement on specific issues. For example, the Alaska School Boards Association is part of the education lobby, but it may not always see eye to eye with (and may often be diametrically opposed to) teachers and other education groups on how best to promote education in the state.

The confusing thing is that both scholars and the general public often use the terms "interest group" and "lobby" interchangeably. Other commonly used terms are interest, special interest, political interest group, and pressure group.[3] But for our purposes, we need only bear in mind the definitions we have given for interest group and lobby, which are widely accepted definitions of these terms today among scholars.

We first consider the setting of interest group activity in the state, including public monitoring of interest group activity. Then we examine the types of groups that operate in the state, the types of tactics interest groups employ to achieve their goals, and the role and function of lobbyists. Next we make some observations about what are perceived as the most effective groups in Alaska. The final two sections make comparisons between Alaska and other states, and discuss the past, present, and anticipated future role of interest groups in Alaska politics.

FACTORS INFLUENCING INTEREST GROUP ACTIVITY

Interest groups are products of the political, social, economic, religious, and natural environments of states or nations. Thus we can't understand the

role interest groups play without first understanding the setting or environment in which they operate.[4] Much of that background information on Alaska
is provided in other chapters in this book. However, there are some things
about the Alaska setting that need particular emphasis because they bear on
interest group activity in the state.

Probably the most important of these factors is that, compared to political
parties in states like Massachusetts, New York, and Wisconsin, Alaska's parties are weak in their organization, campaign participation, and, in particular,
in their enforcement of party discipline in the legislature. These weaknesses
are in part a consequence of the high percentage of independent voters in the
state, the blanket primary, and strong regional and local ties that take precedence
over party loyalty. (See further discussions of these points in the chapters on
Alaska's political parties and elections.) Invariably, in states with weak
parties—Oregon, Texas, and New Hampshire are other examples—interest
groups are correspondingly strong. Together with prominent individual politicians, these groups fill the power vacuum left by a relatively weak and un-
disciplined party system.[5]

A second factor in recent years has been the state's oil revenues. The unprecedented flow of petroleum revenues meant that virtually all groups, even
poorly organized ones, were successful in securing some funding. Oil wealth
in part also accounts for the proliferation of groups stalking the halls of the
capitol over the past decade. The most successful groups from the late 1970s
to the mid-1980s were those whose objective was to get funds. On the other
hand, those with strong philosophical and especially controversial goals (such
as the National Education Association's attempt to secure binding arbitration
for Alaska teachers) had as difficult a time as they would have had without
the oil bonanza, or would have experienced in any other state.

We have already alluded to the third factor that helps explain interest group
activity—the existence of regional and local interests. Alaska is one of the most
regionalized of all states—witness the long, drawn-out conflict over the proposed capital move, and the tensions that exist between urban and rural Alaska.
In the absence of strong parties, legislators are free to respond to their constituents and local group interests, which are the most immediate pressures on
lawmakers. Hence extensive "pork-barrelling" is a dominant fact of political
life in Alaska's legislature. This was particularly true when oil revenues peaked
at the start of the 1980s. (See the chapter on Alaska's legislature.)

The fourth factor is the personal nature of politics in Alaska. In contrast
to practices in large states like California, and even medium-sized ones like
Indiana and South Carolina, Alaska legislators and members of the executive
branch are still very accessible to the public. As one lobbyist, a veteran of

both the California and Alaska legislatures expressed it: "If a California legislator has his home phone listed he's crazy; if an Alaska legislator doesn't, he probably won't get re-elected."[6] Individual Alaskans can and often do influence public policymaking. This importance of the individual has consequences for lobby group tactics. It means that lobbying is not the sole preserve of sophisticated and organized groups, and that Joe and Mary Citizen can and sometimes do stymie, thwart, or undermine well-planned and carefully executed lobby efforts.

Finally, another significant factor affecting interest group and lobbying activity in Alaska is government's role as the major employer and a dominant economic influence. Approximately 70,000 Alaskans, or just under one-third of the state's labor force, work for federal, state and local government.[7] As we shall see, the government's powerful role affects the type and power of interest groups and lobbyists operating in the state and gives such activity in Alaska much of its uniqueness.

There is one more important aspect of the setting for Alaska interest groups that we need to consider. That is to see how interest group activity is sanctioned and regulated in the state. We also need to make a distinction between registered and non-registered groups. This distinction is particularly important in explaining the impacts of groups and lobbies on state politics.

CONSTITUTIONAL AND REGULATORY PROVISIONS: REGISTERED AND NON-REGISTERED GROUPS AND LOBBIES

Section 6 of Article I of the Alaska constitution states: "The right of the people peaceably to assemble, and to petition the government, shall never be abridged." Then in Section 12 of Article II, the constitution says: "The legislature shall regulate lobbying." Prior to 1977, this regulation simply took the form of each lobbyist registering his or her name and employer with the lieutenant governor's office. Before that date the law provided for no financial disclosure by lobbyists.

Then, in 1976, as part of a national trend in the post-Watergate period, Alaska extended its monitoring of lobbying activity. The responsibility for administering the new regulations was transferred to the Alaska Public Offices Commission (APOC), which already administered laws relating to campaign disclosure and conflict of interest.

The lobby law requires that both legislative and administrative lobbyists and their employees register with the commission if they seek to influence legislative or administrative action, spend more than four hours in a thirty-day period engaged in this activity, and receive any salary, reimbursement for expenses, or other compensation for lobbying. Registered lobbyists must file monthly reports disclosing their employers, specific subject areas they seek to influence, and, most important, their lobbying incomes and expenses. Employers are also required to file reports containing similar information. Fines and other civil and criminal penalties are imposed for noncompliance with regulations.[8]

The main thrust of the Alaska law is financial disclosure. It is an attempt to monitor lobbying activity rather than directly control it. It does not restrict, for example, the amount of money that lobbyists can spend on legislators and public officials, or prohibit lobbyists from contributing to political campaigns. Like any private citizen, a lobbyist can contribute up to $1,000 to any legislator's campaign. Nor does the Alaska lobby law place restrictions on lobbyists organizing fund-raisers for legislators.

Alaska's registration requirements do not cover many individuals and organizations that engage in lobbying. About 200 to 250 lobbyists, and about the same number of groups, have been required to register in recent years. There are, however, an estimated additional 250 to 300 groups, organizations, and agencies that unofficially lobby either the legislative or administrative branches of government, but are not required by law to register.

As we might expect in a state where so many people depend directly or indirectly on the state budget, many non-registered Alaska groups and lobbies are government representatives. State and local government officials, both elected and appointed, are specifically exempted by Alaska statute from registering as lobbyists.[9] But if a local government employs a person specifically to lobby, then that person must register with the APOC.

A second category of non-registered groups and lobbyists is the "citizen lobby," composed primarily of volunteers who lobby for _ad hoc_ or loosely organized groups like community associations. A third category is composed of individuals who lobby for pet or personal projects. Both of these kinds of lobbyists can be very influential in the personalized political environment of Alaska.

TYPES OF INTEREST GROUPS

There are a host of different interests represented by lobbyists in Juneau. Table 7.1 lists these groups by category. To get an accurate picture of the full range of interests operating in the capital we must, of course, add the variety of non-registered interests referred to above.

This wide diversity in group activity and representation is a very recent phenomenon in Alaska. Alaska's political style was far less pluralistic in the 1960s and early 1970s than it is today. Major economic, social, and

Table 7.1

Registered Interest Groups and Total Lobby Representation by Group Category, March 1983 (Ranked in Order of Number of Groups in Category)

Type of Group	Number in Category	Total Lobby Representation[1]	Approximate Percentage of Total: Group Representation	Lobby Representation
Trade associations	26	50	12.7%	13.1%
Professional groups, associations, and unions (excluding educational and fishermen's groups)	23	29	11.2	7.6
Educational groups (including student organizations and school districts)	17	41	8.3	10.7
Local governments (excluding school districts)[2]	17	31	8.3	8.1
Oil and gas companies	15	37	7.5	9.7
Native associations, corporations and councils	13	38	6.5	9.9
Banking, finance and insurance	13	32	6.5	8.4
Citizens' groups	12	17	6.0	4.5
Utilities and communications companies	10	17	5.0	4.5
Health groups	7	15	3.5	3.9
Commerce (excluding banking, finance and insurance	7	8	3.5	2.1
Airlines and transportation companies	5	5	2.5	1.30
Fishermen's groups	4	5	2.0	1.30
Lumber and pulp companies	3	8	1.5	2.1
Manufacturing (miscellaneous)	3	4	1.5	1.0
Mining companies	2	4	1.0	1.0
Environmental groups[3]	1	4	0.5	1.0
Agricultural groups	1	2	0.5	0.5
Arts groups[3]	1	1	0.5	0.25
Religious groups	1	1	0.5	0.25
Veterans groups	1	1	0.5	0.25
Miscellaneous and other groups	23	32	11.0	8.4
TOTAL	205	382	100.0%	100.0%

[1]Total lobby representation does not refer to the total number of individual lobbyists representing a category but to the total number of contracts or agreements between employers and lobbyists. Some lobbyists work for more than one employer. Thus, although there were 220 individuals registered as lobbyists in 1983, there were 382 separate lobby contracts or agreements.
[2]This figure includes three lobbyists for the Alaska Municipal League.
[3]This group is a coalition of groups in this interest area.

Source: Alphabetical listing of employers or clients of employers registered with the Alaska Public Offices Commission as of March 3, 1983.

demographic developments in Alaska since statehood have been reflected in a proliferation of interest group activity.

The federal government was the overshadowing force in Alaska at the beginning of the statehood period. The dominant political interests in the state were the salmon canners, the lumber and pulp companies, and the mining interests. Statehood helped break the power of these interests and also helped foster the development of new interest groups in Alaska as decisionmaking powers were transferred from Washington, D.C. to Juneau. Another important change that came with statehood was the emergence of local government as a political force, both as a consequence of the development of the local government system itself and of the rapid increase in population.

But by far the most significant forces for the proliferation of interest groups were the discovery of oil at Prudhoe Bay in 1968, the construction of the trans-Alaska pipeline, and the phenomenal increase in state revenues. Those developments led directly and indirectly to the emergence of Native political and economic power, the rise of labor interests (particularly the Teamsters Union), the burgeoning and success of environmental groups, and the mushrooming of state government.

Table 7.1 shows that the largest categories of registered groups are trade and professional associations and unions. These kinds of groups accounted for one in four registered lobbyists in Juneau in 1983. They include such organizations as the Alaska Air Carriers Association, the Alaska Cabaret, Hotel and Restaurant Association (CHAR), the Alaska Dental Society, the Alaska Public Employees Association, and Teamsters Local #959.

One in every six registered groups in the early 1980s was either an educational group or a local government unit (including school districts). Local governments have been one of the most rapidly expanding interests in Juneau in recent times. Numbers of lobbyists for Native groups, including the Alaska Federation of Natives (AFN) and Native regional corporations such as Sealaska and Cook Inlet Region Inc., have also increased sharply. There are also lobbyists for those groups typically associated with Alaska—oil and natural gas companies and lumber, pulp, and mining companies.

The rest are a miscellany of social service, health, public interest, and other groups. They include the Alaska Network on Domestic Violence and Sexual Assault, the Alaska Environmental Lobby, the Consortium for Alaska Municipal Training, and the Alaska Council of Seventh Day Adventists.

Table 7.2 shows that the dominant spending groups in recent years have been oil and gas companies. They accounted for one dollar in every four spent on lobbying during the 1979 and 1980 legislative sessions. In a distant second place were local governments. Prominent among these were the North Slope Borough and the City of Valdez, both of which enjoy large tax revenues from oil properties. The Alaska Municipal League, whose membership includes all major cities in the state, is also an important representative of local government. If any one trend could be discerned in recent times it was the increase in lobbying funds expended by local governments and school districts. Many hired lobbyists in the scramble to grab a greater share of the state's capital

Table 7.2

Top Ten Interest Group Spenders in the 11th Alaska Legislative Session, 1979-80

	1979			1980		
Group	Amount in $	Percentage of Total Lobby Expenditures	Rank	Amount in $	Percentage of Total Lobby Expenditures	Rank
Chevron USA	141,940	7.10	1	146,709	4.90	2
Alascom	141,002	7.00	2	150,000	5.00	1
Exxon	129,104	6.50	3	92,012	3.10	4
Pacific Alaska LNG Associates	109,779	5.50	4			
North Slope Borough	91,550	4.60	5	136,959	4.55	3
Northwest Alaska Pipeline[1]	90,490	4.50	6			
Alaska Oil & Gas Association	71,992	3.60	7			
Alaska Municipal League	69,113	3.50	8	84,827	2.80	5
Atlantic Richfield	68,938	3.45	9	59,177	2.00	9
Mobil Oil	66,166	3.30	10	74,473	2.50	8
City of Valdez				82,375	2.80	6
Sohio				78,752	2.60	7
Alaska Mutual Savings Bank				55,142	1.85	10
TOTAL	$980,074	49.05%		960,426	32.10	
	Total Lobby Spending for 1979: $2.1 mill.			Total Lobby Spending for 1980: $3.0 mill.		

[1]Northwest Alaska Pipeline was aided by a booster group, Alaskans for the Gas Pipeline, which spent $60,280 for lobbying.

Sources: APOC records for 1979 and 1980; *Anchorage Daily News*, April 3, 1980, January 31, 1981, and March 10, 1981.

budget. The third highest spender in 1979 and 1980 was the communications lobby, headed by Alascom, the state's long distance telephone and communication company. Alascom was the largest individual spender in the eleventh legislature.

Among non-registered groups, the major category is government and government agencies. The influence of the federal government has been gradually reduced over the past fifteen years, largely because of the degree of fiscal independence afforded the state by its oil revenue. Nevertheless, the federal presence remains substantial; about 60 percent of the state's land area is still controlled by Washington, and the federal government has in recent years provided about 10 percent of the state's revenue.[10]

Virtually all federal agencies have some dealings with Alaska, but several are particularly important: the military, the Forest Service, the Bureau of Indian Affairs, and the Bureau of Land Management. These agencies in general attempt to make effective presentations on issues to legislative and administrative personnel, but they keep a low profile. That low profile is evidenced by the fact that approximately 60 percent of legislators interviewed in 1984 and 1985 said they had never been contacted by any federal agency representatives.[11]

Probably the most active sector of government engaged in attempting to influence public policy in Alaska is the state government itself. Although most state employees are not allowed to lobby in their official capacities, the governor's office, the various departments, commissions, and other state agencies usually employ at least one person as a legislative liaison. Of these numerous agencies, six are particularly active: the Departments of Education, Transportation and Public Facilities, Fish and Game, Natural Resources, and Environmental Conservation, and the University of Alaska.

Local governments, in addition to hiring contract lobbyists, also lobby state government themselves. On any day in the legislature and in the various departments, there is likely to be a host of elected and appointed officials from Kake to Kotzebue, lobbying for funds for fire trucks, airport extensions, dock facilities, community centers, and more. Legislators, particularly those from small and rural communities, are well aware of the fact that operating and capital project funds from the legislature are a major source of income to most local governments in the state. This local government pressure is augmented by the work of contract lobbyists employed by organizations with similar goals—such as the state's Department of Community and Regional Affairs, the Alaska Municipal League, and the Alaska chapter of the National Education Association.

Another category of non-registered groups includes nonprofit, social service and public interest and some special interest groups. These include the state chapter of the National Organization for Women and other women's groups, community and neighborhood organizations, the Anchorage Social Services Coalition, the state Parent-Teacher Association, groups representing gifted and handicapped children, and alcoholism and drug prevention groups, among others. What these groups have in common is that they are largely staffed and run by unpaid volunteers. They form the core of Alaska's "citizen lobby." Because of abundant public revenues these groups were probably more successful in Alaska than in most other states in the early 1980s.

The "citizen lobby" shades into a final category of non-registered lobbyists we consider. In this category there are fewer groups than individuals—people who lobby for pet or personal projects. All state and political communities have an elite network of influential citizens. In Alaska, "the world's biggest little town," as one lobbyist has expressed it, and where politics is highly personalized, legislators are highly accessible to individual citizens.[12]

LOBBYISTS

Five types of lobbyists make up the Juneau lobbying community: contract lobbyists, in-house lobbyists, legislative liaisons, citizen lobbyists, and individuals. Since the latter two types were discussed in the last section, here we will concentrate on the first three.

Of the 220 lobbyists registered with APOC in March 1983, approximately one-third could be classified as contract lobbyists—those hired by clients on a contract basis specifically to lobby. This figure is somewhat misleading, however, because law firms that engage in contract lobbying may list several of their members, even though most of them do not usually lobby. Therefore, 30 to 35 contract lobbyists would be a more accurate figure. Tables 7.3 and 7.4 list the major lobbying firms and contract lobbyists in Juneau in recent years, and the fees received by the highest paid ones.

The largest category of registered lobbyists is in-house lobbyists. These are persons who are employed by or are members of organizations and engage in lobbying as part—often a major part—of their duties. This is a very broad category embracing the paid executive directors of organizations such as the Alaska Oil and Gas Association and the United Fishermen of Alaska, as well as representatives of the United Veterans of Alaska and the Anchorage Police Department Employees Association, whose lobbyists receive reimbursement for expenses only.

Because they are not officially lobbyists, and because they often have euphemistic or misleading job titles, it is more difficult to estimate the exact number of legislative liaisons working the halls of the legislature. Also, since most senior agency staff will deal with the legislature at some time, it is often difficult to determine who is and who is not technically a liaison. During recent sessions, there have perhaps been about 60 such liaisons, 90 percent representing state agencies and the rest various federal agencies.

While the specific functions of legislative liaisons vary from agency to agency, most monitor bills affecting their agencies, represent their agencies to the legislature and often to the governor's office, and prepare information requested by these bodies. Others are no more than messengers or conduits between their agencies and the legislature. Some are much more than spokespersons and have authority to make statements at committee hearings and to individual legislators. They may coordinate a client-group's lobbying effort in the legislature or administration.

What are the backgrounds of Juneau's lobbyists and legislative liaisons? A 1984 survey showed that almost all contract lobbyists had prior experience with the legislature or a state agency. Only 15 percent had been lobbyists for more than ten years. About 25 percent were attorneys, including Norman Gorsuch, who later became attorney general. About 50 percent had been either elected or appointed officials at the state level (including legislative aides). For example, Lew Dischner had been a commissioner of labor, and Wes Coyner and Kent Dawson had both been aides to governors. The remainder had a variety of occupational backgrounds, ranging from a former executive director of the United Fishermen of Alaska to a dental hygienist.

In-house lobbyists shared even fewer common background characteristics, except that about 50 percent had worked in the occupation they were representing. Most—75 percent—had little or no previous experience of lobbying before they took up their legislative roles. The majority of legislative liaisons had no previous legislative experience; most rose through the ranks of their agencies, most often from the professional staffs. Of all the members of the lobbying community surveyed in 1984, only five, or less than 3 percent, had lobbied outside Alaska.[13]

Contrary to popular public conception, Alaska legislators view lobbyists positively. Studies in other states suggest that other state legislators feel the same way about lobbyists. Legislators see lobbyists as major sources of information and technical assistance. This usefulness is enhanced by the fact that in Alaska, as in other states, there is a high turnover of elected officials. (Of the 60 members of the Fourteenth Alaska Legislature, a third had never served previously.) Former senate president Clem Tillion, for example, considers lobbyists very important sources of information, and former representative Russ Meekins sees them helping legislators avoid making mistakes.[14] As Mike Miller, a fourteen-year veteran of the house expresses it, "The legislative process would be hard-pressed to exist without them."[15]

Former lobbyist Norman Gorsuch reinforces that view by describing lobbying as "99 percent information and about 1 percent advocacy." Alaska lobbyists (and those in other states) believe that having rapport with legislators, knowing their subjects, being truthful, and not demanding too much are the keys to success.[16] Over 90 percent of legislators responding to a 1984 survey saw trustworthiness and honesty as the principal personal attributes of a successful lobbyist. To quote Representative Miller again: "If I find out that a lobbyist has lied to me, I cross him off my Christmas card list."

GROUP AND LOBBYING TACTICS

The purpose of lobbying is to influence public policy. To succeed in this task a group must gain access to those who make policy—legislators, members of the executive branch (including bureaucrats), and in some cases, the

Table 7.3
Lobbyist and/or Lobby Firms with Five or More Clients, March 1983
(Listed in Order of Number of Clients)

Lobbyist/Firm	Clients
Trust Consultants (9 clients)[1]	Alascom, Inc.
	Alaska International Industries
	Alaska Medical House, Inc.
	City of Valdez
	Enstar Corporation
	North Slope Borough
	Pt. MacKenzie Farmers Association
	Rainier Bancorporation
	Teamsters Local 959
Mitchell D. Gravo, Law Office of (9 clients)	Alaska Association of Realtors, Inc.
	Alaska Cable Television Association
	Alaska Optometric Association
	City of Homer
	City of Unalaska
	Consulting Engineers Council of Alaska
	Cook Inlet Region, Inc.
	Petroleum Equipment Suppliers Association
	Wheelabrator-Frye, Inc.
Sam Kito, Jr. (8 clients)	Alascom, Inc.
	Alaska Dental Society
	Alaska Federation of Natives
	Arctic Slope Regional Corporation
	City of Fort Yukon
	Cook Inlet Region, Inc.
	Multivision, Inc.
	Sealaska Corporation
Ely, Guess & Rudd (7 clients)	Alaska California LNG Company
	Alaska Independent Insurance Agents and Brokers
	Alaska Surplus Line Brokers Association
	Pacific Alaska LNG Company
	Shell Oil Company
	Totem Ocean Trailer Express
	Tesoro

(Continued)

[1]One of the two partners in this firm, Lewis Dischner, also represents Alaska Airlines on an independent basis.

Table 7.3 *(Continued)*

Lobbyist/Firm	Clients
David Gray (6 clients)	Ahtna Regional Corporation Alaska Arts Alliance City of Wrangell Mechanical Technology, Inc. Resource Development Council Tlingit/Haida Central Council, Inc.
Burr, Pease & Kurtz (5 clients)	Alaska Bank of Commerce Eklutna, Inc. Eklutna Utilities, Inc. Peninsula Savings & Loan Associations Toghotthele Corporation
Dawson and Associates (5 clients)	Alascom, Inc. Alaska Cable Television Association Association of Regional Aquaculture City of Seward Cominco Alaska, Inc.
W.L. Kubley (5 clients)[2]	Alaska Air Carriers Association Alaska Distributors Company Louisiana Pacific Corporation Odom Corporation Western Airlines Western Airlines
Smith & Gruening (5 clients)	Alaska Native Commission on Alcoholism and Drug Abuse (ANCADA) Alaska State Homebuilders Assoc. Alaska Visitors Association City of St. Paul Tanadqusix Corporation
Southeast Regional Resource Center (5 clients)	Chugach Schools Klawock City School District Pelican City School District Skagway City School District Wrangell City School District

[2]As a partner in Kubley Consultants, Kubley also represents: the City of Haines, City of Metlakatla, Ketchikan Gateway Borough, and Northern Oilfield Services.

Table 7.4
Lobbyists and/or Lobby Firms Earning Over $50,000 in 1979

Lobbyist and/or Firm	Major Employer(s)/Client(s)	Earnings in $	Approximate Percentage of Total Lobby Fees[1]
Eugene Wiles	Chevron USA	110,000	7.0
Trust Consultants Lewis Dischner Kim Hutchinson	Alaska Airlines Alascom North Slope Borough City of Valdez American Express	205,000	14.0
Ely, Guess & Rudd Norman Gorsuch Joseph McLean	Pacific LNG Associates	125,000	8.0
Wes Coyner	Alaska Bankers' Association Blue Cross-Blue Shield of Washington and Alaska	53,000	4.0
Emmitts L. Wilson	Alaska Hospital and Medical Center	52,750	4.0
C. Waco Shelley	Mobil Oil	51,432	4.0
	TOTALS	597,182	41.0

[1]Lobby fees refers to fees or salaries paid to lobbyists and excludes reimbursement for expenses. In 1979 the total of lobby fees was $1.44 million; an additional $0.7 million was expenses.

Sources: APOC Records for 1979; also, *Anchorage Times*, March 30, 1980; *Anchorage Daily News*, April 3, 1980 and July 29, 1980.

judiciary. The most crucial and difficult parts of lobbying are the tactics of gaining access to decisionmakers and then exerting influence over them.

There are many tactics available to groups, from aiding the election of candidates with money or workers, to writing letters and sending people to the legislature or government departments to lobby directly, to hiring lobbyists and filing amicus briefs with the courts. A large body of literature describes group tactics.[17] Rather than retrace that ground, here we briefly consider some tactics that represent trends or variations in tactics in Alaska.

Because political parties are relatively weak in Alaska, we might assume that there would be considerable group support of candidates at elections. In one indirect way this is the case: as in several other states, major contract lobbyists in Alaska often hold fund-raisers for candidates. We might also assume that political action committees (PACs) would abound. While PACs have certainly been on the increase over the past ten years, Alaska has not witnessed the explosion in numbers and in importance to campaign financing that PACs have evidenced in states like California, Idaho, and Washington. In part this limited growth of PACs in Alaska is due to the $1,000 limit on campaign contributions to candidates by any individual organization or group. The legislature imposed this limit in 1975 in an attempt to stop big oil companies and other large-scale contributors from dominating the state's politics. While PACs like those of the oil companies, the state Chamber of Commerce, and the United Fishermen of Alaska do exist, they are not major vehicles of group tactics.

One result of weak parties, however, is that groups rarely align themselves with one particular party. When an organization like the National Education Association makes campaign contributions, endorses candidates, or provides campaign workers, it does so on the basis of which candidates support its issues, whether they be Democrats, Republicans, or Libertarians. In a weak party state like Alaska, there is more flexibility to build coalitions of support among legislators the groups have helped elect.

One very effective tactic used by groups lobbying during the session is capitalizing on the personal nature of Alaska politics. Using group members to contact legislators in person is a common tactic, perhaps more common than in most states. Alaska legislators—and other public officials—are very accessible, as we noted earlier. Direct personal contact has proven especially successful for Native groups and communities because of the key positions held by Natives in the legislature. Our 1984 survey of legislators also suggested that letter-writing is an effective technique in Alaska.

One interesting trend in lobby tactics in recent years has been an increase in group coalitions and alliances. The various arts groups and environmental groups in the state have formed such alliances; there is also a coalition of women's groups. In February 1981 a coalition of "railbelt" communities—those close to the Alaska Railroad stretching from southcentral Alaska to Fairbanks—was formed to try to increase the railbelt's share of state funding.[18]

One final point about changes in the methods lobbyists are using to influence legislators and other public officials: in the past decade, a new breed of lobbyists who are strictly oriented toward technical and other information has emerged. Unlike the old-style lobbyists, who have generally been in the state for many years and have extensive networks of influential contacts, this new generation places much less emphasis on fund-raising, wining and dining, and personal friendships. Rather, they present extensive technical and other information and use networking and other modern techniques of lobby campaigning. This is not to say that the new breed is any more successful than the veterans, because often they are not. It is simply to say that the style and technique of Alaska lobbying and lobbyists is changing, just as it did in California in the 1960s and as it has in all states as they grow larger, diversify their economies, become more socially and politically complex, and expand the role of government.

In general, while most lobbying tactics used in other states are also used in Alaska, group tactics and campaigns in Alaska are not as sophisticated as in many other states. For example, networking, media and public relations campaigns, and PACs are less widely used. This situation is partly a result of the state's newness and consequent political underdevelopment and the personalized nature of politics.

INTEREST GROUP POWER AND EFFECTIVENESS

In the lingo of the legislature, we now consider which groups in Alaska have the most "juice"—the power to achieve their goals. It is not our purpose here, however, to attempt to rank the most powerful groups in the state. Rather it is to present some brief observations about group effectiveness as viewed by legislators, other public officials, and interest group officials and lobbyists. "Effectiveness" as used here refers to *perceptions* of group power among the various participants in the policymaking process.

Since the oil industry provides the lion's share of state revenues and accounts for over 25 percent of lobby spending, we might assume that big oil is the dominant interest in Alaska. Yet, in the estimation of many observers, the oil industry is not even in the top five most effective lobbies. One reason for this assessment is that there is no sizeable oil industry constituency in the state. Unlike the situation in Texas, Louisiana, and other oil-rich states, in Alaska almost all oil is pumped from state-owned land. Another reason is that the industry itself is often divided over specific issues. (There are 37 members of the Alaska Oil and Gas Association.) Also, according to one ex-representative, oil lobbyists often do not relate well to legislators, and, according to a current representative, they often do not visit those legislators opposed to their position.[19] Perhaps more important is that the public appears to have an ambivalent attitude toward the oil companies—an aspect of the general ambivalence that exists toward big business in the nation and particularly in Alaska. Moreover, oil representatives find it difficult to convince legislators that they are in need of money, or that an increase in taxes would deter them from further explorations. Consequently lawmakers can resist many of their pressure tactics, especially as legislators are very cognizant of the potential adverse political consequences of giving major concessions to the oil companies.

The Teamsters Union was a powerful political force in Alaska in the late 1960s and during the construction of the oil pipeline in the mid-1970s. Dogged by scandals and an expose of union operations in the late 1970s, and more important, by a sharp decline in membership after the pipeline was completed, the union's power has waned. Currently the Teamsters keep an extremely low profile in the state. While 10 of the 51 legislators who responded to our 1984 survey saw the oil industry as one of the top five most powerful lobbies, only two mentioned the Teamsters.

What registered groups have been perceived as effective in Alaska in recent times, and what are the reasons for their success? We can single out three such groups: The National Education Association (NEA-Alaska); the Alaska Municipal League (AML); and the Alaska Public Employees Association (APEA). According to the executive director of the NEA, Bob Manners, that organization has been successful in obtaining funding for education in the state on a per capita basis, funding of special education, teacher bargaining, and an excellent retirement system. This success is attributable to high membership (about 80 percent of those eligible); to the fact that there are members in virtually every community in the state; to an excellent organization involving networking and endorsing of candidates; and to the fact that many legislators are or have been directly involved with education. According to several legislators, the association's two major lobbyists use this last factor skillfully.[20]

The AML has been seen as a very effective group primarily because of its widely distributed membership and skillfully executed lobbying by its former executive director. Also, many legislators have been local officials themselves and they see the political advantage of supporting local governments. AML's close cooperation with government agencies, particularly the Department of Community and Regional Affairs, has also helped. These factors have aided the league in helping to achieve reforms in state laws relating to local governments, among other successes.[21]

APEA represents the majority of the 17,000 state employees. Its major efforts have been directed toward increasing pay and benefits of its members, and it has been particularly successful. Even after adjustments for the higher costs of living, Alaska state workers are the highest paid in the nation.

By consensus of those surveyed, these three organizations are among the five most effective registered lobby groups in Alaska. Others receiving mention were various Native groups, environmentalists, agricultural interests, fishermen, and the state Chamber of Commerce.

Agriculture is an interesting case because it is only a token part of the state's economy. Nevertheless, those promoting agriculture have secured some very large appropriations to subsidize farm operations. Farmers are not without "juice" in Alaska. This can be explained in part by the fact that they have some powerfully placed advocates in the legislature and the executive branch and have employed some effective lobbyists. Other reasons are that agriculture is very much part of the ethos of a frontier state, and many politicians see it as one way to diversify the economy. To quote one representative, "Even as an urban legislator it's hard to be against agriculture in a state like Alaska."[22]

The environmentalists present another interesting case. In the ever-present conflict between those who want to develop the state and exploit its resources to a much greater extent, and those who wish to limit development, the "greenies" (as their opponents have dubbed them) have scored some successes. In part their success is due to grass-roots support from the sizeable number of people who moved to Alaska because they see it as the last frontier and want to keep it that way. It is also a consequence of the creation in 1981 of the environmental lobby, a coalition of environmental groups established to pool resources, build a more effective organization, and present a united front to the legislature. But most of the environmentalists' successes—such as passage of the Alaska lands act[23]—have been achieved primarily at the federal rather than at the state level. One reason for this is that the federal government has had primary jurisdiction over lands and resources of interest to this lobby.

The effectiveness of individual state agencies as lobbyists is more difficult to assess, but we can make several observations. First, some state agencies have functions that bring them into conflict with the functions of other agencies. These conflicts tend to diffuse their power. A case in point is a three-way—often intense—conflict between the Department of Fish and Game, the state's habitat protector, the Department of Environmental Conservation, attempting to ensure a safe environment, and the Department of Natural Resources, the trustee, guardian and landlord of the state's natural resources. Agencies not involved in such conflicts will tend to be more effective lobbyists. Larger budgets also help increase agency client-group support. This is true of the Departments of Education and Transportation and the University of Alaska. Because of their broad-based constituency, the ethos of education, and the fact that capital projects for educational facilities mean jobs in many areas of the state, the education lobbies are potentially the most powerful lobbyists in Alaska.

Major power in the state lies with those groups that depend directly on or represent government. Perhaps the two most significant, though not necessarily the dominant, forces are the education lobby and the local government lobby. Other significant lobbies are public employees, Native groups, and environmentalists.

In conclusion, who then are Alaska's most effective lobbyists? The answer is not simple; there are no lobbyists who can deliver on all issues at all times. The answer to this question depends on the type of issue, the nature and current status of the group being represented, and the current political climate.

A COMPARATIVE PERSPECTIVE

In this section we concentrate on comparisons between the Alaska interest group system and those of other states, and try to place Alaska in perspective. Several scholars have developed theories that help explain the relationship of groups to the political, social, and economic lives of states. Here we briefly explore to what extent comparisons derived from these theories do or do not apply to Alaska—and where they don't, we try to explain why. Finally, since Alaska is a western state, we can see how it fits in or contrasts with recent developments in interest group trends in that region.

Political scientist Harmon Zeigler has identified business groups as the most prevalent interest attempting to influence state governments nationwide. That is also the case in Alaska. He also argues that in states where interest groups are strong, active groups are generally dominated by business, and that legislators perceive business interests as strong.[24] As we have shown, business interests have not been dominant in Alaska in recent years.

Zeigler also contends that pluralism is not a factor in the overall strength of groups in strong-lobby states, and that such states tend to have small bureaucracies.[25] Once again, neither of these generalizations fits the contemporary situation in Alaska. The state is, in fact, quite pluralistic, and a 1982 survey found that Alaska had more state employees per 10,000 inhabitants than any other state.[26] Zeigler also argues that the more professional the bureaucracy and the legislature (particularly in terms of adequate staff and research services) the less powerful interest groups will tend to be.[27] This certainly does not seem to be true in Alaska, where the legislature and the bureaucracy are adequately staffed and interest groups are still strong. Other factors give lobbyists power—particularly access to state officials but also contributions to campaigns and the potential power of groups lobbyists represent. These factors may enable lobbyists to maintain considerable influence even in the face of professionalized legislatures and administrative agencies.

Certainly, the type and activity of Alaska's groups reflect the general political economy of the state. Their strength can be partly explained by weak parties and by the political infancy of the state. Yet strong interest groups are usually associated with low per capita income and low urbanization. Not so in Alaska. True, strong interest groups have also historically been associated with low levels of industrialization and low party cohesiveness in the legislature, but even here Alaska does not fit the traditional pattern. In Alaska lack of industrialization does not mean reliance on agriculture, low urbanization, and low per capita income, as it usually does in other states. Neither is lack of party cohesiveness associated with lack of party competition in Alaska, as is the case in many other states.[28] (See elections chapter.)

Both Zeigler and fellow political scientist Sarah Morehouse argue that in strong interest group states the number of professionals in the workforce tends to be low, income distribution tends to be relatively uneven, and there are relatively few urban and suburban areas of population.[29] Alaska fits this observation only insofar as it has few urban and suburban areas. And even so, almost seventy percent of the state's population lives in the handful of urban areas. Morehouse also contends that strong interest group states are often dominated by one interest.[30] While this may have been true in Alaska in the past, it is no longer the case.

Overall, interest group activity in Alaska is somewhat aberrant compared with activity in the other forty-nine states, particularly with respect to factors that help explain the strength of interest groups in other states. But according to a recent study of interest groups in just the western states, groups in Alaska tend to fit the pattern of that region.[31]

Like Alaska, all other western states have undergone tremendous expansions in economic, social, and, consequently, political pluralism since World War II, and particularly since the 1960s. These changes have resulted in the rise of some interest groups and the decline of others. Another common experience among the western states has been the continued presence of the federal government as the dominant landowner. In the late 1970s dissatisfaction with the federal government's land ownership role led to the so-called "Sagebrush Rebellion." No development has had more influence on interest group activity in the western states over the past twenty-five years than has the increased role of government at all levels.

Government is now the major employer in most of the thirteen western states. So what we have seen in Alaska—the rise of groups related to or directly dependent on government—has been a trend throughout the West in recent years. Most notable are the rise of the education lobby in most states (and especially of public teachers' unions), the growth in membership and political power of public employee unions, and the increase in significance of local governments and local government organizations. There is also the tremendous expansion of state government and its myriad agencies as a lobbying force. A secondary development has been the expansion in the number of business, minority, and public interest groups that have gotten involved in the political process. Environmental groups have risen in influence in almost all western states. We have seen parallel developments in Alaska.

So in recent years a considerable transformation has taken place in the types of group activity and the configuration of group power in the West. Overall, business groups, agricultural interests (with the exception of corporate agriculture), and traditional labor groups have tended to lose power to the new governmental and other interests. Perhaps the most significant aspect of these power realignments resulting from expanded pluralism is that there is no longer a dominant interest in any western state. The Anaconda Company no longer dominates Montana politics, nor does the sugar industry dominate Hawaii, the Union Pacific Railroad has been eclipsed in Wyoming, and the canners have very little influence in Alaska today.

Developments in lobbying and group tactics in Alaska also parallel those in the western region. This is particularly true of the trend toward more technically-oriented lobbyists and the decline of the so-called "super lobbyists" of the old wining and dining school. Probably the most significant development in lobbying, however, has been the tremendous increase in the number of elected and appointed officials who attempt to influence public policy in the thirteen western states. These "hidden lobbyists" (so called because most states do not require government officials to register as lobbyists) have an increasing influence, especially in western states.

In general, while all thirteen western states require some form of lobby registration, the thrust of the laws is to provide public information about who is lobbying and how much they spend, rather than to attempt to restrict lobbying activity. Moreover, there is a trend toward simplifying these laws. Hawaii did so in 1980 and the Alaska Legislature in 1985 reviewed the Alaska Public Offices Commission's regulations on lobbying.

There are some ways in which Alaska is less part of the mainstream of lobbying activity in the West. While important, political action committees have not developed in Alaska to the extent that they have in the rest of the region. Coalition-building between groups is less common in Alaska, as is the use of the initiative and the referendum as vehicles to achieve group goals—although these practices are sometimes used. Unlike most states—Idaho being one other exception—Alaska has seen little increase in the number of groups and lobbyists registered in the last five years. Perhaps the two major differences between Alaska and the other western states are the power that Native groups wield in Alaska and the tremendous revenues that oil has provided in recent years. We discussed the consequences of both these factors earlier in this chapter.

We should now be able to answer the question posed in the introduction: How different are interest group politics in Alaska? The short answer is that they are quite different from patterns in the nation as a whole, but quite similar to patterns in the western states.

Many of Alaska's political aberrations can be explained by local circumstances. These, as we have seen throughout this chapter, are intense regionalism and the personalized nature of Alaska politics, but primarily the state's recent oil bonanza. Mainly as a result of phenomenal oil revenues in the early 1980s, almost all groups that sought funding, even the less sophisticated ones, were successful. Moreover, interest groups in Alaska have probably been more successful in obtaining funding than groups in any other state.

CONCLUSION:
INTEREST GROUPS AND THE ALASKA POLITICAL SYSTEM

What does interest group activity mean for the way the Alaska political and governmental system works, and what kinds of interest group activity can we expect in Alaska in the future?

In the most general sense, interest group activity has certain advantages and disadvantages in Alaska as it does in any other state. On the positive side, groups act as vehicles of representation for their members between elections. This is the so-called aggregation and articulation function that is of immense value to legislators and other government officials. Also, the more groups that participate in the policy process, the less chance of any one interest dominating. This was James Madison's basic argument, in The Federalist Number 10, for preventing tyranny or control by a few interests.

On the negative side, not all people are represented by groups. As Zeigler points out, middle and upper-middle class people tend to join groups much more than do working class people.[32] So there is a distortion in representation by groups. Perhaps a more important factor is that, as Morehouse points out, interest groups are by definition narrowly focused; they are special interests which represent a small—often very small—segment of society and do not speak for or represent the whole society.[33]

In most Western democracies and in several of the American states, political parties act as mediators of various group demands. Parties can promote national or state interests much more than any other organizations because they aggregate more interests and factions.[34] But this only happens when political parties are strong and where interest groups are subordinated to them. In states like Alaska, where parties are weak, groups dominate—and groups represent only fragments of society. Such states lack the overall coordinating influence normally provided by political parties. Hence it is difficult both to develop overall state plans of action and to hold any one group ultimately responsible for government actions.

The dominance of a political system by interest groups can have detrimental consequences in both the long and the short term. As in Alaska in recent years, it can lead to an uncontrolled scramble for influence and funds, a lack of coordination of planning and prioritization of needs, and a fragmentation of political power. These effects were less of a problem in the years of high revenues—but what will happen as revenues drop sharply, as they have begun to do in the late 1980s?

Together with a continued increase in pluralism, declining revenues will probably have the most influence on the type and nature of future group activity in the state. Competition between groups is likely to intensify, which in turn will force many groups to improve their organizations and explore new tactics, particularly forming coalitions with other groups. And, ironically, as a result of declining revenues more groups will likely enter the political arena. As with the recent experience in most other western states, those groups not normally politically active join the political fray to protect their interests. Groups are going to have to deal more with the bureaucracy as the complexity of government increases in Alaska, professionalism in the bureaucracy itself increases, and more public policy decisions are made by bureaucrats. Government and government-related groups are likely to maintain or even enhance their influence.

Whether or not interest groups constitute a third house of the legislature in Alaska, as has been suggested by one observer, is a debatable point.[35] But if there were a heaven or a Shangrila for lobbyists and interest group leaders, that place would surely be a lot like Alaska has been in recent times.

ENDNOTES

[1]This assertion is supported by Sarah McCally Morehouse, *State Politics, Parties and Policy*, (New York: Holt, Rinehart and Winston, 1981), p. 108. She places Alaska in the category of states where interest groups are strong.

[2]David B. Truman, *The Governmental Process* (New York: Knopf, 1971), p. 33.

[3]For some definitions and distinctions between these terms see Henry W. Ehrmann, "Interest Groups," *International Encyclopedia of the Social Sciences*, VII, (1954), p. 486.

[4]L. Harmon Zeigler, "Interest Groups in the States," in Virginia Gray, Herbert Jacob and Kenneth N. Vines ed. *Politics in the American States: A Comparative Analysis*, 4th ed. (Boston: Little, Brown and Company, 1983), pp. 111-117.

[5]Zeigler, "Interest Groups in the States," pp. 115-117.

[6]Interview with Dennis L. DeWitt, president, Alaska State Hospital Association, (since re-named Health Association of Alaska), November 29, 1984.

[7]*Alaska Economic Trends*, vol. 3, issue 2. (Juneau: Alaska Department of Labor, February 1983), p. 9; and *Alaska Planning Information* (Juneau: Alaska Department

of Labor, January 1983), pp. 16-17. This figure excludes military personnel but includes all educational personnel.

[8]Much of the information concerning the role, operation and functioning of the APOC was obtained in interviews held between January 18 and March 10, 1983 with APOC staff—in particular Theda Pittman, the executive director.

[9]Over the years there have been many attempts to require public officials of all types to register if they engage in lobbying. In fact, there was a bill before the legislature in 1983 that would have required just that. The bill was killed, but according to APOC staff, if passed, such a law would be very difficult to administer and enforce in Alaska.

[10]See, *Revenue Sources FY 1984-1987*, Quarterly Update, September 1984. (Juneau: Alaska Department of Revenue), p. 8.

[11]This figure is taken from a survey of legislators conducted by the author during 1984 and 1985. It was part of an extensive study on interest group activity and lobbying in Alaska, which included surveying or interviewing almost two hundred elected and appointed officials, lobbyists and members of the press corps. Much of the information in this and the following sections is drawn from that survey.

[12]Interview with Dennis L. DeWitt.

[13]It is interesting to note that lobbyists in Alaska have their own organization, Pioneer Alaska Lobbyists' Society (PALS), which serves both professional and social functions.

[14]*Anchorage Times*, March 30, 1980. This quote and others are from this informal, but extensive, investigative article on lobbyists and lobbying in Alaska.

[15]Interview with Representative Mike Miller, March 20, 1984.

[16]*Anchorage Times*, March 30, 1980.

[17]A good overview of the various tactics available to groups and lobbyists is provided in, Ronald J. Hrebenar and Ruth K. Scott, *Interest Group Politics in America* (Englewood Cliffs, N.J.: Prentice Hall, Inc., 1982), chapters 4 and 5.

[18]*Anchorage Times*, February 8, 1981; and the *Anchorage Daily News*, February 7 and March 7, 1981.

[19]Interview with Representative Jim Duncan, November 6, 1984.

[20]Interview with Bob Manners, February 28, 1983.

[21]Interview with Ginny Chitwood, February 7, 1984.

[22]Interview with Representative Jim Duncan.

[23]The Alaska National Interest Lands Conservation Act (ANILCA) of 1980, among other things, designated almost 100 million acres of Alaska—27 percent of the state— as additions to parks and other conservation units.

[24]Zeigler, "Interest Groups in the States," p. 99.

[25]Ibid., p. 122.

[26]U.S. Bureau of the Census, Employment Division, (October 1982).

[27]Zeigler, "Interest Groups in the States," p. 11.

[28]L. Harmon Zeigler and Hendrik van Dalen, "Interest Groups in State Politics," in Herbert Jacob and Kenneth N. Vines, *Politics in the American States: A Comparative Analysis*, 3rd ed. (Boston: Little, Brown & Co., 1976), p. 94; and Zeigler "Interest Groups in the States," pp. 111-115.

[29]Zeigler, "Interest Groups in the States," pp. 111-113; and Morehouse, *State Politics*, p. 112.

[30]Morehouse, *State Politics*, p. 112.

[31]The information on this comparison between Alaska and the western states is taken primarily from the concluding chapter in, Ronald J. Hrebenar and Clive S. Thomas, ed., *Interest Group Politics in the Western States* (Salt Lake City: University of Utah Press, 1986). This book contains chapters on the politics and interest group activity of the thirteen western states.

[32]Also, when working-class groups do organize, these organizations do not last as long; see Zeigler, "Interest Groups in the States," p. 98.

[33]Morehouse, *State Politics*, p. 101.

[34]Ibid., p. 95.

[35]Interview with Charles Sewell, *Anchorage Times*, March 30, 1980.

8

Public Opinion and Political Attitudes in Alaska

Richard L. Ender

Alaska's relatively short political history reveals examples of the impacts of public opinion on policy, of the mobilization of public attitudes in the name of causes, and of significant changes in public opinion with demographic shifts in Alaska's population. Public opinion in Alaska and the role political attitudes have played in the state's development are the focus of this chapter.

Public opinion is an integral part of politics today, and a key link between the governors and those governed. But defining "public opinion" is an elusive task, because it can be measured and assessed in many different ways. In this chapter, we define public opinion as an expressed attitude about public policy shared by a group of individuals. Attitudes may be held by the general public, a majority, an interest group, the people of a region, or the members of an organization. Opinions can be latent—unmeasured or undetected—and have little effect on policy, or they can be active and directive, with significant effects on public policy. Opinions can demonstrate divisions in the political arena, thereby reflecting conflict. They can trigger substantial institutional action or reform or act as political norms for behavior. Those holding power can court public opinion or ignore it. How opinions toward public objects are formed, persist, and change has been studied extensively.[1]

Because of the prevalence in recent times of polls and surveys "taking the pulse" of the country, we tend to view interest in public opinion as a purely contemporary phenomenon. Reading of history suggests that leaders have always wondered about and listened to the opinions of their constituents. The torchlight political rallies of nineteenth century America and election of Andrew Jackson as the "people's president" are examples of public opinion and its mobilization. Aristotle's writings in *Politics* were the earliest acknowledgement that the collectivity had advantages over "the quality of the few best." He noted that the opinions of the group offered greater chance for success than those of the powerful individual.

Democratic institutions like our American ones rely on the citizen for their existence. Policymakers and others will always try to measure, guess, or assume the public's feelings about some issue or action. For example, even as the Alaska Senate began its historic 1985 proceedings to determine if Governor Sheffield would be impeached, Senator Bill Ray of Juneau said that the state legislature would lose on the issue no matter what it did—that there would be a significant public opinion backlash, no matter what the outcome of the proceedings.[2]

One major difficulty in studying public opinion is defining how attitudes influence public policy. Three models reviewed by analysts Jerry Yeric and John Todd suggest ways the relationship between public opinion and public policy can be explained. The majority rule model "is based on the idea that public officials should enact policies that reflect the wishes of the majority of the citizens."[3] While this model is seldom believed to work in practice, it provides a useful starting point. An applied example of this model may be the unwillingness in 1986 of most Alaska officials to directly attack the popular Permanent Fund dividend program, which makes direct cash distributions to Alaskans, even though the state's petroleum revenues are declining. A second model, the consistency model, is based on the notion that opinion and policy move in parallel directions, never far from each other, though unlikely to be perfectly congruent. This model leaves more room for minority and interest group influence on public policy and assumes stability of patterns. Finally, the "satisfying" model attempts to explain apparently incongruent policy and opinion. That model assumes initial policy is a reaction to public demand, but that public interest wanes once institutions have responded. A satisfied public doesn't voice as much active support for a policy that it initially demanded.[4]

MEASURING OPINIONS AND ATTITUDES

Successfully capturing public attitudes requires blending science and art. The use of the opinion poll has become so common that we easily forget it is a relatively recent technique. A 1969 *Anchorage Times* editorial talked about the emergence of polling and the importance public officials have historically attached to public opinion:

Measuring and therefore using public opinion in the political process has become an ever dominant feature of Alaskan politics. Candidates, interest groups, agencies, and academics spend ever increasing resources attempting to find out "how the public feels." The business of scientifically measuring attitudes is a relatively new phenomenon in Alaska, but the politician keeping his or her "ear to the ground" is nothing new. Politicians are strong consumers of media information as an indicator of the public's mind. In addition, they listen to constituents, lobbyists, and others in a constant form of informal interviewing.[5]

American fascination with the public opinion poll tends to hide the fact that this technique is only one way of measuring and defining attitudes. While polling provides a quantitative and relatively acceptable way to measure opinions, the citizen forms views and expresses them in any number of ways, including joining organizations, petitioning officials, attending public meetings, or simply discussing issues with friends. Despite these other ways Americans express their opinions, the sample survey remains the most important method of understanding people's opinions.

There are two major types of public opinion polls: straw polls and scientific polls. Straw polls are informal polls in which a relatively small number of persons not necessarily representative of the broader public are asked their opinions about some issue. Persons interviewed for straw polls could be those who happen to be in some particular place (coming out of a grocery store, for instance) at the same time the interviewer is, or those who happen to respond to a mail-out questionnaire that most recipients ignore.

Scientific polls, on the other hand, specifically try to choose a sample of persons with a mix of characteristics that is representative of characteristics in a broader population. Various methods are used to try to capture a representative sample of public opinion; for example, a pollster who wanted to find out how many voters in a city agreed with the mayor's policies might try to choose a sample in such a way that all voters had an equal chance of being selected.

While some scientific opinion polls were conducted in Alaska in the 1960s (notably Governor Keith Miller's commission of surveys dealing with how the state should use its $900 million from the sale of Prudhoe Bay leases), they were not used with any frequency until the mid-1970s. Even then, those surveys that were carried out varied substantially in quality and scientific accuracy. In fact, the efforts in Alaska in the 1970s were similar to the development of national scientific polling in the 1930s and 1940s by such men as Elmo Roper and George Gallup. Methodologies were still being developed and sampling techniques were highly variable. The construction of the trans-Alaska pipeline in the mid-1970s provided the financial base and institutional interest to increase public opinion polling, particularly polls assessing the social and economic effects on Alaska communities of pipeline construction. In addition, political polling, begun as a means for some firms to garner publicity, emerged as a strategic campaign element for candidates from statewide to district races.

Straw polls are quick ways of testing public opinion, but users must be aware of their limitations. In 1966, for example, the *Anchorage Times* used a straw poll as the basis of an article subtitled, "Random Polling Speaks Well for Incumbent." In the text the reader discovers that the article about the re-election chances of the incumbent governor is based on a dozen man-on-the-street interviews and described as "newsworthy if not necessarily scientifically accurate."[6] Other examples of informal straw polls are those undertaken by politicians and interest groups who send out newsletters asking interested constituents their feelings on some particular topic. The quality of such efforts ranges from blatantly biased to honest soundings of voter opinion. The state government has also undertaken informal polls. In 1976, for instance, 1,100 Alaskans responded to a state-distributed questionnaire on land management. But in press reports about the survey, one had to read closely to find that about 200,000 copies of the survey had been distributed. No effort was made to point out that the results were based on the opinions of a small and likely unusual group of Alaskans.[7]

Use of scientific opinion polls is widespread in Alaska in the 1980s, but Alaska conditions pose some special problems. The heterogeneity of Alaska's urban and rural populations not only creates wide differences in attitudes, but also difficulties in sampling and measurement. Language barriers, the lack of telephones in many rural communities (in 1986 some villages still had only one telephone), high field costs, and inadequate and out-of-date population figures are only some of the problems associated with survey research in Alaska. The mobile and changing character of Alaska's population also produces problems in study control and accuracy. One 1975 study, using a panel technique (which involves interviewing the same group of people at different times), found that eleven percent of the 599-member panel had moved during a 45-day period.[8] Another study made six months after the 1980 census found that up to 40 percent of the population in some blocks in Anchorage had not lived in the same places at the time of the census.[9]

The opinion survey technique used most often in Alaska is the telephone survey. High coverage in large and small towns makes telephone contacts feasible. But poor sampling frames and failure of interviewers to call back persons who were not at home bias many surveys using this approach. Proper telephone surveys use a random digit dialing of a fixed proportion of each included prefix, calculated on the proportion of residential ties each prefix represents in the population. Numbers selected are called back several times to keep response rates at about 85 percent. Rural prefixes are weighted in relation to the proportion of total households they cover. In villages where there is just one phone, the single phone is used to summon randomly selected residents. Successful use of the telephone requires cooperation by local telephone companies statewide, which is not always easy to get, or extensive preliminary analysis of population data, which varies in its accuracy. In some cases, statewide samples are actually nothing more than telephone samples of the three largest communities (Anchorage, Fairbanks, and Juneau), which limits interpretive use of the results.

Because of high costs, researchers use face-to-face surveys in Alaska only for long, complex questionnaires or when visual presentation of material is critical. Recent examples of face-to-face surveys include the resource development and impact surveys conducted by the Anchorage Urban Observatory and Institute of Social and Economic Research, both parts of the University of Alaska. Statewide data bases, such as the 10-year federal censuses, quickly become out-of-date, which makes accurate sampling difficult for face-to-face residential surveys.

The mail survey is seldom used in Alaska. Low response rates make this approach unworkable for general population surveys. However, mail-out surveys to specialized populations with high stakes in responding are feasible. Examples of such surveys include the Alaska Judicial Council's periodic surveys of Alaska attorneys about selection and retention of judges, and the survey of military personnel after the 1980 census for legislative redistricting. Successful use of the mail survey requires greater attention to format, clarity, and ease of use for respondents.

Whatever approach is used, it is difficult for the average citizen to evaluate scientific polls. Press reports often leave out key methodological information, and reporters lack the training to assess the credibility of the survey effort. For example, in 1979 the *Anchorage Daily News* reported on an Alaska Public Forum poll that showed the forum's televised public hearing show was widely accepted. The report was based on a sample of 80 households, of which a few over 40 actually watched the show and responded to the questions. The survey failed to ask those not watching for their views on the value of the forum's show. Also, the potential survey error, even if the sampling frame had been correct, exceeded 15 percent. None of these points were alluded to in the newspaper article.[10] In a 1982 article, the *News* reported that 80.4 percent of a statewide sample believed "Alaska should celebrate its 25th anniversary of statehood." While that response could mean anything, the poll sponsors used it to suggest that there was overwhelming support for their proposed exposition. Again the reporter did not question the methods or conclusions.[11]

Poll results are more often questioned or not reported because of controversial findings than because of methodological weaknesses, which are more common. For example, a 1977 poll suggesting that the public was concerned about the political power of the Alaska Teamsters Union was either not reported, or equal coverage was provided to a union vice-president who said that several citizens he had interviewed at union headquarters were not worried about the Teamsters' political power.[12]

Of course, the media has recognized the problem of manipulation of survey results. For example, the *Anchorage Times* in the 1980s has said that it will refuse to publish stories about election-related polls unless pollsters divulge all findings and methodology.[13] However, candidates routinely withhold some results and strategic information, while news outlets, including the *Times*, continue to report political polls.

Polls not only measure opinion but can play a role in creating opinion. Surveys are conducted largely because public interest has already defined certain questions as worth asking. When a public policy is talked about and debated, it is apt to become the subject of an opinion poll. The press has always played a significant role in defining what issues are important and, some analysts suggest, in defining how to think about issues.[14] (See discussion of this point in the chapter on Alaska's press.) But when poll results are presented in extensive articles and analyses, the results themselves become parties in and can influence the ongoing debate. Interest groups sometimes attempt to take the measurement of opinion one step further by taking polls on topics that are not yet of wide interest and using the results to make them items worthy of discussion and media coverage.

And pollsters themselves have become a focus of reporting in recent years. This is particularly true in the area of political polling. Headlines such as "Dialing for Dollars: Polling Becomes Big Business,"[15] "Polls Brought Attention to Randolph Campaign,"[16] and "Pollsters' Fight Seen As Sideshow to Race,"[17] are indicative of the growing interest in the role of pollsters in public policy in Alaska.

PERSPECTIVES IN THE DISCUSSION OF PUBLIC OPINION

The next sections discuss public opinion in Alaska as it relates to traditional survey categories, such as political culture, specific policy issues, and political attitudes. These topics give us insight about differences and similarities in the Alaska polity. Differences include regionalism and socioeconomic and demographic divisions. Though Alaska is a relatively small and young community, its sheer size and wide environmental differences serve to differentiate and define attitudes. Regionalism in Alaska can take many forms— competition between regions, urban versus rural areas, Anchorage versus the rest of Alaska, and others. This regionalism is reinforced to some degree by lifestyle, income, and racial differences within Alaska. Residents of rural regions are more likely to be Native, poor, and dependent on subsistence resources than are urban residents. These differences in economic status, race, and lifestyle can also divide individual communities and regions.

Another factor affecting public opinion in Alaska is length of residence: newcomers versus oldtimers. The rapid increase in Alaska's population since 1970 also changed its demographic character and influenced the dominant values of residents.

CULTURAL VALUES AND LIFESTYLES

As discussed in the chapter on political culture, the heterogeneity of Alaska's population would appear to make it unlikely that common social values would exist. Despite that heterogeneity, there exists a widely discussed but rarely measured "Alaskan" value system. Individualism, living close to nature, and following an easygoing, unhurried lifestyle are the kinds of attributes included in that value system.

While little systematic data exist on this subject, a 1975 study did look at these values in Anchorage, Alaska's largest urban area. A majority of Anchorage residents surveyed said that opportunities to hunt, fish, and camp were important to them, and also that they wanted to live close to nature and follow unhurried lives. That attitudinal profile sounds closer to that of a rural community than that of the business and financial center of the state. So the powerful mystique of the Alaskan culture affects most of its citizens, at least attitudinally. Interestingly, the survey found these Alaskan values to be just as prevalent among new residents as among oldtimers, and throughout all socioeconomic levels.[18]

But holding a particular set of values and acting them out are not necessarily the same. The survey also found that while many Anchorage residents felt these values were important, only a small percentage believed Anchorage actually offered opportunities for unhurried lifestyles and other "Alaskan" values.[19]

A 1976 survey in Fairbanks brought similar results. When 400 residents were asked their reasons for coming to Fairbanks, 50 percent cited "a chance to be independent, to start something new" and 46 percent thought that "being close to a wilderness environment" was important. But only 20 percent came "to live a pioneer's life, be self-reliant." What seems to differentiate urban and rural residents in their opinions about Alaskan values is the level and intensity of expectations. Urban residents are more likely to value "opportunities" to encounter Alaska's wilderness, while rural residents often follow daily lifestyles that incorporate natural forces. Most urban residents want to participate in wilderness activities that are less rigorous than the subsistence activities of rural villagers.[20]

The survey findings in Anchorage and Fairbanks contrast sharply with those of a 1980 village survey in the Yukon-Kuskokwim area, where traditional Alaskan values were not only widely held, but also available and practiced.[21] The relatively greater importance of traditional Alaskan values to rural residents was also indicated in a 1982 study of opinions of rural and urban residents about an offshore petroleum lease sale. Native and rural speakers stressed cultural, social, and biological issues that highlighted their concern about the possible effects of petroleum development on traditional lifestyles and subsistence activities. In contrast, urban residents discussed the economic benefits of development and the scientific implications of possible biological and environmental damage.[22]

A 1985 survey found approximately 48 percent of all Alaska households had participated in hunting and 76 percent in fishing activity at least once that year. Hunting ranged from a low of 38.8 percent among Anchorage residents to a high of 58 percent among residents in the Mat-Su, north to the Fairbanks area. Differences in proportions of Alaskans who fished were even smaller. Regional differences are more obvious when we look at levels and methods of participation. Rural and Alaska Native diets include more of the products of hunting and fishing than do those of other residents. While the average Anchorage household fished 12.6 times and hunted four times that year, rural residents fished 22.8 times and hunted 6.9 times.

Overall, while the interpretation and acting out of "Alaskan" values vary substantially in urban and rural areas, there is agreement that those values exist and are important. But studies of both urban and rural populations suggest that ability of Alaskans to actually follow the "Alaskan" lifestyle is increasingly tied to income. The high costs of travel and equipment for both urban and rural residents make traditional subsistence activities and sport fishing and hunting more readily available to those with higher incomes. This finding tends to contradict a popular conception that those who follow the "Alaskan" lifestyle have lower incomes.[23]

MODERN AMENITIES

Notwithstanding their widespread adherence to "Alaskan" cultural values, Alaskans also want improved public services and other modern amenities. Between 1975 and 1980 a number of surveys in urban railbelt communities (the railbelt extends from Seward on the Kenai Peninsula to Fairbanks in the interior) asked questions on the kinds of services and amenities respondents wanted. The results showed strong demand for and general interest in such standard "quality of life" indicators as financial security, good schools, health care, public safety, good roads, recreational opportunities, and adequate retail outlets.[24] Residents expected efficient delivery of utility services, adequate fire protection, and most of the services Americans enjoy. When state oil revenues peaked in the early 1980s, Alaskans showed their interest in recreational and other amenities by approving construction of stadiums, hockey rinks, and numerous other projects throughout the state.

And the desire for modern conveniences is not restricted to white city residents. Recent surveys in rural Alaska have consistently recorded demand for reliable air transportation, better airports, improved satellite television, more telephones, improved utilities, police and fire protection, more playgrounds and community centers, and upgraded village roads and road maintenance.[25] These desires differ from those of urban residents only insomuch as the existing infrastructure in rural areas is much less developed. Otherwise, expressed needs for services and conveniences are remarkably similar.

That Alaskans hold seemingly conflicting values about traditional "Alaskan" and "modern" lifestyles is not surprising. People always prefer to have the best of both worlds, if possible. Most urban residents superimposed "Alaskan" values on existing expectations about services found in most communities in the United States. As new schools, television, utilities, and other services were extended to rural Alaska, expectations of rural Alaskans increased. The question for Alaska's political culture is the appropriate balance between these two value systems.

BALANCING TRADITIONAL AND MODERN

How urban and rural interests in pursuing traditional and modern lifestyles can be accommodated is becoming a more important political issue as resources diminish relative to the growing population. Urban hunters and fishermen in the 1980s have fought with rural subsistence users in the legislature and in the courts over access and relative share of fish and game. The 1982 gubernatorial election swung heavily on specific issues, one of which was the ballot item on subsistence. Urban interests proposed an initiative that would have abolished existing subsistence use preference for rural Alaskans. Polls suggest that the vote was influenced significantly by the candidates' respective stands on that and other issues.[26] (Alaskans voted to leave the rural subsistence preference intact.)

But perhaps the most significant thing pollsters have found about urban-rural differences over resource use is that the differences are not as sharp as one would guess. A late 1985 study of this issue suggested that a substantial percentage of Alaskans acknowledged a need for a rural subsistence priority. In a statewide sample of 555 residents, 80 percent said subsistence hunting and fishing is important to the economies of rural communities and 57 percent favored giving rural residents priority over urban residents in taking fish and game for personal consumption. This finding held also in just urban areas: the majority of respondents in Anchorage and the Kenai Peninsula and a plurality of those in the Mat-Su and Fairbanks areas supported subsistence priority for rural Alaskans.[27]

One reason for the debate over access to fish and game is that a large share of Alaskans believe that the quality of hunting and fishing in the state has declined in recent times. In the same 1985 survey cited above, 44 percent of respondents said the quality of hunting and fishing was getting worse, and overwhelming majorities in both urban and rural areas supported bag limits and said dependence on fish and game should be a criterion in determining allowable take.

There are a number of related issues that involve public demand for both protection of "Alaskan" values and provision for "modern" lifestyles. Those demands have been politically effective. Rapid growth in state population in the 1970s and early 1980s and the changing demographic character of Alaska, concurrent with growing petroleum wealth, made "catch up" a common phrase. Policymakers began the process of replicating services found in more mature areas of the country. At the same time, there was a strong public sentiment for protecting subsistence lifestyles and providing access for urban residents to enjoy "Alaskan" experiences.

The balance between those idealizing the "Alaskan" lifestyle and those actively living it has changed in recent years. The proportion of actual subsistence practitioners has been declining with the urbanization of the state's population and the influx of new residents who are more used to suburban living than subsistence hunting and fishing. As this trend continues, the long-term impact on public policy is likely to be a lessening of the political clout of things "Alaskan." However, the persistent strength of opinions about the importance of these values, even among urban Alaskans who never practice them, suggests that their political importance will continue for the foreseeable future.

OPINIONS ON PUBLIC POLICY ISSUES

Public opinion on issues important to Alaskans is often sharply divided, reflecting the conflicting agendas of state residents. A 1977 survey in Alaska's three largest communities illustrates that point. When asked about important issues facing the state, 28 percent of the respondents mentioned unemployment and the need to create more jobs, but 11 percent were concerned over rapid and uncontrolled growth. While 18 percent criticized the influx of new people, another 23 percent were concerned because the economy was slowing down or called for faster economic development.[28]

Issues commanding public attention in Alaska change with changing economic conditions and other factors. Public concern over rapid growth reached its high point in the mid-1970s during construction of the trans-Alaska pipeline, when Alaska's population swelled by thousands almost overnight. It was one of the issues raised most often in two 1977 surveys that asked residents of Alaska's three largest urban areas what issues they were most concerned about.[29] Two years later, in the wake of the economic slowdown and population decline that followed completion of the pipeline, less than one percent of respondents surveyed in Anchorage and Fairbanks were concerned about too much growth. Concerns about the economic slowdown dominated the answers of a Fairbanks sample, while those concerns shared top priority with road and public safety concerns in Anchorage.[30]

By late 1983, Anchorage residents asked to name the single most important issue facing the state cited state spending more often than any other issue; that survey was taken at a time when high oil revenues had resulted in massive state spending. Other issues respondents most frequently cited were the need for economic expansion and more employment.[31]

ISSUES OF GROWTH, DEVELOPMENT AND THE ECONOMY

Growth and development issues generate the most debate and contradiction in Alaska. At the risk of oversimplifying the issue, we can observe that Alaskans are likely to oppose growth in the size of their own communities and the increases in population that accompany development. In contrast, they tend to favor general economic development, and are even more supportive of many specific development options.

In a 1978 statewide survey respondents were asked to rate their interest in development on a seven-point scale, with 1 being no development and 7 being extensive development. The result was a mean score of 4.6, with about twice as many respondents on the pro-development side of the scale as on the anti-development end. Anchorage (4.9 mean) and Fairbanks (4.7 mean) residents favored more development than did residents of southeast and rural Alaska (4.1 mean).[32] Support for development, while strong throughout the state, varies in intensity and focus from region to region. Urban-railbelt residents are more supportive of development, particularly of resource development, than are rural Alaskans. In addition, each region has its own agenda based on its location and development options. Interest in fisheries is less intense among Fairbanks residents than among Kenai residents, while agricultural development is more important to Mat-Su residents than to Bethel residents.

In a 1977 statewide survey, 38 percent of respondents felt that the state was moving at about the right pace in developing Alaska's resources and one-third thought the state was proceeding too slowly. Only 18 percent thought the state was moving too fast.[33] A large statewide poll in 1982 found that 55 percent of respondents favored tax incentives to attract industry to Alaska.[34]

Attitudes about growth and development are in part specific to the history of the time. The mid-1970s was a period of unprecedented growth that strained services but brought prosperity to many. Alaskans at that time were worried about too much growth, as is illustrated by an anecdote from a survey on closed entry in the state's commercial fisheries (that is, restricting numbers of fishermen entering the commercial fisheries) in the mid-1970s. When asked how they felt about "closed entry," a significant number of respondents supported closed entry because they thought it meant closing Alaska's borders to further immigration. The decline in economic activity in the late 1970s and again in the mid-1980s lessened the public's concern on this issue. Also, at any given historical period Alaskans have been divided between those calling for more economic growth and those opposed to it. What makes each period different is the differing proportions of Alaskans favoring and opposing development.

In summary, Alaskans, particularly those in cities and towns, strongly support economic development as a matter of political philosophy. That general support has not changed substantially in the last two decades. What has emerged is a debate over specific proposals and over the appropriate extent of state involvement in development projects.

OIL AND GAS DEVELOPMENT

Since the Prudhoe Bay lease sale in 1969, oil and gas has been the most debated and fought-over development option in Alaska. This high public interest is largely due to petroleum's fiscal importance to the state government and the potential and historical impact of petroleum development on local communities.

A 1979 poll found public support for further oil development.[35] In 1980, 83 percent of respondents in a survey of five Alaska cities said oil and gas development had been good for Alaska.[36] In 1982, 67 percent of respondents in a statewide poll favored more oil exploration. However, there were differences by region. While 74 percent of Anchorage respondents favored further exploration, only 51 percent of rural residents agreed.[37]

One reason for the broad support for petroleum development is that residents see the oil industry as very important to Alaska. In a 1985 statewide survey, Alaskans were asked to rank five major resources in order of importance to Alaska's economy. About 66 percent rated oil and gas as the most important and only 17 percent mentioned fishing. A majority of respondents from every region of the state, except rural areas, saw petroleum as Alaska's most important resource. Rural Alaskans placed fisheries first and oil second.[38]

Another major reason for support of petroleum development is that most residents believe Alaska generally is better off because of that development. A statewide survey in 1977 found that 80 percent of respondents believed Alaska was better off for oil development.[39] Experience with oil and gas development also influences Alaskans' support. A 1977 study of five communities on the Kenai Peninsula suggested that a community such as Kenai, where petroleum development, processing, and transport are long-time economic activities, had a fairly realistic view of the changes (including negative ones) oil and gas development bring to a community and still strongly supported it. In contrast, Homer, a fishing and recreation community with little experience with petroleum activities, opposed development.[40] Homer residents may have felt that the possible economic benefits of petroleum development did not outweigh the potential negative effects.

Alaskans do not accept all oil industry activity without criticism, however. Surveys have found, for example, that large proportions of Alaskans believe the oil companies wasted money while building the trans-Alaska pipeline and that the companies were not sincere about wanting to solve the energy shortage. But despite those criticisms, more than 60 percent of the respondents in a 1985 survey had a positive view of oil companies in the state. And even the most controversial form of oil and gas exploration—on the outer continental shelf—receives majority support. In a 1984 survey 68 percent of respondents statewide opposed a moratorium on oil and gas exploration in offshore areas of the United States. But 41 percent of rural respondents said they would like to see all offshore exploration stopped. Residents of the coastal areas of western and northern Alaska generally oppose offshore development because of its potential effects on fisheries and other subsistence resources.[41]

Still another reason why Alaskans support oil and gas development is that they often don't anticipate direct negative impacts from such development. When they do expect direct negative effects and have little experience with the industry, their opposition can increase. How perceived direct effects can influence attitudes is illustrated by the results of a 1982 study of how residents of the Mat-Su Borough felt about proposed development of a petrochemical plant. When Dow Chemical was considering sites for a potential petrochemical facility, the Mat-Su Borough assessed community opinion on this issue. While 73 percent of the respondents felt petrochemical development was important to Alaska's future, only 63 percent saw it as important to the future of the borough. Also, Mat-Su residents ranked petrochemical development well below other development priorities, such as agriculture, hydroelectric projects, and tourism. When asked if they would like a petrochemical facility located in the borough or in some other Alaska location, the respondents were divided, with 48 percent supporting a local site and 46 percent wanting some other location.[42] These study results indicate that while Alaskans may support a development in general, they do not necessarily want that development in their backyards. (In this case, Dow Chemical decided construction of a petrochemical facility in Alaska was not economically feasible.)

Though specific petroleum-related projects have engendered controversy, Alaskans have generally supported most oil and gas proposals. For example, in a 1978 survey, 72 percent of respondents statewide favored establishment of a petrochemical industry to process Alaska's royalty share of Prudhoe Bay oil, and 28 percent opposed it. With changing economics and other factors, a 1982 survey found a smaller proportion of respondents (55 percent) for developing a petrochemical industry in Alaska.[43]

In another example, 67 percent of respondents in a 1985 statewide survey said they would be more likely to support a political candidate who favored construction of an all-Alaska gas pipeline.[44] Legislators, particularly those from the railbelt, got the same message in straw polls and constituent soundings.

One proposed explanation for these positive attitudes toward petroleum-development projects, at least in urban areas and along the railbelt, is the substantial public relations effort made by the Alaska Oil and Gas Association and individual companies. Since those efforts reinforce already existing positive attitudes toward the industry and are matched with apparent economic imperatives, the oil industry has been generally successful in maintaining favorable public opinion. However, rural Alaskans still tend to oppose oil development—particularly offshore development—and some specific proposals have not found favor with Alaskans.

OTHER DEVELOPMENT OPTIONS

Options for development in Alaska are many and vary by region and community. In theory, Alaskans support a wide range of resource and other economic development alternatives. In practice, the majority would rather have "clean" development in their own communities but still be able to enjoy the benefits of all forms of development elsewhere in the state. In a 1978 statewide poll, 61 percent of the respondents supported energy-intensive industries, and over 70 percent favored timber, fisheries, tourism, and agricultural development.[45]

Regional development priorities vary. In a 1977 survey Kenai Peninsula residents placed commercial fishing and processing first.[46] Mat-Su Borough residents surveyed in 1982 placed agriculture first.[47] Anchorage residents in a 1977 survey favored most industrial options, but showed highest interest in the service, trade, and transportation industries that provide the community's economic strength.[48] In a 1984 survey in the Upper Kuskokwim area, residents voiced highest support for small-scale mining, agriculture, timber, and fur tanning as local development options. However, priorities even varied from village to village, depending on local economic activities. Also, villages with largely Native populations showed an interest in subsistence and renewable resources, while communities with mixed Native and non-Native populations had a greater interest in mining.[49]

One major development option that has received substantial public scrutiny in the 1980s is the proposed Susitna hydroelectric project. By 1986, the State of Alaska had spent $135 million studying the project's feasibility and had provided for substantial public input about the project. Proponents and opponents of the project have attempted to use and influence public opinion in the battle over funding. Political polls taken by office-seekers in southcentral Alaska in the early 1980s showed consistent support for the project.[50] Anchorage residents were asked in a 1983 survey to select one of five power projects in which to invest future dollars. A plurality (40 percent) selected "major hydro-electric development" first and another 23 percent said it was their second choice.[51] Even with the economics of the project in question and reduced state revenues, a majority of southcentral Alaska residents surveyed in 1985 strongly supported the Susitna project, while residents of Fairbanks, southeast, and rural Alaska were evenly divided over it.[52] In mid-1986, Governor Sheffield announced that because of falling oil revenues, all feasibility studies and other work on the proposed dam would be halted.

In summary, Alaskans' support for development is largely related to the perceived possibility for success, the mix of the existing economy, and the fear of development-induced change.

THE PUBLIC'S VIEW OF PUBLIC INSTITUTIONS

By and large, Alaskans have been at best skeptical and more often hostile toward public institutions. The old adage that says Americans' esteem for politicians is just below that for used car salesmen seems especially applicable in the 49th state. There are, however, differences in public attitudes about different levels of government. A 1983 survey asked Anchorage residents to rate how well federal, state, and local governments delivered services. About 66 percent rated service delivery by the municipality as good or very good, but only 48 percent thought state government was doing a good job delivering services. About 36 percent said federal service delivery was good.[53]

The performance of the state legislature is a particularly tempting target for Alaskans (as is also discussed in the chapter on the Alaska Legislature). In a 1977 statewide poll, 16 percent of the respondents said legislators were doing an excellent or good job, 42 percent said they were doing just fair and 26 percent said they were doing poorly.[54] A 1983 study found 10 percent of a statewide sample rated leadership in the House of Representatives as very good or good, while 43 percent saw it as poor or very poor. By comparison, 20 percent of the respondents saw the state senate leaders as doing a good job while 32 percent said they were doing poorly.[55]

Alaska's governors have also had their problems with public images in recent years. Governor Jay Hammond's performance in office was rated excellent or good by 39 percent of the respondents in a 1977 survey, but 35 percent said he was doing just a fair job and 22 percent called his performance poor.[56] Governor Bill Sheffield's performance ratings began declining after he took office in 1982. In a 1983 survey in Anchorage, 30 percent of the respondents rated Sheffield's performance positively, while 35 percent rated it negatively.[57] By late 1985, after the state senate had held hearings on whether Sheffield should be impeached for his role in a controversial lease for state offices in Fairbanks, a statewide poll found 23 percent of respondents felt Sheffield was doing a good job, while more than 47 percent said his performance had been poor.[58] In the same poll, three-quarters of the respondents said it was time to give a new governor a chance to do a better job.

But even though Alaska governors have not always had good public images that has not meant they were not re-elected. Hammond, for instance, was re-elected to a second term. This phenomenon has also held for individual legislators who are regularly sent back to Juneau, despite the low ratings accorded the state house and senate in general. Federal officeholders from Alaska also tend to receive high personal ratings and perform well in elections, despite the low public esteem for the federal government's service delivery. In 1983 and 1986 surveys, Senators Ted Stevens and Frank Murkowski and Representative Don Young all received strongly positive ratings.[59]

The third branch of government, the judiciary, has also had its public image problems. A 1977 Criminal Justice Planning Agency survey of Alaskans found only 27 percent who rated their general impressions of the court system as positive; the other 73 percent had largely negative impressions.[60]

The critical attitude Alaskans have toward government appears to have its underpinnings in the generalized values of individualism and self-reliance in both American culture as a whole and Alaska's unique blend of it. It may also be due to the love-hate relationship Alaskans have with government and their dependence on it despite their professed "go-it-alone" attitude.

A further explanation of the low esteem of Alaskans for state institutions is the state's handling of oil wealth. Alaska has a long history of government as the prime economic player in the state. First the federal and now state government is seen as the provider of not only essential and traditional services but also of economic growth and stability. The oil wealth of recent years greatly increased state government activity. It also generated conflicting public demands—for more state spending and for more state saving for the future, when oil revenues would decline. The public debate over the best use of oil money has raged since the first Prudhoe Bay lease sale in 1969, and it was stepped up with rapid growth of oil revenues in the early 1980s.

A 1977 survey reported that only 28 percent of those responding felt the state would find an acceptable way to use oil wealth for the benefit of all Alaskans. The majority of the respondents (54 percent) who thought the state would fail to make the most beneficial use of oil wealth said the state would squander the money, or that poor state leadership would mean poor money management, or that the money would go to special interests.[61] Polls taken as oil revenues grew showed that citizens generally favored investing the oil wealth, using it to create permanent funds, or generally treating it as capital.[62] But at the same time the state faced sharply increasing demands for services, amenities, and capital improvements. In the late 1970s, with the rising tide of oil income, the state tried to accommodate demands for both saving and spending.

A Permanent Fund to act as a savings account for a portion of state oil revenues was established in 1976, and public support for maintaining that savings account has consistently been high. State senate leadership began the 1986 legislative session by calling for protection of the Permanent Fund. One senator remarked that a sample of the opinions of 1,000 of her constituents who strongly supported maintaining the fund had convinced her to follow that policy.[63]

This public support for saving some oil wealth conflicts with the public's support for a vast subsidy system that has been built on oil revenues. In the early 1980s the public supported the legislature's repeal of the state income tax and the use of oil revenues for a myriad of capital projects, infrastructure investments, local government relief, service programs, loan programs, and direct subsidies. But three out of four respondents in a 1979 survey favored spending cuts and 80 percent said that they would not be willing to pay more taxes even if more government services were provided.[64] Such conflicting public attitudes created a confusing atmosphere for policymakers. Requests for spending for specific purposes have by and large outweighed the general public opinion that favors reduction in state spending and greater emphasis on saving for the future.

One interesting aspect of the saving-spending controversy involves the Permanent Fund dividend program; this program was established in 1982 and makes annual direct cash payments to Alaskans from the earnings of the Permanent Fund. Until the program was established, there was little indication of majority support for the concept. A poll in 1977 asked respondents if a portion of the fund earnings should be returned to the people and taxes raised if more state revenues were needed. Only 37 percent of the respondents supported that alternative.[65] A 1979 poll found only 27 percent of respondents statewide in favor of the distribution of cash dividends from interest money.[66] After several years of receiving dividend payments, Alaskans widely support the program and it is politically difficult to attack, even in the face of declining state revenues.

Another question that has frequently been raised in recent years is the extent to which the oil industry should be taxed to maintain or increase state revenue. The industry has made substantial investments in Alaska attempting to persuade citizens that it is a good neighbor and that they should not "kill the goose that lays the golden eggs" by raising taxes to a level that would make further development uneconomic. The success of this approach has changed over time. For example, nearly half the Alaskans questioned in a 1977 survey favored legislative action that raised the severance tax on oil and gas.[67] By 1979, only 19 percent of residents surveyed in Alaska's five largest communities wanted oil taxes raised.[68]

In the mid-1980s, calls for increased taxation on the oil industry by political and interest groups have not received strong legislative support. This lack of support has generally been attributed to the effectiveness of the oil industry's efforts. The issue at least appears to be stalemated. When a number of Alaska residents were asked in 1985 if they would be more likely to vote for candidates who supported higher oil taxes, the outcome was split. While 39 percent of the respondents said they would be more likely to vote for such candidates, 38 percent said they would be less likely.[69] In another 1985 survey respondents were asked how they would like the state to deal with declining oil revenues. The most popular response (34 percent) was reducing the operating budget. Only 18 percent preferred increasing oil industry taxes. A related point is that Alaskans in recent times have consistently rated oil companies more positively than they rated other private entities, political parties, and interest groups.[70] Sharply declining oil prices in 1986 probably also reduced support for increased petroleum taxes.

Overall, Alaskans have been critical of the way state officials handled recent oil wealth—but the citizens themselves have given policymakers very mixed signals about managing the oil wealth. The state's attempts to accommodate demands for both spending and saving have met little public approval.

THE UNDERPINNINGS OF POLICY: POLITICAL BELIEFS

The direction and content of public policy in Alaska is related to the political beliefs of its citizens. Alaskans do not fit well into easily defined categories and seem to thrive on a sense of political independence. Yet despite these attributes, the political ideologies of Alaskans do not look unusually different from national trends. Four 1985 statewide polls asked Alaskans to rate their political ideologies: between 43 and 47 percent of those answering labeled themselves moderate, 22 to 24 percent liberal, and 29 to 34 percent conservative.[71]

National polls show similar patterns, though in recent years the proportions who consider themselves conservative have been somewhat higher.[72] While historical evidence is not easily comparable, it would appear that the proportion of self-identified moderates in Alaska has increased in recent years, at the expense of either liberals or conservatives, particularly the latter. Nationally, the trend has been a decrease of moderates and a shift to conservatives.

There are some differences in the distribution of conservatives, liberals, and moderates in Alaska regions. Several surveys in 1985 found the highest proportion of conservatives (approximately 40 percent) in the railbelt area. Southeast and rural areas had the lowest proportions of conservatives (about 28 and 25 percent respectively). Those describing themselves as liberals ranged from 19 percent in the Mat-Su Borough and rural areas north to Fairbanks to 24 percent in southeast. While the proportion of liberals seemed quite stable among respondents in various surveys, moderate and conservative preferences shifted up to ten percentage points, suggesting a blurring of the lines between these two designations.[73]

Defining political party identification in Alaska is difficult. The open primary system and a political culture stressing independence mean that the majority of Alaskans refer to themselves as independents. The remainder are almost evenly divided between Republicans (24 percent) and Democrats (23 percent), with the balance Libertarian (3 percent). Democrats hold an advantage in southeast and rural Alaska, while Republicans hold the edge on the Kenai Peninsula and in the cities of Anchorage and Fairbanks.[74] Party preferences have changed over time in Alaska. Immigration and national politics have reduced the historical strength of the Democratic party in Alaska while increasing the strength of the Republican party and of those referring to themselves as independents.

The term independent, however, does tend to hide the real party divisions within the state. Independents may in fact identify with a party or lean toward one, depending on what questions they are asked. A 1977 Anchorage survey examined that point and found that 55 percent of those referring to themselves as independents did favor one of the two major parties.[75] This finding is consistent with national studies and suggests that the proportion of unaffiliated voters in Alaska is closer to one-quarter than to one-half the total. Party affiliation is related strongly to interest in politics. About one-third of the population could be characterized as very interested in political campaigns, and one-fifth not interested. Those who identify themselves with parties are more interested in political activity and participate more than do those describing themselves as independents. Party and political ideology are still strong predictors of voting behavior. However, Alaska's electoral framework, in conjunction with the general blurring of party lines, makes party a less important guide in determining political support or opposition than was true historically. The 1982 election highlights that point. Polls showed that the capital move and subsistence issues influenced voters more than did party affiliation.[76] (The chapter on elections discusses party identification, election results, and other issues in more detail.)

SUMMARY

With improved communications, the role of public opinion in society has become more obvious and recognized. Whether it is through the individual entreaties of citizens to legislators, the act of voting, or the publication of opinion polls, the role of the citizen in the policymaking process is important to the American democratic system.

Powered in recent years by oil revenues, Alaska's state government has grown and its ability to respond to citizens in a clear manner has diminished. That does not mean that public opinion has played no part in the policy arena. In fact, its role has been sharpened. Much of the expanded state program development in the 1970s and 1980s was a response to public demand. A major problem for government in the 1980s has been the conflicting signals received from its citizens. On the one hand, the public has called for cutbacks in spending and elimination of waste, but on the other has supported maintenance and even expansion of programs and projects well beyond the long-term fiscal capacity of state government. Declining revenues in the mid-1980s have exacerbated these problems and brought increased policy debates over state priorities, with various interest groups and other parts of the public influencing the debate.

Declining revenues have also aggravated natural differences of opinion in Alaska. Bush and urban interests have clashed over such issues as state spending for education, which urban legislators have suggested favors rural districts. Other differences—including differences related to race, length of residence, and socioeconomic status—have become more apparent. State revenues are no longer adequate to permit papering over differences in outlooks, lifestyles, and philosophies of Alaskans.

As policymakers come to grips with the need to set priorities on spending, the mobilization and manipulation of public opinion in Alaska has become more obvious. Whether it is the Anchorage Organizing Committee using a poll to indicate public support for Anchorage as a site for the winter Olympics or the oil and gas industry advertising about the need for rational tax and development policies, citizens find themselves in the middle of major efforts to influence their opinions and attract their interest. Several 1986 gubernatorial candidates began large-scale advertising as early as January 1986, in an attempt to win votes for a primary eight months away.

These examples provide just a glimpse of many efforts to sway, probe, or change the opinions of Alaska's citizens. Those efforts alone are testament to the importance of the citizen in the policy process. However, we should recall that opinions are rarely unanimous or sufficiently specific for direct policy application. Also, opinions are formed outside the complex policymaking process and often conflict with a myriad of interests, demands, precedents, and personalities that can constrain actions that may seem to be supported by the majority.

ENDNOTES

[1]Examples include: Martin Fishbein, ed., _Attitude Theory and Measurement_, (New York: John Wiley & Sons, 1967); M. Brewster Smith, Jerome S. Bruner and Robert W. White, _Opinions and Personality_, (New York: John Wiley & Sons, 1955); Anthony Downs, _An Economic Theory of Democracy_, (New York: Harper & Row, 1957); and Bernard C. Hennessy, _Public Opinion_, 3rd edition, (North Scituate, MA: Duxbury Press, 1975).

[2]KBYR radio interview with Senator Bill Ray, July 16, 1985.

[3]Jerry L. Yeric and John R. Todd, *Public Opinion: The Visible Politics*, (Itasca, IL: F.E. Peacock Publishers, Inc., 1983), pp. 13-14.

[4]Ibid.

[5]*Anchorage Times*, "How Will Scientists Find the Answer?" Editorial, February 10, 1969, p. 4.

[6]*Anchorage Times*, "Public Picks Egan to Win Governorship," by Josef Holbert, July 11, 1966, p. 1.

[7]*Anchorage Times*, "1,100 Reply to Survey," March 24, 1976.

[8]Richard L. Ender, *Citizens' Attitudes Towards Anchorage Local Government and Issues of Public Policy: A Collection of Reports*, University of Alaska, Anchorage, Anchorage Urban Observatory, 1976.

[9]Richard L. Ender, report for the Municipality of Anchorage, September 1980.

[10]*Anchorage Daily News*, "Forum Directors Claim High Public Acceptance," by George Bryson, October 25, 1979.

[11]*Anchorage Daily News*, "Alaskans Favor Statehood Celebration, Poll Results Show," by George Bryson, February 18, 1982.

[12]James Brelsford, "Anchorage Voter Attitudes Toward the Teamsters Union," Anchorage, Alaska: Alaska Public Interest Research Group, June 1977.

[13]*Anchorage Times*, "Poll Shows Candidates Nearly Tied," by Ellis E. Conklin, September 9, 1981, p. A1.

[14]Peter B. Clark, "The Opinion Machine: Intellectuals, the Mass Media and American Government," *The Mass Media and Modern Democracy*, Harry M. Clor, ed., (Chicago: Rand McNally College Publishing Co., 1974).

[15]*Anchorage Daily News*, "Dialing For Dollars, Polling Becomes Big Business," August 8, 1982.

[16]*Anchorage Daily News*, "Polls Brought Attention to Randolph Campaign," November 1, 1982, p. B1.

[17]*Anchorage Daily News*, "Pollsters' Fight Seen as Sideshow to Race," September 11, 1981, p. A1.

[18]Richard L. Ender, "Local Government Attitudes In A Highly Mobile and Transient Urban Setting," University of Alaska, Anchorage, 1976.

[19]Ender, *Citizens' Attitudes Towards Anchorage Local Government*.

[20]Jack Kruse, *Research Note: Fairbanks Community Survey*, University of Alaska, Institute of Social and Economic Research, December 1976.

[21]Richard L. Ender, *Economic and Social Information for Coastal Zone Planning In the Coastal Resource Service Area, Western Alaska*, prepared for Nunam Kitlutsisti for the Alaska Coastal Management Program, June 1981.

[22]Richard L. Ender and John Choon K. Kim, "The Effects of Social Impact Assessment Through Public Involvement on Outer Continental Shelf (OCS) Oil and Gas Development Policy: A Comparative Study Between Alaska and California," University of Alaska, Anchorage, paper presented at the American Society for Public Administration National Conference, Honolulu, Hawaii, March 21-25, 1982.

[23]Hellenthal and Associates, Inc., "Alaska Public Opinion Research Survey," Anchorage, Alaska, December 1985, discusses how the level of hunting and fishing varies among Alaska regions, and Richard L. Ender, et al., *Bering Norton Petroleum Development Scenarios*, prepared for the Bureau of Land Management, OCS Socioeconomic Studies Program, June 1980, reports on the relation of income to the "Alaskan" lifestyle.

[24]Ender, *Citizens' Attitudes Towards Anchorage Local Government*; Kruse, *Fairbanks Community Survey*; Diddy R. Hitchins, et al., *A Profile of Five Kenai Peninsula Towns*, University of Alaska, Bureau of Management and Urban Affairs and the Anchorage Urban Observatory, 1977; Richard L. Ender, *Matanuska-Susitna Housing and Economic Development Study: Survey Findings*, prepared for the Alaska Department of Community and Regional Affairs, May 1980.

[25]State of Alaska, *Western Arctic Area Transportation Study, 1980.*

[26]This assessment is based on a series of political polls conducted by Hellenthal and Associates, Inc., between 1980 and 1985.

[27]Hellenthal and Associates, "Alaska Public Opinion Research Survey," December 1985.

[28]Rowan Group Report, *Alaskans Talk About Oil Taxes and Government*, prepared for Arco, Sohio, Exxon, and BP-Alaska, October 1977.

[29]Ibid.; and Richard L. Ender, *The Opinions of the Anchorage Citizen on Local Public Policy Issues*, University of Alaska, Anchorage, Anchorage Urban Observatory, December 1977.

[30]Richard L. Ender, "Federal Communications Commission Survey," unpublished, December 1979.

[31]Hellenthal and Associates, "Anchorage Marketing Research Survey," Anchorage, Alaska, November 1983.

[32]Dittman Research, 1977/1978, jas reported in *The Economic Development Program for the Matanuska-Susitna Borough*, Volume II, July 1980.

[33]Rowan Group, *Alaskans Talk About Oil.*

[34]Marc Hellenthal and Richard L. Ender, "Statewide Political Attitudes Study," unpublished, Anchorage, Alaska, July 1982.

[35]*Anchorage Times*, "New Dittman Poll Indicates More Development Is Wanted," prepared for the Alaska Oil and Gas Association, April 25, 1979.

[36]*Anchorage Times*, "Poll by Dittman Research of 541 Alaskans," April 22, 1980.

[37]Hellenthal and Ender, "Statewide Political Attitudes Study."

[38]Hellenthal and Associates, "Alaska Public Opinion Research Survey," Anchorage, Alaska, September 1985.

[39]Rowan Group, *Alaskans Talk About Oil.*

[40]Hitchins, et al., *A Profile of Five Kenai Peninsula Towns.*

[41]Sources for this paragraph are: Rowan Group, *Alaskans Talk About Oil; Anchorage Times,* April 22, 1980; Hellenthal and Associates, "Alaska Public Opinion Research Survey," December 1985 and July 1984.

[42]Richard L. Ender and Donald Lyon, "Citizens' Attitudes Toward Petrochemical Development In the Matanuska-Susitna Borough," prepared for the Mat-Su Borough Assembly, January 1982.

[43]Hellenthal and Ender, "Statewide Political Attitudes Study."

[44]Hellenthal and Associates, "Alaska Public Opinion Research Survey," Anchorage, Alaska, April 1985.

[45]Dittman Research, *Economic Development Program.*

[46]Diddy R. Hitchins, et al., *A Profile of Five Kenai Peninsula Towns.*

[47]Ender and Lyon, "Citizens' Attitudes Toward Petrochemical Development."

[48]Ender, *Opinions of the Anchorage Citizen.*

[49]Richard L. Ender, *Survey Results of the Upper Kuskokwim Regional Strategy Project,* prepared for the City of McGrath, May 1, 1985.

[50]Based on a review by the author of political polls done by Hellenthal and Associates between 1980 and 1985.

[51]Richard L. Ender, "Anchorage Municipal Utility Survey," prepared for the Municipality of Anchorage, September 1983.

[52]Hellenthal and Associates, "Alaska Public Opinion Research Survey," April 1985.

[53]Richard L. Ender, "Anchorage Municipal General Government Survey," prepared for the Municipality of Anchorage, November 1983.

[54]Rowan Group, *Alaskans Talk About Oil.*

[55]Hellenthal and Associates, "Anchorage Marketing Research Survey," November 1983.

[56]Rowan Group, *Alaskans Talk About Oil.*

[57]Hellenthal and Associates, "Anchorage Marketing Research Survey," November 1983.

[58]Hellenthal and Associates, "Alaska Public Opinion Research Survey," September 1985.

[59]Hellenthal and Associates, "Anchorage Marketing Research Survey," November 1983 and 1986.

[60]Criminal Justice Planning Agency and Dittman Research, "Public Opinion About Crime and Criminal Justice in Alaska," Anchorage, Alaska, January 1977.

[61]Rowan Group, *Alaskans Talk About Oil.*

[62]Rowan Group, *Citizen Feedback No. 2: A Survey of Alaskan Citizens*; Ender, "Citizens' Attitudes Towards Anchorage Local Government."

[63]*Anchorage Daily News*, "Senate Leaders Seek to Protect Fund Earnings," by John Lindback, January 17, 1986.

[64]*Anchorage Times*, "New Dittman Poll Indicates More Development Is Wanted."

[65]Rowan Group, *Citizen Feedback No. 2.*

[66]*Anchorage Daily News*, "Poll Samples Opinion on Statewide Issues," by John Greeley, September 11, 1979.

[67]Rowan Group, *Alaskans Talk About Oil.*

[68]*Anchorage Times*, "New Dittman Poll Indicates More Development Is Wanted."

[69]Hellenthal and Associates, "Alaska Public Opinion Research Survey," April 1985.

[70]*Anchorage Daily News*, "Senator Grills Pollster," by John L. Lindback, January 24, 1986; and Hellenthal and Associates, "Alaska Public Opinion Research Survey," April 1985 and December 1985.

[71]Hellenthal and Associates, summary of findings from four consulting reports dated April, September, September, and December 1985.

[72]For example, see *Anchorage Times*, "Survey Shows President Still a Public Favorite," by R.W. Apple, Jr., January 28, 1986, pp. A1 and A12. This national poll found 37 percent considered themselves conservative and 21 percent liberal.

[73]Hellenthal and Associates, summary of findings from four consulting reports dated April, September, September and December 1985.

[74]Ibid.

[75]Ender, *Opinions of the Anchorage Citizen.*

[76]Hellenthal and Ender, "Statewide Political Attitudes Study."

9

The Press and Alaska Politics

Richard A. Fineberg

The stories the press reports—and how it reports (or fails to report)—can have significant effects on how the public perceives government and politics, on how government responds to issues, and on who is elected. Alaska's relative isolation and small population create a unique backdrop for considering the roles played by the media in public policy.

This chapter discusses some of the major changes in the Alaska press during the first 25 years of statehood and offers examples of how the press covered a number of important political issues in that period. We also describe the challenges the press in general faces and how it tries to meet those challenges.

We use the term "press" to refer broadly to both print and broadcast media, but most of the examples of press coverage we use are from Alaska's three largest daily newspapers. We focus on newspaper coverage of public policy issues for several reasons. Daily newspapers in Anchorage and Fairbanks have historically been important sources of state news for a large share of Alaskans and remain influential in shaping public opinion. A 1985 survey found, for example, that 75 percent of Anchorage's adult population reads one or both of the Anchorage newspapers daily.[1]

Until the late 1970s, news coverage by Alaska television and radio stations was, by and large, an echo of coverage by newspapers. This is no longer the case. In recent years broadcasters in Alaska have become much more active and competitive in gathering and reporting news. However, it is difficult to review broadcast news coverage because permanent records are not readily available. Back issues of newspapers, on the other hand, provide concrete and easily available evidence of how reporters and editors dealt with particular issues. Although we focus primarily on print media examples, we do discuss trends in news coverage by Alaska's radio and television stations in the years since statehood. And by showing the ways in which newspapers can influence public opinion and government action, we also show by implication the influence of the press in general.

213

THE CRAFT OF JOURNALISM

In their 1981 analysis of the press in the United States, political scientists David Paletz and Robert Entman observe that the press functions in a dual role as both critic of and aide to government.[2]

It is easy to see that reporters joust with those in power by (a) spotlighting the decisions and actions of politicians and officials, causing them to change priorities and reducing their ability to control events; and (b) heightening public discontent by focusing on discord, debate, delay and confusion in the political arena.

But beneath the clashes that often occur when press meets government, Paletz and Entman find a countertheme. They observe that the press may also serve as the unwitting handmaiden of those in power by (a) relying on and therefore giving credence to the statements and views of elites; (b) oversimplifying complex events and focusing on immediate conflicts rather than significant patterns of political behavior, thereby reducing the public's ability to understand and respond to the actions of political elites; and (c) legitimizing (through the appearance of critical reportage) the economic and social systems controlled by those elites.

The Paletz-Entman dichotomy provides a useful framework for understanding the social functions and consequences of journalism. By and large, however, press people do not see themselves in these terms. Professional press people do not see their purpose as either lambasting or legitimating the institutions they cover.

When asked what his aims were, reporter Bob Woodward, whose coverage of the Watergate scandal of the early 1970s earned a Pulitzer Prize, replied with one word: "truth." Veteran reporter Jim Deakin, who covered six presidents in the White House for the *St. Louis Post-Dispatch*, commented: "Truth? God help us. There must be something easier."[3]

For many in the journalism field, there is no absolute knowledge. Deakin, for example, starts from the premises of mathematician-philosopher Jacob Bronowski, who wrote, "All information is imperfect...that is the human condition." Since there is no absolute truth, Deakin explains, journalists substitute standards such as accuracy, completeness and fairness to portray a world that is "confused, untidy and dangerous."[4]

How well journalists meet these standards is, of course, subject to debate. Deakin does not shrink from criticizing the craft in which he has worked for a quarter century. "[I]f completeness is one approximation of truth," he writes, "only a few newspapers take even a few faltering steps toward Olympus." On a national average, about two-thirds of American newspapers are occupied by advertisements. The remaining one-third, Deakin notes, includes comic strips, sports pages, people columns, recipes for brandied spareribs, advice to the lovelorn, and bridge columns. "The amount of space that is left for actual news...is pitifully small."[5]

The typical wire-service story, Deakin continues, is boiled down to 400 words; an exceptionally long news story is 800 to 1,200 words long. (By comparison, this page contains approximately 500 words.) Crammed into that space are both (or many) sides, in that peculiar see-saw pattern in which reporters approximate the truth. The TV reporter, Deakin notes, has even fewer words. CBS-TV anchorman Dan Rather describes the problem: "There is no way I...can come out there (for) a minute and fifteen seconds and give the viewer even the essence, never mind the details or the substance (of a story)."[6]

The thoughtful reporter, Deakin writes, recognizes that the daily story is liable to be incomplete. The deadline forces the reporter to cut off research and start writing too soon. "The conscientious reporter...leaves the office each night with nagging knowledge that there was not enough time to talk to enough people." Taking comfort in the hope that the story was the best that could be managed on deadline, Deakin concludes, the reporter goes home and pours a strong drink.[7]

Much of the condensed material that does get into the news is from establishment sources. A 1973 study by researcher Leon V. Sigal showed that 58.2 percent of the news in the _New York Times_ and the _Washington Post_ came from press conferences, press releases, and other official sources. Another 25.8 percent came from interviews and other activities that in many cases served official purposes. In sum, in the two newspapers usually considered among the most critical of government, more than four-fifths of the news came from government.[8]

One other point needs to be made here. Veteran _New York Times_ columnist Tom Wicker notes that he has "always considered it ludicrous to speak of how 'left-wing' the press is, when [t]he people who run the press are owners of large, capitalized institutions who are likely to share a broad common perception with the people who run major businesses and government."[9] Despite the frequent appearance of conflict between press and government, on closer analysis it appears that the operating procedures of the media combine with institutional and economic forces to make the press part of mainstream political life.

But what about Watergate coverage and other intensive press investigations of recent years? Doesn't this kind of reportage represent a pattern of press against government? This notion may be too simplistic. Edward Jay Epstein analyzed the Watergate coverage that helped topple a president, earned the *Washington Post* a Pulitzer Prize, and inspired the popular book and movie, *All the President's Men*. Epstein concludes that many accounts unduly magnified the role of the press. In large part, he writes, the press simply fed on facts unearthed and developed by government institutions—the Federal Bureau of Investigation, federal prosecutors, the grand jury, congressional committees, and government sources such as the mysterious "Deep Throat," an apparently well-placed unidentified government tipster.[10]

While Epstein is correct that the press role in Watergate cannot be understood without looking at the under-emphasized role of various government institutions, it is important to note that those institutions might not have been able to play their roles without the press. It is reasonable to speculate, for example, that the Senate Select Committee that brought the highest cabinet officials and presidential aides to the dock could not have done its job without eager newspaper reporters and national television coverage.

One aspect of press-government relations merits special mention: the interplay between press and bureaucracy. Press coverage frequently encourages bureaucrats to consider problems they would otherwise prefer to ignore. Canny bureaucrats readily acknowledge that part of their job is to make the boss look good. And one important place for looking good is in the press. Bureaucratic preoccupation with the press is so great that even the possibility that a critical memo *might* leak can cause top executives to reprimand employees severely.

At the highest levels of decisionmaking, two major forces seem to be the desire for positive press coverage and avoidance of "bad press." The latter term encompasses any critical reportage that implies inaction, misguided or improper action by elected officials, bureaucrats, and political actors outside government. The common ingredient in bad press is the appearance of a problem. Decisionmakers are liable to be more concerned with an issue's effect on their image than with the issue itself. Thus the willingness or ability of the press to pick up a story may be an important factor in whether or not administrative or legislative bureaucracy will respond to problems.

Whether its role is primary investigator or secondary catalyst, the press constantly faces deadlines, severe space limits, and restrictive conventions that can affect accuracy and completeness. But despite its shortcomings, the necessarily truncated version of reality we call "news" plays a very important part in current events and strongly influences our attitudes toward government.

JOURNALISM ON THE LAST FRONTIER

ALASKA NEWSPAPERS

In 1985, 42 newspapers were published in Alaska. The number of newspapers in the state changed little in the 1970s and early 1980s, although Alaska's population increased sharply.[11] Outside Anchorage and Fairbanks, most Alaska newspapers are relatively small community publications that focus on local issues. How government actions and public policy issues are covered in small Alaska newspapers varies greatly, with many examples of resourceful and insightful reporting and many examples of uncritical reporting that can be the result of sparse population, remoteness, and the corresponding lack of competition in remote communities.

It is the three largest daily newspapers in Alaska that are the most influential sources of state government news. The *Anchorage Daily News*, the *Anchorage Times*, and the *Fairbanks Daily News-Miner* reach a large share of Alaska adults every day. A 1985 survey found that 75 percent of adults in Anchorage and about half the adults in nearby areas of southcentral Alaska read one or both of the Anchorage newspapers daily. And the Anchorage newspapers are also flown into the state capital in Juneau daily. The *News-Miner*, the only metropolitan daily newspaper in the northern half of Alaska, reaches an estimated 70 percent of households in the Fairbanks North Star Borough daily.[12]

BROADCAST MEDIA

The number of television and radio stations in Alaska doubled in just over a decade. In 1973, the *Alaska Blue Book* listed eighteen AM radio, three FM, and seven television stations. By 1985, the edition of the *Blue Book* identified 35 AM, 23 FM, and 13 television channels. Many of the new stations were in rural communities. In addition, by 1985, cable television was installed or planned in 72 communities, including 50 not served by other local media. Until the late 1970s, broadcast journalism in Alaska took a back seat to newspapers when it came to generating news about state government. But in recent years, broadcasters have become a significant part of the Alaska news scene.

Several factors account for that development. First, the state's establishment of telecommunications facilities allows Alaska to follow the Lower 48 in the increasing use of television. In 1969, when American astronauts walked on the moon, Ketchikan (with a cable feed from Canada) and Anchorage (with its first live satellite connection to the Lower 48, specially arranged for the occasion) watched on television. The rest of Alaska—along with Russia and China (which were blacked out)—did not participate in this special event.[13]

But the satellite connection established for Anchorage soon became commonplace for much of Alaska, which now watches the national network nightly news the same day it is broadcast.

Another factor in the emergence of broadcast media in Alaska is the support the state and local communities have put into public radio and television. In 1973, there was one public radio station in Alaska (KUAC-FM, Fairbanks). By 1985, 16 public radio and four public television stations were operating in the 49th state. Most of these outlets carry national, statewide, and local news; many serve areas that previously had little (or no) news coverage. The Alaska Public Radio Network (APRN) is one of four non-Juneau media outlets that now maintains a year-round reporter in Juneau.

Local television news varies considerably from channel to channel. One station may break a significant story that another misses altogether; the second station may lead with a rewrite of a newspaper or wire service headline. When one station gets a major story, other outlets will likely pick it up—although more slowly than they would from a newspaper, where hard copy quickly finds its way into the newsroom of the competition.

It is difficult to assess the impacts of electronic media growth in rural areas. A reporter who spent the summer of 1985 in small northern communities concluded that Alaska villagers tend to regard Juneau as a foreign capital, perhaps as remote as Bangkok or Baghdad.[14] In this milieu, it appears that radio political news may call a community's attention to problems in common with other communities, or may otherwise heighten political awareness in remote regions.

A final aspect of changing electronic media coverage that deserves mention is coverage of the Alaska Legislature. Since 1978, the state legislature has contracted with reporting groups to cover the legislature. But the television camera may provide too much insight into legislative workings. In 1981, after a stormy leadership battle in the House of Representatives, the new leaders terminated the coverage. The reporting group managed to save its job with the Alaska Senate by offering coverage of that body without commentary, editing, or analysis.

This pattern continued until 1985, when a new legislature restored bicameral coverage. The 1985 thirty-minute program was slow-paced, providing extensive hearing and floor coverage with little analysis or interpretation.

NEWSPAPERS AND PUBLIC ISSUES

BACKGROUND: ANCHORAGE AND FAIRBANKS NEWSPAPERS

From before statehood until the end of the 1970s, the *Anchorage Times* was the most widely read and influential newspaper in Alaska. In 1977, the *Times* had more readers than the other Alaska dailies combined.

The newspaper and its publisher, Robert Atwood, have historically pushed for economic development in Anchorage in particular and in Alaska as a whole. The _Times_ was one of the leaders in the fight for Alaska statehood, which Atwood and others saw as a necessary step for economic growth in Alaska. Over the years, the _Times_ consistently took editorial positions in favor of proposed large development projects in the state, and some researchers have charged that the paper's editorial positions frequently influenced its presentation of the news. (See later discussion of the _Times'_ support of moving the state capital from Juneau to southcentral Alaska.)

A second Anchorage newspaper, the _Anchorage Daily News_, has been published since the late 1940s, but until the 1980s, its circulation was only a fraction of that of the _Times_. Norman Brown started the _News_ to give Anchorage "a second voice, some diversity."[15] He sold the struggling newspaper to Larry and Katherine (Field) Fanning in 1967. Fanning, who had previously edited newspapers in San Francisco and Chicago, had helped train a number of prominent journalists, including Mike Royko, Nicholas Von Hoffman, and Joseph Kraft. Fanning believed the role of the press was to provide the reader with both facts and analytical interpretation, and the _News'_ attempts to probe the social issues behind the news stood in contrast to coverage by other Alaska media.

Under Larry Fanning, the _News_ explored the implications of the events that were sweeping Alaska in the late 1960s—the Native land claims movement and the discovery of oil at Prudhoe Bay. The Fanning approach to journalism produced some quality reporting that cut through the miasma of official rhetoric, but the interpretive mode also produced some egregious errors of judgment. (See later discussions of specific instances of _News_ coverage.)

When Larry Fanning died in 1971, his widow Kay took over the newspaper.[16] In the late 1970s, the _News_ continually suffered from lack of operating money and a shrinking circulation; at one point, it had just five reporters.[17] In 1979, after an ill-fated joint operating agreement with the _Times_ had dissolved, Kay Fanning sold 80 percent of the _News_ to the California-based McClatchy newspaper chain. The McClatchy group immediately began pumping money into the _News_—and the great Anchorage press war was born. Competition between the _Times_ and the _News_ in the 1980s has been among the most robust and intense in the nation and has sparked noticeable improvements in news coverage by both papers. The circulation figures in Table 9.1 help tell the story.[18] In 1985, the circulation of the _News_ exceeded that of the _Times_.

The third largest daily in the state and the only daily in the northern half of Alaska is the _Fairbanks Daily News-Miner_.

Table 9.1
Anchorage Newspaper Circulation

Year	Anchorage Population	Circulation	
1967	100,000	Times 22,000	News 18,000
1978	200,000	Times 46,000	News 12,100
1985	248,000	Times 40,000	News 50,000

Founded shortly after the turn of the century, the *News-Miner* served Fairbanks and the outlying mining camps that flourished with interior's mining boom. In 1949, owner A.E. "Cap" Lathrop brought a management consultant to Fairbanks to find out what it would take to turn the newspaper into a money-maker. The consultant, C.W. Snedden, told Lathrop it would take a sizable capital investment. Lathrop sold the paper to Snedden, who turned the little daily into a profitmaker and established an employee stock ownership plan in the early 1970s. The paper had an average daily circulation of nearly 19,000 in 1985 and reached about 70 percent of households in Fairbanks and nearby areas.

Like his Anchorage counterpart Robert Atwood, the conservative Snedden was active in the statehood drive. Critics have observed that *News-Miner* coverage has frequently reflected the development-oriented perspective of its publisher.

SAMPLES: OMISSIONS, DISTORTIONS, AND GOOD REPORTING

The following examples from Alaska's three largest newspapers illustrate a number of ways in which press coverage can influence government action and public awareness. We picked samples from different periods and on quite different subjects. They are intended to show both good and bad reporting; how editorial positions of newspapers can slip over into news coverage; how persistent publicity can force government action; how completeness and accuracy on a subject can vary in different stories by the same newspaper.

Anchorage Times: Move the Capital. Proposals to move Alaska's state capital from Juneau to southcentral Alaska were on the ballot five times between 1960 and 1982. Reviewing the *Anchorage Times* coverage of the capital move campaigns of 1960, 1962, 1974, 1976, and 1982, researcher Clifford John Groh found that political leaders of both parties—and on both sides of the capital move issue—viewed *Times* publisher Robert Atwood as the leader of the pro-movers.[19]

If "move it" was the message, the *Times* was the medium. The day after the 1960 move initiative lost (by a vote of 23,972 to 18,865) the *Times* editorialized, "Capital Issue Down but Far from Dead." The lead article the next day was headlined, "Pledge Drive for New Capital."

In 1962, when the move lost by a similar margin, the *Times* responded similarly. When the capital move appeared again on the 1974 ballot, the *Times* managed a capital move editorial every three days for over a month, while 33 of 36 news stories were on the pro-move side. The capital move was approved by voters in 1974, subject to selection of a site in southcentral Alaska. In a 1976 vote, the stipulation was added that costs of moving the capital also had to be approved.

In 1982, *Times* coverage of the capital move issue emphasized public opinion polls that indicated the capital movers were in danger of losing. Some observers regarded this approach to the issue as an attempt to stir up community support for the capital move through ostensibly objective news columns. In 1982 voters essentially voted down the move by failing to approve its calculated costs.

Overall, Groh concluded that during the periodic drives to move the capital, the *Times* used its news columns at times to promote the move concept and appeal for campaign funds; to play up support and play down opposition (or vice-versa, depending on the situation); and to publish just selected information about Juneau's physical conditions and the costs of moving the capital compared with maintaining the capital in Juneau.[20]

While the *Times* pro-move coverage undoubtedly reflected the sentiment of many Anchorage community leaders, the newspaper also exerted a major influence on general public awareness and perception of the issues. Here both press roles described by Paletz and Entman can be seen: aide to powerful Anchorage community leaders and critic of state leaders in Juneau.

Authors John Hanrahan and Peter Gruenstein, whose book, *Lost Frontier: The Marketing of Alaska*, described the political forces at work in Alaska during the 1970s, wrote that Atwood and the *Times* had the power "to set the parameters of discussion on any issue and to mold public opinion through its news coverage."[21] Those authors reported that in general the *Times* was inclined to give short shrift to liberal and conservationist viewpoints while giving favorable coverage to development forces—of which the pro-movers could be considered an example.

Anchorage Daily News: Native Land Claims. In the late 1960s, the aboriginal land claims of Alaska Natives and their economic plight became increasingly prominent issues in Alaska. The *Anchorage Daily News* ran a series of articles that documented for urban readers the poverty, disease, and tides of change that were running in rural Alaska. Then, in December 1969, the *News* devoted extensive coverage specifically to the land claims issue. Spurred by the discovery of oil at Prudhoe Bay, the U.S. Congress was seriously deliberating resolution of this long-standing question: what compensation should Alaska Natives receive for the taking of their aboriginal lands? The state government at that time was opposed to a large cash settlement.

In front-page news articles, the land claims series ripped the state's resistance to a large cash settlement as "utterly frivolous...despicable...inept, desperate...frantic." The state approach suffered from "incompetence... rivaled only by its deviousness." This blatant editorializing was carried in news columns and was not even tagged "analysis," according to Groh.[22]

When state officials complained about that editorializing, the *News* also gave those criticisms front-page play. Moreover, the newspaper ran an editorial that apologized for its previous reporting excesses. The editorial still criticized state policies but promised to confine its criticisms to the editorial columns. By its own account, the *News* had:

> ...strayed well beyond the bounds of sound journalistic practice. We allowed opinion (in contrast to useful interpretation) to invade the news columns—and we are sorry.[23]

This episode clearly demonstrates the distinction between fact and opinion—as well as the manner in which the press attempts to honor that distinction by restricting opinions to the editorial page.

Anchorage Daily News: The Alaska Teamsters Story. In 1975, at the height of the pipeline boom, the *Anchorage Daily News* assigned a team to investigate the most powerful union in Alaska: the Teamsters' Union. One of the reporters was Anchorage-born Howard Weaver, now managing editor of the *News*. The Teamsters controlled trucking along the overland supply lines to the pipeline camps strung out along the 800-mile corridor, Weaver recalls. Nevertheless, the union's operations were shrouded in mystery. Federal investigators puzzled through allegations of racketeering while reports of job-selling, extortion, drug-dealing, and contract murders spread through the rumor mills of the pipeline camps, where everything was for sale.

"We have the hammer," Teamster leader Jess Carr boasted. The oil companies were neck-deep in debt and had to keep the project moving; the nation needed the oil. In addition to trucking, the Teamsters controlled the warehouses.

It was a tough story to crack. And it was quite a gamble for a newspaper with a small staff to put three reporters on a long-term assignment.

"Nobody would talk on the record," Weaver recalls.[24] It took countless interviews to chart the size and scope of the Teamsters' operation.

The wealthier *Fairbanks Daily News-Miner* put its business reporter on the same assignment. Then the *Los Angeles Times* sent a four-reporter team to Alaska; one of its targets was the Teamsters. The *News*, well along in its research, held its breath. The *News-Miner* got some good quotes from Jess Carr, but its lone reporter on the assignment only had time to pay lip-service to the nuts-and-bolts of the story—the pension funds, the union ties to the business community, all the seamy things that swirled around the violence in the pipeline camps.

The *News* kept digging. Three reporters had files of information, but no tangible evidence of union involvement in illegal activities. Finally, they reached a point of diminishing returns on their investigative effort; they were ready to package the story and go with it. Their massive research spun out into a nine-part series.

The story didn't overturn the Teamster leadership or send anybody to jail, but the editors did submit the series for a Pulitzer Prize in local reporting. To their surprise, the Pulitzer judges plucked the story from that reporting category to honor it with the most coveted of all press awards, Pulitzer Prize for Public Service. One of the factors in their award, the judges said, was that a newspaper with such limited staff resources devoted that much effort to a special project. The *News* had laid out for the consideration of its readers the power of the union and connections between the union and Alaska's political and economic elites.

"Hard work...not brilliant," Weaver says of that story. "What we tried to do was to shine a little light in a dark spot."

Fairbanks Daily News-Miner: Miners and Mud. Press treatment of siltation of interior Alaska streams as gold prices spiralled skyward at the close of the 1970s involves the classic Alaska confrontation between resource development and environmental values. The issue continues to spark controversy—and legislative scrutiny.[25]

Many mining proponents believe environmental regulations needlessly strangle their development; advocates of stricter regulation claim placer mining activities jeopardize wilderness, recreation, and subsistence resources.

In July 1980, the *News-Miner* carried a front-page aerial color shot of a stream near Fairbanks winding its way past a mining claim. Upstream from the mining activity, the stream is clear. Downstream, the water is brown, evidently choked with silt from the placer-mining operation. A companion picture shows canoeists enjoying a white-water stream.[26]

Taken alone, these photos and accompanying story might be regarded as an example of good reporting on a controversial issue, spotlighting both sides. But in earlier stories, between 1978 and mid-1980, as gold prices rose and mining activity increased, the *News-Miner* had disregarded or downplayed widespread reports of stream problems associated with mining.

In September 1978, for example, the newspaper extensively quoted a miner who castigated public officials attempting to reduce water quality problems resulting from mining.[27] The following year, as the sudden rise in the price of gold brought still more miners to the streams of interior Alaska, the *News-Miner* frequently focused on the economic benefits to miners and merchants.[28] During this period, the *News-Miner* covered the tough environmental protection questions associated with stream protection only after other Alaska newspapers had reported on this issue.[29]

In summary, the 1980 story presenting both sides was a change from one-sided news coverage that tended to deflect readers' attention from this issue for more than two years.

Review of *News-Miner* coverage of this story demonstrates the difficulty of generalizing from a single article. Paletz and Entman's observations concerning the dual role played by the press also are relevant. On one hand, the *News-Miner's* coverage exposed government environmental efforts to criticism. On the other hand, the same coverage also tended to legitimize government activity by giving readers the impression extensive stream protection was taking place; in fact, however, monitoring of mining activities during this period was rather limited.

Fairbanks Daily News-Miner: The Fairbanks State Office Lease. In 1985, a *News-Miner* series led to the first gubernatorial impeachment inquiry in the United States in 47 years.

The state government had leased a building for state offices in Fairbanks. The *News-Miner* questioned whether state officials had followed required leasing procedures. The newspaper's early inquiries prompted bureaucrats to turn over pertinent materials on the lease procedure to state attorneys. Because state procedures governing bidding appeared to have been violated, a grand jury was convened. Although the grand jury found no indictable offense, it also opined that the procedures used in leasing the building warranted public consideration in the form of an impeachment inquiry of the governor. A special session of the legislature was called and the senate rules committee decided, on a 3-2 vote, that the evidence did not warrant an impeachment proceeding against the governor.

In the process of the inquiry, the governor's chief of staff resigned when it was disclosed that he had destroyed documents and lied to the press, apparently in an effort to insulate the governor from potential criticism.[30]

In sum, the *News-Miner's* balanced and cautious investigation of alleged favoritism by the governor and key aides in steering a state lease to a political contributor of the governor focused public attention on the conduct of state power holders. The coverage also brought the *News-Miner* national press awards.

ALASKA'S JOURNALISTS

We cannot look at what news is produced in Alaska without looking at who produces it. Who writes and edits the stories? How do their actions and their products affect the process they chronicle? How does the Alaska journalist differ from his counterpart in the Lower 48?

AGE, TURNOVER, AND SALARY

Compared with reporters in the Lower 48, Alaska reporters are relatively young and inexperienced. These characteristics are exaggerated by the fact that the Alaska press corps has a relatively high turnover rate. The Juneau press corps is no exception to this pattern. When the 1984 legislature began, a majority of the ten reporters working for newspapers or major broadcast outlets outside Juneau had never covered the Alaska Legislature. Three were in their second year and only one had more than five years of capital experience. Most were relative newcomers to Alaska. If the age of 30 were a fulcrum, reporters younger than 30 would have balanced those over 30; only two were over 40.[31]

High turnover in the Alaska press corps results from several factors. First, Alaska is no exception to the general rule that reporters tend to move around in the early years of their career, working up to assignments of interest and responsibility. Second, the reasons why turnover is high in other sectors of Alaska society apply also to journalism: harsh climate, remoteness and distance from family, for example, affect reporters in the same way these factors affect others who come North; many leave.

But the major factor that explains the turnover rate is money. The reporters' guild is not strong in Alaska (only the *Anchorage Times* has an organized bargaining unit) and press salaries are relatively low—far lower, in fact, than state government or oil industry public relations salaries, both of which snag many of the reporters who stay in Alaska.[32]

FEW REPORTERS, MANY ISSUES

One of the most striking characteristics of the Alaska press corps is that the issues are big, but the reporters and media outlets, by comparison, are few. The area north of the Alaska Range, for example, is a vast territory, larger than the second largest state in the country, with the largest oil field in the United States. Yet this region has only one daily newspaper.

Reflecting Alaska's sparse population, the number of reporters covering state government is relatively small. In 1976 in the capital city, for example, only the hometown *Juneau Empire* and the Associated Press provided year-round newspaper coverage. Three newspapers sent reporters to Juneau for the annual legislative session. By comparison, in the Texas capital of Austin, more than a dozen newspapers had year-round reporters, while eight Illinois newspapers had full-time bureaus in Springfield.[33] Coverage in Juneau has improved considerably in recent years. During the early 1980s, both Anchorage dailies established year-round reporters in Juneau. But the basic fact remains: The relatively large role of state government, the rapid changes in the 49th state, and the effects of the oil boom of the early 1980s created a wide range of issues and potential news stories for a reporting crew that was relatively small in comparison to those in other state capitals.

LEGAL AND CONSTITUTIONAL ISSUES

Three aspects of the legal system have special impact on press conduct in Alaska and elsewhere. These are (1) libel laws, (2) press shield laws and (3) open meeting and public information laws.

LIBEL AND SHIELD LAWS

Alaska's libel and shield laws are basically similar to those of other states. Libel laws give an erroneously maligned citizen the right to collect damages, if it can be demonstrated that the press reported in error and in reckless disregard of the truth. Shield laws protect reporters from being forced to disclose sources of information that might dry up if the reporter could not guarantee confidentiality. While the national trend toward broader application of libel statutes has undoubtedly been noticed by Alaska editors, Alaska has not seen a significant increase in libel activity in recent years. Alaska reporters and editors seldom find themselves in jail or court to protect their sources. Robert Atwood of the *Times* and Tom Snapp of the *All-Alaska Weekly* attribute this fact primarily to the moderate conduct of the Alaska press.[34]

OPEN MEETING AND PUBLIC DOCUMENT LAWS

Editors Howard Weaver of the *Anchorage Daily News* and Tom Snapp of the *All-Alaska Weekly* report spending far more time working on public access to government meetings and documents than on libel and shield issues.[35]

The open meeting laws of the state provide that all meetings of state and local government bodies must be open to the public, unless specifically excepted by law. Only limited subjects, such as personnel matters and topics that could directly and adversely affect the state's finances, are exempt from this requirement.[36] While this statute embodies the principle that the public's business should be done in public, this legal framework does not prevent public officials from discussing public affairs with which they are concerned in informal and nonpublic settings. If two publicly employed persons have a brainstorm while eating a hamburger, does the public have the right to be there? Not necessarily. But a private meeting of public officials to make specific plans about the course of action to be taken at a subsequent public meeting is another matter. The Alaska Supreme Court has held that such meetings are illegal. In general, the impropriety of any action taken at a meeting held in violation of public meeting statutes can be overcome by calling a meeting with proper public notice and considering the issue anew before taking action.[37]

With limited exceptions (for certain vital statistics and medical records, for example), Alaska statutes guarantee access to public documents.[38] According to Snapp, public officials frequently use the state's constitutional guarantee of privacy to withhold information otherwise public under the freedom of information law.

In 1983 a reporter sought access to agency budget request documents after he was denied access to scheduled meetings in which aides to the governor discussed the coming year's budgets with agency representatives. (The governor's office traditionally tries to keep such meetings closed in order to discuss agency problems privately, and because reports of contemplated cuts would unduly alarm agency staff.) Although state sunshine laws (open meeting laws) would appear to guarantee press access to both, the reporter was denied access to both the meetings and the preliminary budget documents.[39]

In 1986, the issue of public access boiled over near the end of the legislative session when the League of Women Voters, the *Anchorage Daily News*, and the *Fairbanks Daily News-Miner* took the Alaska State Legislature to court. The league and the newspapers charged that the legislature was holding closed-door meetings to avoid making budget decisions in public. As of the end of the regular 1986 legislative session, the courts were still considering the issue.

In sum, although the public meeting and sunshine statutes serve as a deterrent to backroom conduct of public business, these legal remedies do not guarantee access to discussions of public matters.

CONCLUSIONS

In a state characterized by rapid change and polarization on key issues, the Alaska press corps writes the first draft of history in the face of serious handicaps, including daily deadlines, limits on available space, and at times difficulty of access to government meetings and documents. A relatively small press corps routinely handles stories of major magnitude from remote locales in which local pressures are frequently evident. The relatively few reporters covering Alaska state government may not generate the diversity of coverage on which a pluralist society normally depends.

The interplay between press and bureaucracy affects reporting in all states, but these factors may be more important in Alaska than elsewhere. Because government in Alaska plays a relatively larger role than it does in other states, the manner in which the press handles its coverage of government assumes greater importance to the Alaska political process. At the same time, by virtue of its relative size and isolation, the Alaska press faces extraordinarily difficult challenges.

In recent years it has become fashionable for both political scientists and press columnists to criticize the press as elitist and out of touch with the mainstream of society. Few of the critics appear to understand what it is the press attempts to do, how the press goes about accomplishing these ends, or the constraints under which reporters and editors operate.[40] For example, an official who cares about his job is liable to despair of the way the press sledgehammers the story; often, the reporter simply does not have the time to do a better job. On other occasions, the reporter accused of unfairness or malice may be following the requirements of the craft in a thoroughly professional manner. The conventions that require the reporter to ferret out and highlight salient facts often place the reporter in the position of holding up a mirror to society. When warts appear, the press is blamed.

"We're often accused of sensationalism, even when we're as deliberate, balanced, and careful as we know how to be," says Howard Weaver, managing editor of the *Anchorage Daily News*. "When people say we run an expose just to sell papers, that makes me mad—it just doesn't work that way." In-depth reporting about the misdeeds of officials may be important, Weaver explains, but these stories just don't sell papers. "The *National Enquirer's* circulation is something like 17 million papers; the *Wall Street Journal* has a circulation of 2 million. If we just wanted to sell newspapers, which kind of stories do you think we'd write?"[41]

It appears simplistic to say that the press is in conflict with the government. Although there are often conflicts, it appears that the fundamental power struggle is not between government and the press. Rather, the struggle is between government and alternative views, with the press as the conduit for both.[42] The manner in which the press plays its role is a major determinant of the issues with which state government deals, and with the way in which the government makes decisions.

ENDNOTES

[1]The Belden Continuing Market Study, 1985. Conducted for the *Anchorage Daily News* by Belden Associates, Dallas, Texas.

[2]David L. Paletz and Robert M. Entman, *Media Power Politics* (New York: The Free Press, 1981), pp. 6, 17, 21, 184.

[3]James Deakin, *Straight Stuff: The Reporters, the White House and the Truth* (New York: Morrow, 1984), p. 98.

[4]Ibid., pp. 97-99.

[5]Ibid., pp. 94-96.

[6]Ibid., p. 96.

[7]Ibid., p. 97.

[8]Ibid., p. 102.

[9]*Harper's* (January 1985): 48.

[10]Edward Jay Epstein, *Between Fact and Fiction: The Problem of Journalism* (New York: Vintage, 1975), pp. 19-32. See also Paletz and Entman, pp. 158-165.

[11]For a listing of Alaska media outlets in the early 1970s and mid-1980s, see *Alaska Blue Book*, 1973, pp. 135-136; 1985, pp. 191-196. The book is published biennially by the Alaska Department of Education, Division of State Libraries.

[12]The Belden Continuing Market Study, 1985; and the Branham Data Sheet, 1985.

[13]Television coverage of the moon walk was described in the *Anchorage Daily News*, July 20, 1969, p. 1.

[14]Interview with Annabel Lund, 1985.

[15]Clifford John Groh, unpublished manuscript. I am indebted to Groh for sharing the extensive information he has compiled on the Anchorage press during the first two decades of statehood.

[16]In 1983 Kay Fanning was named editor of the respected *Christian Science Monitor*. For her biography see "Kay Fanning: Who would play her in the Movie?" by Margery Eagan, in *Boston* Magazine (January 1984): 87-89, 164-169.

[17]For an interpretive analysis of the *Times* and the *News* in the 1970s, see Michael Parfit, "Anchorage," in *New Times*, (September 18, 1978): 31-34. This article was part of a special edition: "Alaska: Eleventh Hour for America's Wilderness."

[18]Sources of circulation figures: 1968 figures reported in "A Cheechako Takes Over," in *Time* (June 30, 1967): 43; 1978 figures from Audit Bureau of Circulation Reports, September 1980; 1985 figures for the first quarter of 1985 from Audit Bureau report, as reported in the *Anchorage Daily News* (May 28, 1986), p. A-6.

[19]Clifford John Groh, unpublished manuscript.

[20]Ibid.

[21]John Hanrahan and Peter Gruenstein, *Lost Frontier: The Marketing of Alaska* (New York: Norton, 1977), p. 45.

[22]Again, my thanks to Groh for making his materials on the Anchorage press available.

[23]C. Robert Zelnick, "The 91st Congress Will Settle Native Land Claims," December 7, 1969, p. 1; subsequent articles December 8, p. 1 and December 9, p. 1. See also, "Governor's Aide Raps Series in Daily News," December 10, 1969, p. 1, and "The Sorry Saga of Alaska's Response" (editorial), December 10, 1969, p. 4.

[24]Interview with Howard Weaver, April 1984.

[25]See, for example, the 1984 debate over rechanneling the Tuluksak River in southwest Alaska ("Miners Plan to Divert River Enrages Villagers," *Anchorage Times*, January 19, 1984, p. A-1; "Village Fights Proposed Rechanneling of River," *Anchorage Daily News*, May 10, 1984, p. C-1; "River Permit Granted," *Anchorage Daily News*, May 12, 1984, p. A-1).

[26]*Fairbanks Daily News-Miner*, July 26, 1980, p. 1.

[27]*Fairbanks Daily News-Miner*, September 2, 1978, p. 2.

[28]For examples of *News-Miner* enthusiasm for mining in 1979, see "Gold!", September 7, p. 4 (editorial) and Associated Press, "Gold Market Goes Berserk," September 14, 1979, p. 1.

[29]*News-Miner* coverage of stream siltation was reviewed by the author in "The News-Miner Today," *Alaska Advocate* (November 23, 1978, p. 5), and in "Mining and Mud: What Happens to Alaska's Streams When Gold Hits $400 per Ounce," *Interior/North Alaska Media Project Newsletter* (vol. 1, no. 1, October 1979). When the *Anchorage Daily News* ran a front page story by the author on mining in the Fairbanks area October 22, 1979, the *News-Miner* picked up a condensed version from the Associated Press.

[30]For examples of the *News-Miner's* coverage, see, "Attorney General Investigates $9 Million State Office Lease," April 2, 1985, p. 1; "Blackout of Office Lease Ex-

tended," April 4, 1985, p. 1; "Grand Jury Investigates Office Lease; Sheffield's Chief of Staff Steps Aside," and "Chronology Shows How State Lease was Signed," April 24, 1985, pp. 1-3.

[31]For a press feature on the Juneau press corps, see *Anchorage Daily News*, January 23, 1983, p. A-1.

[32]Groh manuscript. Between the November 1982 elections and the end of 1984, five reporters (including the author) left the Juneau press corps for state jobs.

[33]Hanrahan and Gruenstein, p. 57; William T. Gormley, Jr., "Coverage of State Government in the Mass Media," *State Government* (Spring, 1979): 47.

[34]Atwood's comments were made at a University of Alaska, Taft Seminar in Fairbanks in June 1985. Snapp discussed constitutional aspects of press operations with the author in September 1985.

[35]Interview with Howard Weaver, April 1984; interview with Tom Snapp, 1985.

[36]AS 44.62.310-.312.

[37]*Brookwood Area Homeowners Assn. v. Anchorage* (702 P.2d 1317). See also *Johnson v. State of Alaska* (3 KN 83-386 Civil; Decisions February 11, 1985 and May 14, 1985). In 1984 the attorney general's office prescribed the remedy the courts later applied in *Brookwood* and *Johnson* when an action by the Alaska Resources Corporation was taken at a meeting that was held without a quorum.

[38]AS 09.25.110-220.

[39]The preliminary budget numbers were held by the attorney general's office to be draft or working documents; the meetings, the attorney general decided, were exempt from the statute because no final decisions were taken. The *Anchorage Times*, whose Juneau reporter raised the issue, did not take the challenge to court.

[40]Deakin quotes columnists David Broder and Joseph Kraft, p. 345; political scientists Thomas R. Dye and L. Harmon Ziegler pan the press in *American Politics in the Media Age* (Monterey, CA: Brooks/Cole, 1983), pp. 126, 133-141, 358-360. See also "Journalism Under Fire," *Time* (December 12, 1983): 76-93, and "Westmoreland vs. CBS: The Media on Trial," *Newsweek* (October 22, 1984): 60-72.

[41]Interview with Weaver, April 1984.

[42]Deakin, *Straight Stuff*, p. 47.

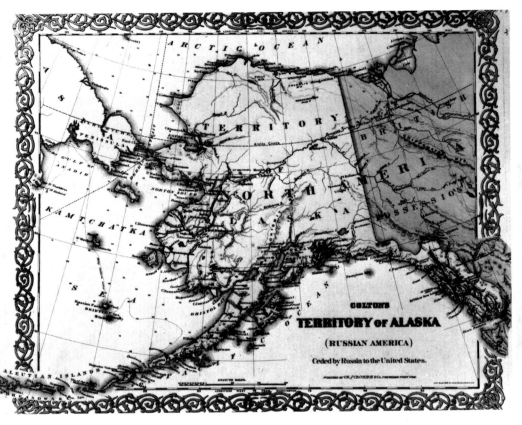

Alaska at the time the United States bought the huge territory from Russia. (Rare Map Collection, Archives, University of Alaska, Fairbanks.)

New Archangel (Sitka), which in the mid-1850s was the seat of government and center of commerce for Russian America. (Siberia-Alaska Collection, Archives, University of Alaska, Fairbanks.)

The signing of the 1867 Treaty of Cession of Russian America to the United States, as rendered by the artist E. Leutze. (General Historical Collection, Archives, University of Alaska, Fairbanks.)

Anthony Dimond (left), Alaska's territorial delegate to Congress from 1933 to 1944, and his successor, E.L. "Bob" Bartlett. Both introduced unsuccessful statehood bills in Congress in the 1940s. (E.L. Bartlett Collection, Archives, University of Alaska, Fairbanks.)

Delegates to Alaska's constitutional convention of 1955-56 pose in Constitution Hall, the site on the Fairbanks campus of the University of Alaska where delegates met. (R. Griffin Collection, Archives, University of Alaska, Fairbanks.)

Elijah Kakinya, a dancer from Anaktuvuk Pass, performs at the 1984 Festival of Native Arts. The Native culture is a distinct part of Alaska's political culture. (Brian Schneider, *Fairbanks Daily News-Miner.*)

President Dwight Eisenhower and other federal and Alaska officials look on as the U.S. flag with 49 stars is hung on January 3, 1959—the day Alaska became the 49th state. (E.L. Bartlett Collection, Archives, University of Alaska, Fairbanks.)

Alaska's first U.S. Senators, Ernest Gruening (left) and E.L. "Bob" Bartlett. *(Fairbanks Daily News-Miner.)*

Jay Hammond, Alaska's governor from 1974-1982, talks with Alaska villagers in the late 1970s. Many Alaskans saw Hammond as representing the "individualist" aspect of Alaska's political culture. *(Fairbanks Daily News-Miner.)*

Picketers at a 1978 demonstration in Fairbanks protest President Jimmy Carter's administrative imposition of wilderness and other strong conservation measures on large areas of Alaska land. Federal land management in Alaska has historically been a source of state-federal conflict. *(Fairbanks Daily News-Miner.)*

This poster for E.L. "Bob" Bartlett's successful campaign to become one of Alaska's first U.S. Senators illustrates a number of the points Alaska political candidates historically emphasized— including long-time residence and support for statehood. (E.L. Bartlett Collection, Archives, University of Alaska, Fairbanks.)

Alex Miller, named national committeeman for the territorial Democratic Party in 1955, speaks during the 1956 Alaska elections. *(Fairbanks Daily News-Miner.)*

E.L. "Bob" Bartlett, U.S. Senator from Alaska during the 1960s (left), and his wife Vide (right) meet with President Lyndon Johnson and his wife Lady Bird in the White House in 1965. (E.L. Bartlett Collection, Archives, University of Alaska, Fairbanks.)

Alaska's congressional delegation and the widow of E.L. Bartlett examine a bust of Bartlett at the 1969 dedication of the Bartlett Memorial Auditorium in Washington, D.C. Pictured left to right are Representative Howard Pollock, Alaska; Senator Ted Stevens, Alaska; Vide Bartlett; Senator Mike Gravel, Alaska; and Senator Warren Magnuson, Washington. (Nate Fine Photos.)

Several of the most highly-paid lobbyists in Alaska meet in the halls of the capitol in the early 1980s. Pictured left to right are Sam Kito, Lew Dischner, Alex Miller, and Henry Pratt. (Paul Helmar.)

Alaska voters mark their ballots in the privacy of election booths. (Mike Belrose, *Fairbanks Daily News-Miner.*)

Ernest Gruening, elected U.S. Senator from Alaska in 1958, greets former President Harry Truman. As president in the late 1940s, Truman had supported statehood for Alaska. (Archives, University of Alaska, Fairbanks.)

Television cameras film Steve Cowper (seated left) during an interview in his run for governor in the 1982 primary election. (Jimmy Bedford, for *Fairbanks Daily News-Miner.*)

Robert Atwood, publisher of the *Anchorage Times*, addresses a gathering in the late 1970s. Throughout the statehood period the *Anchorage Times* has been one of the most influential newspapers in Alaska. (Marc Olson, *Fairbanks Daily News-Miner.*)

C.W. Snedden (foreground), publisher of the *Fairbanks Daily News-Miner,* shown in 1984 receiving an award for his work on behalf of Alaska Statehood Day. Shown with Snedden are (left to right) William R. Wood, former president of the University of Alaska; William Sheffield, Alaska governor; and Don Young, U.S. Representative from Alaska. *(Fairbanks Daily News-Miner.)*

The Territorial House of Representatives
poses in Juneau in 1925. (Alaska Historical Library, courtesy of the *Fairbanks
Daily News-Miner.*)

The Alaska House of Representatives at
the opening meeting of the 1984 session.
(Eric Muehling, *Fairbanks Daily
News-Miner.*)

Representative Hugh Malone (center), often credited with shepherding legislation to create the Alaska Permanent Fund through the house, is shown meeting with Representatives Mike Miller (left) and Jim Duncan in an early 1980s legislative session. (Eric Muehling, *Fairbanks Daily News-Miner.*)

Legislators, staff, and lobbyists bustle around the halls of the capitol during the Thirteenth Alaska Legislature (1983-1984). (Eric Muehling, *Fairbanks Daily News-Miner.*)

Jay Kerttula, president of the Alaska Senate from 1980 through 1984, talks with other legislators during the 1982 session. *(Fairbanks Daily News Miner.)*

The Alaska Senate meets in a historical special session in July 1985 to consider impeaching Governor William Sheffield. (Brian Wallace, *Fairbanks Daily News-Miner.*)

Keith Miller (center), who assumed the governorship of
Alaska in 1969, when Walter Hickel was named U.S.
Secretary of the Interior. Pictured with him in this 1969
photo are Representative Howard Pollock and Senator Ted
Stevens of Alaska. *(Fairbanks Daily News-Miner.)*

Jay Hammond,
Alaska governor
from 1974-1982, is
shown in his office
just before the end
of his second term.
*(Fairbanks Daily
News-Miner.)*

William Egan, Alaska's first state governor, is shown here addressing the Alaska Legislature in 1983, with another former governor, Walter Hickel, looking on. Egan was governor from 1959 through 1966 and again from 1970 to 1974. *(Fairbanks Daily News-Miner.)*

Walter Hickel, elected governor of Alaska in 1966, is shown meeting with a delegate at the Republican National Convention in 1968. (**Josef Holbert,** *Fairbanks Daily News-Miner.*)

William Sheffield, elected governor of Alaska in November 1982, is shown here receiving the endorsement of former Governor William Egan. *(Fairbanks Daily News-Miner.)*

Governor Sheffield meets with his cabinet in 1983. (Eric Muehling, *Fairbanks Daily News-Miner.*)

The Alaska Supreme Court justices in 1985, from left to right: Allen T. Compton, Daniel A. Moore, Jr., Edmond W. Burke, Jay A. Rabinowitz (chief justice), and Warren W. Matthews. The state's top court has a reputation as being among the most progressive in the nation. (Malcolm Lockwood Photography.)

10

The Alaska Legislature

Stephen F. Johnson

The Alaska Legislature in its basic form is quite similar to the other American state legislatures. The most important contrast between Alaska's legislature and those of other states is not in form, but in content: the Alaska Legislature is unique and interesting primarily because of its historical context, institutional and social environment, membership, organization, and actual operation.

Shaped by familiar constitutional principles, the Alaska Legislature is intended to perform a number of important functions:

- Lawmaking: establishing the formal rules for the society.
- Representation: acting in the interest of constituents; responding to their requests, needs, and concerns.
- Checking and balancing the other branches of government, particularly the executive.
- Overseeing administration, through the power of the purse and through hearings and investigations.

Alaska's legislature can be understood in a limited way by studying how its formal rules relate to these functions, as well as by comparing its rules with those in other states. Such an examination will, however, tell only a part of the story. While we will pay some attention to formal rules, they are not the focus of this chapter. The chapter instead focuses on the more dynamic elements that make the Alaska Legislature unique and help explain its growth and change. One of the most important of these elements is the huge influx of oil money in the late 1970s and early 1980s. How the legislature responded to that bonanza will be an important part of our discussion.

BACKGROUND

Alaskans seem to pay closer attention to their legislature than do citizens of other states. But greater attention does not mean greater approval. Alaskans, like other Americans, do not think much of their state legislature. Legislators are keenly sensitive to this disapproval; in a 1978 survey, 76 percent of Alaska legislators said they believed that the public's image of the legislature was poor.[1]

Legislators often fault the press for their low public esteem. Alaska papers, particularly Anchorage's, tend to be critical of the legislature.

Senator Bill Ray's response to one 1985 *Anchorage Times* editorial was:

> The Times is so idiotic in its editorial policy and thought process that I can't believe it. Some of this stuff is just plain stupid. I am the target of that paper at least once a week in their editorials in some disparaging manner....[2]

The Alaska press may tend to emphasize the legislature's weaknesses and abuses but in any case the citizenry is attentive to state politics. Historical as well as contemporary factors help explain this interest.

Prior to statehood, Alaska's legislature was weak for a number of reasons discussed more fully in the history chapter. Many of the decisions that affected Alaska were made in government offices and corporate headquarters in Washington, D.C., New York, and Seattle. Territorial legislatures and governors were dominated or ignored by the federal government. As a result, when the new state legislature came into being in 1959, many Alaskans saw it as an institution that would help Alaska take control of its destiny.

Alaska's constitutional framers supported measures to make the legislature influential within an effective government structure. One expert on Alaska's constitution has observed, "A major expression of confidence in the legislature is the broad discretion the constitution gives it to fashion the details of government structure and operation (details which are specified in the constitutions of many states)."[3] The framers also approved annual unlimited sessions (although sessions are now limited as a result of a 1984 constitutional amendment), established a system of pay for legislators, and established a legislative council to support the legislature's work and manage its affairs. (More detail on the constitutional provisions for a state legislature is in the chapter on Alaska's constitution.)

Overall the legislature was designed as an institution concerned with protecting vulnerable and isolated Alaskans from powerful outside interests, as well as an instrument for developing the state's natural resources. So in the early days of statehood Alaskans were very interested in their legislature. That interest endures today, but for different reasons.

Alaska in the mid-1980s is a wealthy state, no longer dependent on federal handouts to provide its basic services. But it is a wealth overwhelmingly controlled by government and dependent on one resource: oil. Eighty-five percent of government operations were paid for by oil taxes at the start of the 1980s. The legislature divides and distributes oil revenues. Not surprisingly, the process of distribution became the central feature, and most important factor, in the legislative process in the early 1980s. We look closely at legislative operations during the years when oil revenues were at their peak, but first we look at the composition of the legislature. The legislature after all is made up of 60 individual human beings, and their characteristics and behavior go far toward defining it as an institution.

COMPOSITION OF THE LEGISLATURE

CHANGES IN REPRESENTATION

The legislature changed rapidly in the first 25 years of statehood. The growth in urban areas of the state, particularly Anchorage, and the relative decline in rural population affected the character and composition of the legislature. With each 10-year census the number of urban representatives has increased.[4] Anchorage legislators now make up a significant block, with 19 of 40 members in the house and 8 of 20 senators. Nonetheless, the power of rural areas, particularly if defined broadly to include most of the non-Anchorage portions of the state, has not seriously eroded in the 1980s. In fact, rural legislators have tended to be disproportionately influential, often allying with legislators from other regions of the state to form ruling coalitions. Non-Anchorage legislators on the whole have long tenures in office, particularly in the senate. Non-Anchorage members of the senate in the mid-1980s averaged twice as long in office as did Anchorage area members and often held the balance between Republican and Democratic majorities. In the 1984 Alaska Legislature, for instance, tenures of legislators ranged from less than 2 years to more than 20 years. None of the legislators with the longest tenures were from Anchorage—but a large share of those with the shortest tenures were.

This long tenure in office translates into power for the rural areas of the state. During the fourteenth legislature (1984-1986), for example, one senator from a non-Anchorage region got an appropriation for his district reinserted by threatening future action. He reportedly said that while he was in the minority now, he would be in the majority in the future and would not forget those who had voted against him on an issue so vital to his district. The majority members of the committee changed their votes and allowed the appropriation to stand.[5]

The influence of rural legislators has also been reinforced by Native corporations. The corporations are important entities whose land holdings, economic activities, and constituents are basically oriented toward rural Alaska and have close ties to some rural legislators. During the fourteenth legislature, a significant indicator of the influence of rural Alaska was the fact that both the senate and house finance committees were chaired by Natives from rural Alaska. (The co-chair of the senate finance committee was from Anchorage.) Demographic change alone does not tell the whole story of regional power and representation. In the end the legislature is made up of individual men and women, and we must look to them and their characteristics to understand it.

THE LEGISLATORS

"All of this is discouraging normal people from running for the legislature."
Comment by Rep. John Lindauer, R., Anchorage, during floor debate on adjournment of the thirteenth (1982-1984) legislature.

Knowing who serves in Alaska's legislature is important to understanding its behavior. The legislature is made up of sixty individuals who vary in education, occupation, and other personal characteristics. These Alaskans have different ideological perspectives, come from diverse districts, and relate to their constituents and interest groups in different ways. Once they are elected to the senate or the house, they assume roles and adapt to the norms of these institutions. One of the most pressing issues they face is whether they are legislators first and citizens with private pursuits second, or whether they are private citizens who as a civic duty spend some time as legislators. They must also decide to what extent they should conform to and support the wishes of people in their districts, or attend primarily to their own feelings about what is right or good for the state as a whole.

A "typical" Alaska legislator in the 1980s is a white male, who, if in the house, is likely to be in his 40s, and if in the senate, in his 50s. He is most likely to be a businessman, to have been born outside the state, to have served one previous term in the legislature, and to have a college degree. But there is still considerable variety in the legislature. Women constitute about 10 percent of the membership, Alaska Natives 10-15 percent, and other minorities about 2 percent. A majority of legislators describe themselves as businessmen, but 20 percent are from the professions (law and education, mostly) and a small proportion are fishermen, miners, and farmers. (See Tables 10.1 and 10.2.) The businessmen tend to be Republicans, and the lawyers and educators are almost all Democrats.

Demographically the Alaska Legislature is thus not very representative of the general population of the state. Women, minorities, and the young are under-represented, while men, business people, and professionals are over-represented. Social background, however, is not a completely reliable indicator of legislative behavior. Every representative has a series of relationships with

Table 10.1
Alaska State House of Representatives Occupational Categories

	1985-86	1983-84	1981-82	1979-80	1977-78
Professional (total)	(10)	(11)	(8)	(9)	(9)
Attorneys	5	2	2	1	3
Medical		1	1	1	1
Educators	4	6	3	5	3
Engineers		1	1	1	1
Accountants	1	1	1	1	1
Government	2	1	2	3	5
Writers	2	2	1	3	1
Farmers			2	1	
Real Estate/Insurance	3	2	2	2	
Business	18	20	20	15	20
Fishermen	1	2	3	5	4
Miners	1	1	1	1	
Legislators	1	1	1		
Other	2			1	1

Source: Alaska Department of Education, *Alaska Blue Book*, 1977-1978 to 1985-1986.

Table 10.2
Alaska State Senate Occupational Categories

	1985-86	1983-84	1981-82	1979-80	1977-78
Professional (total)	(5)	(7)	(6)	(4)	(5)
Attorneys	3	4	2	2	4
Medical					
Educators	2	3	4	4	1
Engineers					
Accountants					
Government			1	1	1
Writers					
Farmers	1	1			
Real Estate/Insurance	1		1	1	2
Business	11	11	11	12	10
Fishermen	2	1	1		
Legislators					1

Source: Alaska Department of Education, *Alaska Blue Book*, 1977-1978 to 1985-1986.

many other individuals and groups, and these relationships may influence his behavior.

In other states, "birthright" characteristics—race, religion, and ethnic and national background—tend to be very important attributes in the recruitment of legislators. In Alaska such characteristics are generally less important, although still present. This is particularly true in the Native regions of the state. About 14 percent of the state's population is Native, but in some regions Natives are a majority. Being a Native from some rural regions can be an important and even critical factor in electoral success. By contrast, in urban areas birthright characteristics seem relatively unimportant. Alaska's urban population has diverse origins, and its settlement patterns are not clearly defined by ethnicity or religion.

Other criteria that voters elsewhere use in selecting legislators are place and length of residence. Legislators in other states tend to have strong roots in their constituencies, with districts seldom electing "newcomers" with less than twenty or twenty-five years of residence. One study found that even in the highly mobile state of California 56 percent of legislators had been born in their districts or had lived in them over 30 years.[6] In Alaska, long-term residence is less significant. Alaska grew 33 percent in the decade from 1970-1980, and migration into the urban areas constituted nearly half the total growth in this period. The thirteenth Alaska Legislature included only seven members born in Alaska, and of these six were Natives. In a state of newcomers, long-term residence isn't critical—although those candidates who have been in Alaska a long time often emphasize that fact in their campaigns.

Alaska legislators in general are employed in higher status occupations and have more education than the population as a whole, but they are not necessarily members of an upper class of inherited wealth and influence. One reason for this is that the "upper class" as such is not well defined in Alaska, the state's affluent being "new rich."[7] Because the state does not have a significant group of distinguished old families of great wealth and social stature, being a legislator may be a position of greater social recognition and prestige in Alaska than in other states.

Many legislators subscribe to or personify aspects of the Alaska political culture described in the chapter on that topic. In particular, Alaska voters may be inclined to elect officials who project an image of self-reliant individualism. Jay Hammond, who was Alaska's governor from 1974 to 1982, is a strong example of this image; Hammond is a bearded trapper, guide, and fisherman who was popular with voters throughout the state.

Tables 10.1 and 10.2 show that Alaska legislators, like those in other states, tend to come from occupations with flexible work schedules and the free time to devote to legislative service. Business people, attorneys, educators, and fishermen are the dominant professional groups in the legislature. Business people generally have the necessary financial resources, contacts, and concern about public policy decisions. Attorneys have a natural interest in lawmaking, and serving in the legislature gives them exposure and contacts. The number of attorneys in the legislature declined in the late 1970s, due in part to the effects of the state public disclosure law which requires legislators and other public officials to reveal sources of income and business involvement.

Because of the attorney-client relationship, attorneys found these disclosure requirements difficult to comply with. In 1973, before the law was in force, there were nine attorneys in the legislature. This number had dropped to three by 1979-80. In the 1980s the number of attorneys in the legislature has grown again, perhaps because the disclosure law is not as much of a problem as attorneys had anticipated.

Fishermen have free time in the winter and have always been an important political group in Alaska. Historically, one of the pressures limiting the length of sessions has been the desire of fishermen/legislators to leave Juneau in time for the salmon runs. Educators are generally politically active, and are an important interest group. Most of those who serve are retired, because state law in Alaska does not allow public employees to retain their jobs and hold state office. Alaska has more public employees than any other state, so a significant sector of the population is not eligible for elective office because they hold public sector jobs.[8] Former public employees who are members of the legislature may, however, reflect the interests and concerns of that group.

Overall, Alaska legislators, like their counterparts elsewhere, possess certain social characteristics expected by their constituents. They are a mixed group reflecting the highly diverse regions of the state, both in ethnic and racial terms and occupational backgrounds. It seems that Alaskans, like citizens of other states, elect local boys who have made good and share their values, but who are not necessarily mirror images of themselves.

RECRUITMENT AND ELECTIONS

As interesting as the question of who runs for the legislature is the question why. What makes a citizen decide to be a legislator? It is very difficult to discover the motives of office seekers, and there is no systematic information on the motives of Alaska legislators. Legislators themselves often don't understand all the reasons why they seek public office.[9]

Alaska seems to have a proportionately larger than normal pool of people who are interested in running for public office. The high level of interest in and salience of state government in Alaska, and the fact that government is such an important segment of the economy, may create more interest in running for state office in Alaska than in other states. Nationally, political scientist Alan Rosenthal sees increases in communication about politics as an important factor in recruitment. He also attributes higher interest in running for state legislatures to increasing education of the population and more opportunities for minorities and women to enter politics.[10] In Alaska, the lack of party control over nominations, due to liberal electoral laws and the blanket primary, encourages entry into electoral politics. Moreover, the state's small population makes public offices more visible, and with three times as many legislators per capita as its nearest neighbor, Washington state, Alaska provides more electoral opportunities.[11]

Alaska's legislators generally describe their motives for running for the legislature in terms of an interest in public affairs or sense of obligation to the public. Legislators surveyed in 1978 responded to the question of why they were serving with statements like "It's satisfying to be able to have an impact— to be able to help constituents" and "There are personal satisfactions in being able to help people." Civic duty and community service are public-spirited reasons and are obviously more likely to appeal to voters than are statements about seeking private power or status. There seems no reason, however, to believe that Alaskans don't also run for the legislature for personal reasons. One senator, for example, said he enjoyed "the prestige and recognition" that went with being a senator.[12]

Regardless of the motivation, the desire to be a legislator is not something that in most cases comes suddenly. Political scientist James Barber found two categories of state legislators he called "spectators" and "reluctants" making up a large part of the Connecticut legislature in the late 1950s. Generally middle-aged or elderly and possessing modest achievement, limited skills and restricted ambitions, these types of people were recruited to run for office in small, non-competitive towns. The Alaska Legislature of today seems to have only a few members who fit this description. Rather, Alaska legislators are more like Barber's other types, the "advertisers" and "lawmakers." These types are younger, more energetic, and ambitious; they seek nominations, rather than being recruited by party leaders.[13] Most Alaska legislators interviewed in 1978 talked in terms of policy and service, characteristic postures of "lawmakers" rather than of the passive "spectators."

As difficult as it is to determine what motives Alaskans have to run for the legislature, it is almost as hard to specify the circumstances. Many claim they were prevailed upon by friends, constituents, backers, or party officials to run for office. As the chapters on political parties and elections indicate, the role of parties in Alaska is not strong. While political scientist Frank Sorauf has found that the "party is obviously the chief stimulus to candidacy in Pennsylvania" and other states, this is not the case in Alaska.[14] Candidates for the legislature often have little contact with the party before they run for office. Almost never in recent years can it be said the party was the "chief stimulus" for a legislative candidate's decision to run for office. One reason for this is that the parties in Alaska have historically had few assets to help candidates. Alaskans seem to be primarily "self-starters" who decide to run for office independent of party influence and often without much persuasion by others.

One form of recruitment that does exist in Alaska is recruitment by individual or organizational backers. Insiders talk about offers by interest groups and wealthy individuals to fund campaigns. Given the weakness of political parties and the presence of well-funded interest groups and lobbies prepared to fill this political vacuum, such recruitment undoubtedly takes place. The chapter on interest groups concludes that interest groups in Alaska are among the most influential of those in any state. One senator interviewed for this chapter said he had been offered a campaign war chest of $20,000 in contributions, to be organized by a former legislator/lobbyist, in exchange for support of a future organization of the senate. Clearly, interest groups and power brokers play a role in recruitment, though the extent and significance of those factors can only be estimated. Some legislators have gained reputations as representatives of particular interest groups as much as of their districts, blurring the distinction between legislator and lobbyist. And some legislators have emerged from interest groups such as the chambers of commerce, and been elected with their backing.[15]

Finally, a significant source of recruits is former legislative staff members. Already familiar with the legislature and in touch with the sources of campaign support and financing, such candidates for the legislature seem to do well in campaigns. In the 1984 election, no less than five of the house candidates from the Anchorage area were former legislative staff members, and nineteen members of the 1985-86 legislature were former staff members. Close to the legislative process, staff members no doubt harbor some sense that they can do a better job than the incumbents they have observed at first hand.

Legislative elections in Alaska are not nearly as competitive as might appear from looking at the overall turnover in legislators. The chapter on elections finds that while the state had nearly equal numbers of Republicans and Democrats in recent years, the regions tended to be dominated by one political party or the other, reinforcing the staying power of incumbents. In any case many of those who don't return to Juneau have chosen not to run again. The reasons for this failure of some incumbents to run vary, but include long sessions and frustration with the process. Representative Rick Urion, in announcing on the house floor in 1978 that he would not run again said, "For those of us who have lives outside this body, it is very difficult to decide whether to run again."[16]

The capital is a long way from the state's population centers, making service there a mixed blessing, particularly for legislators with families. Juneau is 600 air miles from home for a legislator from Anchorage and more than 1,000 for one from Kotzebue. Perhaps there is some geographical significance to the fact that the two representatives and one senator from Juneau have served an average of 16 years in the legislature, and all three ran unopposed in their last election. At the same time, no member from Anchorage is senior to the most junior member from Juneau, and eleven of sixteen house members from Anchorage were freshmen in 1985. The remoteness of the capital is not the only factor, however. Anchorage, and to some degree Fairbanks, are growing mid-size urban areas, which are undergoing more rapid change than the non-Anchorage areas of the state. This change is reflected in the greater competitiveness of Anchorage's elections and higher rates of turnover.

PROFESSIONALIZATION

In addition to the questions of who legislators are and why they choose to pursue legislative office is the question—what is a legislator? Is he or she a citizen on temporary duty, or is a legislator a professional—an expert in the making of law and policy? Professionalism can apply to legislators as individuals, to the organization itself, and to the adequacy of its staff, information, and other facilities. The definition of professional carries the connotation of skill or quality of work and that this work is a serious, predominant activity. It is also clear that there is some ideological coloration to the designations "professional" and "citizen" legislature. By and large "citizen" legislatures are conservative legislatures in the sense that they tend to favor slow change and preservation of the status quo. "Professional" legislatures tend to favor change and are a product of change. Various studies that have evaluated the Alaska Legislature give a mixed picture of its "professionalism."[17]

Deciding if a legislature is "professional" in part depends on the criteria used to make the judgment. One of the most frequently cited criteria is whether the legislature is part-time or full-time. Because the issue of limiting session length by law has been heavily debated in Alaska, it presents an opportunity for examining the whole issue of legislative professionalism.

In much of the United States, legislatures have in the past been seen as part-time affairs. Fifteen states provide for regular legislative sessions only every other year.[18] Thirty-four, including Alaska, have a limit on session length. The philosophical underpinning of these limited sessions is that legislators should be private citizens who come together infrequently and for short periods, make the few necessary laws, approve the budget, and go home. In some states, the time limits no doubt reflect the generally negative view of state legislatures among Americans, giving rise to the now well-worn expression "No man's life, liberty or property are safe while the legislature is in session." Alaska's legislature has never been subject to the type of scorn that greets the Texas legislature, about which the state agricultural commissioner said, "It only meets for 140 days every two years and most Texans think it'd be better if it only met for two days every 140 years."[19]

In spite of the popular saying that the public considers a good legislature a legislature not in session, national organizations that evaluate state legislatures take a different view. They judge legislatures with limited sessions as "less professional," based on criteria that pertain to overall legislative functions. Conversely, urbanized, heavily populated states like California and New York with full-time legislatures are considered to be "highly professional." One study rated eight state legislatures as "highly professional"; only one had any restriction on session length, and none had biennial sessions.[20]

In 1984 Alaskans voted to amend the constitution to limit legislative sessions to 120 days. Legislative sessions had become longer and longer since the 1968 Prudhoe Bay oil discovery, until they reached a record 165-day session in 1982. The public and many legislators were upset with the wrangling, alleged cases of conflict of interest, and appearance of time-wasting and disorganization that characterized the long sessions. Some legislators seemed willing to stay in session as long as necessary, while others saw this and the growth of interim (between sessions) committees as turning the legislature into a de facto full-time, year-round organization.

The debate over full-time versus part-time legislatures frequently focused on the label "citizen legislator." Speaker of the House Joe Hayes and others who favored a citizen legislature argued in 1984 that such long sessions made service by Alaskans who were not "...retired, independently wealthy, or employed in seasonal industries impossible. There must be some assurance that citizens who undertake public service will be able to return to private sector jobs and families in a reasonable amount of time."[21]

In a 1978 debate on this issue, Representative Russ Meekins said, "We need a citizen legislature to keep in touch with the people." Another legislator, in announcing he would not run again due to the length of the session, said, "It's really important for legislators to have employment outside the legislature. It puts them in the real world."[22]

Legislators who opposed a limit on session length argued in 1978 that it might strengthen the hand of the governor, who could wait out the legislature on policy questions, and have discretion handed to him when the legislature was forced to adjourn. Mike Miller, a Juneau representative, maintained that limited sessions were "made to order for the special interests, whose major job is to block legislation."[23]

Underlying the debate over session limits and citizen legislators versus unlimited sessions and professionalization may be some sense that the former favors the status quo, and is thus unpopular with liberals, while the latter favors change and is thus unpopular with conservatives.

In the end, the length of the session as such is an important issue primarily because of the way it affects the ability of the legislature to carry out its constitutional purposes. The National Conference of State Legislatures (NCSL) was asked by the Alaska Legislature in 1983 to examine this issue and a number of others. The NCSL did not recommend limiting session length but said the legislature could make more effective use of its time by establishing deadlines and scheduling its work better. Such proposed reforms were highly charged politically, in that they would directly impact leadership discretion, control of the process, and its legislative outputs. But the proposals did suggest that a session limit might have been the wrong target, if its purpose was to improve the performance of the legislature. Inability or unwillingness of legislative leaders to make the reforms proposed by the NCSL left the focus on session length.

A number of recent studies have found a change in the makeup of state legislatures, with the newer group of legislators being better qualified than legislators of the past. This professionalization of state legislatures is also evidenced by their changing occupational makeup. Minnesota, for example, has seen a dramatic change in composition of its legislature. The lawyers, independent business owners, and farmers who once dominated the legislature have been replaced by young people; one-sixth of the Minnesota legislators in 1983 depended on their legislative pay.[24]

More and more legislators nationwide are describing themselves in their biographies as "legislators." For example, Alan Rosenthal noted in 1981 that "Ten years ago only one New York senator and not a single assemblyman listed himself as a legislator. Today, however, nearly a third of the members of each house identify themselves as such."[25]

In Alaska between 1976 and 1984 only one senator and one house member listed their occupations as "legislator." Yet observers of the legislature know that some members consider being legislators their primary jobs, and also in many cases their major source of income. One legislator who was part of the large group of new young legislators who came into office in 1974 said, "Hell, we didn't have any jobs other than the legislature, but [publisher Robert] Atwood and the [*Anchorage*] *Times* would flay you alive if you listed your job as legislator.'' That Alaska legislators avoid listing ''legislator'' as their occupation thus reflects more the public's attitude toward legislative professionalism than realities of interest and activity.

In states such as New Hampshire, Nebraska, and Wyoming, legislators continue to be citizen amateurs. Change in these state legislatures is very slow. Without oil development Alaska's legislature would probably be similar to them. Alaska legislatures of the 1960s had many of the elements of amateurism. In Alaska, the arrival of the oil bonanza signaled change, and Alaska's legislature changed rapidly. At that critical moment in the state's history, the Alaska Legislature came to be dominated by a new group. They were the first wave of Alaska's professional legislators. But they were also a uniquely Alaska first wave—they were green troops, they were eager, they won some important battles, they suffered high casualties, and they probably won't be seen again. We look next at those legislators.

THE SUNSHINE BOYS

> Who are the sunshine boys? Well, they are legislators who don't have
> anything, they don't want anything, and don't want you to have anything.
> Senator Bill Ray

In 1974, in the aftermath of the national Watergate scandal, large numbers of new reform-oriented and mostly Democratic legislators swept into Congress and the state legislatures. In Alaska the new legislators took control of the House of Representatives. This new breed of Alaska legislator was not, however, identical with the Watergate class elsewhere, and the public response to Watergate was not the only factor that propelled them into office.

In Alaska in 1972 and 1974 there was a crystalization of attitudes about dealing with the impending oil bonanza. Some politicians and others claimed the $900 million lease sale down payment the state had received for Prudhoe Bay leases in 1969 had been wasted by earlier legislatures. Many people were also afraid of and hostile to the oil companies, whom they saw as descending on the state. A 1974 editorial in the *Anchorage Daily News*, at the end of what critics considered a pro-oil development legislature, noted that Alaska had always supported development and growth of almost any kind:

> ...because our state's economic footing was very much in doubt and an
> economic base was essential...But now things have changed...This ''year
> of the pipeline'' is also a political year, a time for candidates to consider
> the questions of uncharted growth and ill conceived promises that fulfill
> only bureaucrats' or developers' dreams and do nothing to improve the
> quality of our lives.[26]

The 1974 campaign charges that the eighth legislature had given the oil companies too much, and that its members had also refused to pass open government laws and campaign finance regulations, reinforced the reformist mood in Alaska. Alaska had also just undergone a redistricting, which created opportunities for new candidates, particularly from Anchorage. Many of these new candidates were young idealists who had cut their teeth as part of the "Ad Hoc Democrats," an anti-Vietnam war and pro-political reform movement within the state's Democratic party. Along with Republican populist Jay Hammond, this new group hit a responsive chord with the electorate. In a major change of direction, the state elected a new Democratic majority in the legislature and a Republican governor who shared many of the views articulated by the reform Democrats on the critical issues facing the state.

Once in office, these young reformers—labeled the "sunshine boys" for their support of "sunshine" laws dealing with open meetings, financial disclosure, and conflicts of interest—dominated the house Democratic majority. Their agenda and the issues they had campaigned on were legislation for clean government and management of the oil bonanza in the interests of Alaska. In 1975 they passed the state's campaign finance disclosure law. They also put a popular referendum on the ballot regulating conflict of interest. In 1976, concerned by the strength of the oil industry's lobby, they passed a lobbying regulation law. These measures gained the support of some Republicans and the senate majority, and Governor Hammond signed them into law.

The sunshine boys thus completed the "open government" part of their agenda. Idealistic, energetic, and mostly inexperienced, they at first puzzled senior legislators. In the political terms of the past, "they didn't want anything," and thus were difficult to deal with. In fact they wanted certain things badly, and were highly issue-oriented. According to one of them, what really brought them together was the sense that "A flood of money was about to descend on the state, and that it was very likely to be wasted or be diverted out of the state" by the oil companies. The way to prevent that from happening was first to open government up so the public would know what was going on, and second to focus on capture, control of, and management of the oil bonanza.

For the rest of the period they were in power in the legislature, the sunshine boys were preoccupied by the issue of oil money. Representative Hugh Malone, speaker of the house in 1977-78, became the legislative father of the Permanent Fund, a proposed special fund to save part of the state's oil revenues for the future. With the support of Governor Hammond, the Permanent Fund was established in 1976.

The sunshine boys and other legislators and the governor had succeeded in providing a mechanism to control and preserve the benefits of the oil bonanza. Some of the sunshine boys' liberal critics in the Democratic party charged that their single-minded crusade to capture and manage the oil wealth caused them to neglect other social issues and priorities of the period. Nevertheless, the sunshine boys demonstrated that a highly motivated group of legislators could, on an issue they perceived as critical to the state's future, consciously choose a course of action, have it debated publicly, and implement the public policy choice.

By 1981, the era of the sunshine boys was over. Democrats lost control of the House of Representatives in a coup that saw a Republican-led coalition take power. In a number of ways the rise and fall of the sunshine boys were among the most significant developments in the legislature since statehood. They changed the legislature by opening the process to public scrutiny. Where executive sessions of committees, in which deals were cut by insiders, had been frequent in the past, they became less frequent, at least before the largest volume of petroleum revenues began to flow. And as a result of their efforts, the public now had access to more information about who was using money in what ways to influence election of members and passage of legislation. Moreover, to some degree the composition of the legislature may have been changed by discouraging from service those who were unwilling to disclose their personal or campaign finances. The most enduring impact of the sunshine movement, however, was surely that it helped establish the Permanent Fund and may have extracted a higher return to the state of Prudhoe Bay wealth.

The sunshine boys brought significant change to the legislature, but their effects on professionalism were mixed. In some areas the legislative process is more open and better informed. In others, notably developing the state's budget, they not only failed but certain of them may have contributed to the breakdown of collective review in the process. It was one of the sunshine boys, for example, who initiated the practice of divvying up control of the state's capital budget so that all legislators could allocate their individual shares as they saw fit—a case of "openness" in government running its full circle. (See discussion of the budget process below.)

The Alaska Legislature is currently a mix of people who would consider themselves citizen legislators and professionals. Citizen legislators may care less about just satisfying constituents and campaign contributors, because they care less about winning. But they also are probably less able, in the sense of knowing the technical issues and process, than those committed to a long career in the legislature. Professionals, on the other hand, may be too reluctant to take risks. The rewards of office may have become too important to them. Having made a choice of a career in politics, they may take care of their districts, offend as few people as possible, and do little to disturb the process. What was unique about the sunshine boys may be that they were neither citizen legislators nor professionals. Instead they were idealists who used the process to achieve something they thought was important.

ORGANIZATION AND LEADERSHIP

Like those of most legislative bodies, the Alaska Legislature's leadership and organization are determined by a simple majority of the members of each chamber. On June 12, 1981, near the end of a long session, the Alaska House of Representatives switched from a Democratic majority to a Republican-dominated coalition. In many states close majorities have led to coalitions and intense maneuvering at the beginning of sessions. Seldom, however, has a mid-session change in the majority taken place without a change in the legislature's composition.

One hundred and fifty days into the session, the Republican minority was dissatisfied because it believed it was not getting the consideration minorities had traditionally received. Many legislators felt that the legislative session had dragged on too long. There was bitter debate over priorities in spending the state's oil wealth, and over the shares each member was to receive for his or her district. Representative Russ Meekins, the leader of the dissident Democrats, conferred with the leadership of the Republican minority, formed an insurgent coalition, and secretly moved onto the floor of the legislature. Meekins took the speaker's chair, excused all members not present, and entertained a motion to remove the current speaker. A disorderly scene ensued, with an almost complete breakdown in decorum and parliamentary procedure.

The whole scene was characterized by Representative Mike Miller of Juneau, when he finally got a chance to address the body:

> ...this kangaroo session is beneath contempt, and it's a disgrace to the history of the Legislature of Alaska. I just can't express to you my disappointment in the people who would participate in an event such as this. It's just a total abrogation of your responsibility under the constitution.[27]

Regardless of the intense feelings of the legislators involved, the mid-session reorganization (opponents called it a ''coup,'' and pundits called it ''banana republicanism'') was sustained by the courts, which refused to question another branch's internal organization. The new majority coalition directed the rest of the twelfth legislature (1981-82).

That event graphically illustrates two points: that it is the majority, however constituted, that organizes and holds leadership in the legislature, and that party discipline is extremely weak in Alaska. Party discipline is the ability of party leadership, and the willingness of party members, to agree on and enforce the party's perspective and priorities. An absolute minimum evidence of party discipline is agreement on controlling and organizing legislative bodies, where the party's members are in the majority.

Leadership in the Alaska Legislature operates on two levels. There are formal leadership positions, and there are informal. Informal leaders may be deferred to in subject areas where they are expert, such as former Representative Hugh Malone, who was little known outside the legislature but was respected inside for his expertise on the Permanent Fund issue. That expertise gave him considerable influence on matters related to the fund. Besides subject area leadership, individual legislators may be respected for their fairness and integrity, taking what amount to moral leadership roles in the legislature.

It is the formal leadership, however, that controls the day-to-day operations of the legislature and determines its overall direction. These positions are roughly parallel in the senate and house. The presiding officer of the senate is the president. Elected by a majority of the membership in a step which also dictates how the body will be organized, he or she is one of the state's most powerful figures. Once selected, the president appoints a committee or committees consisting of five members, including the president. This committee nominates the chairs and members of the standing committees in a report that must be approved by a majority vote of the senate. Who will be nominated is generally settled as part of a long and complex bargaining process prior to the session. The central feature of that bargaining is selection of the all-powerful president.

The house is presided over by the speaker. His selection is also a key factor in the majority's organization, but is likely to be simpler and more straightforward than in the senate, particularly if there is a clear party majority. Under the uniform rules of the legislature, the speaker's powers are similar to those of the president of the senate. These include the authority to refer bills to committees. This is a significant power in that the committee or committees to which a bill is referred can determine its fate; many bills "die in committee." In the 1985 legislative session Senate President Don Bennett used the State Affairs Committee, chaired by Senator Mitch Abood, for exactly this purpose, causing that committee to be referred to as "Abood's Tomb."

Standing committee jurisdiction is specified and bills are normally assigned according to their subject. Because bills often deal with more than one subject, or a subject in which committee jurisdictions are not clear, the speaker's discretion can significantly affect the outcome. Another power the presiding officers have is ruling on parliamentary questions. Use of parliamentary rulings is a powerful tactic that a skillful house speaker or senate president can employ with considerable effect.

The speaker and senate president are influential in determining the majority party membership on the standing committees. Legislators eagerly seek out particular committee appointments, either because particular committees are important to their constituents, or so they can pursue particular policy goals, or because the committee assignment enhances their political objectives. The finance committees in Alaska are so important that virtually all legislators seek positions on them. The power of the chairs of the finance committees in fact rivals that of the presiding officers.

The presiding officers can also use their power over appointments to reward friends and punish enemies, as well as to create obligations to be called in later. Such control over the organization of the legislative process, the fate of legislation, and other important aspects of the system become levers that effective presiding officers use to pursue their own policy priorities and political objectives.

In addition to the presiding officers, there are the majority party leaders in each house. Majority leaders act as lieutenants in assisting the speaker and president in the conduct of legislative business. They are usually more partisan than the presiding officers, who generally attempt to appear more impartial. In the 1982-1984 legislative sessions, many considered the house speaker and majority leader to be excessively partisan and arbitrary in their actions. The defeat of Representative Ramona Barnes, the Republican majority leader, in the Republican primary in 1984 may have resulted in part because of this partisanship. Voters responded to her challenger's promise to bring "civility" back to the legislature. Further, her Republican challenger was backed by many Democrats who considered Barnes to be excessively partisan.

Leadership and the requirements of legislative organization interact to create much of the character of a given legislative session. Some speakers and presidents seem to have had far greater personal impact on the process than others. Sometimes this impact is a result of circumstances, but more often it is attributable to the personal qualities of the leaders. Different styles may be effective—quiet persuasion by a well-liked speaker or president is sometimes judged as effective as the maneuvering and "bullying" that have also brought results for presiding officers.[28]

THE LEGISLATIVE BUDGETING PROCESS

"No money shall be withdrawn from the treasury except in accordance with appropriations made by law." Article IX, Section 13 of Alaska's constitution gives the legislature its most significant power: the power of the purse. Money is what makes government work and turns policy statements into concrete actions and services.

In Alaska, the legislative budgeting process was radically affected by the oil bonanza of the late 1970s and early 1980s. Huge increases in expenditures took place, with the total budget growing from less than $400 million in 1974, before the oil money began to flow, to over $5 billion in 1981, when oil revenues peaked. The state in the mid-1980s depends on oil revenues for 85 percent of its non-federal revenues. Price declines in the world oil market send shock waves through the legislature. Because the legislature appropriates in *anticipation* of revenues for the coming fiscal year, changes in revenue forecasts lead to frantic attempts to revise the budget, or force cuts in existing agency expenditures. Much of the behavior of the Alaska Legislature in recent years can be seen as an effect of the ups and downs of oil prices. The budgeting process has come to overshadow the rest of what the legislature does. As a result, examination of the legislative budgeting process will help us understand the contemporary Alaska Legislature.[29]

Each year the governor submits to the legislature executive operating and capital budgets. The executive operating budget can be extensively revised by the legislature. Much of the final capital budget will be expenditures authorized and appropriated by the legislature itself. The executive budget may best be viewed as a planning document. While there is no state plan as such, the governor's budget is the opportunity for the executive branch to lay out in one place its priorities and plans for the coming year. Consistent with this concept, the executive budget took the form of a "program budget" system from 1971 to 1981. This meant that requests for appropriations came to the legislature not as individual items, but as program packages, a practice followed in many other states.

During the years when program budgeting was being used, the legislature developed a system for review of the budget. Public hearings took place before the finance committees over a number of months. Each program was reviewed in considerable detail. After budgets were passed by the house and senate, the inevitable differences required appointment of a conference committee with members from both houses. Often this was a "free" conference committee that rewrote sections of the budget from scratch. The free conference committee had vast powers to make changes in the budget, and it met in closed session. In 1974 the "sunshine" movement succeeded in requiring that meetings of the committee be public, and other reforms in 1982 virtually eliminated use of the free conference committee. (The legislature also has a Legislative Finance Division that helped coordinate and rationalize the budget process.)

In 1978, as part of an extensive year-long special project evaluating the legislature, the Alaska League of Women Voters issued a report that found little wrong with the budget process:

> The main difficulty with the budget process as currently instituted is the great amount of time that is involved for legislators and administrators alike.[30]

The league recommended further computerization of the budget and consideration of biennial budgeting. In the same year, the legislature passed a statute requiring the state to publish a summary of the budget to make it more understandable to the public.[31] Thus, until oil prices went up dramatically at the end of the 1970s, critical observers took a relatively benign view of the way the legislature set spending priorities. The "sunshine" movement's major objective was to open the process to public view, rather than to change the procedures used. The process, while far from perfect, was reasonably understandable and responsible.

When the state's oil revenues climbed sharply in 1979, in the wake of the Iranian revolution, the existing budget process began to break down. Observers seemed inclined at first to accept this breakdown as an understandable consequence of the first impact of large amounts of money, but as time went on the situation seemed to get worse. The state's newspapers and editorial writers became increasingly critical of the way the legislature was handling the budget. A banker-economist wrote in the *Anchorage Times* in April 1984:

> The spending is not only out of control, which in itself is bad, but there are two other dimensions to it that cause it to be unacceptable. First, the spending pattern by the state has absolutely no rhyme or reason. There is no logic whatsoever to the capital expenditures proposed by the legislature and approved by the Governor. Second, and most important, the behavior in Juneau is the ultimate insult to us well-meaning conscientious average citizens. Somehow each individual legislator has made the erroneous assumption that we constituents have a predisposition toward "bringing home the bacon."[32]

On the same Sunday, the *Anchorage Daily News* editorialized about the terrible state of budget information, with accurate figures being virtually unobtainable, and the widely held assumption that:

> ...numbers are at least partly political, and only as credible as their political source. People pick the budget numbers that best support their contentions.[33]

In the same paper two legislators warned of the coming decline in oil revenues and bemoaned the lack of an overall financial plan to guide the state's saving and spending habits.[34]

Before 1979, home district state-funded capital spending projects which could be considered "pork barrel" were not common. The state had very little money in comparison with its needs. According to one veteran legislator, legislators recognized that only the high priorities could be met, so legislative districts tended to receive capital projects on a cooperative rotational basis. (Veteran legislators have a saying for this: "what comes around goes around.") One school or road might account for most of a year's capital budget. The scarcity of money forced legislative review and cooperation to meet genuine needs.

A significant "reform" in 1979 probably did more to reduce review and accountability and fragment this policymaking process than any other event, aside from the discovery of the oil itself. After the big money began to arrive, the chairman of the house finance committee, Russ Meekins of Anchorage, established a precedent. He gave each member of the house $750,000 to spend as he wished in his district. This allocation system survived for several years, until rapid declines in world oil prices stemmed the flow of state revenues. Some legislators regularly referred to these allocations as "my money" and objected to any review by the finance committees of "their projects." For example, when asked about the need for public review of allocation formula spending in his district, Representative Ray Metcalfe of Anchorage—while acknowledging the need for public review—said, "I don't want to see my stoplights or playgrounds delayed."[35]

In a variation of traditional log rolling, the ruling ethic became not questioning other members' projects. Richard Fineberg, a researcher and reporter who investigated the budget process in 1982, found that Representative Meekins had created a monster: "Individual legislators did not want the finance committee to review their projects. As soon as they had the money they said in effect: stay out of my district."[36]

Meekins later said he had never intended that the allocation system would do away with overall review by the finance committee, and in fact, as chair of the finance committee, he sought collective review of the projects based on allocated funds. But legislators would not tolerate interference with their priorities. This was log rolling with a vengeance. Members were reluctant to question each others' pet projects, for fear their own might be voted down. In a legislature where strong party discipline does not exist, log rolling becomes virtually inevitable. In Alaska in the early 1980s, the abundance of money also removed the discipline provided by scarcity of revenues.

In a logical complement to the allocation system that developed in the legislature, negotiations with the governor led to an "allocation" system for each branch. The house, the senate, and the governor each got one-third of the capital budget. This strategy was intended to veto-proof the budget. It led to more fragmentation of the process. The mechanisms provided in the past to insure public review and attention to the priorities of the society as a whole were subverted. Each branch said to the others, "We will forgo our constitutional responsibilities to review the areas of the budget you wish to control, so long as you will do the same for us."

Another move away from accountability in the budgeting process occurred in 1981 when Senator Ed Dankworth of Anchorage pushed through legislation that took the state off program budgeting. Program budgeting's rational organization of the budget by program (for example, primary education) got in the way of capital items desired by legislators (say, a school in their district). The legislature did not seriously consider reform of the program budgeting system. It just did away with it, because it restricted capital project spending that could not be tied to programmatic needs.

The arrival of the bonanza also brought other legislative changes. In both the house and senate it was widely understood after 1981 that the real decisions were made behind closed doors despite open meeting laws. One legislator, who claimed he opposed such behavior, pointed out that the very computerization that the League of Women Voters in 1978 had seen as virtually the only needed reform of the process now facilitated "backroom deals." In the past, the complexity of large numbers of projects had required more participation, consultation, and meetings just to deal with the budget mechanics. Computerization largely removed those constraints.

Another effect on the legislature of big oil money was an increase in charges of conflicts of interest. In 1981, Senator George Hohman of Bethel was sentenced to prison after he was convicted of offering a bribe to another legislator to support purchase by the state of Canadian-made airplanes. Legislators interviewed by the author uniformly said they thought such blatantly unethical behavior was probably rare. On the other hand, there were also widespread and persistent charges of conflicts of interest of a less blatant variety.

In 1984, the legislature passed a new law on conflict of interest. It defined such a conflict as existing:

> ...when a person...takes or withholds official action or exerts official influence that could substantially benefit or harm a financial matter in which the person has a direct or indirect private interest.[37]

The committee on legislative ethics charged with enforcing this statute is made up of legislators, plus one public member selected by the legislature. Whether this new legislation will deal with the problem remains to be seen.

Perhaps one of the most important explanations for the breakdown in the budgeting process in the legislature in the 1980s is the lack of accountability in a financial system not based on taxation of individuals. The legislature in recent years has not spent individual taxpayers' money. The legislature did away with the state personal income tax in 1979. Governor Hammond opposed ending that tax, proposing instead that it continue, with refunds, to maintain a connection between legislative expenditures and the public. In the mid-1980s, most state monies came from taxes on oil companies. The Permanent Fund, by providing dividends to the public, has created a constituency interested in protecting that fund. But there is no clear constituency of taxpayers supporting fiscal responsibility with the rest of the state's money.

The effect of the oil bonanza on party discipline cannot be overlooked either. Party control of legislative organization broke down almost completely in the senate, and to a considerable degree in the house. The weakness of Alaska political parties, and regional politics, were major factors in this breakdown. It is noteworthy that a "bush caucus" of rural and Native legislators, defecting primarily from the Democratic party, has been the most important element in recent house coalitions. The oil bonanza seems to have been the critical catalyst in this "disorganization."

Before 1979, coalitions occurred almost exclusively when there were ties between Democrats and Republicans in the house and senate. In these legislatures the defection of only one member was required to create a majority. In the early 1980s, however, mixed party coalitions involving large numbers of defectors, and in situations where one party had a clear majority of members, became the rule rather than the exception in both the house and senate. (See Table 10.3.) The scramble for pieces of the capital budget, combined with the already weakened political party system, produced a system for organizing the legislature based on opportunism rather than party.

The power of legislative leaders is based in part on an understanding of how the confused and irrational budget process works. Like the mechanics in Crozier's study of a French factory—who destroy the manuals to the machines they repair so that only they can fix them—the ruling leadership in the first half of the 1980s had little incentive to make the confused process of appropriations more rational and understandable to outsiders. In the house, "bush caucus" members held the balance of power, dominated the body, and controlled the all-important finance committee. Without party control, leadership

Table 10.3
Party Makeup and Organization of Alaska Legislature Since Statehood

Year	HOUSE OF REPRESENTATIVES Rep	Dem	Other*	Organization	SENATE Rep	Dem	Other*	Organization
1959-60	5	34	1 (I)	Democrats	2	18	0	Democrats
1961-62	20	19	1 (I)	Coalition (R)	7	13	0	Democrats
1963-64	20	20	0	Coalition (R)	5	15	0	Democrats
1965-66	10	30	0	Democrats	3	17	0	Democrats
1967-68	25	15	0	Republicans	14	6	0	Republicans
1969-70	18	22	0	Democrats	11	9	0	Republicans
1971-72	9	31	0	Democrats	10	10	0	Coalition (R)
1973-74	19	20	1 (NP)	Coalition (R)	11	9	0	Republicans
1975-76	9	31	0	Democrats	7	13	0	Democrats
1977-78	15	25	0	Democrats	8	12	0	Democrats
1979-80	14	25	1 (L)	Democrats	11	9	0	Coalition (R)
1981-82	16	22	2 (L)	(Dem to 6/16) Coalition (R)	10	10	0	Coalition (R)
1983-84	21	19	0	Coalition (R)	11	9	0	Coalition (R)

*I = Independent;   NP = Non-partisan;   L = Libertarian

domination of the capital budget became the mechanism for disciplining and controlling the legislative process.

CONCLUSIONS

This examination of the Alaska Legislature has focused on legislators and their behavior, and the impacts and consequences of the "sunshine" movement and the oil bonanza. Much more could be said about these subjects and the legislature as a whole. In the end, the important thing is how these dynamic elements affect the long-term functioning of the legislature. Lawmaking, representing the people, overseeing administration, and balancing the other branches of government are the intended purposes of the legislature. How do the realities of the legislature's composition and operation affect these purposes?

The legislature's responsibility to make laws can only be evaluated in a subjective way. The key question is whether the legislature recognizes the important issues facing the state and passes laws to deal with them in the public interest. Legislative professionalism and reforms that make the legislature more functional seem to serve this purpose. The establishment of the Permanent Fund, though not without controversy, is a clear example of the legislature acting to address what were perceived to be the general and long-term interests of the state. The subsequent continued fragmentation of power in the legislature, however, due to weak party discipline and the parceling out of authority over the capital budget, raises serious concerns about the legislature's ability to function effectively in this way in the future.

The Alaska Legislature appears to serve the function of representation well. While the legislature is far from being a mirror of the population in terms of race, sex, occupation, or economic status, most elements of the state's population appear to have a voice in the capital. Moreover, constituents appear to have adequate access to legislators, and legislators seem to respond to constituents. A troubling question is whether the legislature's many points of access and responsiveness are skewed toward organized interests. The sunshine movement's efforts to open up the process and publicize sources of campaign funds were intended to make the legislature more representative and to check the power of organized interests. It cannot be demonstrated that the Alaska Legislature today is any more representative because of the sunshine movement, nor that organized interests are less influential, but the sources and beneficiaries of financial contributions to legislative campaigns are clearer.

Balancing the other branches of government, particularly the executive, and overseeing government's proper administration, are the two functions most dependent on the legislature's professionalization. Only a legislature with experienced and informed members can responsibly review and oversee the complexities of modern administration. Moreover, a professional legislature unfettered by arbitrary constraints and amateur membership will be able to better balance the constitutionally and institutionally powerful Alaska governor. At the same time, professionalism may adversely affect representation. Too long a tenure in office, and limited daily experience in the real world back in the district, may breed detachment.

The final picture of the Alaska Legislature is not a clear one. Elements of professionalization and reform were arrested by the oil bonanza and the resulting scramble for pieces of the huge capital budget. The institution of the allocation system, giving each member unilateral control over large sums of money, helped destroy party control and influence. The increased fragmentation of the legislative policymaking process has been most clearly reflected in the rise of coalition government. The question for the future is whether the legislature can recover the degree of coherence and direction it will need to deal effectively with new challenges brought about by declining oil revenues. The effects on the legislature of huge increases in revenues were profound. It seems likely that the decline in revenues will have equally profound, though unpredictable, effects.

ENDNOTES

[1]League of Women Voters, "The Alaska Legislature," September 1978, p. 3, (unpublished).

[2]Senator Bill Ray, quoted in the *Juneau Empire*, January 14, 1985, p. 6.

[3]Gordon S. Harrison, *A Citizen's Guide to the Constitution of the State of Alaska* (Anchorage: University of Alaska, Institute of Social and Economic Research, 1982).

[4]The authors of the state constitution foresaw that shifting population could distort representation in the legislature and devised a system based on both geographic area and population. That system was overturned by a 1962 U.S. Supreme Court decision. See complete discussion in Victor Fischer, *Alaska's Constitutional Convention* (Fairbanks: University of Alaska Press, 1975).

[5]Related to the author by several observers who were present. This event has been often referred to and has become part of the folklore of the Alaska Legislature.

[6]Peter Rossi, "Community Decision-Making," in Roland Young (ed.) *Approaches to the Study of Politics* (Evanston: Northwestern University Press, 1958).

[7]Gaetano Mosca, *The Ruling Class* (New York: McGraw-Hill, 1939).

[8]*Alaska Blue Book: 1983* (6th edition), Department of Education, State of Alaska, p. 267.

[9]John C. Wahlke et al., *The Legislative System* (New York: John Wiley and Sons, 1962), p. 488.

[10]Alan Rosenthal, *Legislative Life* (New York: Harper and Row, 1981), p. 57.

[11]*Alaska Blue Book: 1983*.

[12]League of Women Voters, "The Alaska Legislature," p. 4.

[13]James David Barber, *The Lawmakers* (New Haven: Yale University Press, 1965), pp. 217-233.

[14]Frank Sorauf, *Party and Representation* (New York: Atherton Press, 1963), pp. 94-103.

[15]A close review of Alaska Public Offices Commission records and a series of articles on campaign finance in the *Anchorage Daily News* provide abundant circumstantial evidence in support of these observations.

[16]Quoted in the *Alaska Advocate*, June 1, 1978, p. 4.

[17]John Burns, *The Sometime Governments: A Critical Study of the Fifty American Legislatures* (New York: Bantam, 1971). This study was updated by the Alaska League of Women Voters in their 1978 report, "The Alaska Legislature," (unpublished).

[18]Council of State Government, *Book of the States* (Lexington, KY: 1984).

[19]Quoted in *Washington Post Weekly*, January 10, 1984, p. 16.

[20]Thomas R. Dye, "State Legislative Politics," in Herbert Jacob and Kenneth Vines, *Politics in the American States*, Second Edition, (Boston: Little, Brown & Co., 1971).

[21]Senator Joe Hayes in *State of Alaska Division of Elections, Official Election Pamphlet: 1984*, p. 101.

[22]Quoted in *Alaska Advocate*, June 1, 1978, p. 4.

[23]Ibid.

[24]"Power Shifts in State Capitals as Professional Law Makers Take Over Leadership Spots," in *Congressional Quarterly* (September 3, 1983), pp. 1767- 1769.

[25]Rosenthal, *Legislative Life*, p. 58.

[26]*Anchorage Daily News*, April 19, 1974, p. 6.

[27]Transcript of House Session, June 12, 1981, (quoted in *Anchorage Daily News*, June 13, 1981).

[28]Past leadership in the Alaska Legislature has sometimes been equated with aggressive behind-the-scenes dealmaking. See, for example, *Anchorage Daily News*, editorial, April 8, 1984, decrying that practice.

[29]Richard Fineberg and his report, *Chaos in the Capital: The Budget System in Crisis*, issued by the Alaska Public Interest Research Group, 1982, provided much of the background for this section.

[30]League of Women Voters, "The Alaska Legislature," 1978 (unpublished).

[31]Although passed in 1978, the Governor's Office did not publish *Budget in Brief* until 1982.

[32]Robert Richards, in the *Anchorage Times*, April 8, 1984.

[33]*Anchorage Daily News*, editorial, April 8, 1984.

[34]Hugh Malone and Mike Szymanski, "Front Loading the Permanent Fund Will Help Control Spending," *Anchorage Daily News*, April 8, 1984.

[35]*Anchorage Daily News*, July 23, 1982, p. 6.

[36]Fineberg, *Chaos in the Capital*, p. 25.

[37]AS 24.60.030.

11

Alaska's Governor

Gerald A. McBeath

In most American states, the governor has become head of state and chief policymaker only after reforms strengthened the office. Alaska's constitution was a state-of-the-art document which incorporated these reforms, and from inception the governor of Alaska was designed to be a powerful figure in state government. Framers of the state constitution in 1955-56 pictured a governor who would overcome the weaknesses of the territorial executive. They wanted a governor who would deal forcefully with federal officials and with other powerful interests. They also wanted the governor to be the equal of the legislature in influence, which set up a basic tension between the state's two premier institutions of government.

This chapter examines the distinctive aspects of the Alaska governorship, both from the comparative perspective of government and politics in the 50 states and over three decades of statehood. The chief question it asks is whether the Alaska governor has lived up to the expectations of the constitutional framers. Also investigated are styles of governing Alaska and the capacity for change of the Alaska governorship. We turn to these several themes after looking briefly at the way in which governors of Alaska have come to office.

ELECTING ALASKA'S GOVERNORS

Gubernatorial elections in most American states are competitions between parties and issue positions as well as contests between power-seeking individuals and their supporters. This is also the case in Alaska, where candidate organizations have increasingly dominated statewide elections since 1970. Outside Anchorage, home to half the state's population, "friends and neighbors" politics is still important.

CAMPAIGNS FOR GOVERNOR

The state has had seven campaigns for the governorship since the first election in 1958. Although parties played significant roles in the 1958, 1962, and

1966 races, the most prominent feature of campaigns since 1970 has been the organizations formed around the candidates—for example, the Hammond for Governor campaign groups in 1974 and 1978. These groups have generally been run by those with personal and professional relationships to the candidates. Functions in the groups have included managing finances, developing and researching issues, organizing volunteers, and carrying on related housekeeping activities. Those operating campaign offices, raising funds, representing the candidates, and performing other activities were often old friends and associates of the candidates—for example, Bob Palmer and Clem Tillion in the Hammond organization. In 1982 the Sheffield for Governor organization had a steering committee of seven, each with long-term relationships with the candidate. Chief of the campaign staff was Sheffield's business partner. Democratic party officials occupied only two spots on the committee; two other officials had previously been registered as Republicans.

Studies of American national politics have chronicled the rise of candidate organizations in presidential politics and the decline of other forces.[1] The same pattern appears to have developed in state electoral politics. The emphasis on and importance of candidate-centered organizations in the Alaska election process appear greater than in other states, largely because of the reduced importance of political parties and the very large non-partisan registration—over half the Alaska electorate in 1984.

Alaska's gubernatorial campaigns are different from those of other states in another respect: their high cost. The 1982 per/vote cost of $19 in Alaska was the highest in the nation. Several states recorded much higher total campaign expenditures that year, but Alaska's $3.7 million in expenditures was high indeed for a state with the smallest voting population. Amounts spent in the previous six Alaska gubernatorial campaigns, although much less than the 1982 figure, were still approximately 15 percent higher on a per capita basis than spending in other states.

Factors that make goods and services more expensive in Alaska than in the other states also drive up the costs of gubernatorial elections. These higher costs are illustrated by advertising costs, which account for a large part of election campaign expenses. Purchasing a 30-second ad on Fairbanks television, for instance, is about 30 percent more expensive than in Seattle. In Fairbanks, as in all cities but Anchorage, there is little commercial competition, and this lack of competition has had the effect of substantially inflating the advertising prices paid by political candidates. Travel costs are of course also greater in America's largest state. Although nearly 75 percent of the state's population lives within 20-mile radiuses of Anchorage, Fairbanks, or Juneau, votes of rural Alaskans are also important; the outcome of more than one statewide race has hinged on the bush vote. Travel to these regions is expensive and time-consuming and usually feasible only in small planes.

Costs of gubernatorial election campaigns will probably continue to rise, driven by advertising cost increases and other forces. The first Alaska woman to announce her intention to run for governor, state senator Arliss Sturgulewski, said that it would cost her around $1.5 million to campaign for the 1986 elections—nearly $750,000 to get through the Republican primary and another $500,000 to $750,000 for a statewide general election race. Such costs seem likely to rise faster than population increases.

Under campaign reform legislation of 1974, the Alaska Public Offices Commission (APOC) requires candidates to file regular reports, listing in considerable detail the sources of their campaign contributions. Analysis of these records suggests that there have been three main sources of support for gubernatorial candidates in recent years: out-of-state political action committees (PACs), Alaska PACs, and individual contributions, including those of the candidates themselves. An increasing percentage of total campaign contributions in Alaska has come from out-of-state sources. (This observation also applies to sources of contributions for Alaska's U.S. Senate and House seats.) Oil and gas companies have been major contributors in recent gubernatorial races, and they have favored incumbents over challengers—including Jay Hammond in the 1978 election, even though Hammond had been critical of some oil and gas development schemes.[2]

Substantial shares of gubernatorial campaign expenditures in recent times have been met by political action committees in the state, with oil and gas companies and other resource extraction industries (such as mining, fishing, timber) contributing the most. Professional groups, such as teachers, public employees, health care professionals, and lawyers have also been large contributors, as have labor unions—with the Teamsters and the AFL-CIO making the largest contributions.[3]

Although limited by law to $1,000 per candidate, contributions from individuals have often provided the critical margin, but they have been less important in gubernatorial than in state legislative races. Loans from candidates to their own campaigns have also become a necessary aspect of running for the state's highest office. All three gubernatorial candidates in 1982 spent considerable parts of their personal wealth on the campaign, with Bill Sheffield, the winner, spending about $500,000.

These high costs of gubernatorial elections have excluded poorer candidates. Candidates have become more dependent on wealthy donor groups, leading to conflicts of interest. A recent example was a controversy early in the Sheffield administration. To recover personal loans he had made to his 1982 campaign, the new governor attended fund-raisers held on his behalf by oil company representatives in Houston. Governor Sheffield had been in the nation's capital just before this visit, presenting the state's position on proposed oil and gas lease sales and development in the Norton Sound area. The timing of his trip (as well as his being accompanied by the state attorney general and commissioner of the Department of Natural Resources) raised ethical questions, especially when the purpose of the fund-raiser was to pay off campaign debts to himself.

VOTING FOR GOVERNORS IN ALASKA

The single most important factor in election (or re-election) in Alaska seems to be the candidate's image and appeal (including name recognition, and the support of "friends and neighbors"). Second, issues influence gubernatorial election outcomes, particularly when two or more issues produce an ideological choice for most voters and when candidates' positions on those issues are clear, as occurred in the 1982 election. Third, political party identification has an influence—although a declining influence—in Alaska state gubernatorial elections.

It may be a myth of Alaska politics that citizens have direct personal relationships with political leaders, but candidates act as though this were the reality. Candidates for public office regularly mention their histories in the state, emphasizing length of residence and local ties. A candidate for governor who has adequate resources, but no established credentials as a long-time resident and no name recognition, is not likely to fare well at the polls.[4] Name recognition alone, however, is insufficient for electoral victories, as illustrated by Jay Hammond's defeat of ex-governor Walter Hickel in the 1974 Republican primary and his subsequent defeat of incumbent governor William Egan in the general election. Before he became Alaska's governor, Hammond was a relatively unknown bush pilot, guide, and former state legislator.

The positions gubernatorial candidates take on issues can strongly influence their electoral chances, and the 1982 election is a case in point. What distinguished the candidates, and what led to the electoral coalitions deciding the race, were the candidates' positions on two state ballot propositions—the capital move proposition and the subsistence repeal initiative.[5] The influence of these two issues in the 1982 election is discussed in detail in the elections chapter; here we briefly describe the candidates' positions on these issues and how those positions influenced voters.

Both Republican Tom Fink and Libertarian Dick Randolph supported the proposition that would have approved the costs of moving the state capital from Juneau to a site near Willow in southcentral Alaska. Democratic candidate Sheffield opposed it. In doing so, he won nearly unanimous support from southeast Alaska—without sacrificing much support in interior Alaska, where there was also substantial opposition to the move. Sheffield's base in Anchorage was weak, and no issue position he took was likely to significantly improve his chances against Fink.

The second major ballot proposition in 1982 was the subsistence law repeal initiative, which would have repealed the state law that gives rural subsistence users preference in the allocation of fish and game.[6] By supporting the 1978 subsistence law, Sheffield gained the very strong support of rural Alaskans, particularly Natives. Fink and Randolph supported the subsistence repeal; that support did not significantly increase their electoral bases, which were already strong in urban areas.

The votes Alaskans cast for governor on November 6, 1982 were strongly influenced by these two ballot propositions. Statewide the capital move proposition lost, with 53 percent of voters opposing it. In Anchorage and southcentral precincts, the vote was overwhelmingly for the capital move. Voters in southeast Alaska and rural areas overwhelmingly opposed the move, as did over 62 percent of the Fairbanks and other interior voters. The subsistence repeal initiative lost by a comparable margin statewide—58 percent con to 42 percent pro. Again, rural areas and southeast Alaska were almost unanimous in rejecting the proposition. Fairbanks and interior Alaska divided on this issue too. In Anchorage, about 50 percent of the voters opted for repeal of the law.

In winning the governorship with 45 percent of the three-way vote, Sheffield received critical support from the areas which opposed the capital move and subsistence repeal propositions: southeast Alaska, rural areas of the state where Natives are in the majority, and interior Alaska (including a large number of Fairbanks voters). Fink carried Anchorage handily.

Political party identification has had declining significance in determining the Alaska governorship in recent years. An important factor in that decline is the increased "independence" of the majority of Alaska voters from parties. Notwithstanding the Republican preference of Alaskans in national elections, Republican candidates do not do quite so well in legislative races. And Alaska has had the nation's most vibrant branch of the Libertarian party.[7] This second factor played a prominent role in the 1982 election, when Libertarian candidate Randolph was the spoiler, splitting the nominal Republican vote and giving the election to Sheffield. In Republican Jay Hammond's two gubernatorial races in the 1970s, party likewise played an insignificant role. Alaska's open primary system permitted a large number of Democrats to cross over and vote for Hammond, the moderate candidate who did not stress party affiliation. In fact, Hammond was challenged from the more orthodox section of his own party in the 1978 election race, when former governor Hickel staged a strong write-in campaign.

The fact that there have often been more than two candidates in gubernatorial election campaigns sets Alaska races off from those in most other American states. Obviously, the presence of third party, independent, and write-in candidates on the ballot reduces the impacts of traditional Republican and Democratic party forces. The large number of candidates also makes more prominent the roles of personalities and issues.

BACKGROUND OF GOVERNORS

No pattern seems to describe the backgrounds of Alaska's chief executives, and despite the discussion above, no proposition explains the elections that brought them to power. It is necessary to look at each case briefly.

The state's first governor, Democrat Bill Egan, was a life-long Alaskan whose immediate experience before entry into a life of politics was as a Valdez storekeeper. He served first on the Valdez city council, then 13 years in the territorial legislature, and in 1955 was chosen by other delegates as president of the constitutional convention. In 1958, he ran for governor in the state's first gubernatorial election and won. Egan's unsuccessful opponent, John Butrovich, was a Fairbanksan who had served in the territorial legislature from 1945 to 1957. (Butrovich returned to the state legislature, serving from 1963 until his retirement in 1979.)

An *Anchorage Times* staffer, in a post-election evaluation of the state's first gubernatorial campaign, said, "It's still difficult to find any real issues developed by any of the candidates."[8] Egan was elected because of his greater experience (and name recognition). Another factor was the Democratic landslide of that year, which brought into office all the Democratic candidates for federal and statewide office.

Egan's opponent in his second gubernatorial race in 1962 was Mike Stepovich, an attorney from Fairbanks who had served in the territorial legislature from 1951 to 1957 and was the territory's last governor. Stepovich had nearly defeated Ernest Gruening in the 1958 U.S. Senate campaign. Four years later, he campaigned against the record of the Egan administration, charging that it had "turned our statehood dream into a nightmare."[9] Neither this charge nor Stepovich's slogan "Alaska must grow or die" brought him sufficient support, and Egan was re-elected by a margin of 1,350 votes, or 2.5 percent.

Egan tried to succeed himself again in 1966, but primary opponent Wendell Kay, an Anchorage attorney, said it was "time to eliminate the bungling, stumbling, fumbling mediocrity of the whole Egan crew."[10] A second charge, of importance to many voters, was that Egan's quest for a third term violated the spirit and intent of the constitution, which limited governors to two consecutive full terms. (Egan's first term was 34 days short of a full term.) The divisiveness of the primary soured Egan's general election race against Republican Walter Hickel.

Hickel had come to Alaska in 1940 with a background of experience in construction. He developed businesses in Fairbanks and Anchorage, including hotels, and cultivated contacts that gave him a leading position in the state Republican party. He was Republican party national committee chair for Alaska from 1956 to 1964.

Hickel took appropriate advantage of concern over Egan's attempt to gain a third term. His campaign ads put the voter's choice as "A Third Term or New Leadership." The ads emphasized the need to limit Egan to two terms:

> Our state constitution limits a governor to two terms lest an administration become too secure, too powerful, or too dictatorial. The measure of two terms is more than a technicality—isn't a few days short of the eight years really two terms, for the next step means a total of twelve years.[11]

Hickel also fought a strong campaign for economic development. He won the race with a margin of 1,100 votes (2 percent).

Hickel left the governorship in 1969, to become Secretary of the Interior in President Richard Nixon's cabinet. Hickel's secretary of state (the post is now called lieutenant governor), Keith Miller, succeeded him. Before coming to Alaska, Miller owned and operated a collection agency in Seattle. He worked for the Internal Revenue Service in Anchorage, and for an oil heating firm in Fairbanks. First elected to public office (the state house) in 1962, he became secretary of state in 1966 and governor in 1969—a meteoric rise to power. The 1970 gubernatorial election pitted Miller against former governor Bill Egan. Egan successfully campaigned against Miller's limited experience and skill. A secondary issue was Miller's position on the unresolved Native land claims issue, which Egan called the primary problem facing Alaska. Miller believed land claims were a federal responsibility[12] and focused his campaign on "orderly development" of the state's resources and prudent fiscal policy—topics a majority of voters did not find appealing. Egan won by over 3,000 votes, a 6 percent margin.

The 1974 race pitted Egan, seeking a fourth term as governor, against Jay Hammond, who won a close race and occupied the governor's mansion in Juneau for the next 8 years. Hammond came to Alaska in the 1940s. He had been a licensed guide, air taxi operator, agent for the U.S. Fish and Wildlife Service, and proprietor of a fishing lodge before he was first elected to the state house (as an independent) in 1958. He switched to the state senate in 1967, becoming majority leader in 1970 and senate president in 1971-72. Hammond was mayor of the Bristol Bay Borough and had become a Republican (although he did not emphasize party affiliation) at the time he staged his successful campaign for the governorship. Hammond defeated four opponents (including former governor Hickel) in the Republican primary. He then outpolled Egan, who had won an easy primary victory.[13]

The 1974 general election focused on the age of the Egan administration and the need for new faces. Egan charged Hammond with being negative on a series of state development issues—and with voting against earthquake assistance for Anchorage, against the Equal Rights Amendment (ERA), against formation of the state Departments of Environmental Conservation and Community and Regional Affairs, and against reducing the voting age to 19.[14] However, Hammond gained the support of rural, Native, and commercial fishing interests. His most notable support (in the context of the Prudhoe Bay discovery and the construction of the oil pipeline) was from the developing environmental constituency in the state. The state's newspapers, in a rare show of unanimity, endorsed Hammond, who squeaked into office with a 100-vote margin (less than 1 percent) over Egan.

The 1978 Republican primary featured a neck-and-neck race between Hammond and Hickel, with the former winning by only 103 votes. The fight over that tight race went to the state supreme court. The close race also inspired a Hickel write-in campaign that, with the independent candidacies of Tom Kelly and others, and the Democratic opposition of Chancey Croft,[15] made the race crowded. The Hammond administration's performance during the previous four years was the chief issue of the campaign, with attention again focusing on the pace of economic development. Opponents charged Hammond with having "locked up" Alaska's land and slowed economic growth. Hammond failed to win a majority in the multi-candidate race; his plurality of the vote was 39 percent.

The 1982 gubernatorial election had more color in the primary race than in the general election. Lt. Governor Terry Miller, a Fairbanksan with long experience in the state house and senate (and at 38 the youngest candidate for governor in the state's history), was favored to win the race. In the Democratic primary was Steve Cowper, a Fairbanks lawyer and former state representative and chair of the house finance committee. Neither candidate made it to the general election, however. That race was dominated by the three-party contest between Bill Sheffield, Tom Fink, and Dick Randolph.

Sheffield, who won with 47 percent of the vote, was a hotelier with no experience in politics before his gubernatorial campaign. He came to Alaska in 1953, initially working as an appliance repairman. In the 1960s he bought his first hotel in Anchorage and over a period of ten years added other hotels in Anchorage, Juneau, Canada's Yukon Territory, and in regional centers of rural Alaska. An active member of the Anchorage business community, he headed the state chamber of commerce and was the founding vice-chairman of Common Sense for Alaska, a strong development-oriented association of Anchorage business and political leaders. Sheffield was active in the Democratic party from the late 1960s on, but was not a leading party figure until the late 1970s. He began a race for the governorship in 1978, but withdrew before the primary due to the ill health of his wife.

His chief opponent in 1982 was Tom Fink, an Anchorage insurance man and former speaker of the Alaska House of Representatives. Fink's issue positions were distinctive and controversial. He supported capital punishment and pro-life initiatives, and he was the only primary candidate who supported the capital move and repeal of the subsistence preference law. Those positions, as well as suspected cross-over votes of some Libertarians and Democrats, brought him success in the primary. The general election, however, included another candidate—the head of the Alaska Libertarian Party, Dick Randolph; Randolph was a Fairbanks insurance man and former legislator.

Personalities and issues (including incumbency as an issue) do figure prominently in Alaska's gubernatorial races, as this review shows. The prevalence of close races, however, such as the 1962, 1966, 1974, and 1978 elections, points out the importance of idiosyncratic forces. The "fluke factor" cannot be discounted in explaining who wins or who loses.

POWERS OF ALASKA'S GOVERNORS

We turn now to the chief question of the Alaska governorship: whether those who have held the office have been strong governors, as the authors of Alaska's constitution intended, and if not, why not. The general belief of Alaskans in the 1950s was that the slow pace of economic development was due to federal control over the territory and to the indifference of absentee corporations that exploited Alaska's resources. Statehood promised sufficient authority to change those conditions, but the framers of the constitution wanted to insure that government would be unified and could act quickly with force. Thus, they designed a governorship that was stronger than that in most of the American states at the time, but they also created a strong legislature. The governor and the lieutenant governor are the only statewide elected officials, and voters in recent elections have not diluted the governor's power by making the positions of any executive officials, most notably the attorney general, elective rather than appointive.

POWERS OF APPOINTMENT AND REMOVAL

A significant part of executive authority is the governor's power to appoint. Section 25 of Article III of the state constitution provides:

> The head of each principal department shall be a single executive unless otherwise provided by law. He shall be appointed by the governor, subject to confirmation by a majority of the members of the legislature in joint session, and shall serve at the pleasure of the governor.

Two of the state departments—Education and Fish and Game—are formally headed by boards, as a result of strong lobbying by those interest groups at the constitutional convention.[16] The board members who recommend selection of a commissioner, however, are appointed by the governor. The other commissioners (and in some cases, deputy and assistant commissioners and division directors) as well as all exempt members of the governor's office are direct gubernatorial appointees, serving at the governor's pleasure. Commissioners are subject to legislative confirmation. The governor appoints more than 500 members of state boards and commissions, some of whom are subject to legislative approval. (The structure of the state administrative system is described in detail in the chapter devoted to Alaska's administrative system.)

The governor also appoints all state judges, using the Missouri system of recommendation through a judicial council and retention elections. (This system is described in the chapter on courts.) In sum, the governor appoints or can veto the selection of nearly 1,000 state officials and board members.

The clear intent of the constitutional framers was that the governor should use his appointment powers to create a unified and responsive administration. This intent, however, did not preclude the use of patronage appointments, for citizens could hold political appointees responsible through the electoral process (that is, they could vote the governor out of office). There has been some interesting variation over the statehood period in the "political" use of the appointment process. Two governors—Bill Egan and Walter Hickel—were known for their strongly partisan appointments. In the Hammond administration, however, patronage played a somewhat smaller role. Whether because of the more bipartisan nature of Hammond's administration or its estrangement from Republican party leaders (and especially competition with the Hickel forces in the party), Hammond made appointments on other grounds—such as personal relationships, the desire to represent different groups, and professional competence.

The Sheffield administration in 1982 provided an interesting contrast to previous administrations' appointment policies. Sheffield adopted the "executive search" as a model. During his campaign, Sheffield promised jobs to few. When he was elected, his transition team said that no one would be hired without submitting a resume, and called on qualified Alaskans to apply. The response was overwhelming: within two weeks, transition team offices were flooded with more than 1,000 resumes, letters, and calls.[17]

This approach, however, did not work as planned. Some key positions were ultimately awarded on patronage and personal grounds, as in previous administrations, and several officials got jobs without submitting resumes. The fifteen cabinet-level appointees did not hold a consistent philosophy of management;[18] state and federal cabinets very seldom do.

In conclusion, Alaska governors do not appear to have used their appointment powers to create a unified senior executive staff. Partisan factors have been given some attention in each administration, and each new governor has paid off some personal debts with senior positions. Additionally, the pool of leadership talent in Alaska is smaller than that in other states, and on occasion the executive needed for a particular position is not available in Alaska.

BUDGETARY POWERS

Two articles of the state constitution give the governor extensive budgetary powers. Article IX, on finance and taxation, obliges the governor to submit an annual executive budget to the legislature specifying all expenditures and expected income of the state. Simultaneously, the governor is to submit general appropriations bills to provide for expenditures and to develop new revenue sources. These are not unique features of the Alaska constitution; they had been recommended by reformists over a period of 50 years as means of fostering responsible state fiscal practices. Their effect is to cast the governor in the role of activist (at least in a formal sense), and put the legislature in the position of having to react.

Combined with this power is the provision of Article II in the constitution that allows the governor not only to veto bills, but to "strike or reduce items in appropriation bills"—the line-item veto. Most state constitutions provide this power for the governor; what makes the Alaska network of powers somewhat more formidable is the combination of the line-item veto with strong budget-making authority.

If Alaska's executives had followed the "strong governor" model, we would expect to see a very close relationship between the budgets they have proposed and those the legislatures have passed into law. There has been some variation over the period of statehood, but in recent years, the state legislature has "made the budget over from scratch"—in the words of several legislators—so that the result does not bear a close relationship to what the governor's budget officers had developed. The state's operating budgets have generally borne the closest relationship to the governor's original proposals.[19] In the early 1980s (at the end of the Hammond administration and on into the Sheffield administration), there were very large capital budgets that were only partially dependent on executive planning. The so-called "equal thirds" method of budget construction, with the governor, the house, and the senate each determining a third of the final capital budget, shows the extent to which executive budgetary authority was weakened during this period, particularly by the coalitions ruling the legislature. (See the chapters on legislature and administration for more discussion of the points raised here.)

An interesting example of the limits on executive budgetary authority took place in 1983, early in the Sheffield administration. In his budget and "state of the state" addresses, the new governor took a stance of confrontation toward the legislature. He asked the legislature to submit to executive budget priorities that neglected the special interests on which legislative coalitions were founded.

In drawing up his capital budget, the governor accumulated requests for capital projects and then established a list of priorities. This top-down process created conflict between the executive and legislature, and the legislature changed his proposals very substantially. Too, the contradiction between the governor's endorsement of a huge capital projects budget and projections that the state faced falling revenues surprised seasoned observers of state government. The controversy over the governor's fund-raising trip then intruded on legislative-executive relations, further weakening the governor's position. The administration was forced to restore "equal thirds" as the method for allocating capital projects, and to drop its objections to other fiscal items.

Alaska's governors have had significantly greater success in their use of line-item veto authority, because of both constitutional and procedural factors. The constitution makes the governor's vetoes of appropriations items very difficult to override. Three-fourths of the legislators meeting in joint session must agree to restore funding cut by the governor. And the legislature tends to save consideration of the budget until the very end of the session each year, and then adjourn immediately after it is completed. Thus, the governor vetoes appropriations when the legislature is not present to countermand his actions. In few cases has the governor's use of the line-item veto been overridden.

STATE POLICYMAKING

The state constitution enables the governor to set the agenda of action for the state, to serve as the state's major opinion leader, and to lead the state through crises. These several powers give the governor more to say about the policies made in Alaska than any other individual.

The governor's formal lead in agenda setting is provided for in Section 18 of Article III:

> The governor shall, at the beginning of each session, and may at other times, give the legislature information concerning the affairs of the state and recommend the measures he considers necessary.

The "state of the state" message delivered by the governor on the first day of the legislative session is given a large play by the Alaska press, and is usually followed by submissions of bills to the state legislature. However, governors in the state's history have had indifferent success at setting the legislative course of action of the state. One of the more successful uses of executive agenda setting powers occurred in the mid-1970s when Jay Hammond urged the legislature to adopt an Alaska Permanent Fund, as one means of protecting the state against a future without large oil revenues. The Permanent Fund was established in 1976. A contrasting example took place in the Sheffield administration. In his first "state of the state" message in 1983, Sheffield called for rationalizing capital spending, voiding the Permanent Fund dividend program (which makes direct cash payments to Alaskans), altering state loan and benefit programs based on residency requirements, and reorganizing the executive, particularly through setting up a Department of Corrections. All of the large-scale reforms failed to pass the legislature. Two years later, however, the governor won a large number of items on that year's legislative agenda.[20] The independence and power of the legislature (which were also intended by the authors of the constitution), seem to ensure that Alaska's executives get less than the whole loaf in dealing with the legislature.

The governor's opinion leadership, on the other hand, is more visible and more likely to be effective. Like the American presidency and executive offices in the other states, the governorship of Alaska provides a "bully pulpit," and problems in which the governor takes an interest often become public issues. In fact, governors in Alaska would appear to have had greater success in bringing items to the *public agenda* (the list of public problems about which there is general discussion and debate) than to the *government agenda* (the list of issues given attention by the legislature and agency bureaucrats).

Examples of gubernatorial opinion leadership are easy to find in Alaska's short history of statehood. Governor Egan became a champion of the state's disadvantaged and sought to direct attention to their needs and concerns. Governor Hickel was a strong advocate of economic development; he mobilized opinion for active state policies that would encourage speedy growth. Governor Hammond developed support for balanced growth and protection of environmental values in the state. Not only did he popularize the Permanent Fund concept,[21] he also focused public attention on renewable resource development, with outcomes such as agricultural development in the Delta area and enhancement of state fisheries. Governor Sheffield called for limits on government growth and spending, and sought to prepare the state for a future less dependent on oil.

Some of these proposals and other causes championed by Alaska's governors made their way onto the government agenda of the state. But in general, governors have had greater success in popularizing issues and bringing them into debate than in gaining approval for their policy preferences. In this respect, Alaska's executives are similar to those of other states.

Finally, Alaska's governors have opportunities for crisis leadership, based on two constitutional provisions. First, the governor is commander-in-chief of the armed forces of the state (the Alaska National Guard), and he may proclaim martial law. Under these military leadership powers, the governor may deal with natural emergencies such as floods and earthquakes, as well as occurrences of insurrection and terrorism. To the present, use of this provision has not been significant; governors have called on the national guard only for help in providing disaster relief.

A second, extraordinary power of the governor is described in Section 17 of Article III:

> Whenever the governor considers it in the public interest, he may convene the legislature, either house, or the two houses in joint session.

Alaska's executives have used this provision on several occasions since statehood. In 1973 the state legislature passed a liberal series of measures that heavily taxed the oil and gas industry and regulated industry developments. Representatives of the oil industry claimed these measures would have a deleterious effect on future oil and gas development at Prudhoe Bay, and Governor Egan responded by calling the legislature into special session to revise oil and gas severance tax policy. In 1982, Governor Hammond objected to the legislature's dismissing his call for a constitutional cap on state spending. He called the legislature back into session, and in exchange for the governor's lifting the lid on capital budget funding, the legislature adopted a spending limit amendment that went to the voters for approval in that year's general election. These are examples of governors effectively using their powers to convene the legislature to enact policies. Not all special session calls have been so effective. The *threat* to call a special session is made more often than it is carried out. But as Governor Sheffield discovered as the legislature prepared to adjourn in 1983 (without having acted on his request to establish a Department of Corrections, among other items), legislators do not necessarily believe the governor will act on the threat. The legislature did not act on the governor's request, and he did not call it back into session.

The governor's role in policymaking is constitutionally very strong indeed, but that role is shared with the legislature and other political actors in the state (and some forces outside Alaska, such as the U.S. Congress). The most effective policymaking initiatives have come from the governor's leadership of public opinion. The governor's ''power to persuade'' is the only power not checked by others, and it is the key power of Alaska's executive.

STATE GOVERNMENT ORGANIZATION

Several provisions of the state constitution emphasize the unity of the Alaska executive and the authority of the governor over the governmental bureaucracy of the state. Section 1 of Article III vests the ''executive power'' of Alaska in the governor. Section 16 makes the governor responsible for ''the faithful execution of the laws,'' even permitting the governor to intervene in or launch lawsuits of interest to the state, a provision not commonly found in state constitutions.

The constitution protects unity of the executive in three other ways. First, it limits the number of executive departments, to prevent the dilution of executive power by spreading it among countless agencies and bureaus. The state is limited to 20 principal departments, a number that has not yet been reached. Second, the constitution provides for the appointment rather than the popular election of officials such as the attorney general, commissioner of education, and other officials. The governor and lieutenant governor are the only two statewide elected officials, and through the mid-1980s proponents of the strong governor system have successfully resisted proposals that the attorney general's position be made elective. And third, as noted above, the governor has direct power to appoint most commissioners and veto power over suggested heads of the departments of Education and Fish and Game.[22]

The extent to which state administrations have been united in fact as opposed to just in constitutional theory has varied over statehood. The Hammond administration was characterized by competition, some conflict, and even occasional acrimony among some commissioners, which the governor tolerated in the belief that through these means a myriad of interests would be represented. The Sheffield administration began with obvious attempts to induce a team spirit among commissioners, and egregious failures to toe the line led to dismissals. The potential for executive centralization is as great in Alaska as it is in any other state, but its practice depends on the will of the governor as well as on other forces in the political environment.

The constitution does not limit creation of boards and commissions, and since statehood these have proliferated greatly. (See the discussion in the chapter on administration.) To the extent that boards participate in policymaking, as is true of the Board of Education, Board of Game, and Board of Fisheries, they divide executive authority. Regulatory boards such as the Alaska Public Offices Commission and the Alaska Power Authority have this effect too.

A final power of the Alaska executive is that of executive organization. Under Section 23 of Article III of the constitution, the governor is empowered to:

> ...make changes in the organization of the executive branch or in the assignment of functions among its units which he considers necessary for efficient administration.

The governor makes changes in the form of executive orders, but the legislature may respond to the governor's actions within 60 days.

Governors have used their reorganization power on several occasions since statehood. For example, in the Hammond administration, the Departments of Highways and Public Works were merged to create the Department of Transportation and Public Facilities. This was done to eliminate duplication by offices engaged in comparable kinds of construction and maintenance activities and planning. The most recent reorganization was the creation of the Department of Corrections in 1983. The legislature at that time was preoccupied with the governor's budget requests and embroiled in the fund-raising controversy, and it held the reorganization request hostage along with other high priority items sought by the governor. Ultimately, the department was established through an executive order of Governor Sheffield after the legislative session ended.

With respect to governmental organization in Alaska, the intent of the strong governor model has been achieved. The state administration is more streamlined than those in most American states, and the opportunities for executive influence through the bureaucratic system would appear to be greater.

Nonetheless, the governor's influence is offset by civil servant protections and by the influence of large agencies with allies in the legislature and the public. These limitations on gubernatorial power figured prominently in the state's historic impeachment proceedings of 1985.

IMPEACHMENT: A TEST OF EXECUTIVE-LEGISLATIVE RELATIONS

The high drama of Alaska's executive occurred in 1985, when the state senate met to decide whether to impeach Governor Bill Sheffield. Although the senate decided against impeachment, the historic proceedings seem likely to have impacts on executive-legislative relations and on the evolution of the governorship.

The governor was charged with having illegally influenced the award of a lease on a building in Fairbanks where state offices were to be consolidated. The lease went to a building partially owned by a man who had raised substantial funds for the Sheffield campaign.

The process used to award the lease became an issue when the *Fairbanks Daily News-Miner* began an investigation and raised questions about possible bidrigging and other improprieties. Those charges led to a grand jury investigation; the jury issued a report implicating the governor in violating state lease procedures. The grand jury decided against filing a criminal indictment. Instead, it opined that the governor had violated the public trust, and that the legislature should consider impeaching him—which was an unusual step for a grand jury to take.

Leaders of the state senate and house responded by calling the legislature into special session. The senate rules committee established procedures and carried out hearings over a two-week period. Both the governor and the senate showed that they were taking the accusations seriously: they both hired attorneys who had been involved in the 1974 Watergate hearings. Sheffield's chief of staff admitted that he had asked the Department of Administration to change bid procedures to favor the owners of the building that had been awarded the lease; he later resigned. The governor himself testified that he could not recall attending meetings at which changing the bid documents was discussed.

Four of the five rules committee members were Republicans, and observers expected a partisan hearing and outcome. Rules committee members could count, however, and they saw insufficient support in the senate for impeachment. The committee's report noted that lack of support and called for establishment of an ethics code covering the executive branch and revisions to state procurement policy. The senate approved three moderate resolutions. The first requested study of grand jury powers. The second established a committee on procurement practices and procedures. The third resolution expressed the sense of the senate that there was no "clear and convincing evidence that William J. Sheffield has committed an impeachable offense."[23]

Depending on one's perspective, the 1985 impeachment proceedings were a "tempest in a teapot," a partisan attack on the governor, or a serious indictment of the ethics of the Sheffield administration. The event seemed to alter legislative and executive relations, but whether the change was short- or long-term remains to be seen.

POWERS AND ROLES OF ALASKA'S GOVERNORS

In 1982, the 46 surviving members of the 1955 Alaska constitutional convention were asked their observations about the results of their handiwork. One of the questions asked all delegates concerned the "strong governorship," and their opinions about constitutional theory and political practice. They were nearly unanimous in their belief that the constitution in the 1980s remained what it had promised to be in the 1950s—a vehicle for a strong governor, if one could be found. Complaints (in part reflecting partisan considerations) were that recent governors of the state had not exercised the authority of the office, that they had not actively led the state, and that as a result policymaking had foundered.

Comparing Alaska's governors to those of other states gives us another view of this matter. States whose governors seem to have weaker formal powers than those of the Alaska executive, such as California, have in practice had strong executive leadership. To understand how Alaska's executive operates, then, we need to go beyond discussing formal powers and briefly observe the styles of governing Alaska.

POLITICAL LEADERSHIP: STYLES OF GOVERNING ALASKA

Alaska has had only five governors since statehood, too few to enable us to draw comparative observations on patterns of executive effectiveness. It is possible to gain a sense of executive leadership, however, by reviewing two aspects of governors' performances—their activity and orientation toward the job: how much time they devoted to it and whether they projected images of positive or negative political leadership.[24]

The state's first governor, Bill Egan, set an example of activity in the governorship. An ebullient personality, Egan devoted long hours to the office during his three terms, and was involved in all aspects of the administration. Egan was willing to let government grow to accomplish social welfare purposes.

Egan was strongly positive in his orientation toward government and the executive, an attitude that influenced his dealings with the legislature and the state administration. He commented on these relationships in an interview in 1983:

> I have always felt that it's [legislative-executive relationships] been pretty much of a tug of war. It's due to the make-up of things. Alaska has a strong governor by the constitution. Many times you're better off to go to the legislature; don't give them the impression that you're trying to bulldoze them. Take their ideas and let them start it; let it appear it is their idea. Working this way, together with them, you can get your own program through. You have to have the human touch. That's how to get it in. Think of the other guy; recognize his importance, his obligations.[25]

Egan's style of governing was active and positive. These are dimensions associated with "strong" leadership.

Egan's successor in 1966, Walter Hickel, was similar to him in several important respects. He was even more active as governor, and projected an image of dynamic movement. However, Hickel had an entirely different vision of the size and role of government. In 1983 Hickel talked about his gubernatorial experience:

> The most important thing I thought about [as governor] was to get a hold of the reins of government in a hurry and take charge.... The governor is supposed to be a strong leader.... In a vacuum of leadership, the legislature acts. That is what happened in the last eight years.... I made contact with legislative leaders. They had access.... In Alaska you have to move very fast on issues.... Tactically, well, I do it [relate to the legislative leadership] by personality. It is just like how you court your wife; you just do it, you're at it all the time.[26]

Hickel commented at some length on the difference between leadership in Alaska when he was governor and in the 1980s:

> I'd say that it's easier to lead now.... Greatness comes out of leadership when it is pressed. Alaska is pressed now. This unique piece of real estate, this unique piece of world real estate, will founder without leadership.... Here you have to be a very active leader. The governorship of Alaska has to be entrepreneurial, it has to be creative. When you are young, you have to innovate. The opportunities for leadership in Alaska are fantastic. I don't see any obstacles. Nature doesn't present any obstacles. There weren't any obstacles to building a pipeline to tidewater. Obstacles are only in a person's mind. But whatever you do, don't change the system. It'll work, if you find the right people it will work. I believe in that. You have to keep the window open.[27]

However, Hickel spent barely two years in the governorship before accepting President Nixon's call to serve as Secretary of the Interior. His successor in office, Keith Miller, took a different approach to leadership. Miller's approach to government was far less expansive than Hickel's, as he indicated in responses to questions during the 1970 race about his philosophy of government:

> The state's fiscal policy should continue to respond to the needs of all Alaskans while maintaining a responsible investment policy.... Alaska's financial condition is the main concern of government. It will require astute and alert management.[28]

Prudential accounts and a careful, cautious approach to issues were common during Miller's administration. Miller was lambasted by legislators for being negative, primarily because of the large number of vetoes he cast.

Jay Hammond, who took office in 1974, had a leadership style quite different from Miller's. Although physically active and energetic, Hammond was relatively non-directive as governor. State commissioners were essentially autonomous, as were some special assistants to the governor. The governor intruded little on legislative affairs, but he did veto legislation to gain bargaining leverage and was active in the introduction of bills.

Although Hammond was not a particularly active governor, it would be a mistake to view him through the lenses of another ex-governor who said Hammond would have been "a good governor for an established state, like Massachusetts, but [was] a poor governor for a new state like Alaska." Hammond's leadership was important in developing support for environmental values during the tremendous impacts of construction of the trans-Alaska pipeline in the mid-1970s. He did develop a consensus on some issues, particularly establishment of the Permanent Fund, and he was willing to approach problems from the standpoint of their "human" aspects, which was important given Alaska's divergent cultural groups.

Hammond's own observations about leadership in the state reflect his hands-off style of government management:

> I concluded long ago that you can't handle all the details of government yourself. Get yourself top notch talent and convey responsibility to them. You need to avoid the Jimmy Carter style. Those things can bleed you white....
>
> I was asked why I thought I could administer the state better than my predecessors. They said I had no experience. I said I had an advantage.

I could get anyone to work with me. There were no partisan obligations, payoffs to make. So, I got people with disparate points of view. The main thing is to get top talent and keep your fingers out of affairs....

I'm concerned about campaign promises. They elevate expectations. I made no promises in either campaign. The only one was, if re-elected, I would govern less. The first two years I took no time off.[29]

Governor Sheffield presents a different style of leadership. In contrast to some passivity of the previous governor, Sheffield is a model of activity. He works long, hard hours and is extensively involved in the decision processes. He is willing to focus on detail, perhaps sometimes at the expense of the broader picture. His style is that of the manager turned politician. This style promises greater control of government and perhaps a realistic harnessing of expectations, but appears less positive than that of his predecessor.

In discussing his views of the governorship, Governor Sheffield has presented these ideas on the purposes of executive leadership:

As governor, it's in my job description to be looking into the future at the same time I'm trying to manage the day-to-day details of a big and complex government. It's not an easy job, and quite frankly I can't do it all myself. That's why we've brought into the administration not only people who are good managers, but also people who have promising and exciting ideas about the future.

And in making long-range plans and setting goals, the Sheffield administration intends to temper idealism with realism. As I said in my inaugural speech, Alaska is not immune to events occurring outside her boundaries. The slide in world oil prices is a good example of that. But we do have a tremendous opportunity to shape our own future if we manage our wealth in a wise manner.[30]

The "management of wealth"—as opposed to its creation, expansion, or distribution—is an important theme in the Sheffield governorship. His concern about controlling resources implies a distrust of expansive government and a sense of responsibility to the future, however uncomfortable or difficult that might be and however negative it might make his leadership seem.

Recent governors have not been both active and positive in their orientations to power, as were Governors Egan and Hickel. This may account for the feeling of some observers that the state in recent times has lacked strong governors. The personality and management styles of state leaders would seem to have an impact on policymaking, but without further information it would be hazardous to comment on the direction and degree of that relationship.

EXECUTIVE LEADERSHIP: CAPABILITY OF THE ALASKA GOVERNORSHIP

In 1958, the Alaska governorship was a new institution. Nearly three decades after statehood, irrespective of who happens to serve as governor, we have come to expect a pattern of activity from the office. This is an indication of the institutionalization of executive authority in Alaska, and we turn now briefly to two examples of this process: development of an executive staff system and management of the gubernatorial transition.

STAFFING THE ALASKA GOVERNORSHIP

The chapter on Alaska's administrative system describes the development of a career civil service in Alaska, and this is perhaps the most significant sign of strength in the executive branch of government. Yet the formation of an established bureaucracy challenges the governor's ability to set new directions in state policy. Preserving the governor's freedom of action is the ability to develop a gubernatorial staff that extends the reach of the executive.

Governor Hammond praised his staff as "enormously helpful.... They perform the functions better than I can." However, critics believed that special assistants to the governor had too much influence in the Hammond administration, to the extent that they functioned as though they were commissioners. In fact, a complaint during that administration from commission staffs was that commissioners had less access to the governor than did his special assistants.

It was partly in response to this kind of criticism that in the early days of the Sheffield administration special assistants to the governor had limited influence. There were attempts to curb the natural growth of their influence as they developed their contacts with the governor, on the one hand, and enhanced their knowledge of agency operations, on the other. These limitations brought some confusion in the executive office as no clear pattern of command was evident.

Soon, however, a pattern of influence similar to that of special assistants in the Hammond administration developed, with the chief of staff holding sizable influence, and with the staff specialized by function. Significantly, in quite different governorships, the staffing system has developed along similar lines.

TRANSITION MANAGEMENT

A second example of the development of executive government routines in Alaska is seen in the way transitions across administrations have been handled. The management of transition is composed of two parts: research on problems and policies of state government, and implementation of change in administration in a short period.

In preparing for his own departure from office, Governor Hammond ordered each of his agencies to prepare transition materials for the new administration, documenting the chief issues that the new administration would face and suggesting options for action. Upon taking office in November, 1982, Governor Sheffield formed six transition task forces, drawn from a wide range of groups and interests. Then he dispatched these private citizens into the state bureaucracy, with a mandate to find out what was wrong with government and how it might be righted in terms of his campaign promises.[31] The teams produced task force reports and a large transition study, that the governor took quite seriously.

Of course, there were questions about the kind of research done by the transition team, and the objectivity of the data collection. Nevertheless, a good deal of information was collected in a short period, and several important problems of state government were highlighted.[32]

In moving from administration to administration, Alaska's new governors have learned to act quickly and with force. The transition team concept will likely be used in future changes of government.

CONCLUSIONS

In an editorial written one week before the first statewide election in 1958, the _Anchorage Times_ said:

> The new state of Alaska is going to almost certainly have the most powerful governor of any state.
> This could be a means to smooth, highly efficient government. It could also mean the development of as powerful a political machine on the state level as the country has ever seen.[33]

Alaskans have had high expectations about the governorship from those early days to the present. However, neither the promise (a highly efficient government) nor the threat (a powerful political machine) of a strong governorship has materialized. Why?

This chapter points out constitutional and legal impediments to a strong governorship. The state legislature is the chief constitutional obstacle; it was designed to check governors' power. The state bureaucracy on the one hand and the strong network of private organizations (including the media) in Alaska also limit executive power. Not all governors have sought to enhance executive powers. For example, Jay Hammond as governor was accused of ceding influence to the legislature. And some governors have lacked the skill necessary to aggregate influence. The first year of the Sheffield administration provided several examples of the need for more skill in gubernatorial politics.

How do powers of Alaska's executive compare with those of the other states? A 1985 study by political scientist Keith Mueller provides interesting comparative data. Mueller created an index of the formal powers of governors, including their tenure potential and appointive, budget, and veto powers. He found that from 1960 to 1982 the powers of governors increased overall, and that variability in those powers among the states decreased.[34] Although the Alaska governorship increased in power over this period too, it did so at a slower rate than in many other states. Stated differently, in 1960, governors of 20 states possessed formal powers greater or equal to those of Alaska's governor. By 1982, governors of 32 states held greater or equal powers. A new state with a reformist governorship has, in its second generation, fallen behind states that have overhauled their executives.

Mueller's second observation commands attention: power struggles between legislatures and governors are particularly important in active states.[35] Although governors' powers have grown in most states, legislatures have become more professional and have demanded greater roles in spending and raising state resources. Alaska closely resembles other states in competition and conflict between legislature and executive.

ENDNOTES

This study of Alaska's governorship began in 1982 as part of a comparative study on gubernatorial transitions in the American states. Sources used in preparing the chapter include: documents prepared for the Alaska gubernatorial transition by the Hammond and Sheffield administrations; interviews with staff members of both administrations, with the Sheffield transition team and task forces, and with all Alaska's governors; review of published works on Alaska's executive and extensive review of Alaska's newspapers from 1958 to 1985. Thanks are due Dr. Thomas A. Morehouse for his constructive criticism of several drafts. Drs. Gordon Harrison and Richard Fineberg also provided several useful suggestions for revision.

[1]James Q. Wilson, *Political Organizations* (New York: Basic Books, Inc. 1973).

[2]This indicates the importance of incumbency and not the affinity of interests. Over 50 percent of Hammond's contributions came from out-of-state fund-raisers in New York, Washington, and Texas, according to the *Anchorage Times*, July 14, 1978.

³See Alaska Public Offices Commission annual reports, 1978, 1982.

⁴However, the large number of newcomers voting in elections since construction of the trans-Alaska pipeline in the mid-1970s has depressed the importance of candidates' having deep Alaska roots.

⁵The Alaska ballot, like that of other western states, is usually crowded with propositions initiated by interest groups or the legislature itself. The November 1982 ballot contained eight propositions. The other six propositions were:
— a "tundra rebellion" initiative, to assert state ownership over federal lands in the state
— a proposition calling for a state constitutional convention
— a measure to withdraw state funding for abortions
— a proposed constitutional amendment to redesign the judicial qualifications commission
— a proposed constitutional alteration in the veterans' loan program
— a proposed constitutional amendment to put a cap on state spending

⁶As aboriginal residents of Alaska, Natives are protected by federal law in their aboriginal occupancy and use of land. Native claims to land were resolved in the Alaska Native Claims Settlement Act of 1971 (ANCSA). Native rights to subsistence use were incorporated as a section of ANCSA, and specifically provided for in the Alaska National Interest Lands Conservation Act of 1980 (ANILCA). For interpretations of ANCSA see Robert Arnold, _Alaska Native Land Claims_ (Anchorage: Alaska Native Foundation, 1976) and Gerald A. McBeath and Thomas A. Morehouse, _The Dynamics of Alaska Native Self-Government_ (Lanham, MD: University Press of America, 1980). For information on Native sovereignty issues, see David S. Case, _Alaska Natives and American Laws_ (Fairbanks: University of Alaska Press, 1984).

⁷The Libertarian presidential candidates did better in Alaska than in any other state. Three Libertarians have been elected to the Alaska state legislature since 1978.

⁸Bob Kederick, in _Anchorage Daily Times_, November 24, 1958.

⁹_Juneau Empire_, September 8, 1962.

¹⁰_Anchorage Times_, July 29, 1966.

¹¹_Anchorage Times_, November 7, 1966.

¹²_Juneau Empire_, August 24, 1970.

¹³_Fairbanks Daily News-Miner_, September 29, 1974.

¹⁴_Fairbanks Daily News-Miner_, October 15, 1974.

¹⁵Croft was an Anchorage attorney who had served in the state house (1968 to 1970), state senate (1970 to 1978), and served as senate president in 1975-76.

¹⁶See Victor Fischer, _Alaska's Constitutional Convention_ (Fairbanks: University of Alaska Press, 1975), for a discussion of this process.

[17]By the start of the legislative session over 16,000 resumes came in, roughly four applications per post but with the greatest interest, obviously, in positions of commissioner, deputy commissioner, and directors with the division office.

[18]Most were Democrats, and fewer than half were Republican or nonpartisan. Two women sat in the cabinet as did two members of minorities (several Natives held subcabinet positions). A striking characteristic was lack of experience in state government. A larger number of businessmen were selected as commissioners than had been the case in the Hammond administration.

[19]The relationship was weakest for a period in the 1970s when additions and deletions to agency expenditures by free conference committees changed executive intent very substantially. See Richard Fineberg's account of this in *Chaos in the Capital: The Budget System in Crisis*, (Anchorage: Alaska Public Interest Research Group, 1982.)

[20]Attorney General Norman Gorsuch said the governor won "6 1/2 of 7 items," but this observation was somewhat biased. Statement to Taft Seminar, University of Alaska, Fairbanks, June 20, 1985.

[21]Mentioned first by Governor Keith Miller in the 1970 campaign.

[22]The Board of Education, Board of Fisheries and Board of Game *recommend* names to the governor, who decides upon commissioners.

[23]*Fairbanks Daily News-Miner*, August 6, 1985.

[24]The account is based on James D. Barber's *Presidential Character*, a creative analysis of presidential leadership. Barber has not been successful in establishing a tight linkage between character (or personality) type and policy outcomes. His typology is useful chiefly as a way of organizing information about leaders' personalities and speculating on the impact that different motivational states might have.

[25]Personal interview with Bill Egan, January 13, 1983, Anchorage, Alaska.

[26]Personal interview with Walter Hickel, February 17, 1983, Anchorage, Alaska.

[27]Ibid.

[28]*Fairbanks Daily News-Miner*, October 13, 1970.

[29]Personal interview with Governor Hammond, in Juneau, November 30, 1982.

[30]*Juneau Empire*, January 12, 1983.

[31]The departments reviewed by the transition team task forces were:
Resources (Department of Fish and Game, Department of Natural Resources, Department of Environmental Conservation)
Human Services (Department of Health & Social Services, Department of Education, University of Alaska)
Public Protection and Labor (Department of Public Safety, Department of Labor, Department of Military Affairs)
Business Management (Department of Revenue, Department of Commerce and Economic Development)

Revenue Transfer (Department of Transportation & Public Facilities, Department of Community & Regional Affairs)

General Government (Office of the Governor, Office of the Lt. Governor, Department of Law, Department of Administration, Boards and Commissions).

[32] Among the problems were the lack of a maximum security prison, the need to transfer the Alaska Railroad to the state, problems in the state accounting system, and problems with the state's subsistence law.

[33] *Anchorage Times*, November 19, 1958.

[34] Keith J. Mueller, "Explaining Variation and Change in Gubernatorial Powers, 1960-1982," *Western Political Quarterly*, Vol. 38, No. 3 (September 1985), p. 427.

[35] Ibid., p. 429.

12

Alaska's Administrative System

Gordon S. Harrison

Alaska's state administrative system is the aggregation of governmental departments and agencies that comprises the executive branch. Most of these public agencies are elements of the centralized administrative structure that is directly accountable to the governor. Others, such as many boards and commissions and the sprawling University of Alaska, are designed to operate with a large measure of autonomy. But however they relate to the governor's office, whether tied directly to it or orbiting only loosely within its gravitational pull, these agencies share a common purpose, which is the constitutional underpinning of the executive branch: they implement the laws and administer the statutory programs of the state.

Another name for the administrative system is the "bureaucracy." The term is slightly pejorative; it reflects the popular image of government as an enormous and Byzantine network of offices housing high-paid workers carrying out vague, self-justified tasks according to inflexible, often irrational and inefficient procedures. Perhaps because of this image, and because the bureaucracy is not a regular source of high public political drama, the administrative system is very dimly perceived and poorly understood by most people. Yet knowledge of this system, and how it interacts with the legislative branch, is critical to an understanding of what state government is and how it works.

This chapter provides a broad view of the administrative system and its role in making and carrying out public policies of the state. Specifically, the chapter:

1. Provides an overview of the structure and operations of Alaska's administrative system;

2. Points to distinctive features of Alaska's system in contrast to those of other states; and

3. Assesses the overall character and effectiveness of the system.

OVERVIEW OF ADMINISTRATIVE STRUCTURE

Essential to a survey of Alaska's administrative system is a description of the main structural elements of that system. This section gives a brief overview of these structural elements.

PRINCIPAL EXECUTIVE DEPARTMENTS

The discussion of the principal departments below treats mainly their evolution since statehood rather than their current duties and functions. The reader who is interested in knowing the full range of activities and organizational subdivisions of each department has at least three good reference sources available.[1]

State Organization Act of 1959. Article III, Section 22 of the Alaska constitution states, in part:

All executive and administrative offices, departments, and agencies of the state government and their respective functions, powers, and duties shall be allocated by law among and within not more than twenty principal departments, so as to group them as far as practicable according to major purposes.

A major task confronting the first session of the Alaska Legislature was to create from the tangle of territorial executive bodies a streamlined and efficient administrative structure as envisioned in the constitution. Three organizational schemes were proposed: one by the governor's office, which recommended 15 executive departments; one by the Legislative Council, which recommended 13; and one by the Public Administration Service (consultant to the statehood committee), which recommended 11. A compromise bill was adopted and signed into law on April 15, 1959. Known as the State Organization Act of 1959 (Chapter 64 SLA 1959), this bill created 12 executive departments in addition to the Office of the Governor. These departments consolidated within general functional areas all the related boards, commissions, offices, authorities, and departments that existed under territorial status. For example, the new Department of Labor assumed the responsibilities of the territorial Employment Security Commission, the Alaska Territorial Employment Service, the Territorial Advisory Council, the Alaska Safety Council, the territorial Department of Labor, the Alaska Industrial Board, and the Board for the Care of Sick and Disabled Fishermen.

Special treatment for the Department of Fish and Game and the Department of Education was the major controversy in deliberations over the organization act. The interest groups associated with these departments wanted to insulate their programs from "politics" by vesting control of the departments in quasi-independent boards, rather than commissioners appointed by the governor. These interests had been represented at the constitutional convention and had succeeded in securing permissive language that allows the legislature to designate a board as the head of a department (Article III, Section 25). Now they pressed their case. A compromise was finally reached that created a Board of Education and a Board of Fish and Game, members of which were appointed by the governor for fixed, overlapping terms. The boards were to have policy oversight and rulemaking authority, but their powers explicitly excluded "administrative, budgeting, and fiscal" affairs. These were to be the prerogative of the commissioners of the departments. However, these commissioners were not simply to be appointed by the governor, like all the others; rather, they were to be appointed by the governor from a list of qualified persons nominated by the board, subject to the right of the governor to request additional nominations.[2]

An important feature of the state's administrative system today is the result of the legislature's decision in the State Organization Act of 1959 to centralize in the Department of Administration responsibility for personnel and labor relations matters, and for purchasing and leasing. Centralization for policy making in these areas potentially imparts a large measure of efficiency to the management of state government in Alaska. Uniformity in personnel policies and procedures among the departments would otherwise be impossible to enforce, as each unit of government tends to consider its circumstances and its personnel management problems unique. Centralization of purchasing authority avoids the duplication and inconsistency that would result from independent purchasing agencies within each department. It also enhances the opportunity for discounts on volume purchases.

Principal Executive Departments Today. Despite the growth in the size and complexity of the executive branch since passage of the State Organization Act of 1959, the number of principal departments has not changed substantially. There are currently fifteen departments (five fewer than authorized by the constitution), and there have never been more than fifteen. The current departments are Administration, Commerce and Economic Development, Community and Regional Affairs, Corrections, Education, Environmental Conservation, Fish and Game, Health and Social Services, Labor, Law, Military Affairs, Natural Resources, Public Safety, Revenue, and Transportation and Public Facilities.

Twice single departments have been split into two separate departments and then merged again into single departments. In 1962 the Department of

Economic Development and Planning was created from the Division of Tourism and Economic Development, which was located in the Department of Commerce. In 1975 these two departments were consolidated into the Department of Commerce and Economic Development.

Also in 1962, a new Department of Highways was created from the Division of Highways in the existing Department of Public Works. In 1977, these two departments were put back together as the Department of Transportation and Public Facilities. In addition to these changes, three new departments have been established since 1959. In 1971 the Department of Environmental Conservation was created. It was built mainly from the environmental health and sanitation programs in the Department of Health and Social Services. In 1984 the Department of Corrections was created from the Division of Corrections, which had also been located in the Department of Health and Social Services. In 1973 the Department of Community and Regional Affairs was created from the Local Affairs Agency, which had been put in the Office of the Governor by the State Organization Act of 1959. This agency is the only executive agency (except the University of Alaska) whose existence is mandated by the constitution (Article X, Section 14).

These changes in the organizational structure of the executive branch are summarized in Table 12.1.

Meanwhile, the departments have grown in size and complexity. In 1959, for example, there were 7 assistant attorneys general; in 1984, there were 95. In 1959, the governor had 3 special assistants; in 1984, he had 13. The number of divisions within the principal executive departments grew from 56 in 1959 to 110 in 1985. See Table 12.2.

Increases in the number, size, and functional specialization of administrative agencies represent several forces of growth since statehood. Nationwide, state government has grown rapidly over the past several decades. For example, the Advisory Commission on Intergovernmental Relations reports that in 1957 there were 67.4 full-time equivalent state employees per 10,000 persons in the United States, and in 1982 there were 133.2 (an increase of almost 100 percent).[3] Americans have come to expect higher and higher levels of service from state government, and increasingly we look to state government to help solve social and economic problems.

A good example in Alaska of this reliance on state government to solve problems is the limited entry program in the commercial fisheries. That program was created to help alleviate financial hardship among fishermen by restricting numbers of fishermen. Substantial administrative machinery (the Commercial Fisheries Entry Commission) is required to implement this very complicated program. Another example is the Alaska Public Offices Commission,

Table 12.1
Departments of the Executive Branch: Evolution to 1984

1959	1984
Office of the Governor ———————————————————————	Office of the Governor
Local Affairs Agency ——————— [Became in 1973] ———————	Community and Regional Affairs
Administration ———————————————————————————	Administration
Commerce ———	
Division of Tourism and Economic Development	
1962 Became the... ——— [Merged in 1975]	Commerce and Economic
Department of Economic Development and Planning ⌟	Development
Education ———————————————————————————	Education
Fish and Game ———————————————————————	Fish and Game
Health and Welfare ———————————————————	Health and Social Services
Division of Environmental Health and ——— [Became in 1971]	Environmental Conservation
other sanitation and related engineering programs ⌟	
Division of Corrections ——————— [Became in 1984] ———	Corrections
Labor ———————————————————————————	Labor
Law ———————————————————————————	Law
Military Affairs ———————————————————	Military Affairs
Natural Resources ———————————————	Natural Resources
Public Safety ———————————————————	Public Safety
Revenue ———————————————————————	Revenue
Public Works	
Division of Highways ———	
1962 Became the ——— [Merged in 1977]	Transportation and Public
Department of Highways ———	Facilities

a body created by the legislature in the wake of the Watergate disclosures to administer state campaign financing disclosure and lobbyist registration laws. All things considered it is not surprising to see substantial growth in Alaska's administrative system since the legislature passed the State Organization Act of 1959: there has been a general trend of increasing reliance on state government to solve social problems; Alaska's population increased 78 percent between 1960 and 1980; Alaska has assumed management responsibility for about 100 million acres of land since statehood; and the state government has taken control of virtually all the rural schools formerly run by the U.S. Bureau of Indian Affairs.

Also, of course, growth of the administrative system has been fueled by Alaska's petroleum revenue, beginning with the famous lease bonus payments of $900 million in 1969. State administrative machinery for monitoring developments of the oil industry has expanded, as has our machinery for computing and collecting taxes and royalties. More important, however, petroleum revenues have funded many new state programs.

Table 12.2
Number of Departmental Divisions 1959, 1970, and 1984

Department	1959	1970	1984
Administration	4	6	14
Commerce	7	4	—
Economic Development and Planning	—	2	—
Commerce and Economic Development	—	—	9
Community and Regional Affairs	—	—	4
Education	3	7	5
Environmental Conservation	—	—	5
Fish and Game	7	5	8
Health and Social Services	4	6	7
Corrections	—	—	3
Labor	4	4	4
Law	2	2	3
Military Affairs	6	6	4
Natural Resources	3	5	8
Public Safety	3	3	5
Revenue	6	6	7
Public Works	7	6	—
Highways	—	6	—
Transportation and Public Facilities	—	—	24
	56	68	110

This table lists only activities of the departments organized as divisions. It excludes many offices, authorities, and agencies that might otherwise be regarded as divisions of a principal department.

Finally, initiatives of the federal government have led to significant growth of Alaska's administrative apparatus. Because of new federal programs in the last several years, for example, the Department of Environmental Conservation now has responsibility for clean air and water programs that it did not previously have; the Department of Health and Social Services has expanded responsibility for health care programs; the Office of Management and Budget has a Coastal Management Program, and so on.

OFFICE OF THE GOVERNOR

There are three main components of the Office of the Governor: the governor's personal staff and administrative support, which we shall refer to as the

Executive Office of the Governor; the Lieutenant Governor's Office; and the Office of Management and Budget. In addition, a few boards and commissions are attached to the governor's office for administrative purposes, and there are from time to time special projects run from the governor's office.

The Executive Office of the Governor consists of a chief executive assistant (presently called the chief of staff), an assistant for legislative relations, a press secretary, an assistant to oversee the appointment of citizens to the numerous boards and commissions and to special committees and task forces created by the governor, and several special assistants who are responsible for policy issues concerning the departments assigned to them. The special assistants facilitate communication between the commissioners and the governor, as well as between other public officials and private citizens and the governor.

Traditionally, secretaries of state and lieutenant governors (Alaska's lieutenant governor was called the secretary of state until 1970) are given the job of overseeing the state's elections. This is the case in Alaska, where the Division of Elections is the only administrative responsibility of the lieutenant governor.

The Office of Management and Budget (OMB) was created in 1983 from three divisions that formerly reported directly to the governor: the divisions of Budget and Management, Policy Development and Planning, and Internal Audit. There are currently four divisions within OMB: Budget Review (coordination of executive budget preparation); Strategic Planning (economic, fiscal, and other policy analysis for the governor); Management (financial and performance audits, management assistance to agencies); and Governmental Coordination (interagency coordination of resource development proposals and permit applications). The various activities of these divisions have found their way over the years into the governor's office as a result of problems created by the bias of a single agency perspective which tends to occur when the activities are performed in a department. For example, the Division of Budget and Management was moved from the Department of Administration in 1976, partly to eliminate the appearance of "advantage" of one commissioner over the others in budgetary competition.

At the present time four commissions are affiliated with the governor's office: the Human Rights Commission, the Alaska Women's Commission, the Alaska Land Use Council, and the Alaska Coastal Policy Council. Over the years, however, a large number of agencies, boards, and special commissions have been attached to the governor's office. These special boards seek the visibility and symbolic importance that seem to be conferred on them by affiliation with the governor's office. Typically, if a newly created commission established in the governor's office survives its first few years of existence, it will be moved to a principal department. For example, just those agencies that have moved from the governor's office to the Department of Administration over the years include Pioneers Homes (1969), Office of Telecommunications (1982), Office of Equal Employment Opportunity (1978), Alaska Council on Science and Technology (1982), Public Defender Agency (1967), and Alaska Public Offices Commission (1980).

BOARDS AND COMMISSIONS

There are currently about 120 boards and commissions that are part of the executive branch of government. Each one is attached to one of the principal departments for administrative "housekeeping" purposes. Over 1,000 persons, most of whom are private citizens, serve on these bodies. The majority of these boards and commissions are of little general significance, and they function on the periphery of government. Others, however, perform vital executive functions and make significant administrative decisions involving expenditure of money and granting of valuable permits, licenses, and authorizations. With two notable exceptions—the Board of Education, which is the head of a principal department, and the Board of Regents, which is the head of the University of Alaska—Alaska's boards and commissions fall into one of three general categories: advisory, regulatory, and public corporation. Most boards are advisory. Advisory boards and commissions deal with such things as the management of natural areas, federal land issues, state libraries, pioneer homes, safety, tourism, litter control, and historic sites. As a group the advisory boards are the least significant politically, but they can be very useful to their parent agencies. For example, they can be a source of information for decisions, provide legitimacy for policy decisions, and help develop public support for their programs.

Regulatory boards serve a very important administrative function by making allocative decisions that the line agencies of government are not structured, equipped, or politically suited to make. The most important of these boards in Alaska may well be the Board of Fisheries, which must allocate the state's valuable fishery resources among commercial fishermen (whose own ranks are often rent with bitter conflicts between those who exploit the same stocks with different types of gear and even between those who use the same types of gear but at different locations), sport fishermen, and subsistence fishermen. Other important regulatory boards are the Alaska Public Utilities Commission, the Alcohol Beverage Control Board, the Commercial Fisheries Entry Commission, the Board of Game, and the Alaska Public Offices Commission.

Like other states, Alaska also has numerous (28) occupational licensing boards. These are a subset of the regulatory category. Each board typically has several members who are practitioners of the profession the board oversees, and several members from the general public. Thus the boards bring specialized expertise as well as the layman's perspective to the task of setting and monitoring minimum levels of professional qualifications and standards.

The national concern about all regulatory boards is that they are really handmaidens to the professions they purport to regulate, and that they neglect the public interest. For example, licensing boards are accused of fostering anticompetitive practices through restrictions on advertising (especially price advertising) by doctors, dentists, lawyers, opticians, morticians, and others. They are also accused of restricting entry into the professions to keep supply and demand for services in balance at high prices. For example, a public accusation was recently made that the qualifying examination administered by the Alaska Board of Dental Examiners was designed to fail a disproportionately large number of those seeking admission to practice in Alaska.[4]

Responsibility for insuring that Alaska's occupational licensing boards function well and adequately protect legitimate professional and public interests falls to the Division of Occupational Licensing within the Department of Commerce and Economic Development, which performs staff functions for the boards. It also falls to the special assistant within the governor's office who is responsible for recruiting and screening applicants for positions on the boards, for ultimately the quality of the boards' performance is a function of the people who serve on them.

Alaska's public corporations are an interesting and politically significant category of state boards and commissions. These are the Alaska Housing Finance Corporation (AHFC), Alaska Power Authority (APA), Alaska State Housing Authority (ASHA), the Municipal Bond Bank, the newly formed (1984) Alaska Railroad Commission, and the Permanent Fund Corporation. As public corporations, these agencies have a legal identity separate from the State of Alaska. The main rationale for this separate standing is to limit legal liability to the state from their dealings, such as the selling of revenue bonds. Also, it gives the organizations certain management ("business-like") flexibility. For example, most employees of the corporations are exempt from the rules governing the classified service.

Generally speaking, the creation of public corporations and the granting of significant policymaking responsibilities and administrative functions to other boards and commissions (such as administration of the $65 million-per-year student loan program by the Commission on Postsecondary Education) erodes the power and prerogative of the governor.[5] Alaska's governors have not been unmindful of this, of course, and they have sought to maintain as much control over the public corporations as possible. It is significant, for example, that a majority of the boards of directors of the "big three" public corporations—AHFC, AIDA, and APA—are the heads of principal departments. This insures consistency with the governor's policies and coordination with the programs of the departments with responsibilities in related areas.

MEANS OF ACCOUNTABILITY

A fundamental question about all administrative systems is the degree to which they are *accountable*. In its most expansive sense, administrative accountability refers to the linkage between acts of the bureaucracy and the will of the electorate. In its practical application, the concept of accountability underlies these familiar questions: Was this administrative act arbitrary or unreasonable? Did it exceed the discretionary authority of the official responsible for it? Did the public have a chance to comment on the action before it became final? On what legal grounds was it based? In short, mechanisms of accountability are intended to insure that the bureaucracy serves the public rather than its own interests.

Alaska's administrative system is structured in hierarchical fashion to facilitate accountability: subordinates are answerable to superiors at all levels, and the governor is ultimately answerable for all actions of his administration, both to the public—which elects him—and to the legislature—which gives him statutory direction and the money to operate. Also, numerous administrative procedures and means of legislative oversight help guarantee the system's responsiveness to the public and the legislature.

ADMINISTRATIVE ORGANIZATION AND PROCEDURE

The administrative reform movement of the first half of this century urged states to enhance the accountability of their administrative systems by increasing gubernatorial control. This objective is achieved by structuring these systems hierarchically in accordance with modern principles of organizational management (such as the integration of functionally related units, limited span of control, and clear chain of command). The authors of Alaska's constitution so structured the executive branch, and Alaska's administrative system has been widely considered a model of modern, effective, and accountable bureaucratic organization.

Article III, Section 24 of the Alaska constitution states simply: "Each principal department shall be under the supervision of the governor." Thus the governor is ultimately answerable for the actions of his agencies. Accountability is greatly impaired in the administrative systems of other states that are characterized by "plural executives"—that is, directly elected cabinet officers and independent boards and commissions with significant administrative authority. This fragmentation of executive power reduces the accountability of the system by dispersing responsibility for official acts.

In Alaska, the governor has a free hand to set administrative policy. He gives policy direction to the commissioners, who communicate it to deputy commissioners and division directors, who in turn work with program managers to implement it throughout the departments.[6] With this power to control the bureaucracy comes the undiluted responsibility for its successful performance. Alaska governors can and do fire commissioners, deputy commissioners, and division directors who are unreceptive to their policies, or are unsuccessful in securing compliance with them by subordinates.

Administrative accountability requires not only that supervisors are liable for the actions of subordinates, but that there is a clearly discernible legal basis for all actions that occur. Several procedural safeguards exist in Alaska that work to keep administrators within the narrow confines of the law, and to prevent them from making decisions that are arbitrary, unreasonable, self-serving, or improperly influenced by special interests. These procedural guidelines are not unique to Alaska,[7] but their stringency and enforcement by the courts mark Alaska as a leader among the states in the degree of public accessibility to administrative decisionmaking and the record of administrative decisions.

Preeminent among these safeguards is the Administrative Procedures Act (AS 44.62). This act sets forth steps that administrative agencies must follow when they engage in "rulemaking"—that is, when they issue legally enforceable administrative regulations that implement laws. These procedural steps are intended to prevent administrators from exceeding their authority and from being unreasonable and arbitrary. Key provisions of the act require administrators to: 1) cite the statutory authority upon which the regulations are based; 2) allow the interested public to comment on the proposed regulation at an open hearing; and 3) give the public notice 30 days prior to a hearing on the proposed regulation.

Another important provision of the Administrative Procedures Act requires open meetings (AS 44.66.310). All formal meetings of state and local government bodies must be open to the public. Only three exceptions are permissible: when the meeting involves: 1) "matters, the immediate knowledge of which would clearly have an adverse effect upon the finances of the governmental unit; 2) subjects that tend to prejudice the reputation and character of any person...; and 3) matters which by law, municipal charter, or ordinance are required to be confidential.'' A long series of court cases and opinions of the attorney general interpret this law very strictly, so that virtually no meeting of a public body, however informal, escapes it, and actions taken in disregard of it are void.[8]

A final procedural safeguard that is noteworthy in this discussion of administrative accountability is Alaska's freedom of information statute. AS 09.25.120 begins: "Every person has a right to inspect a public writing or record in the state...." With few narrowly specified exceptions, the law allows public access to all of the written work of state and municipal officials.

LEGISLATIVE OVERSIGHT

We have noted that Alaska law requires public servants to do their work in full public view, and makes the governor ultimately answerable for their performance. In addition, the administrative system is answerable to the legislature, for after all, administrators exist to implement the laws the legislature passes. In Alaska, legislators rely on several mechanisms to monitor administrative activity and insure its compliance with legislative intent.

Not surprisingly, the exercise of legislative oversight often leads to border skirmishes between the legislative and executive branches of government, as each is protective of its constitutionally-demarcated line of jurisdiction.[9] This has been the case with legislative review of regulations, for example. Also, the exercise of legislative oversight often results in legislative directives that contradict administrative policy, and administrators and program managers are frequently required to juggle as best they can two different sets of goals and priorities. Even when it is clear to the administrator that a legislator's interest in the management of a program is a vested one and does not reflect statutory intent, he knows it can be foolhardy to ignore this interest altogether. (There is, for example, always the prospect of budgetary retaliation in the next legislative session.)

Appropriation Process. Through the appropriation process the legislature exercises its strictest and most effective power of review over administrative actions. Every agency must get its budget approved, and the members of the house and senate finance committees sit in judgement of what each agency has done, is doing, and seeks to accomplish. An agency is in an uncomfortable situation, and probably in serious trouble, if its performance has fallen short of or deviates from the expectations of key finance committee members.

No program of any significance can be implemented without public funding, so the annual appropriation process can be as important as the law that originally called the program into existence.

Legislative Post-Audit. Article IX, Section 14 of the Alaska constitution directs the legislature to appoint an auditor to conduct "post-audits as prescribed by law." This requirement is fulfilled by the Legislative Audit Division, which reports to the Legislative Budget and Audit Committee, a permanent interim committee of the legislature. Although initially the division concerned itself exclusively with financial compliance audits, which determine if executive branch agencies have expended money in compliance with applicable laws, regulations, and statements of legislative intent, it has since 1971 been authorized to conduct performance audits. Performance audits are evaluations intended to determine how effectively and efficiently a program or agency is run. Harsh criticism in a report by the legislative auditor is something every administrator wants to avoid, because it can put his own job in jeopardy, as well as the financial and statutory future of his program.

Review of Regulations. Legislation initiating new programs is typically broad and conceptual in nature, leaving an administrative agency wide latitude to fashion the detailed provisions of the program necessary to make it work. In effect, the legislature delegates part of its lawmaking power to the agencies, which exercise this power through the adoption of administrative regulations. Legislators often complain that the agencies are not faithful to legislative intent when they adopt regulations. As a consequence, they have asserted the right to annul offensive regulations by passing resolutions, which are not subject to the governor's veto.[10] The executive branch has regarded this unilateral attempt to annul regulations as an encroachment on its constitutional authority, and the courts have agreed that it is.[11] To overcome this obstacle, the legislature has twice put before the voters a proposed constitutional amendment that would explicitly permit a "legislative veto" of administrative regulations, and twice it has been rejected.[12]

Even without the power to annul regulations, the Alaska Legislature monitors the rulemaking activity of the agencies through the Regulations Review Committee. This legislative vigilance has the desired effect of keeping statutory intent in the forefront of the minds of administrators who are preparing to promulgate regulations. When disputes arise, they are settled through consultation between legislators with an interest in the offending regulation and the agency head, and, if necessary, the governor. (The issue of legislative-executive conflict over regulations is also discussed in the chapter on Alaska's constitution.)

Ombudsman. Alaska's ombudsman is an agent of the legislature (AS.24.55.010). His job is to investigate complaints of administrative wrongdoing, mismanagement, lethargy, and caprice—all the elements of "bureaucratic despotism." The ombudsman does not possess the authority to reverse administrative actions or sue to enforce compliance with laws and procedural regulations. Rather, his ability to chastise an errant public servant stems from the eager attention his reports get in the press and legislative hallways. Unfavorable publicity is one of the bureaucrat's worst enemies, and an investigation by the ombudsman (or by the legislative auditor) is something that all seek to avoid. There seems little doubt, although no formal evaluation documents this conclusion, that the Alaska ombudsman is an effective mechanism for enhancing the overall accountability of administrative agencies and their responsiveness to individual citizens.[13]

Sunset Review. In 1976 Colorado adopted the first "sunset law," and a year later Alaska enacted its own. Today, 35 states have some variation of sunset legislation on their statute books. Sunset laws threaten automatic termination of state agencies at certain intervals unless the legislature takes positive action to renew their charters. Alaska's sunset law (AS 44.66.010; 08.03.010) reaches all boards and commissions and every state program as well, whereas laws in most other states apply only to boards and commissions. Sunset laws strengthen the legislative oversight function. In Alaska, the legislative auditor begins the scheduled review process (usually every four years for each agency) with a performance audit. Approximately 50 agencies have been reviewed since 1977. The legislative auditor has recommended termination of 12 boards or commissions, and the legislature has terminated three and merged two others.

Evaluations of the sunset process in Alaska and in the U.S. as a whole conclude that, while wholesale elimination of government agencies has not been achieved, the periodic reviews have generally increased agency efficiency and public accountability.[14]

Informal Intervention. A citizen with a grievance against an agency may complain to the ombudsman, or he may complain directly to his or her legislator. Legislators and their staffs tend to be very responsive to these complaints, because they are opportunities to demonstrate interest in the problems of constituents and to show the legislators' influence and ability to "get results" from the system. Informal intervention by a legislator in the work of an agency is, however, at best an imperfect method of enhancing the accountability of the system. Too often the intervention can be disruptive and destabilizing to otherwise sound administrative decisions. A health care agency, for example, might have made a careful assessment of its resources and the areas of greatest need, only to be confronted by a legislator furious that a decision has been made to transfer a staff position from a clinic in his district to a clinic with a heavier workload outside his district. His threats may not be ignored, even if he does not have a powerful position in the legislature; he might come back as Speaker of the House in the next organization. Conflicts of this type may ultimately require involvement of the governor, and they can be very costly in administrative time and energy.

Confirmation of Appointees. Alaska's legislature, sitting in joint session, must approve by a majority vote the governor's cabinet appointments (Alaska Constitution, Article III, Section 25). This provision is one of several constitutional "checks and balances" on the executive branch by the legislature. It is a basic safeguard of accountability built into our constitutional system of government.

Normally, the governor is afforded the privilege of appointing whom he pleases to his cabinet, provided the credentials of the appointees are at least minimally plausible for the position. Nonetheless, legislators individually may use the confirmation process to communicate their concerns about the operation of the department to the nominee. Occasionally these discussions can become quite high-pressured, and a nominee may direct a number of his staff people to the casework of the legislator, or he may reach an explicit agreement on a policy issue of special interest to a legislator or committee.[15] Recently, an appointee to the head of a major department was led to believe by key legislators that his confirmation was in doubt, and he publicly took a position favored by these legislators on a sensitive issue but which contradicted the governor's own position. There have been occasional open conflicts between the legislative and executive branch regarding confirmation, but these have not involved quarrels over the qualifications and suitability of proposed department heads.[16]

ROLE IN MAKING LAWS

The American scheme of constitutional government assigns to the legislature the responsibility for making laws, and to the executive branch the responsibility for enforcing and implementing those laws. Through the system of checks and balances, each branch exercises specified, limited powers in the sphere of the other. In the day-to-day operation of our system of government, however, the functional roles of the two branches are blurred to a much greater extent than is suggested by a textbook explanation. We have seen from the foregoing discussion of legislative oversight that the legislature can become very deeply involved in the administrative details of state programs. The administrative system is also deeply and directly involved in the lawmaking function.

When agencies are given new programs to administer, they typically face many decisions that were not anticipated in the statute, or which were deliberately left to the agency to resolve. Thus, through the implementation of laws the agencies routinely make public policy decisions. These decisions are usually codified in regulations. However, the choice of implementation methods by the agencies usually amounts to a less significant contribution to making public policy than their direct involvement in drafting laws in the first place. This is because laws set policy: the latitude for agency discretion in carrying them out is typically quite narrow when viewed in perspective. Thus, in the opinion of the author, we should look to the administrative role in the development of legislation for an understanding of how the responsibility for making public policy is really shared between the two branches of government.

A large number of the bills that are on the legislative agenda every session are submitted by the governor—134 of the 854 bills introduced in the 1985 legislative session, for example. These are of two general types: "housekeeping" bills, and major policy initiatives of the governor. Both are prepared by administration officials. Housekeeping bills are technical amendments to statutes that are necessary to overcome problems encountered by program administrators. Some bills that may appear to be housekeeping measures can actually involve very significant policy issues, such as expanding or changing eligibility requirements, distribution formulas, exemptions, or exclusionary provisions. In fact, a strategy sometimes used by agency staffs (as well as lobbyists and legislators), is to portray their really important bills as technical housekeeping measures that no one needs to be concerned about, and to write the bills themselves and supporting statements in language that is incomprehensible to laymen.

Bills that represent priority policy initiatives by the governor are developed either by the governor's key policy staff or by the commissioner and staff of the relevant department. The Department of Law drafts and reviews all legislation that is formally introduced through the house or senate rules committee at the request of the governor.

Occasionally during the legislative session, when a bill with provisions that the governor opposes begins moving in committees, the governor's office may hurriedly put together an alternative or revised bill and have it introduced as a committee substitute by a friendly legislator. In these situations the Department of Law (and other agencies with some substantive interest in the subject matter) may or may not have a look at it before it appears in print. What is interesting about this practice of "farming out" legislation to a cooperative, like-minded legislator (or one who may want the governor to sponsor one of his bills) is that it is an avenue sometimes used by agency officials to circumvent the governor's review of their legislative proposals. Agreements between administrator and legislator are usually not publicized, so the full extent of the practice is unknown. It is important to realize, however, that significant legislation bearing the name of a senator or representative may well have originated from within the administrative system.

Executive branch employees also usually have a hand in crafting legislation that originates on the legislative side. Most legislation directly affects the programs and activities of one or more departments. These program managers are the best qualified to assess the impacts and effectiveness of the proposed legislation. At a minimum, they testify at committee hearings about technical aspects of the bill, and, unless the governor opposes the measure (and even when he does, depending on their own interests), they commonly work closely with legislators and committee staffs to perfect the concept and language of it.

All bills that are passed by both houses of the legislature come to the governor for his signature or veto.[17] At this point the administrative agencies typically have a final opportunity to review bills and make a recommendation to the governor. Here many an inexperienced legislator has realized that he should have consulted the agencies about his bills, or have been more receptive to the advice they gave. Unless the governor has made a prior commitment to sign a bill, he is very likely to follow the veto recommendations of his departments.

BUDGET PROCESS

All of what government does requires the spending of money. The annual process of apportioning the state's available revenue among the agencies is therefore a very important one and it commands a good deal of attention in government circles. The executive branch accounts for most state spending for non-capital items (spending by the legislative and judicial branches is small in comparison) and inter-agency competition for operating funds is a dominant feature of bureaucratic life. An overview of the budget process in this chapter on the administrative system seems worthwhile for this reason, in addition to the fact that the executive branch plays an important formal role in the preparation of the annual budget. (The chapter devoted to the Alaska Legislature also discusses the budget process, but that discussion looks in detail at how the legislature allocates money and in particular at how the huge increases in revenues in the early 1980s affected the legislative budget system.)

EXECUTIVE AND LEGISLATIVE ROLES

Alaska's constitution requires the preparation of an executive budget. Article IX, Section 12 states in pertinent part: "The governor shall submit to the legislature, at a time fixed by law, a budget for the next fiscal year setting forth all proposed expenditures and anticipated income of all departments, offices, and agencies of the State." This basic budgetary responsibility of the governor is elaborated in the Executive Budget Act (AS. 37.07). All state constitutions but three give the governor the same responsibility to prepare an executive budget. (A joint legislative-executive budgeting board oversees preparation of the budget submission in the other states.) The executive branch is considered well equipped (with time, staff, technical knowledge of programs and their interrelationships, and a statewide perspective) to prepare a detailed, comprehensive fiscal plan for the state. In Alaska the legislature reviews the spending proposals submitted in the executive budget and may accept them, modify them, or reject them as it pleases. It may introduce its own appropriation bills. Only a few state constitutions limit the ability of the legislature to exercise full discretion over appropriation proposals of the governor.[18]

When the Alaska Legislature enacts appropriation bills, they go to the governor, who may veto them altogether or reduce specific line items. A three-fourths vote of the legislature meeting in joint session is required to override a line-item veto or reduction by the governor. (Non-appropriation bills can be overridden with a two-thirds majority.) Here again procedures in Alaska are not unusual, except perhaps in the degree of difficulty imposed by the constitution on the legislature in overriding an appropriation veto or reduction. Virtually all governors possess some form of line-item veto power (unlike the president of the United States, who does not have this power) and virtually all require a super majority vote in the legislature to override. [19]

Although all state legislatures possess extensive formal powers of budget review, they differ widely in the effectiveness with which they perform the task. As a consequence, the significance of the executive budget varies enormously from state to state. For various reasons, many state legislatures today play largely a passive role in shaping the budget. This passivity has been characteristic of most state legislatures, although many have become increasingly active in the budgetmaking process in recent years. Alaska's legislature is extremely active in its budget review function. The finance committees hire staff, and the legislature employs budget analysts through its Legislative Finance Division. There has been continuity in recent years in the finance committee leadership, which has permitted these members to acquire considerable expertise in agency programs and budget issues. These and other factors, including the unusually large amounts of money available for capital projects in the early 1980s, have contributed to the legislature's active participation in budgetmaking. While the executive budget is the point of departure for legislative deliberations on spending for non-capital items, it cannot be considered the de facto state budget when it is sent down to the legislature.

In states where the executive budget is, for all practical purposes, the state budget, the internal administrative process of writing that document becomes the focus of agency competition to secure "adequate" levels of funding. In Alaska, agencies get a chance to present their cases before the finance committees if the governor and his budget review committee were not sufficiently generous. This is tricky business, however, and it can be perilous for an inexperienced bureaucrat. All departments—even those that may feel an important activity or line-item was shorted—are presumed to support the governor's budget after it is in final form. Nevertheless, in testifying before the finance committees (and, more important, before the subcommittees that have been assigned their budget) agency heads usually are given or make an opportunity to press the case for restoring items omitted in the governor's budget submission.

DEDICATED AND FORMULA FUNDS

Executive and legislative budgeteers in numerous states actually have discretion over only a very small portion of their revenue because so much of it is dedicated (or earmarked) to specific programs by law. For example, in some states all fuel taxes are earmarked for highway maintenance and all sumptuary taxes are earmarked for support of education. Alaska's constitution prohibits the legislature from earmarking funds (except for deposits to the Permanent Fund and for a few other, minor programs), and consequently budget makers work with an exceptionally high proportion of unrestricted funds.

In Alaska as elsewhere, however, a large portion of unrestricted general fund revenues are claimed by "formula" (or "entitlement") programs. These statutory programs qualify certain individuals, local governments, school districts, and other recipients for payments set by law. The School Foundation Program is the largest of these in Alaska—about $500 million in fiscal year 1985, or a quarter of the entire operating budget. That program makes every school district eligible to receive a payment from the general fund on the basis of enrollment.

The legislature does not, however, have to appropriate money necessary to fund the formula programs, if it wishes to hold back for any reason, and occasionally a formula program is not fully funded. In that case the shortfall is usually prorated among eligible recipients. Generally speaking, however, the formula programs receive the appropriations required to fulfill the obligation of the law. In fiscal year 1985, the formula programs amounted to approximately 40 percent of Alaska's unrestricted general fund appropriation.

THE BUDGET CYCLE

Alaska state government operates on an annual budget with each fiscal year running from July 1 to June 30.[20] This allows the legislature ample time to deliberate on spending decisions for the coming year.

Passing the operating budget is one of the very last actions taken by the legislature before adjournment. Nevertheless, state law requires the governor to submit the executive budget on December 15, a month before the legislature convenes in January.[21]

To meet this schedule, the executive budget preparation cycle must begin in mid-summer, a full year from the beginning of the next fiscal year. This means that only a month or two into one fiscal year the departments must begin preparing for the next. Consequently, to project their needs they must look to past trends and patterns for which data is available. It is not unusual for this data to be two years old by the time an appropriations bill is passed.

Through the Office of Management and Budget (OMB), the governor issues guidelines to the departments about acceptable budget growth. Each departmental budget officer works with an OMB analyst, who provides instruction and interpretation of budget forms and procedures. In the fall, OMB assembles all the agency requests and begins an internal review process with the governor and his budget advisors, who may or may not meet as a formally convened budget review committee. It is important that every department have an opportunity to argue its case before the governor and his budget advisors. This internal review process is brought to a close in time for OMB to print the general appropriation bill and the *Executive Budget Book*, a summary of the governor's proposed spending plan, before the December 15 deadline.

REVENUE ESTIMATES

An important part of the budget process is estimating revenues for the coming fiscal year. In Alaska, as in many other states, this task is assigned to the

Department of Revenue. What is unusual about Alaska in recent years, however, is its extreme dependence on revenues from a single source: about 85 percent of unrestricted general funds in the 1980s derive from taxes and royalties on petroleum. Petroleum revenues are sensitive to the market price of crude oil, which is subject to fluctuation. Therefore, revenue forecasting is largely an exercise in the black art of oil price forecasting.

The department makes quarterly forecasts of oil prices, and small changes in their price assumptions can translate into very substantial changes in expected revenue from one forecast to the next.

To deal with the problem of uncertainty in revenue estimates, the administration and legislature have agreed to use a deliberately conservative estimate in preparing the annual budget.

INCREMENTALISM AND BUDGET REFORM

Like many other states, Alaska has experimented with reforms that seek to "rationalize" the budgeting process. Like other states, Alaska has always reverted to the traditional approach known as "incremental budgeting," in which attention is focused on marginal increases in agency budgets rather than on the overall level of agency requests or the comprehensive programmatic relationship of agency activities.[22]

This persistence of incremental budgeting underscores the ponderous stability of government agencies and programs. Virtually all state programs are set firmly in statute, and each one typically represents a hard-fought political compromise among various interests. To eliminate a program, or even to threaten to slash a program's budget, fractures this fragile political accommodation of interests and can bring grief to a governor or legislative body beyond any possible benefit they might hope to gain from the action.

It can be very destabilizing even to revamp suddenly the administrative details of a program; the clientele of the program as well as its administrators will resist change for fear they will be disadvantaged under the new procedures. In short, things typically are the way they are in the administrative system for important reasons (although not necessarily good ones). While the governor and the legislature can add new programs at will, neither can easily make sweeping changes in programs that already exist.

Given the political weight of the status quo, it is not productive for budget makers to probe annually the rationale for and performance of every program. Instead, they tend to focus on marginal increases in existing program budgets and allocation of incremental revenue to that growth and to initiation of new programs that are so important to politicians.

PUBLIC SERVICE AND PUBLIC SERVANTS

The human dimension of governmental organizations must not be overlooked. People make the system go. Characteristics of state employment are an important feature of every administrative system.

SIZE OF STATE WORKFORCE

Perhaps the dominant characteristic of Alaska's governmental workforce is its size relative to the population of the state. Alaska is reported to have the highest combined state and local government employment per 10,000 of population in the nation.[23] There were approximately 16,000 full-time, permanent state employees in 1984, including employees of the Marine Transportation System and the University of Alaska.

Thus, Alaska's administrative system is very large in relative terms. There are several reasons why this is so. All states with low population densities tend to have higher ratios of public employment to population, in large part because economies of scale in service delivery are limited. But the fact that Alaska state government has had comparatively high revenue from oil development in recent years is doubtless a major explanation for Alaska's large government workforce.

There are important socioeconomic implications of a large state workforce in Alaska. For example, state workers represent a significant electoral force, especially in Juneau and Anchorage. State workers also make a major contribution to the state and local economies.[24]

MERIT SYSTEM

A key feature of the constitutional framework of Alaska's administrative system is Article XII, Section 6, which says, "The Legislature shall establish a system under which the merit principle will govern the employment of persons by the State." Whereas many states have had to struggle against a long tradition of political patronage in state personnel systems, Alaska's constitution mandates the merit principle in state employment.

In 1961 the legislature enacted the State Personnel Act (AS 39.25) to implement the constitutional requirement and to provide a comprehensive personnel system for the state. It establishes three categories of public service: the classified service, the exempt service, and the partially exempt service. The vast majority (about 80 percent) of the state's employees are in the classified service and subject to the state's personnel rules that enforce the merit principle of civil service employment. The act recognizes, however, that policy-level employees and certain other categories of employees should be exempt or partially exempt from those rules, to ensure the political accountability and management efficiency of the system.

COLLECTIVE BARGAINING

Unionism for Alaska public workers began to develop in the 1960s, primarily at the local level. It was not until the 1970s that collective bargaining began to be authorized at the state level.[25] Alaska is a "strong union" state, and it is not surprising that it was among the first states to permit its employees to organize and bargain collectively for wages, salaries, hours, and conditions of employment. In 1972 the legislature passed the Public Employees Relations Act (AS 23.40), which authorized collective bargaining for state workers. The act was also made applicable to local governments, although they can opt out of its provisions by actions of their legislative bodies.

Table 12.3 shows that Alaska is among the states with the highest percentage of full-time employees represented by authorized bargaining units. It is noteworthy that Alaska is so much like the industrial eastern states in this respect, and so unlike our western state counterparts.

Currently, eight unions represent and bargain collectively for state workers. The largest of these is the Alaska Public Employees Association (APEA), which represents about 8,770 general government and supervisory employees. The Confidential Employees Association (CEA) represents about 200 employees who deal with personnel papers and are prohibited from belonging to APEA. These unions represent various categories of some 750 state ferry workers: Inlandboatmen's Union of the Pacific (IBU), International Order to Masters, Mates, and Pilots (MMP), and the Marine Engineers Beneficial Association (MEBA). The Public Employees Local No. 71 of the AFL-CIO covers the 1,500 workers in the Labor, Trades and Craft (LTC) unit.

Three hundred and eighty state troopers are represented by the Public Safety Employees Association (PSEA). Finally, about 60 educators are represented by the Central Correspondence Study Education Association (CCSEA).

REMUNERATION

Alaska's state government workforce is not only the largest in the nation on a per capita basis, it is also the highest paid. In 1982, the estimated annual earning of the average full-time State of Alaska employee was $31,272, 80 percent higher than the national average and $7,236 above that of the second-ranking state, California.[26] The average salary disparity between Alaska and

Table 12.3

Percentage of Full-Time State Employees In Bargaining Units, 1980

	State employees in bargaining units		State employees in bargaining units
Alabama	17%	Montana	43%
Alaska	74	Nebraska	10
Arizona	0	Nevada	0
Arkansas	0	New Hampshire	53
California	0	New Jersey	59
Colorado	0	New Mexico	17
Connecticut	83	New York	83
Delaware	31	North Carolina	0
Florida	47	North Dakota	4
Georgia	0	Ohio	16
Hawaii	70	Oklahoma	0
Idaho	0	Oregon	54
Illinois	19	Pennsylvania	67
Indiana	6	Rhode Island	70
Iowa	32	South Carolina	0
Kansas	20	South Dakota	9
Kentucky	0	Tennessee	3
Louisiana	10	Texas	10
Maine	43	Utah	1
Maryland	3	Vermont	52
Massachusetts	75	Virginia	0
Michigan	35	Washington	39
Minnesota	32	West Virginia	0.2
Mississippi	0	Wisconsin	47
Missouri	22	Wyoming	0
U.S. Average	25%		

Excludes employee associations not recognized for collective bargaining.

Source: Richard C. Ellings, "State Bureaucracies," *Politics in the American States*, Gary, Jacob, and Vines, eds. 4th Edition. (Boston: Little, Brown), p. 262. Derived from U.S. Census data.

California is comparable to the cost of living differences between the two places, but even when this adjustment is considered, Alaska public servants remain among the best paid in the nation. In addition to their comparatively high salaries, public workers in Alaska also receive attractive perquisites, including paid vacations and holidays, health insurance, and retirement pensions. Several explanations for this generous remuneration for public service seem apparent: the high cost of living in Alaska; more than a decade of collective bargaining by employees; the electoral influence of public workers; and the availability of North Slope oil revenue.

A consequence of high state salaries is keen competition to fill vacancies. We may strongly presume, although no statistical measure is available to verify the presumption, that this competition results in a more highly qualified and competent workforce than would be the case if state salaries and benefits were not so appealing.

CAREER PATTERNS

Some general career patterns in Alaska state government are noticeable, although exceptions abound. Administrative departments differ widely in the extent to which they are professional career services—that is, in the extent to which recruitment is typically at the entry level from among graduates of professional schools, and promotion to the higher supervisory levels requires a gradual progression through the ranks on the basis of demonstrated competence.

Generally speaking, the career service departments are those whose activity has little or no counterpart in the private sector or even in the public sector at the local level. Examples of these are the Departments of Fish and Game, Corrections, and Public Safety. The departments that least fit the professional career service model are those whose activities require knowledge and skill that are readily saleable outside government. The Department of Law is perhaps the best example: recruits are mostly young attorneys fresh from law schools who typically spend three to five years in government service acquiring expertise in a specialized field of law and then move into private practice where their earnings can be substantially higher than state salaries. (A stepping stone out of the Department of Law is occasionally a deputy commissionership in the department with which the attorney has been working.) Professional level employees in other non-career service departments move into and out of government service at middle and upper levels where their skills are applicable in the private sector: financial experts and accountants (Departments of Revenue and Administration), architects, engineers, and facility planners (Department of Transportation and Public Facilities), banking, securities and insurance experts (Department of Commerce), among others.

Commissioners are not usually recruited from within the ranks of the departments, although occasionally in the career service departments a person will move through the higher ranks to commissioner. Governors often find it difficult to recruit commissioners, despite many advantages commissioners have. Appointment as a commissioner usually means leaving a well-paid position, being exposed to public criticism, moving to Juneau, disrupting family relationships, and tolerating other inconveniences. At times a commissioner will be recruited from out of state, but special circumstances are necessary. Commissioners are expected to have close ties to at least some of the important client groups of the department they head. Perhaps because the pool of eligible candidates is so small, it is not uncommon for commissioners to be appointed who are not of the same political party as the governor. There have been "coalition cabinets" for many years in Juneau.

At the subprofessional level (for example, secretaries and administrative assistants) and among employees with technical skills (for example, computer programmers, bookkeepers, personnel officers) who have experience in the state system, there is considerable inter-departmental mobility. At this level, there seem to be ample opportunities for advancement for competent and enterprising people.

CONCLUSION

Alaska's administrative system is governed by constitutional and statutory provisions that are widely regarded as modern and progressive. They create an administrative structure that is highly unified and integrated, when contrasted to the executive branch organization of many other states. This centralized structure enhances the accountability of decisionmaking by the executive branch.

Recommendations are made every year by legislators and administrators themselves for structural and functional changes that seek to enhance the efficiency, productivity, and general economy of administrative operations. Many of these are valuable recommendations that are eventually adopted and implemented as part of a slow, on-going evolution of Alaska's executive branch. Noteworthy, however, is that these changes take place at the margin of an administrative system that is generally acknowledged to be well-designed and effective.

During the second half of the decade of the 1980s, as Alaska's oil revenues decline, the challenge of state public administrators will be to accelerate the search for and adoption of management measures that further improve efficiency and productivity. Across-the-board cutbacks and the elimination of some state programs seem inevitable in the face of declining revenues. Constriction of the operating budget, and steep declines in capital spending, will cause personal dislocation for many state workers as well as significant reduction in state-provided public services that have benefited residents throughout Alaska. Also, there is apprehension that reduced spending by the state will be a setback for the health of the entire economy, as state expenditures are thought to have made a major contribution to Alaska's rapid economic growth during the first half of the 1980s. In any case, it seems probable that by the mid-1990s Alaska's administrative system will be more similar in size and pay scales to those elsewhere in the United States. Also, it will doubtless concentrate on the delivery of more traditionally defined "essential" services.

ENDNOTES

[1] These sources are: _Alaska Blue Book, 1985_, and previous editions, published by the Alaska Department of Education; _Handbook on Alaska State Government_, published annually by the Alaska Legislative Affairs Agency; and the _Alaska Report of Performance_, an annual (fiscal year) compilation of agency activities and accomplishments, published by the Alaska Office of Management and Budget (formerly by the Division of Policy Development and Planning).

[2] These provisions continue to govern the Department of Fish and Game (although now there are separate boards for Fish and Game) but they have been changed for the Department of Education. In 1967, the legislature designated the Board of Education "the head of the Department of Education" (Chapter 96 SLA 1967). The number, qualifications, and terms of office of board members were changed, and the board was given the power to appoint the commissioners subject to the approval of the governor. It should be noted that the commissioners of the Department of Education and the Department of Fish and Game are subject to legislative confirmation just as are the other commissioners.

[3] Advisory Commission on Intergovernmental Relations, _Significant Features of Fiscal Federalism, 1982-83 Edition_, Washington, D.C., 1984 p. 127.

[4] Associated Press story July 20, 1984, run in the Anchorage and Juneau newspapers.

[5] A good review and critique of public corporations in general and Alaska's public corporations in particular is available in Institute of Public Administration, _Alaska Public Corporations_: a Report to the Legislative Budget and Audit Committee, State of Alaska, 1982.

[6] The exception to this generalization is the Department of Education. It should be noted, however, that typically commissioners work directly with the governor to develop specific policies concerning their own departments.

[7] See _State Policy Reports_, Vol. 2, no. 3, February 9, 1984, p. 9.

[8] See, for example, opinions of the attorney general of May 11, 1981 (memorandum to Charles Webber, Commissioner of the Department of Commerce and Economic Development), and February 9, 1984 (memorandum to the Board of Directors of the Alaska Resources Corporation).

[9]This is the common consequence of legislative oversight. See Samuel K. Gove, "State Management and Legislative-Executive Relations," *State Government*, Vol. 54, No. 3 (1981).

[10]See Rich Jones, "Legislative Review of Regulation," *State Legislatures*, September, 1982; and Prescott E. Bloom, "Legislative Oversight: A Response to Citizens' Demands and Needs," *State and Local Government Review*, Vol. 16, No. 1 (1984).

[11]Alaska v. A.L.I.V.E. Voluntary, 606 P.2d 769 (1980).

[12]Proposed Alaska constitutional amendments failed to be ratified in the general elections of 1980 and 1984. At the federal level, the U.S. Supreme Court has declared the "legislative veto" over administrative actions unconstitutional (Immigration and Naturalization Service v. Chandra, 1983).

[13]See the *Annual Report* of the Office of the Ombudsman.

[14]See Division of Legislative Audit, *A Special Report on the Sunset Process in Alaska*, May 1984; and Common Cause, *The Status of Sunset in the States*; March 1982.

[15]A good example of this phenomenon at the national level familiar to many Alaskans is the pledge Walter Hickel gave the U.S. Senate Interior Committee in his confirmation hearings that he would not revoke the federal land freeze in Alaska pending a settlement of the Native land claims there. Previously he had said that he would revoke the freeze when he became Secretary of the Interior.

[16]A conflict developed when the legislature asserted the right to confirm deputy department heads as well as department heads. When the governor refused to submit the names of his appointees to these positions, the legislature sued. The Alaska Supreme Court agreed with the governor that the legislature's demand was unconstitutional (Bradner v. Hammond, 553 P.2d 1; 1976). In 1983, the majority faction of the Alaska House of Representatives precipitated a constitutional crisis when its members refused to meet in joint session to confirm the governor's cabinet nominees. The governor called a joint session and compelled the attendance of absent members. The court upheld the legality of the governor's action. In these cases, the motivation of the legislature was not to ensure capable department heads, but to pressure the governor for other political purposes.

[17]There is no "pocket veto" in Alaska; bills not signed by the governor become law (Article III, Section 17).

[18]In Maryland, New York, and West Virginia, the legislature may only decrease appropriations in the governor's budget (except appropriations for the legislative and judicial branches); in Nebraska, a three-fifths vote of the legislature is required to increase appropriations in the governor's budget.

[19]An excellent source of information in summary form about state budgeting processes is Council of State Governments, *Book of the States 1984-85*, Table 1 ("Budgetary Practices") pp. 244-245.

[20]Nineteen states prepare budgets biennially (every two years) although only six use a different fiscal year.

[21]In 1984 the legislature changed the law to require the governor to submit his budget on December 15. In previous years, state law required the governor to submit it on the fourth day of the session. The change was made by the legislature in 1984 in anticipation that voters would approve a constitutional amendment limiting legislative sessions to 120 days. Legislators thought that the finance committees could begin their work before the session began if the governor's budget were available.

[22]See Ira Sharkansky, "State Administrators in the Political Process," in Jacob and Vines, eds. *Politics in the American States*, 2nd Edition (Boston: Little, Brown and Co., 1971), for a good description of the administrative logic of incremental budgeting. Aspects of the experience with budget reforms in other states are similar to Alaska's. For example, the Montana experience with zero-based budgeting is similar to Alaska's attempt to prepare a zero-based executive budget in 1983. See John S. Frizpatrick. "Montana's Experiment with Zero-Based Budgeting," *State Government*, Vol. 53, No. 1, Winter 1980.

[23]A meaningful comparison of levels of public employment in the states requires state and local employees to be combined, because in many states, especially the industrial states, many governmental activities are performed at the local level. In 1983, the U.S. Census Bureau reported that Alaska had 814 full-time equivalent state and local employees per 10,000 population, in contrast to a national average of 465. This data is summarized in a useful compendium of statistics published as *1985 State Policy Data Book*, by State Policy Research, Arlington, Virginia (Table E-12). See also Advisory Commission on Intergovernmental Relations, *Significant Features of Fiscal Federalism, 1982-83 Edition*. Washington, D.C., 1984, p. 128. This report shows 820 and 468 respectively.

[24]National statistics show that state and local payrolls in Alaska amount to 15.7 percent of total state personal income, higher than any other state's percentage and twice the U.S. average. ACIR, *Significant Features of Fiscal Federalism*.

[25]See Richard J. Carlson and Thomas Sedwick, "Collective Bargaining in the Public Sector: A Focus on State Government," *State Government*, Vol. 50, No. 3, Summer 1977.

[26]ACIR, *Significant Features of Fiscal Federalism, 1982-83 Edition*, p. 130.

13
Courts In Alaska

Andrea R.C. Helms

Alaska was one of the first states to adopt a unified court system that includes many of the judicial reforms long advocated by judicial experts. All courts in the state are under the jurisdiction of the Alaska Supreme Court. There are no city, borough, or special jurisdiction courts. Judges are chosen under a merit plan that involves nominations by a judicial council and appointment by the governor—but that still makes judges accountable to the public by providing for periodic votes on retaining appointed judges.

Features similar to those of the Alaska court system have been adopted to some extent in many other states as part of the judicial reform movement of recent decades. This chapter discusses the development of Alaska's judicial system, describes its structure and operations, and compares it with systems in other states.

STATE COURTS IN THE UNITED STATES

Courts affect the daily lives of Americans by defining the limits of government intervention in private concerns. Courts also provide the arenas where citizens attempt to settle disputes. And courts provide for the public safety by trying and sentencing those who have broken the law.

In the United States there are two separate court systems: the federal court system, which operates throughout the country, and state court systems, which operate in each of the 50 states. Federal courts hear mostly cases involving federal laws, interstate disputes, interpretation of the federal constitution, and a few other kinds of cases that affect national interests. These federal cases make up only about 5 percent of all court cases in the United States.

It is the state courts that hear the rest—about 95 percent of court cases brought in this country. These cases heard by state courts range from small traffic violations and divorces to murder and other felonies; they include all kinds of cases not specifically under the jurisdiction of the federal courts. A growing problem for state courts in Alaska and elsewhere in recent times has been the staggering increase in their caseloads. Between 1955 and 1979, the number of cases heard by state courts throughout the United States increased 1,000 percent.[1]

COMMON FEATURES: ALASKA AND OTHER STATE SYSTEMS

The state courts of Alaska and all other states share some features. Cases heard by state courts are of two broad types: civil and criminal. Civil cases generally involve private parties asking the court to settle disputes between them. A civil case can be brought, for instance, by a person who believes that he was injured by someone else's negligence, or that he has lost property through someone else's carelessness. Divorce actions are also civil cases; there are hundreds of other kinds of civil cases.

Criminal cases involve persons accused of breaking the law. The courts decide guilt or innocence and sentence those convicted. It is the most serious criminal cases—murders, or large, spectacular robberies, for instance—that capture public attention, but those cases are relatively few as compared with the number of civil cases and criminal cases involving lesser offenses.

The Alaska system and all other state systems are broadly made up of courts with original jurisdiction and appellate courts. Courts with original jurisdiction hear cases from the beginning; these are trial courts, where juries may be impaneled, witnesses called, and testimony taken. Trial courts may hear either criminal or civil cases.

Appellate courts—as their name implies—primarily hear appeals from parties dissatisfied with decisions of the trial courts. They can either reverse or uphold the decisions of lower courts. Appellate courts are generally panels of judges that review trial records and sometimes listen to attorneys presenting their clients' arguments. They can review either civil or criminal cases. Under unusual circumstances appellate courts can also hear cases from the beginning.

Alaska and other states have legal standards that men and women who serve as lawyers and judges must meet. These standards vary somewhat from state to state, but at a minimum they generally require lawyers and judges to have some legal training and to have been admitted to practice law in their individual states. Also, all state court systems are bound by the fourteenth amendment to the U.S. constitution to provide justice in accordance with rules of procedure developed and enunciated by the Supreme Court of the United States— the highest court in the nation.

STRUCTURE OF STATE SYSTEMS

In the mid-1900s the structure and operations of state court systems around the country varied substantially. Many state systems had a variety of courts with confusing and overlapping jurisdictions and with no single entities that had the authority to administer and regulate all parts of the systems. Critics also charged that the various ways in which state judges were chosen sometimes resulted in unqualified or corrupt judges.

The inefficiencies and inequities in state court systems led to calls for judicial reform. The reformers wanted unification of state courts; they wanted all parts of a state's court system to be under the regulation and administration of a single body. The reformers also called for selection of judges based on merit and for other measures to improve the efficiency and equity of state courts.

Since the 1950s there has been a significant judicial reform movement in many states. According to the Advisory Commission on Intergovernmental Relations, by 1985 court systems in 34 states had been at least partially unified. Many states have also incorporated some aspects of merit systems for selecting judges.[2]

There remain many differences in court systems around the country, but most have a number of similar elements. Most state systems include (1) municipal and county courts, with limited jurisdiction over cases involving lesser offenses or smaller disputes; (2) courts of special jurisdiction, like traffic courts and juvenile courts, that hear cases only within their specific areas; (3) general trial courts with broad jurisdiction; and (4) higher courts that mainly review decisions of lower courts.[3]

Municipal, county, special jurisdiction, and broad trial courts are courts of original jurisdiction. Higher courts are almost entirely appellate courts. A given court may hear either civil or criminal cases or both, depending on its authority and jurisdiction.

As mentioned at the beginning of this chapter, Alaska has no municipal or borough courts or special jurisdiction courts—largely because Alaska's system was modeled on proposed judicial reforms that advocated simpler and more unified systems. Before turning to a detailed discussion of Alaska's court system, below we look briefly at the administration of justice in Alaska before statehood.

THE JUSTICE SYSTEM IN TERRITORIAL ALASKA

Alaska was a territory of the United States from 1867, when the U.S. bought Alaska from Russia, until 1959, when Alaska became a state. During that period federal courts and federal officials administered justice in the giant territory—but that administration was limited, particularly in the early days.[4]

In 1868 Congress gave the U.S. district courts of Washington, Oregon, and California jurisdiction over Alaska court cases. But it was not until 1884 that Congress acted to provide general laws for Alaska—and at that time it simply extended the laws of Oregon to Alaska to the extent that they were "applicable and not in conflict with the laws of the United States.'' Alaska historian Claus-M. Naske has reported that in the early territorial days, residents "could not own property, get married, write a will, or even cut firewood without defying a Congressional prohibition.''[5]

In acts passed in 1899 and 1900, Congress established civil and criminal codes for Alaska, created a district court, and divided the territory into three judicial divisions. By 1909 a fourth judicial division had been added, with one judge in each of the territory's four divisions. Congress approved creation of a territorial legislature in 1912, and over the years the legislature passed various acts affecting the justice system in Alaska.

Those acts of the territorial legislature, together with the congressional acts of 1899 and 1900 and other federal laws and regulations, shaped the justice system in Alaska until 1959. At that time Alaska became a state, and began establishing the new state court system outlined in Alaska's constitution.

Alaska's constitution is the product of a conscious attempt to incorporate the experiences of the older states and to avoid their mistakes. (See discussion in the chapter on Alaska's constitution.) Because only federal courts existed in Alaska before statehood, the authors of the constitution were able to start from scratch in designing a judicial system. That system incorporates many of the provisions that judicial reformers were calling for in the 1950s. The two most important of these are a unified court system and a merit system for selecting judges.

STRUCTURE AND OPERATIONS OF THE ALASKA COURTS

Alaska has four levels of courts. These are—from the lowest to the highest—the district court, the superior court, the court of appeals, and the supreme court. The superior and supreme courts were established in the constitution. The district court and the court of appeals were created by legislative acts.

All the state's courts are unified—that is, they are parts of a single statewide system that is administered and regulated by the Alaska Supreme Court. Figure 13.1 shows the simplicity of the Alaska system; it provides Alaskans with a straightforward means of legal access.

Alaska is divided into four judicial districts. Judges for the district and superior courts, which are the trial courts (or courts of original jurisdiction), are assigned to each judicial district. The court of appeals and the supreme court each consist of one panel of judges that hear appeals from lower court decisions.

Figure 13.1
Alaska State Court System

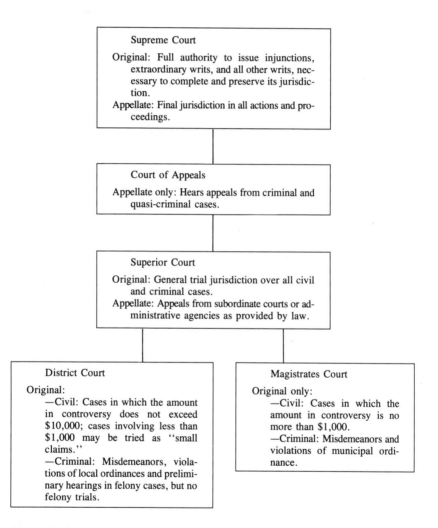

Supreme Court

Original: Full authority to issue injunctions, extraordinary writs, and all other writs, necessary to complete and preserve its jurisdiction.
Appellate: Final jurisdiction in all actions and proceedings.

Court of Appeals

Appellate only: Hears appeals from criminal and quasi-criminal cases.

Superior Court

Original: General trial jurisdiction over all civil and criminal cases.
Appellate: Appeals from subordinate courts or administrative agencies as provided by law.

District Court

Original:
—Civil: Cases in which the amount in controversy does not exceed $10,000; cases involving less than $1,000 may be tried as "small claims."
—Criminal: Misdemeanors, violations of local ordinances and preliminary hearings in felony cases, but no felony trials.

Magistrates Court

Original only:
—Civil: Cases in which the amount in controversy is no more than $1,000.
—Criminal: Misdemeanors and violations of municipal ordinance.

Source: Fannie J. Klein, _Federal and State Court Systems—A Guide_ (Cambridge, MA: Ballinger, 1977), p. 78.

DISTRICT COURTS

District courts are trial courts with limited jurisdiction. In criminal cases they primarily have jurisdiction over minor offenses (misdemeanors) and violations of city or borough ordinances. They can also issue arrest or search warrants, preside over criminal arraignments, enforce orders of the superior court, and carry out miscellaneous other duties.[6]

In general, district court authority in civil cases is also restricted to smaller cases; in 1985, for example, district courts could hear small claims suits for amounts up to $2,000, or suits for recovery of money or property up to $10,000.

There are two classes of judicial officers in district courts—judges and magistrates. The chief difference is that the magistrate's authority is in some respects more limited than that of the judge; for example, in civil cases in 1985, magistrates could award only up to $1,000 for claims or damages. Magistrates handle routine district court matters in many rural areas where there are no full-time district court judges. In some urban areas magistrates help reduce the caseloads of judges. And, as we discuss more in a later section, magistrates are appointed by the presiding judges in their districts and serve at the judges' pleasure.

In 1985 there were 8 district court judges and 54 magistrates in Alaska. The district courts hear several times more cases than any of the other Alaska courts: about 142,000 cases were filed in district courts in fiscal 1984—an increase of 15 percent over the number of cases filed in fiscal 1982. The largest share of cases district courts handle are traffic and vehicle-related violations; in fiscal year 1984 about 70 percent of district court cases fell into that category. The remaining 30 percent of district court cases were mainly a variety of misdemeanors and small claims actions. About 5 percent of district court cases in fiscal 1984 involved felonies.[7]

SUPERIOR COURT

The superior court is Alaska's major trial court with general jurisdiction in both criminal and civil cases. This court has exclusive jurisdiction in all matters involving domestic relations, children's proceedings, probate, and guardianship and civil commitments. It also hears appeals from district court decisions.

In 1985 there were 29 superior court judges in the state's four judicial districts. Cases involving domestic relations (divorces, requests for child support, and domestic violence, among others) made up 44 percent of the superior court caseload in fiscal 1984. Ten percent of superior court cases that year involved children's proceedings, and 14 percent were probate cases (which are in general cases that involve establishing the validity of wills and administering estates). About 10 percent of superior court cases in fiscal 1984 involved felonies (including violent crimes, illegal possession of drugs, robberies, and other crimes against property). The remaining 23 percent of superior court cases were a variety of civil cases—including those dealing with bad debts, damages, and disputed real estate or contract dealings.

About 20,500 cases were filed in superior court in Alaska in fiscal 1984—an increase of 17 percent over the 17,500 cases filed with the superior court in fiscal 1982.

COURT OF APPEALS

The court of appeals was created by the state legislature in 1980 to hear appeals of superior and district court decisions in criminal cases as well as what are known as quasi-criminal cases—those involving, for example, juvenile delinquency, conditions under which prisoners can be held, and matters of probation and parole. Another important responsibility of this court is to determine which cases involve significant issues of constitutional law and should therefore be reviewed by the supreme court.

The court consists of a three-judge panel. It was created mainly to reduce the caseload of the Alaska Supreme Court; the court of appeals was to take on most of the appeals of criminal cases that the supreme court had previously heard, leaving the supreme court to review primarily civil cases. (The supreme court still can and does review some appellate court decisions in criminal cases.)

In 1982, one of its first years of operation, the court of appeals had about 450 pending cases—about the same number as were before the supreme court that year.

SUPREME COURT

The Alaska Supreme Court is the highest state court—the court of last resort in most cases. It is also responsible for regulating and administering the entire Alaska court system. There are five supreme court justices—one chief justice and four associate justices.

The supreme court will hear appeals of any superior court decision in civil cases. It can also, at its discretion, hear appeals of decisions made by the court of appeals in criminal cases. The highest court also reviews cases which the court of appeals has certified as involving substantive issues of constitutional law.

In the first half of the 1980s more than 75 percent of supreme court decisions were in civil cases. The supreme court in fiscal 1984 ruled on about 425 appeals.

Although the supreme court is the administrative head of the Alaska court system, the day-to-day administrative oversight is carried out by the administrative director of the court system. The administrative director, among other responsibilities, makes recommendations to the supreme court on administrative policies and provides the court with a variety of information and advice on legislation and other matters affecting the courts.

RECRUITMENT AND RETENTION OF ALASKA JUDGES

Democratic societies generally choose their judges either by election or appointment. Election insures that judges are responsive to their constituents, but also carries the risks that the judicial process could be influenced by partisan politics or corruption. Appointment of judges ostensibly limits the effects of partisan politics on the judicial process, but it also insulates judges from the public and reduces their sensitivity to community concerns.[8]

Alaska's constitution calls for state judges to be chosen and retained through a combination of appointment and election. This system is a form of what is known as the Missouri Plan (named for the state where it originated). It is designed to reduce the effects of partisan politics in the selection of judges, while at the same time giving the public the opportunity to decide whether they should be retained. This method or some variation of it has been adopted not only in Missouri and Alaska but also in Arizona, Colorado, Indiana, Iowa, Kansas, Nebraska, Oklahoma, Utah, Vermont, and the Territory of Guam.

The basic steps in Alaska's system of selecting and retaining judges are: (1) The Alaska Judicial Council prepares a list of nominees. (2) The governor appoints a judge from the list of nominees. (3) The public periodically votes on whether the judge should be retained.

SELECTION OF JUDGES

The Alaska Judicial Council is a seven-member group that prepares lists of nominees for vacant judgeships. It also recommends changes in the judicial system to the legislature and the supreme court. Another council job is to conduct evaluations of judges facing retention elections.

Three members of the council are attorneys, appointed by the Board of Governors of the Alaska Bar Association, and three are laymen (non-attorneys), appointed by the governor and confirmed by a joint session of the Alaska

Legislature. The council members serve six-year terms. The seventh member is the chief justice of the supreme court. The council is governed by rules of procedure in Article IV of the state constitution. It has an executive director and a small staff.

Various Alaska groups can influence the selection of nominees. Local bar associations, police and other law enforcement agents, individual attorneys, and private citizens may suggest potential nominees, make comments about proposed nominees, and even conduct public campaigns to try to sway the judicial council's decisions. Of these, probably the most effective are the bar associations and the law enforcement groups, because they are experienced in working for or against nominees, and they can mobilize their memberships.

Even though the nomination process is intended to keep partisan politics to a minimum, the men and women who are nominated for judgeships generally have some political records. Past nominees have included some active members of the state's political parties. In 1968, for example, local newspapers gave prominent coverage to the fact that one of the nominees for the state supreme court had served as chairman of Southcentral Alaska Republicans and as general counsel to the Republican Party of Alaska.[9]

At least four council members must agree on nominees for judgeships. The council submits to the governor names of two or more nominees to fill vacancies on the bench. The governor must then choose one of the nominees within 45 days. Nominees for judgeships must be U.S. citizens, meet certain residency requirements, and have practiced law in the state for specific periods.[10]

The judicial council also conducts studies and makes recommendations to the legislature and supreme court on ways to improve the judicial process. Such recommendations are delivered to the supreme court and the legislature at least every two years.

The recommendations can include suggestions for general reforms and improvements in the justice system as well as specific proposals for legislation, personnel actions, or decriminalization of certain offenses. In 1972, for example, the council recommended, among other things, that the supervision of persons on parole or probation be improved, that the court system's request for a law library be approved, and that legislation be enacted that would allow convicted persons to clear their records after they had been rehabilitated.[11]

Many of the changes in Alaska's court system over the years have been the result of recommendations in judicial council reports. The chief justice of the supreme court, who is a member of the judicial council, also has the authority to call superior and appellate court judges to judicial conferences. At such conferences Alaska's judges consider issues confronting the courts and can prepare recommendations to be submitted to the legislature. Past judicial conferences have also made significant contributions to improving the administration of justice in Alaska.

RETENTION ELECTIONS

Judges appointed by the governor can only remain on the bench if the public votes to retain them. Newly appointed judges must stand for voter approval in the first general election held at least three years after their appointments. Names of judges appear on nonpartisan ballots which ask voters to mark either yes or no on the question of retaining specific judges.

After these initial retention elections, supreme court justices serve ten-year terms, appellate court judges eight-year terms, superior court judges six-year terms, and district court judges four-year terms. At the end of these terms, judges can be reconfirmed for additional terms by again placing their names on the ballots at general elections. District court magistrates are different from judges in that they are appointed for indefinite terms by the presiding judges in their judicial districts, and they serve at the pleasure of those presiding judges.

Between 1959 and 1985, Alaskans voted against retaining only three judges. The first judge denied retention was Harry Arend, a supreme court justice, who was voted off the bench in 1964. The Alaska Bar Association had organized an effective campaign against Arend as a consequence of disputes over supreme court decisions in which he had participated.[12] So it is clear that organized groups like the bar association can exert strong influence not only over the initial selection of judges but also over their retention.

In 1982, the Alaska Judicial Council recommended against retaining two district court judges, Joseph Brewer and Virgil Vochoska. Those two judges were in fact voted off the bench in the general election. This was not the first time the judicial council had recommended that specific judges not be retained—it had made similar recommendations in 1976, 1978, and 1980—but it was the first time Alaskans had followed those recommendations.

The difference in 1982 seems to have been that Alaska voters were better informed about the council recommendations than they had been in earlier years and more willing to give the recommendations legitimacy. Although the council did not "campaign" against those judges, it did make its findings widely available. Another important factor was that the peace officers' association and the bar association agreed with the council and made their opinions known to the public. The judges themselves helped publicize the council's recommendations by attacking them. In addition, there was a high level of interest in the general election because of ballot issues that increased voter participation.[13]

The 1964 campaign against Arend has been attributed at least partially to politics rather than to his judicial performance.[14] In 1982, by contrast, opposition to Brewer and Vochoska seemed to be based on more substantive issues raised by the judicial council. While it may still be possible to unseat an Alaska judge for reasons not related to judicial performance, there seems to be a growing sophistication among voters when they decide about retaining judges.

Alaskans often complain that the system for retaining judges is somehow a failure because so few judges are rejected—because almost all incumbent judges are retained on the bench. This attitude does not consider that the initial appointment process is designed to put only well-qualified persons on the bench. A higher rejection rate would indicate that the screening of potential nominees is faulty.

Relatively few judges have been rejected by voters in any of the states using the Missouri Plan, and almost all such rejections have been the result of well-organized opposition from state bar associations. Scholars of the plan believe that the strong retention rate shows that the initial selection process is successful. Of those judges that have been rejected in various states, about 75 percent were rejected for reasons related to judicial competence, philosophy, or conduct, or for making very controversial decisions that inflamed public opinion. Other causes have included criminal or scandalous activities or local politics.[15]

JUDICIAL ACCOUNTABILITY

Alaska judges can be removed from the bench not only through popular vote but also through impeachment by the legislature or through disqualification as a result of disciplinary actions. Disqualification can include suspension, removal from office, forced retirement, or censure. These extreme measures can be taken only on the recommendation of the Commission on Judicial Conduct.

The commission has nine members—three state court judges, elected by their fellow judges; three attorneys who have practiced law in the state for at least ten years, appointed by the governing body of the state bar association; and three persons who are not judges or lawyers, appointed by the governor and confirmed by a joint session of the legislature. Terms of commission members are four years.

ALASKA JUDICIAL PROCESS

REGULATING THE COURTS AND THE BAR

The Alaska Supreme Court supervises the lower courts. Its decisions in appeal cases provide guidelines for operations and deliberations of other state courts. The chief justice can also call judicial conferences (discussed earlier) that bring together the state's judges to discuss changes in the judicial system.

The state bar (meaning collectively all the lawyers who practice in Alaska) is regulated by a combination of the supreme court, the Alaska Bar Association, and the state legislature. The supreme court draws up rules governing the practice of law in Alaska, usually with the collaboration of the bar association. Most of the time, the bar association and the supreme court negotiate the rules under which they will operate; on occasion a dispute may send one or the other side to the legislature for a new law or to a federal court for clarification.[16]

The statutes that establish eligibility to practice law in Alaska are enacted by the state legislature, generally with testimony and assistance from individual lawyers and representatives of the governing body of the Alaska Bar Association. Many of the statutes regulating legal practice in Alaska also originated in judicial conferences or were first proposed by the Alaska Judicial Council.

JUDICIAL-EXECUTIVE RELATIONS

The executive and the judicial branches of state government are in many respects independent but are also entwined in important ways. The governor or his appointee is the chief law enforcement agent in Alaska, through the state Department of Public Safety. Through the Department of Law, the governor or his appointee is the chief attorney for Alaska. And the governor or his appointee is the head administrator of the prison system through the Department of Corrections. The courts are of course concerned—both as arenas within which legal battles are fought and as guarantors of the legality of government actions—with the enforcement of laws and the imprisonment of convicted persons.

The state constitution also grants the governor some near-judicial powers, including the power to impose martial law for a period of up to 20 days without the concurrence of the legislature if "the public safety requires." Under martial law, civilian courts may be temporarily suspended.[17] The governor can also pardon or reprieve convicted persons or commute their sentences, subject to limits imposed by the legislature.[18]

Interactions between the executive and the judicial branches have sometimes led to heated disputes. In one instance in the late 1960s, the court system filed suit in a dispute with the Department of Administration over control of the court system's operating money. The executive director of the court system believed that the independence of the judicial branch was being impaired because the Department of Administration was attempting to control how the court system spent its operating money.[19] The issue was one of separation of powers; the court prevailed and now administers its budget independently of the Department of Administration.

LEGISLATIVE-JUDICIAL RELATIONS

The legislature and the judicial branch interact in a number of ways. The legislature must appropriate operating and capital money for the court system. The legislature passes the laws that the courts administer. The supreme court and the judicial council make recommendations to the legislature for changes in the judicial system. Also, the legislature can attempt to control the freedom of action of the courts through legislation.

A good example of the legislature using public policy to restrict actions of the court is the system it enacted in 1978 "for determining the appropriate sentence to be imposed upon conviction of an offense." This system limits judicial discretion in a number of ways. It requires judges to take into account specific factors when imposing sentences, including seriousness of the crime, record of the defendant, harm done to the victim, and deterrent effect of the sentence. It prescribes minimum and maximum sentences for particular crimes and limits judges' authority to suspend sentences. It allows the state to appeal sentences it considers too lenient.[20]

The legislature imposed this "presumptive sentencing" because of reports of unevenness in sentencing—that is, quite different sentences for the same offense—and because of a public mood favoring tougher law enforcement. Critics of presumptive sentencing have charged that the mitigating factors judges can consider are too limited and that judges can no longer tailor a sentence to the specific circumstances of a case. In the mid-1980s prisoners in one of the correctional facilities near Anchorage filed suit, challenging the legality of the entire presumptive sentencing system. The court found that the system is constitutional.[21]

In an ironic twist, the Alaska courts have recently ordered the Department of Corrections to reduce crowding in the state's prisons. Some observers believe that the overcrowding in Alaska's correctional facilities in recent years can be traced at least in part to the presumptive sentencing system imposed on the court by the legislature—because that system has resulted in more persons being jailed for longer periods.

A NOTE ON ALASKA COURT RULINGS

This chapter has described the structure and operation of the Alaska court system, which is recognized as among the most advanced in the nation. Another aspect of Alaska's justice system is also known for its progressiveness: the decisions of its courts. It is outside the scope of this chapter to discuss court rulings in detail, but below we briefly characterize those rulings.

Alaska's courts, particularly the supreme court, have the reputation of being among the nation's leading courts in interpretation and expansion of fundamental personal rights. Much of this reputation is based on the supreme court's historic 1975 decision (*Ravin v. State*), which held that personal use and possession of limited quantities of marijuana by adults in their own homes would no longer be considered criminal. (The court based this decision on a provision of the state constitution that guarantees citizens the right of privacy. See discussion in the chapter on Alaska's constitution.)

That Alaska is part of the Ninth Circuit of the U.S. Court of Appeals has probably influenced the progressiveness of its courts. The ninth circuit in general has been noted for decisions that are on the leading edge of constitutional interpretation of personal rights. For many years the ninth circuit was under the supervision of Justice William O. Douglas, one of the most liberal members of the U.S. Supreme Court.

But another factor that probably also influences Alaska's courts is the character of the state's population. On average Alaskans are younger, better educated, and more mobile than other Americans. Such citizens probably take more than average interest in court decisions and are less likely to accept what appear to be unfair or arbitrary actions.

On the other hand, because Alaska's population is young and mobile, crime rates in the state are generally somewhat higher than in the country as a whole. That higher crime rate offers more opportunity for testing of laws and sentencing and imprisonment practices against both state and federal constitutional provisions.

CONCLUSIONS

The Alaskans who wrote the state constitution were afforded a great opportunity: to create, from the ground up, a court system that would be free of many of the complexities and inefficiencies that plagued older state court systems.

Alaska's constitution outlines a straightforward system that puts all state courts under the jurisdiction of the supreme court. The district courts handle traffic, small claims, and other minor cases that in other states might be divided among several courts. The superior court is the sole trial court that has broad jurisdiction in major criminal and civil cases statewide. The court of appeals hears appeals of superior court decisions in criminal cases. The supreme court primarily hears appeals of superior court decisions in civil cases, but it can also choose to hear appeals of lower court decisions in criminal cases. The state's top court also reviews all cases that involve substantive constitutional issues.

Alaska's system of selecting judges is a combination of appointment and election designed to insure that well-qualified candidates are chosen but that the people ultimately decide whether they will stay on the bench. In adopting this system, the authors of the constitution took advantage of the advice of top national judicial experts.

Overall, Alaska's justice system is on the frontier of the legal process, both in its structure and in its proceedings.

ENDNOTES

[1]See Chapter 8, "State Court Systems," in *The Question of State Government Capability*, Advisory Commission on Intergovernmental Relations, Washington, D.C., January 1985.

[2]Ibid.

[3]For a more detailed discussion of variations in state court systems see Chapter 6, "The State Judiciary," in Ogg and Ray's *Essentials of American State and Local Government*, Tenth Edition, by William H. Young (New York: Appleton-Century-Crofts, 1969). Also see Chapter 11, "The State Judiciary," in *State and Local Government*, by Joseph F. Zimmerman, Barnes and Noble Outline Series (New York: Barnes and Noble Books, Revised 1976).

[4]Much of this history of the judicial system in territorial Alaska is based on information in the foreword to the *Alaska Rules of Court Procedure*, reprinted in the *Alaska Blue Book, 1985*, compiled and published by the Alaska Department of Education, Division of State Libraries, Juneau. Edited by Scott Foster.

[5]Claus-M. Naske, "The creation of the Alaska state court system," mimeo, 1983; and undated mimeo, "Territorial Alaska's federal judicial system."

[6]Before the district court was created by the legislature in 1970, several different courts—including justice of the peace and recorder's domestic relations courts—handled cases that are now all heard by Alaska's district courts.

[7]Statistics on the district and other Alaska courts are from the *Alaska Blue Book, 1985*.

[8]Fannie J. Klein, *Federal and State Court Systems: A Guide* (Cambridge, MA: Ballinger Publishing Co., 1977), p. 76.

[9]*Anchorage Times*, December 2, 1968, pp. 1-2.

[10]District court judges must be at least 21 years old, have lived in Alaska a minimum of one year, and be licensed to practice law in Alaska. Magistrates are not required to be attorneys. Superior court judges must have lived in Alaska for at least three years and have practiced law for five years. Judges for the Court of Appeals must have lived in Alaska five years and practiced law for eight. Supreme court justices must have lived in the state three years and practiced law for eight. *Alaska Statutes*, Title 22, Judiciary.

[11]*Anchorage Times*, April 4, 1972, p. 2.

[12]Jay Rabinowitz, the current chief justice of the state supreme court, joined the court after Arend was removed. Rabinowitz later attributed Arend's removal to controversial decisions taken by the supreme court. (Quoted in *Anchorage Times*, June 11, 1965, p. 13.)

[13]Francis L. Bremson, "Retention Elections: An Alaskan Update," *Judicature* (1983): 257-58.

[14]See note 12, above. Also, the closeness of the vote on retaining Justice Warren Matthew in 1980 was clearly related to his vote in a controversial "residency" case. See *Anchorage Times*, November 5, 1980, p. A3.

[15]John A. Stookey and George Watson, "Merit Retention Elections: Can the Bar Influence Voters?" *Judicature* (1980): 241.

[16]Such a dispute arose in 1965, when the Alaska Bar Association went to federal court to fight a rule under which the Alaska Supreme Court assumed what the bar association felt was unwarranted power to discipline lawyers. See *Anchorage Times*, February 15, 1965, p. 1.

[17]Alaska Constitution, Article III, para. 20.

[18]Alaska Constitution, Article III, para. 21 and Alaska Statutes 33.20.070.

[19]*Anchorage Times*, June 23, 1967, p. 1.

[20]Alaska Statutes 12.55.120.

[21]*Nell v. State*, 642 P2d 1361 (1982).

Conclusion

In thirteen chapters we have pointed out significant ways that the government and politics of Alaska are both different from and similar to those of the other states. There are irreducible common elements to American state politics, and this is as obvious in the Alaska environment as it is in Alabama or Massachusetts. In other respects, however, the Alaska setting is unique.

First, the natural environment of Alaska government and politics is indeed distinctive. Alaska's geographic isolation and vastness present obstacles to human settlement and have made colonial, territorial, and early statehood history different from that of other states. Second, the constitution of Alaska struck out in a different direction from most state constitutions of the time, because its framers self-consciously intended it to be a "model" basic law incorporating the latest ideas. A third difference is that the attitudes, values, and beliefs of Alaskans concerning the political process and their role in it are unlike those of residents of other states. This is not only because of the individualistic Alaska ethos, but also because there is a traditional Native culture in the state. Fourth, the Alaska governmental setting includes a federal presence that is relatively greater than it is in other states because of federal land ownership, national strategic interests, and the federal trust relationship with Alaska Natives. Finally, Alaska's relatively small population and economy have limited the scale of politics, tending to bring politicians and government closer to the people. Politics have seemed more visible and government more manageable than in the more populous states.

The Alaska political process is also similar to those of other states. The same mechanisms link citizens to government in Alaska as in other states. For instance, elections are held no less frequently in Alaska, and the rules and regulations governing participation show the stamp of national law, standards, and practice. But actual rates of participation in recent state-level contests have been higher than in other states. On issues that are primarily national in focus, the opinions of Alaskans do not diverge markedly from opinions of other Americans. Political parties "sponsor" candidates in general elections, although with fewer claims on candidates' loyalties than in strong party states. Interest groups and lobbyists take their special concerns to decisionmakers and seem to be more dominant than are parties in the political process. The press's influence appears to be greater than that of other non-government organizations and, on occasion, seems to rival that of government institutions.

Institutions of government, the actual nuts-and-bolts of the Alaska political system, are closely modeled on those of other American states. The checks-and-balances system as seen in separate branches of government—legislative, executive, and judicial—that share authority to make policy is the same basic system of rule found in the federal government and in each of the American states. The so-called "fourth" branch of government—the administrative system—also resembles state bureaucracies found elsewhere in American politics. A reading of this book, however, quickly conveys the special Alaska characteristics of state government institutions. The state has a highly unified and more efficient judicial system. The legislature is less professional (and predictable) than those of the larger, industrial states, but it has been professionalizing rapidly, with recent improvements in staff and salary. The Alaska governor appears to be more exposed to political pressures, including those emanating from the legislature, than is the case in other states. Some of these perceived differences may be due as much to the unusual visibility and accessibility of Alaska government as to distinctive Alaska political behavior.

The differences we have identified need to be set in relief. They refer primarily to (1) weaknesses of institutions in the political development of the state, (2) the importance of state government in citizens' lives, and (3) the rapid process of change over the course of statehood, especially the "nationalization" of state government and politics.

In the introduction we discussed the capability of Alaska government in terms of its institutionalization. Since institutional capabilities generally increase with age, Alaska government of the 1980s would likely be more capable than state government was in the 1960s. The real test of capability, however, is the extent to which state government has managed political conflict and change. In this respect, Alaska government institutions have appeared insufficiently developed to deal effectively with crises, particularly the large and rapid economic changes that rocked the state in the 1970s and 1980s. In poorly institutionalized political communities, normal restraints are weak or missing, and action follows the strongest force. The spending frenzy following the state's petroleum revenue windfall, and the crises attending declines in those same revenues, are examples of this.

The second respect in which Alaska's government is unique is in its great prominence in citizens' lives. Part of state government's role is hidden from popular view, because of the decentralization of programs and transfer of funds to pay for them to school districts and local governments. What remains strikes the observer for its reach into all aspects of life. For example, the investment of the state in transportation is mammoth and qualitatively different from that in any other state: the state owns and operates a railroad; it maintains an elaborate marine ferry system; it is responsible for a vast network of airfields; and it is constructing roads where previously there were no overland routes. Although state government is unlikely to maintain so high a profile when revenue declines, Alaska's geographic isolation, other environmental factors, and the relative power of state government itself seem likely to keep it more important than state governments elsewhere.

A final respect in which Alaska politics are distinctive emerges from the process and direction of change. A commonplace of American state politics is that the most distinctive region has been the American South. Politics of the south are becoming less distinctive and more like politics in the rest of the United States. But Alaska's politics are assimilating to the American norm more quickly. The process of change accelerated in response to Alaska's resource wealth of the 1970s and 1980s, which attracted thousands of migrants to the state. The rapid economic and population growth was a basic force for the further assimilation of Alaska as a society into the American mainstream, and it influenced ongoing changes in the character of Alaska's political system as well.

We have noted several important changes in Alaska's political system since statehood that have made it more like those of the rest of the states, particularly the western states. Parties became weaker as organizers of campaigns and elections and as objects of voter loyalties. Elections became more diverse, fragmented means of choosing among candidates and state policy directions. As parties faded, interest groups became more important as organizers and transmitters of constituency demands; these groups were also reduced to more specialized fragments of public interest and opinion. This process of political differentiation, in turn, was reflected in more complex forms of legislative representation and politics, as cross-party coalitions and divided government became the norm. The press, which has traditionally played a prominent role in Alaska politics, became even more important as a transmitter and interpretive filter for statewide political events. And Alaskans' political opinions and electoral choices were increasingly influenced by television as well as by newspapers. In some of these ways, particularly in party weakness and interest group strength, Alaska appears to have surpassed the norm of the American states to the point of occupying a place toward the far end of the national spectrum.

The nationalization of politics in Alaska fulfills hopes of the framers of the Alaska constitution. They wanted to show that the territory was ready for statehood, and thus they drafted a quintessentially American governmental system that would convince Congress and the nation of Alaska's readiness to enter the union. The state's government and politics have rapidly evolved into familiar American political forms.

We have also seen that distinctive qualities persist in Alaska state government and politics, and much of what persists is rooted in Alaska's unique geography and natural environment. Largely because of the small population and sparse settlement outside Anchorage and a handful of medium- and small-sized towns, a "friends and neighbors" form of politics persists side-by-side with modern impersonal forms of media politics. State officials remain relatively accessible, and state government retains its high salience for most interested citizens. And with Alaska's geographic vastness and diversity, regionalism continues as a powerful force in Alaska's political life. A related factor is the unique political culture maintained among Alaska's rural-based Native population.

Underlying these political continuities are Alaska's remoteness, climate, and a natural resource-based economy that is constrained by high costs, subject to booms and busts, and dependent on uncontrollable international market trends and resource discoveries. The volatile pattern of resource exploitation, in turn, has profound political effects: the preceding chapters have shown that it strongly influences, among other things, the conflict between development and preservation; relations between federal, state, and local governments; activities of interest groups and lobbyists; the nature of elections; the organization and behavior of the legislature; and the size and character of the state bureaucracy.

The final issue to which we turn is the future of government and politics in Alaska. Can we expect a continuation of the differences noted—that is, continued weakness in state institutions of government, centrality of state government, and rapid change? Although Alaska seems likely to continue to be vulnerable to the roller coaster of world oil prices, this dependence will increasingly be moderated by the Alaska Permanent Fund. As a dedicated fund that is not directly subject to political change through the legislature, and that can help sustain state programs through leaner years, the fund will lend some needed stability and strength to the institutional basis of the state.

The psychological climate of the late 1980s is sharply different from the heady atmosphere of the late 1970s and early 1980s, when high oil prices made it possible for the state legislature to fund almost any program. Shallowness in the state's revenue stream may re-establish discipline in state institutions. Another likely future development is increased state government direction of local governments. Increasingly, as the federal government attempts to reduce its deficit by reducing programs for states and localities, state governments will be expected to carry this burden, and they will also impose the controls.

Control has been slow to follow the dollar in Alaska, because when there is enough for everyone—as one governor proclaimed at his inaugural—there is little worry about how the dollars are used. But the sharp decline in state oil revenues and in federal aid for municipalities, and the increasing pressure on state government from multiple sources, will encourage greater state participation in local decisionmaking. Local government services, particularly education, are already more dependent on state government in Alaska than is the case in the other states.

Finally, we ask what the future holds for the individualist and progressive traditions of politics in Alaska. The individualist tradition emphasizes Alaskans' distrust of centralized government, but it also reflects their somewhat contradictory demands for government support of private development through various forms of public subsidy. The stresses and strains in this ambivalent individualism were aggravated both during the petroleum boom, when private gains from public spending reached historic peaks, and during the economic downturn and the mounting uncertainties and fear about Alaska's future. The progressive tradition, in contrast, emphasizes Alaskans' belief in positive government, and it reflects a spirit of innovation and optimism about the future. Perhaps the innovativeness of Alaska government has been the obverse side of its poorly institutionalized character. With the maturation of government institutions, the Alaska system of rule could become staid and unresponsive to demands for change. Enlightened political leadership is the key to moving Alaska's progressive tradition forward into the state's second generation.

Glossary

ANCSA-Alaska Native Claims Settlement Act, passed by Congress in 1971, under which Alaska Natives received title to 44 million acres in Alaska and $962.5 million as compensation for extinguishment of their aboriginal land claims. Regional and village corporations were established to manage land and money awarded under the act.

APOC-Alaska Public Offices Commission, created by the Alaska Legislature in the mid-1970s to administer laws relating to campaign disclosure, conflict of interest, and registration of lobbyists.

ARA-Alaska Reorganization Act, passed by Congress in 1936 to extend the provisions of the Indian Reorganization Act to Alaska Natives. (See **IRA**.)

Ad Hoc Democrats-A reform-oriented political organization in Alaska in the early to mid-1970s; it advocated open government, controls on the oil industry, and campaign finance and conflict of interest laws.

Administrative Procedures Act-An Alaska statute that provides guidelines for administrative agencies to follow when issuing legally enforceable regulations to implement laws.

Alaska Permanent Fund-A special state fund established in 1976 as a savings account for a portion of the state government's petroleum revenues. Alaska voters created the fund by approving an amendment to the state constitution, which broadly restricts establishment of special funds. The Permanent Fund is managed by a public corporation that is headed by a board of trustees appointed by the governor and confirmed by the legislature. Since 1982, Alaskans have received annual cash payments (dividends) from the interest earnings of the Permanent Fund.

Appellate Jurisdiction-Authority of a panel of judges to review cases already heard in lower courts. The Alaska Court of Appeals hears appeals of superior and district court decisions in criminal cases and the Alaska Supreme Court has appellate jurisdiction in both criminal and civil matters.

Bail-An amount of money posted with a court in exchange for a defendant's freedom until his case comes to trial.

Bicameral Legislature-A legislature with two houses; the Alaska Legislature is bicameral, with both a senate and house of representatives.

Biennial Legislature-A body of elected representatives that meets once every two years. As a territory, Alaska had a biennial legislature; as a state it has an annual legislature, under provisions of the Alaska constitution.

Blanket Primary-The most open form of primary, in which voters are not required to declare party preference and receive ballots listing candidates of both parties and may vote for either Republicans or Democrats for each office. It is an alternative of the closed or party primary. (See **Closed Primary**.) The Territory of Alaska had open primaries from 1947 through 1958. The State of Alaska closed primary elections from 1960 through 1966 but re-established open primaries in 1967.

Block Grants-Federal grants to states and localities for general uses such as community development or health improvements.

Borough-An areawide unit of local government in Alaska. Similar to counties found in most other states, Alaska boroughs have broader powers that rival those of the strongest municipal corporations.

Bush-Broad areas of rural Alaska (particularly the western, northwestern, and central regions) that are sparsely populated and far from the road systems. The population of bush Alaska is largely Native.

Categorical Grants-Federal grants to states and localities that are restricted to specific uses, such as federal aid for highway construction or the Aid to Families with Dependent Children program.

Citizen Legislator-An elected state senator or representative who has a primary job other than lawmaking and who considers being a state legislator part-time work. Citizen legislators contrast with professional legislators, who consider lawmaking their full-time job.

Citizen Lobby-Collective designation for volunteers who lobby the legislature on behalf of nonprofit, social service, public interest, and other groups in which they have particular interests. These non-paid volunteers, in contrast with paid lobbyists, are not required to register with the state.

Civil Cases-Court cases that involve legal disputes between individuals or organizations but that do not involve criminal matters. Civil cases can be of many kinds, including divorce actions or disputes over sales contracts.

Civil Code-Body of law enacted by a state or nation to define government jurisdiction and rights and obligations of private citizens.

Closed Primary-A form of primary election in which voters must register with a particular party and can vote only for candidates of that party; contrast with **Blanket Primary**.

Coalition-A temporary union between factions from different political parties. Coalitions are formed to create a majority in the legislature. The Alaska Legislature in the early 1980s was generally controlled by coalitions.

Coattail Effect-The ability of a major candidate, such as a presidential or a gubernatorial candidate, to help carry other candidates from his political party into office—for instance, the ability of a Democratic gubernatorial candidate to help bring Democrats into the state legislature.

Collective Bargaining-Negotiations between an employer and an organized group of workers over the conditions of work. Alaska was among the first state governments to authorize collective bargaining for state government employees.

Consensus-General agreement on an issue. Most Native authority systems in Alaska emphasize decisionmaking by consensus.

Criminal Cases-Court cases that involve violations of public laws; criminal cases include robberies, murders, and many other kinds of punishable offenses.

Delegate Representation-The method under which a U.S. territory can have a representative in the U.S. House of Representatives. A territorial delegate elected by citizens of his territory can introduce bills and take part in debates in the House, but cannot vote. Alaska had a delegate to Congress from 1906 to 1958.

Demography-Study of the distribution, density, socioeconomic, and other characteristics of populations.

Despotism-A governmental system under which rulers exercise absolute or arbitrary power; a system not limited by law, custom, or effective opposition.

Direct Legislation-Provisions in state constitutions (including Alaska's) that allow voters the use of the **Initiative**, **Referendum**, and **Recall** processes to change or influence laws; in effect, such provisions give citizens the right to make laws directly.

Double Jeopardy-Being prosecuted twice for the same offense. The U.S. and the Alaska constitutions prohibit double jeopardy.

Due Process-The conduct of legal proceedings according to established principles designed to safeguard the rights of the individual. The U.S. and the Alaska constitutions guarantee rights of due process.

Electoral Demography-Study of the social characteristics of a voting age population; such study may shed light on the political orientations and voting patterns of that population.

Eminent Domain-Government right to take private property for public use, generally with compensation to the owner.

Enabling Act-A congressional act that allows the people of a territory desiring statehood to frame a state constitution.

Equal Protection Clause-A provision of the Fourteenth Amendment to the U.S. constitution that guarantees equal treatment of individuals. Citing this clause, the U.S. Supreme Court in the early 1980s overturned Alaska's original plan for distributing Permanent Fund dividends, because that plan would have favored those who had lived in Alaska longer. (See **Alaska Permanent Fund**.)

Equity-A legal principle requiring fair or just dealings for citizens.

Ex-Officio-Holding an office or position by virtue of holding another office or position; for example, commissioners of state departments are ex-officio members of some boards and commissions.

Federalism-The system of government in which a central (or "federal") government exists side by side with state or provincial governments. Both federal and state governments in the United States derive their powers from a single federal constitution, but each holds independent authority in particular areas.

Felony-A major crime, such as murder or arson; contrast with **Misdemeanor**, which is a lesser offense.

First Organic Act-Congressional act of 1884, under which Alaska was made a judicial and civil district and provided with some federal and territorial officials.

Formula Programs-Programs qualified to receive prescribed payments from unrestricted general fund revenues. The School Foundation Program in Alaska distributes the largest share of formula funds.

Habeas Corpus-A court order to bring an imprisoned person before the court; intended to prevent illegal imprisonment. The right to obtain such an order is guaranteed by the U.S. and the Alaska constitutions.

Home Rule-Power of local governments to modify their charters and run their own affairs with a minimum of limitations set by the state legislature.

Housekeeping Bills-Technical amendment to statutes, intended to correct mostly routine problems of administration.

IRA-Indian Reorganization Act, passed by Congress in 1934 and intended to strengthen tribal governments by providing for land control, means of obtaining loans and legal counsel, and federal charters for tribal businesses.

Impeachment-The process by which a public official is charged with misconduct in office; if an official is charged (impeached), he is then tried on the charges. Grounds for impeachment are specified in the U.S. constitution but not in the Alaska constitution. Motions for impeachment in Alaska must, however, cite the basis for the proceeding.

Incorporated Territory-A designation the U.S. Supreme Court applied to some U.S. territories (including Alaska and Hawaii) in the early twentieth century.

This designation meant the U.S. constitution applied fully in those territories and that they were eligible for future statehood. Other territories were designated as "unincorporated" and therefore not eligible for statehood.

Incremental Budgeting-The approach Alaska and most other state governments have traditionally used to develop state financial plans. It focuses on marginal increases or decreases in agency budgets rather than on major reallocations of revenues among programs.

Independent-a person not bound to or registered as a member of a particular political party.

Initiative-A method voters can use to amend state constitutions or pass laws directly. Proposed constitutional amendments or laws can be placed on the ballot if sponsors obtain signatures of enough voters on petitions. (See **Direct Legislation**.)

Injunction-A court order prohibiting a person or persons from taking some particular action.

Interest Groups-Groups of persons with common interests that attempt to influence the actions of government and to shape public policies in ways that are favorable to them.

Judicial Review-Power of the courts to declare acts of the legislature or the executive to be unconstitutional.

Legislative Veto-A provision of law under which the Alaska Legislature asserts the power to nullify actions—usually regulations adopted to administer laws—of the executive.

Libertarian-A member of the Libertarian Party, an American political party that advocates maximum individual liberty. The Libertarian Party was more active in Alaska and did better in Alaska elections than in most other state elections in the early 1980s.

Line-Item Veto-The power of many state governors (including Alaska's) to strike or reduce particular items in appropriation bills.

Litigant-A party in a lawsuit.

Lobbyist-A person (who may be hired or who may volunteer) that represents the interests of some particular group and who communicates with legislators and administrators and attempts to influence their decisions.

Logrolling-Process by which legislators help each other get favorite legislation passed; it is summarized in the expression "you scratch my back and I'll scratch yours."

Magistrate-A judicial official with limited jurisdiction, especially in criminal cases. Magistrates in Alaska can handle traffic and other minor offenses.

Martial Law-A body of laws administered by military forces and invoked by governments in emergencies when civilian law enforcement agencies are unable to maintain public order and safety. In Alaska, imposition of martial law for an extended period would require a majority vote by a joint session of the legislature; the governor has the authority to impose martial law for up to 20 days without legislative concurrence.

Misdemeanor-A minor offense, such as speeding, that is less serious than a **Felony**.

Missouri Plan-A method of selecting state judges that combines the use of appointments and elections; it is named for the state where the plan originated. Alaska uses a modified form of the plan that calls for judges to be appointed by the governor but to stand periodic retention elections.

Non-Partisan-Without regard to any political party. In elections the term means candidates carry no party labels.

One Man, One Vote Ruling-A 1962 U.S. Supreme Court decision that in the future all state legislatures would be apportioned based on population, so that all citizens had equal representation. Previously, many state legislative bodies had been apportioned based on geographic areas—so that voters in large but sparsely populated rural areas had more representation than did voters in heavily populated urban areas. This ruling invalidated the State of Alaska's original legislative apportionment plan.

Original Jurisdiction-Jurisdiction of a court to hear a case from the beginning, with witnesses called and juries impaneled; contrast with **Appellate Jurisdiction**. In Alaska the superior and district courts are the courts of original jurisdiction.

PAC-Political action committee. Organizations formed to influence the legislative process by contributing campaign funds to political parties or individual candidates. These committees can be either independent organizations or the political arms of corporations, labor unions, or interest groups. Nationwide PACs have become major campaign contributors in recent years.

Partial Preemption-Form of intergovernmental regulation based on the supremacy of national law and the delegation of responsibility. For example, Alaska is permitted to manage fish and wildlife on federal lands in the state, as long as it observes federal laws and standards--such as giving subsistence uses priority over sports hunting and other activities.

Partisan-A supporter of a particular political party—a Republican, for instance.

Partisanship-Strong and often uncritical support of one's political party.

Party Identification-Voters' attachment to specific political parties.

Party-Less Campaigning-Election campaigns in which individual candidates form personal campaign organizations and make individual appeals; they do not align with either major party.

Penal Code-A compilation of various crimes and their legal penalties.

Pluralism-A wide distribution of political power through many groups and institutions than can check, limit, and compete with one another for advantage. American society (and Alaska society) can be described as pluralistic.

Plurality-The largest number of votes garnered by any single candidate in an election, but less than half the total votes cast. In an election where several candidates are running, the leading candidate may win not by a majority but rather by a plurality.

Pocket Veto-Power of the U.S. president and some state governors to kill a bill approved by the legislature by not signing it within some specified period after the end of the legislative session. Alaska's governor does not have the authority to make pocket vetoes.

Populist-One who believes in the rights, wisdom, or virtues of the common people, as against elites and corporate organizations. The political culture of Alaska includes traces of populism.

Pork Barrel-Federal or state funds used to pay for local projects and thus providing political benefits in elected representatives' home districts. After the State of Alaska began collecting large petroleum revenues in the late 1970s, many home district, state-funded capital spending projects around the state were considered pork barrel projects.

Power of Incumbency-The ability of an incumbent elected official to gain re-election by virtue of being able to use the advantages of office to establish himself with voters.

Program Budget System-A system of budgeting whereby appropriations are not made for individual items but rather for a major set of program purposes— such as resource development or child welfare.

Progressivism-A reformist, optimistic social and political movement that emerged in the early twentieth century in the United States; a belief in progress and the possibility of human betterment through government action.

Proposition 13-A constitutional amendment approved by California voters in 1978; it limited local property taxes in the state. That proposition acted as a catalyst for similar tax limitation votes in Anchorage and other U.S. cities.

Public Agenda-The list of public problems about which there is general discussion and debate.

Railbelt Communities-Those Alaska communities along the route of the Alaska Railroad, which runs from Seward in southcentral Alaska to Fairbanks in the interior.

Reapportionment-The drawing of new boundary lines for legislative districts and the reallocation of legislative seats among them, based on the results of new population counts.

Recall-Removal of elected officials from office through votes of the people. The Alaska constitution and most other state constitutions give citizens the right to recall elected officials.

Referendum-A popular vote on a measure passed by or being considered by a legislature, or on a measure put on the ballot through popular **Initiative**.

Revenue Sharing-Funds transferred from one level of government to another with few restrictions. Local governments in Alaska benefitted greatly from state revenue sharing during the era of high petroleum revenues.

Second Organic Act-A congressional act of 1912 that made Alaska a territory and authorized establishment of a territorial legislature.

Shield Laws-State laws designed to protect reporters from having to reveal their sources of information.

Sovereign Government-A government with independent political authority. In the United States, federal, state, and tribal governments all have some sovereign powers.

Standing Committee-A permanent committee of a legislature that considers bills and conducts hearings and investigations. For example, the finance committee of the Alaska Legislature is a standing committee.

Subsistence-In Alaska, a way of life followed by those (primarily Alaska Natives) who gather a large share of their food and other necessities from the land rather than depending solely on the cash economy.

Subsistence Repeal Initiative-An initiative on the general election ballot in Alaska in 1982 that called for repealing provisions of state hunting and fishing regulations giving preference to subsistence users. (The initiative was defeated.)

Sunset Laws-Laws that require periodic review of the continued need for specific programs or agencies. In 1977 the Alaska Legislature passed sunset legislation that requires the legislature to periodically review and extend or terminate boards, commissions, and programs.

Sunshine Laws-Laws that require open meetings of legislative and administrative officials, financial disclosure by candidates for public office, and public access to government documents. Alaska has had such laws since the mid-1970s.

Third Party-Any minor political party organized as an alternative to the two major political parties (the Republican and Democratic parties) in the United States. The Libertarian Party is an example of a third party that was strong in Alaska in the early 1980s.

Ticket-Splitting-In a given election, a voter who chooses Democrats for some office and Republicans for others is splitting his ticket.

Unicameral Legislature-A legislature with only one house, as contrasted with **Bicameral Legislature**.

Utilitarianism-The belief that the purpose of government is to achieve the greatest happiness of the greatest number of people—that the best laws are those that maximize utility or happiness.

Write-In Campaign-A political campaign to persuade voters to write in the name of a candidate who is not listed on the election ballot. Often such campaigns in the general election are carried out by those who have lost in the primary election.

Index

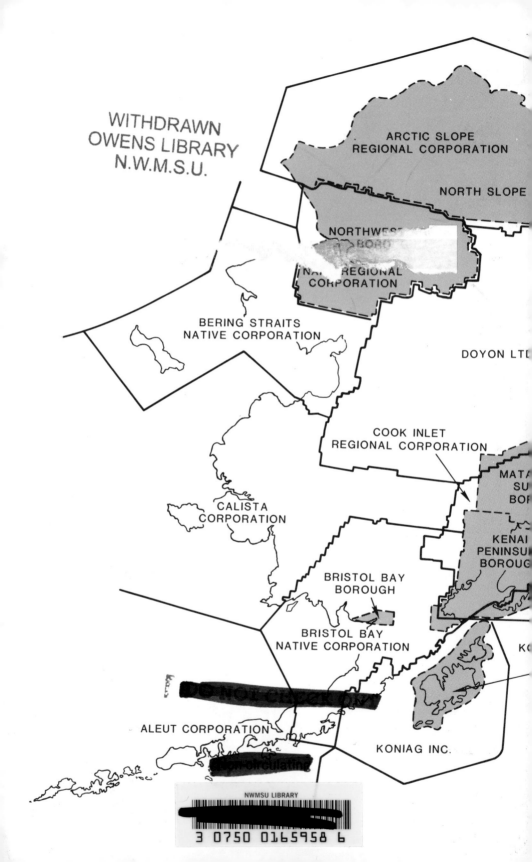

ARCTIC SLOPE
REGIONAL CORPORATION

NORTH SLOPE

NORTHWEST
BORO

NA REGIONAL
CORPORATION

BERING STRAITS
NATIVE CORPORATION

DOYON LTD

COOK INLET
REGIONAL CORPORATION

MATA
SU
BOR

CALISTA
CORPORATION

KENAI
PENINSU
BOROUGH

BRISTOL BAY
BOROUGH

BRISTOL BAY
NATIVE CORPORATION

K

ALEUT CORPORATION

KONIAG INC.

KO